Childhood transformed

Childhood transformed provides a pioneering study of the remarkable shift in the nature of working-class childhood in the nineteenth century from lives dominated by work to lives centred around school. The author argues that this change was accompanied by substantial improvements for many in the home environment, in health and nutrition, and in leisure opportunities.

The book breaks new ground in providing a wide-ranging survey of different aspects of childhood in the Victorian period, the early chapters examining life at work in agriculture and industry, in the home and elsewhere, while the later chapters discuss the coming of compulsory education, together with changes in the home and in leisure activities. A separate section of the book is devoted to the treatment of deprived children, those in and out of the workhouse, on the streets, and also in prison, industrial schools, and reformatories.

In memory of my late wife Barbara, and for my greatly cherished children, Ruth, Hedley, and Valerie.

Childhood transformed

Working-class children in nineteenth-century England

Eric Hopkins

Manchester University Press
Manchester and New York
Distributed exclusively in the USA and Canada by St. Martin's Press

Published by Manchester University Press
Oxford Road, Manchester M13 9NR, UK
and Room 400, 175 Fifth Avenue, New York, NY 10010, USA

Distributed exlusively in the USA and Canada
by St. Martin's Press, Inc., 175 Fifth Avenue, New York,
NY 10010, USA

British Library Cataloguing-in-Publication Data
A catalogue record for this book is available from the British Library

Library of Congress Cataloging-in-Publication Data
Hopkins, Eric.
Childhood transformed : working-class children in nineteenth-century England / Eric Hopkins.
p. cm.
Includes biblographical references (p.) and index.
ISBN 0–7190–3866–9 (hard).—ISBN 0–7190–3867–7 (pbk.)
1. Children—England—History—19th century. 2. Children—England—History—20th century. 3. Education—England—History—19th century. 4. Children—Employment—England—History—19th century. 5. England—Social conditions—19th century. I. Title.
HQ792.G7H67 1993
305.23′0942′09034—dc20 93–45571

ISBN 0 7190 3866 9 *hardback*
0 7190 3867 7 *paperback*

Phototypeset in Linotron Ehrhardt
by Northern Phototypesetting Co. Ltd, Bolton

Printed in Great Britain
by Bell & Bain Ltd, Glasgow

Contents

Preface and acknowledgements

This book is the result of a simple interest in the subject of children at work and in school during the nineteenth century. Originally the plan was to carry out research on the employment of children in the early part of the century, but without any very clear idea as to what should happen next. This helps to explain why the theme of children at work before 1867 is pursued at some length over the first three chapters. Subsequently the growing importance of schooling throughout the century produced the second major theme of the work. At the same time it became apparent that other aspects of children's lives ought to be investigated as well – life at home, the lives of deprived children, and leisure activities. So gradually the whole enterprise took shape. It was not long before the extent of the changes which occurred suggested the main title of the book, *Childhood transformed*. In some ways it can be argued that part of the transformation was the extension of childhood itself, in that at the beginning of the nineteenth century, starting work at so early an age brought an enforced end to infant irresponsibility and the start of a lifetime of earning a living; whereas by 1900 this climacteric had been postponed to the age of twelve at the earliest, and for many till the age of fourteen. At all events, this book takes 'childhood' to span the ages between birth and about fourteen.

It is hoped that this survey of nineteenth-century working-class children in England will make its modest contribution to the social history of the period by providing a useful introductory sketch for students and others attracted by the subject. It makes no claim to originality, but is based on a certain amount of research particularly in the fields of work experience and of elementary education, together with a great deal of information culled from secondary sources. The Bibliography will bear witness to the extent to which I am indebted to the work of many others which is relevant to my subject. I am very grateful to them all. I would also extend my thanks to colleagues in the Economic and Social History Department of the University of Birmingham, especially Mr Peter Cain and Dr Len Schwarz, who have patiently endured my customary chatter about the problems arising from the writing of the book. Of course, I am solely responsible for all the errors of commission and omission, and for all misconceptions and misapprehensions in the following pages. My thanks also go to our two excellent secretaries, Sue Kennedy and Diane Martin.

Prologue

Changing attitudes to children in early nineteenth-century England

In the late eighteenth century, working-class children worked from an early age, and were often treated brutally both at home and at work. They attended school for only short periods of time, if at all, and they frequently died at an early age. They had few, if any, legal rights; and might actually be bought and sold or otherwise disposed of by their parents. Concepts of childhood were still unformed, the child often being regarded simply as a miniature adult, without characteristics distinctive of particular stages of physical and psychological development. Children could be hanged for theft at the age of seven.

By the end of the nineteenth century, all this had changed. Few children under the age of twelve were in full-time employment, and education up to that age had become compulsory and free. The general standard of health had greatly improved, together with the expectation of life, and there was much less physical chastisement; legislation now existed against cruelty to children. Parental authority had been diminished as a result, and also by the appointment of school attendance officers, factory and workshop inspectors, and health missioners. The nature of childhood was better understood, both in respect of relationships with the adult world, and in its influence on learning processes in school. In all these ways, working-class childhood had been transformed during a period of great social change for society as a whole. Perhaps the greatest transformation for the children had been from a life dominated by employment from as early as six or seven (or even earlier) to a life spent at school until twelve or even older. What had brought about this extraordinary change?

There has been no lack of theories in recent years to account for changes in attitudes to children from the seventeenth and eighteenth centuries onwards.[1] It has become accepted by many historians that there was no general concept of childhood before the seventeenth century, and that such a concept developed gradually over the following two centuries, subject only to an increase in parental discipline in the second half of the eighteenth century, due to the spread of Methodism. This more authoritarian approach lasted till the 1870s, and was based on the belief that children were naturally sinful, and their will therefore had to be broken; but it was accompanied by an increased concern for the children's moral welfare.[2] By the third quarter of the nineteenth century, however, this stricter approach to discipline had run its course.

During the past ten years, a new interpretation of the whole subject has been put forward by Dr Linda Pollock, based on a re-examination of a range of basic sources such as diaries (of adults and children) and autobiographies. Her conclusions are certainly challenging: she argues that there *was* a concept of childhood in the sixteenth century, that there were few changes in parental care and child life in the home from then onwards to the nineteenth century, that parent–child relations were not formal and that the majority of children were not subject to brutality – in her own words, 'a large section of the population – probably most parents – were not battering their children'.[3] She does concede, however, that there was an increase in parental strictness in the early nineteenth century.

One problem here is the nature of the source material which Dr Pollock uses to support her arguments. Inevitably, much of it is middle-class in nature, simply because in earlier centuries the working classes did not as a rule record their experiences; literacy in the sense of the ability to write was very limited. Hence it is difficult to know how working-class parents as a whole treated their children, let alone any differences between skilled and better-off working parents and the lumpenproletariat. So there is the danger of assuming that the views and attitudes of working-class parents were little different from those of middle-class parents. In fact, Dr Pollock does not tell us a great deal about working-class attitudes in her book, though her thesis does have a chapter on the State as Protector, in which she declares that 'children who worked during the Industrial Revolution suffered such dreadful hardships because the state at that time was not capable of alleviating their plight, not because they were subject to such economic exploitation by their parents'.[4] In other words, parents were relatively blameless because they disliked their children working (or so Dr Pollock argues), and somehow the House of Commons was unable to produce the necessary remedial legislation. This seems a somewhat naive and over-simplified explanation, which begs many questions, to say the least; but the attitude of parents and the problems of factory reform will be discussed in Chapter Three.

The central fact is that we know very little directly about working-class attitudes to children in 1800, but have to make do with incidental references in the literature of the time, together with an exercise of the historical imagination. Fairly recently Lawrence Stone appears to have done just this, in describing the treatment of children by the poor (it is not clear whether this refers generally to the working classes, or to treatment by only the most impoverished substratum): 'They were in the habit of treating children with rough, even extravagant affection in good times, more often with casual indifference, and not infrequently with great brutality when in drink or in bad times.'[5] This seems an acceptable enough general picture to any reader versed in the literature and in the reports in the Blue Books of the first half of the nineteenth century; and Stone goes on to paint a fearful picture of the increase in the bastardy rates, in infanticide, and in the abandonment of babies in the eighteenth century (all seemingly based on the evidence of a single working-class source, Francis Place's autobiography), but concluding that, in Place's view, matters had much improved by 1820.

The fact remains that we can only make intelligent guesses as to working-class attitudes around 1800, and this in itself does not tell us what we need to know, that is, what changes, if any, were taking place in society's attitudes as a whole at this time. In particular, we need to be informed about middle-class attitudes and beliefs. For this, we must examine the evidence for the growth of humanitarianism in the second half of the eighteenth century, for here, it seems, the seeds of the transformation of childhood which occurred in the following century are to be found. For Stone, the spread of revulsion against cruelty in the eighteenth century seems to have been concurrent with and related to the spread of Enlightenment ideas throughout Europe. This movement was genuinely moral, involving new attitudes and emotions, and stimulating the development of a new ideal type, the Man of Sentiment or Feeling.[6] This is as may be, but in England there were certainly a number of developments which illustrate the growth of interest in the welfare of the working classes and their children. The best known of these is probably the evangelical movement in the Church of England and among dissenters. Its members were active in a number of fields, including the campaign for the abolition of the slave trade, which was achieved in 1807, and later the abolition of slavery itself in the British

Empire in 1833.

Other fields of endeavour included working-class education and the beginnings of the Sunday School movement in Gloucester in the 1780s. In the previous decade the prison reformer John Howard had published three volumes, and his further revised *State of the Prisons* appeared in 1784. In 1788 the first act against the employment of child chimney sweeps was passed. Early in the next century, the famous Quaker, Elizabeth Fry, carried on Howard's work in the prisons, with special reference to women prisoners. Penal reform was also supported by Sir Samuel Romilly, and was given a powerful boost by Sir Robert Peel who exempted about 100 felonies from the death penalty when he was Home Secretary between 1822 and 1827. Meanwhile, Richard Martin campaigned against cruelty to animals (he was nicknamed 'Humanity Martin' by his friend George IV), and the first bill against the ill-treatment of horses and cattle was passed in 1823 (it was not much liked by the working classes who resented interference and sometimes prosecution). In the following year, admittedly against the background of a good deal of opposition and ridicule, the Royal Society for the Prevention of Cruelty to Animals (the RSPCA) was established. Lastly, the factory reform movement may be said to have had its small beginnings in the unease expressed by a group of Manchester doctors in 1784 at the long hours worked by child apprentices in the new cotton factories. This was followed by the local magistrates deciding not to permit any child apprenticeships when the hours were longer than ten hours per day, or with night work. Other magistrates were of the same mind, and in 1802 the first factory act, the Health and Morals of Apprentices Act, was passed, having been introduced by a Bury factory owner, Sir Robert Peel, senior.

Of course, philanthropic endeavour in the last decades of the eighteenth century was not new, but it is suggested that its various manifestations as listed here have a particular significance in their attempts to reduce cruelty and to promote the exercise of human kindness. Moreover, the attempt to do this through legislative action is especially significant. True, in previous centuries it is quite possible to find instances of legislation apparently designed to assist the poor, but on further investigation it turns out that the motive is often to quell unrest and maintain order, or to reorganise poor law relief in a more economical way. This certainly applies to the poor law acts of the eighteenth century. Yet remarkably, one of the most important modifications of poor law practice was the institution of the Speenhamland system in 1795, when the county magistrates of

Berkshire decided to supplement low wages by grants-in-aid from the poor box. Subsequently this so-called system was to be heavily criticised for its expense and the abuses it allegedly encouraged, but at the time it constituted a humanitarian gesture, comparable to the above-mentioned actions of the Manchester magistrates, who were seeking to protect apprenticed children (often from the workhouse and without parents to look after them) from the exploitation of unscrupulous mill-owners and their overseers. It appears that whatever examples of brutality to children at work can be uncovered – and many will be given in the following chapters – there were funds of goodwill among both the middle classes and the working classes; but the middle-classes had the power to take effective steps towards reform, whether in their own localities or on a national scale in the House of Commons. Given the vast social changes resulting from the Industrial Revolution, the task was both necessary and urgent.

The key to understanding the transformation of children's lives in the nineteenth century is really provided very largely by middle-class action, especially in the fields of working conditions and of education. The first four chapters of this book will trace what happened in some detail. The starting point is factory reform, itself triggered by the hapless state of apprenticed labour. At about the same time, church schools were beginning to be established. The first of these reforms may well be ascribed to the philanthropic motive – Richard Oastler's famous words of 1833 come to mind – 'Any old washerwoman could tell you that ten hours a day is too long for any child to labour' – while the second was based on a mixture of motives; apart from the obvious desire that children should grow up as Christians, there was also the strong belief that religious indoctrination would act as a social control, reconciling the working classes to their subordinate place in society.[7] Education for the working classes was certainly not thought of as something good in itself, let alone a right of the individual child, but rather as a means to an end. These views, naturally enough, were to change substantially by the end of the century, by which time the lives of working-class boys and girls had become dominated by school rather than by the workplace.

One further factor in the developments after 1800 must be considered: the creation of government machinery to enforce reform once the reform movement (especially factory reform) was sufficiently advanced. This idea, advanced originally by Professor MacDonagh, was simply that once some intolerable evil had become generally known, and once legislation had been passed, then inspectors would be needed to see that the law was obeyed. The inspectors would report on progress, and a new government department would come into being. In time, a whole new corpus of specialised knowledge would be accumulated, and both Parliament and Government would have to take all this into account when looking to the future. Further reform would become an increasingly complex business in which government officials, with their specialised knowledge, would have an important part to play.[8] It is possible to overemphasise all this, of course, but the suggestion that an administrative momentum was created is useful, and helps to explain why reform continued not merely on the basis of how far, in theory, government intervention as opposed to *laissez-faire* ideas could rightly proceed, but also how it resulted from an ongoing and indeed apparently unstoppable administrative process.

To return to our starting point: the transformation of working-class childhood which took place in the nineteenth century was not the consequence of any profound change in attitudes to children at the beginning of the century.[9] Rather it was the product of philanthropic or compassionate motives, together with a concern for social control, at a time of unprecedented social change – a swelling population, industrialisation, and urbanisation. These last three in concert provided a potentially explosive mixture, and seemed to threaten the destruction of pre-industrial society. In practice, society survived by adjusting to the new social forces, and by the application of pragmatic solutions to problems as they arose, with an admixture, from time to time, of a traditional compassion. Nominally at least, and certainly at times in practice, England was a Christian country. This is not to say that the struggle for reform was not hard and prolonged, especially in the realms of the regulation of working conditions and the ending of child labour. Nor was the outcome reached at the end of the century envisaged by the reformers of 1800. The desire to protect apprentices from the workhouse from cruel treatment in the cotton mills ended with all childhood employment coming under regulation; and the need to assist the churches to provide schools ended in the establishment of a national and secular system of schooling. Moreover, reform was not always the result of the milk of human kindness – as we have seen, motives were mixed, and certainly included a simple middle-class concern for self-preservation. At the end of the nineteenth century, as we shall see, the need for improved measures to ensure national and imperial self-preservation also led to an increasing concern with standards of working-class health and welfare. But somehow, in one way or another, more civilised standards, which were of benefit to society as a whole, emerged during the course of the century.

However, the transformation of the lives of working-class children during the nineteenth century is really part of an extraordinary transformation of the whole of working-class life. Those masses who in earlier centuries had been known merely as the lower orders, or even the mob, had become known generally as the working classes, and by the end of the century the more skilled and regularly employed were respected members of society, having gained the vote, and occupying positions of responsibility as officials of trade unions, members of school boards, and even sitting on the bench of magistrates. All this, of course, did not apply to the lowest rungs of society, where poverty was still acute; but nevertheless, the general improvement in comfort and civilisation is unmistakable. Along with all this there naturally went great changes in the lives of the children, not only in a material sense, but in the respect accorded the child as a human being. If, as older historians have argued, children were formerly shown little consideration as individuals, being regarded merely as miniature adults (even being dressed as such), then great changes occurred by the end of the century, and this book attempts to examine these changes in detail.

Lastly, it might be helpful to conclude by saying something about the organisation of material in the pages which follow. In the first place, it seemed appropriate to deal with children's working conditions, since work bulked so large in their lives in the first half of the century. Further, because of the common misconception that the majority of working children worked in factories in the early nineteenth century, the work of children in agriculture, workshop industry, iron manufacture, mining, and other industries is discussed before work in factories (it might be observed in passing that the majority of working children in the nineteenth century never saw the inside of a factory). Part I, the section on life at work, ends in 1867 – a deliberate choice, because in that year workplaces other than textile factories were brought within the scope of legislation, including domestic workshops. The Factory Act, 1867 and the Workshops Act, 1867, taken together, therefore constitute a milestone in the regulation of working conditions. For reasons of convenience, Part II, which deals with the home, education, and religion, also ends in 1867. Part III surveys the subject of deprived children, and spans the whole century. Part IV picks up the story of the further reform of working conditions, and of continued reform in education and in the home over the period from 1867 to the end of the century, which is sometimes taken to mean 1914 rather than 1900. The last chapter deals with leisure activities over the nineteenth century as a whole, with greater emphasis on the second half of the century than on the first. It is followed by 'Conclusions and observations'.

References

1 See in particular Phillipe Ariès, *L'Infant et la Vie Familiale sous l'Ancien Régime*, 1960, (English translation: *Centuries of Childhood*, 1962); Ivy Pinchbeck and Margaret Hewitt, *Children in English Society, Vol. II: from the Eighteenth Century to the Children Act, 1948*, 1973; J. H. Plumb, 'The new world of children in eighteenth-century England', *Past & Present*, 67, 1975; Lawrence Stone, *The Family, Sex and Marriage: England 1500–1800*, 1977; Linda Pollock, 'The Forgotten Children', St Andrews Ph.D. thesis, 1981, and *Forgotten Children: Parent–Child Relations from 1500 to 1900*, 1983. See also her anthology, *A Lasting Relationship: Parents and Children over Three Centuries*, 1987, though unfortunately this has very little material relating to working-class children in the nineteenth century.

2 This view is set out in detail in Lawrence Stone, *The Family, Sex and Marriage*.

3 Pollock, *Forgotten Children*, 1983, p. 268; this author provides a very helpful general survey in her book under the heading, 'Summary and conclusions', pp. 262 ff.

4 Pollock, thesis, p. 132.

5 Stone, *The Family, Sex and Marriage*, p. 470.

6 *Ibid.*, pp. 237–9.

7 On social control generally, see A. P. Donajgrodski (ed.), *Social Control in Nineteenth Century Britain*, 1977. For a cool appraisal of the subject, see F. M. L. Thompson, 'Social Control in Victorian Britain', *Economic History Review*, XXXIV, 1981, and also his 'Social Control in Modern Britain', in Anne Digby and Charles Feinstein, (eds), *New Directions in Economic and Social History*, 1989.

8 The theory is expounded in Oliver MacDonagh, *Early Victorian Government*, 1977. The basic ideas are to be found in his earlier work, *A Pattern of Government Growth: The Passenger Acts and their Enforcement 1800–60*, 1961. There has been criticism of the theory on the grounds that it does not explain change in the Education Department where new departures were rarely made on the initiative of civil servants: see Anne Digby and Peter Searby, *Children, School and Society in Nineteenth Century England*, 1981, pp. 6, 8.

9 Pollock takes the view that parental care appears to have altered little from the sixteenth century to the present day (*Forgotten Children*, 1983, p. 269), and in her thesis remarks that 'parents have always tried to do what is best for their children, within the context of their society' (thesis, p. 136). Obviously, much will depend (one might well think) on the context of society.

Part I

Working conditions to 1867

Chapter One

Agriculture and workshop industry

When attempting a survey of the vast range of jobs on which children were employed during the nineteenth century, the first problem is to decide where it is best to start. In this chapter the two categories of work which will be examined have been chosen because for many years they had been the two major forms of employment in the national economy – agricultural work and workshop industry. For centuries past, agriculture had been the foundation industry, while what manufacturing existed had usually taken place in the small workshop, often in the home or near it. Some industry, of course, had to be undertaken away from the home – for example, mining, the making of iron, shipbuilding – but before the advent of the factory system, most manufacture was based on the workshop. Child labour in agriculture and in the workshop therefore provide a logical starting point, and in this chapter they will be discussed with particular reference to the ages at which the children were employed, the nature of the work, and working conditions. Having done this, it will then be possible to discuss in more general terms some of the issues which have been raised.

At the beginning of the nineteenth century the employment of children in agriculture was widespread throughout the kingdom. Agriculture had provided the largest single occupation for many centuries, and in 1801 it still employed 36 per cent of the British labour force.[1] Given the importance of this occupation, and also the fact that education was not compulsory for working-class children (and not even thought necessary by many of their parents – an attitude to be discussed in Chapter Five), it is understandable that in rural areas young children often helped their parents with work in the fields as a matter of course. As they grew older and stronger, their hours of work would increase until they were physically capable of a full day's work. This would have been considered entirely natural in 1800 – how else were children to occupy themselves, apart from a brief spell, perhaps, in school in order to obtain the rudiments of reading and writing? There were also important economic considerations: the earnings of young children contributed to the family income, and could be vital if the family was large, and there were many mouths to feed. Thus the employment of children in agriculture was in no way novel or controversial in the early years of the nineteenth century. There was no movement at the time for its suppression or restriction, and it was regarded very much as part of the natural order of things. Outside the towns, boys and girls were born to it, and many spent their whole lives in farm work, often without leaving the neighbourhood of their native village.[2]

The age at which children began work in agriculture depended on their sex, their physical development, and the kind of farming practised locally. As for sex, the employment of girls under the age of puberty on field work seems to have been very limited in the 1840s, because of their lack of physical strength,[3] although they might give occasional help to their parents when younger than this.[4] Both boys and girls helped in this way from about the age of seven. From then on, the employment of boys became more regular as their strength increased. Permanent work would start for them at about nine or ten, and around the age of twelve they would usually be strong enough to take on work with the plough team. All depended on the stage of physical development; it was no use giving a boy a task for which he had insufficient strength.[5] The other determining factor was the type of farming. In most cases farming was arable, pastoral, or a mixture of both, with dairy work indoors for the girls and the women; but there could be more specialised cultivation, as of hops in Kent and elsewhere, or there might be rural industry such as straw plaiting in Bedfordshire. In some parts of East Anglia, children were employed under the gang system.

In more detail, at the age of seven (sometimes earlier) boys were given simple jobs such as bird-scaring, watching poultry or cattle in the fields, couching (clearing weeds and roots), and stone-picking. At nine or ten, they might help with reaping and threshing, corn-raking and stacking, and working generally in the hayfield. A strong ten- or eleven-year-old might lead a horse at the plough, while at ten or after he could himself plough, mow, and ditch and hedge – all tasks requiring something like adult strength. In the hopfields, the more specialised jobs needed a similar amount of strength – 'opening the hills' (digging the mounds of earth at the foot of the vines in order to prune the roots), shimming (horse-hoeing between the vines), poling, pole-shaving, and chog-clearing (clearing the broken ends and shavings of poles). All these tasks required the strength of older boys who might also be used to pick the hops. The types of jobs over the whole range of agricultural employment were surprisingly numerous, but all would depend on the seasons, the kind of farm, the soil, and the strength of the individual child.[6]

How onerous was the work in the first half of the century? In the first place, hours were certainly long – generally from 6 a.m. to 6 p.m., but shorter in the winter when the hours of daylight were limited. They were extremely long at the hay harvest and the corn harvest, when it was essential to get the work done before the weather broke. At other periods of the year, in December and January in particular, there was little to be done in the open fields except for such tasks as turnip lifting (very hard work when the ground was frosty). In these months, any cottage industry available, such as lace or straw plaiting in Bedfordshire and Buckinghamshire, might be a valuable additional source of income. Secondly, agricultural work was not in itself reckoned to be especially laborious, and children engaged in it were not at the mercy of machinery as in a textile factory. It might be dull and monotonous, however – 'irksome' is the word applied by one of the poor law commissioners enquiring into the employment of women and children in agriculture in 1843.[7] One of the most boring jobs, given to the youngest, was bird-keeping (bird-scaring). According to a witness, the Rev. S. G. Osborne, this might appear cruel when the child was so occupied for eight or ten hours at a time, but he thought there was no reason to suppose that boys were injured by it.[8] On the other hand, it was acknowledged that leading or driving horses or oxen could be hard (but not too hard, it was thought). Sometimes overexertion (in this context presumably implying exhaustion) resulted from too much walking. Concern was also expressed by some witnesses at the 1843 enquiry at the fact that some children worked seven days a week, since most tasks except ploughing continued on Sundays; but this practice varied from place to place, and certainly most adult farmworkers had time off to go to church.

All in all, child workers do not seem to have suffered greatly from the nature of their employment in agriculture, at least not by the standards of the time. It was not especially dangerous, and labourer witnesses in 1843 said that although the work might be hard, it was not injurious in itself. Accidents did happen, of course, and were accepted as part of the job. Thus, a twelve-year-old boy, Thomas Hall, reported philosophically on a minor accident:

Yesterday I sprained my wrist; I can move my wrist today. I have never hurt myself before at work in the hop-gardens, but in the summer I sprained my thumb at 'swapping' [swapping is elsewhere called bagging]. I used to be much fatigued when I first went to work . . . One can go on working if one has sprained the wrist if one ties it up, but then one keeps catching of it often; I mean by that it gives sudden pains.[9]

One medical witness suggested that if women and children suffered in health, it was not due to the work, but to sheer want of food. Undoubtedly the standard of living of agricultural families was very low, and their housing extremely poor (see Chapter Four). Damp and insanitary accommodation usually lacked any proper means of drying out wet working clothes, or even of drying wet bedlinen after washing. It is not surprising that agricultural labourers suffered greatly from rheumatic complaints. Yet at the mid-century it appeared that the outdoor life in agriculture helped to keep farm labourers more healthy than their town counterparts. The general level of mortality in urban districts in the period 1851–60 was a quarter as high again as the rate in rural areas – 24.7 per 1000 as against 19.9 per 1000. Over the period 1838–44, child mortality was three times higher in Manchester than in Surrey.[10]

One form of work which on the face of it would appear to be oppressive to child agricultural workers was poor law apprenticeship to husbandry. This was common enough under the old poor law, but seems to have lost importance after the passing of the Poor Law Amendment Act, 1834. After this act, the policy seems to have been to keep pauper children in workhouse schools rather than to apprentice them to local farmers.[11] Nevertheless, poor law apprenticeship continued in some parts, especially in Devon. In this county, children could be taken from parents by relieving officers without consutation, and apprenticed to farmers, (chosen by lot) from the age of nine till twenty-one (or, in the case of girls, until they married, if they did so under twenty-one). In theory, children so apprenticed would be open to exploitation, as were their fellow poor law apprentices in the textile factories and even in workshops. In practice, they do not seem to have been overworked, though by the 1840s this kind of apprenticeship was becoming more and more unpopular with employers. Some Devon farmers expressed strong dislike for the system in the 1843 enquiry. Thus Mr Edward Trood declared 'I am tired of apprentices. I find it better to pay regular wages; you have no control over apprentices; you can't dismiss them; they are a mere plague.'[12] Another farmer claimed that he was the first to oppose 'this improper mode of unpleasant servitude'. However, one middle-class witness in Devon, a surgeon, was actually in favour of apprenticeship, and thought that apprentices were generally better lodged, fed, and clothed than boys and girls living at home and working for wages. Two other farmers, and even two agricultural labourers, one of them an ex-apprentice, also spoke approvingly of the system.[13] They were in a minority. The assistant poor law commissioner for Devon, Mr Alfred Austin, had no doubts himself that apprenticeship of this kind was on balance a bad thing – the apprentice was often forced upon an unwilling master, to whom he was generally a burden and an expense. The poor law apprentice was essentially in a degraded position, according to Austin, looked down upon even by the hired servants, and 'treated by everybody in a manner corresponding with his situation'. Children of the undeserving poor might have the benefit of being apprenticed, he thought, while children of the more meritorious might not be able to find work because the farmer could not afford to pay them. The greatest objections to apprenticeship, Austin declared, were 'its injustice towards the industrious labourer and his family, the separating of children from their parents, [and] its degrading effect upon the apprentice.'[14]

In other agricultural areas, poor law apprenticeship to husbandry appears to have almost died out after 1834. Around Maidstone in Kent, very few had been bound in the ten years preceding 1843 – not more than three in every two years. In Suffolk, Norfolk, and Lincolnshire, the system had been 'almost universally abandoned' since 1834. In Yorkshire, it was 'very rare'. In any case, there really seems to be no evidence to suggest that the working conditions of pauper apprentices in agriculture were noticeably worse in the 1840s than the working conditions of the non-apprentice children. There was no outcry against their treatment as there had been more than forty years previously against the over-long hours and ill-treatment of factory apprentices. On the contrary, it was assumed that agricultural work was healthy for all engaged in it, including the children, whether free or apprenticed. The objections raised were not to overworking, but to the system in itself. It was thought to be wrong in principle, and unfavourable to parents, masters, and apprentices alike. According to Alfred Austin, it was better to discontinue the system than to try to reform it.[15]

However, one form of agricultural employment for children was criticised strongly in the 1843 report. This was the gang system – the employment of gangs of women and young children on field work, often at considerable distances from their homes. It was most commonly to be found in East Anglia, where the farms were often few and far between. Children as young as four, five or six were sometimes employed. The assistant commissioner for Suffolk, Norfolk, and Lincolnshire, Mr E. C. Denison, devoted a considerable part of his report to this system, and referred in particular to the parish of Castle Acre, near Litcham in Norfolk, which he described as a parish which attracted undesirables, quoting a gang overseer's description of it as 'the coop of all the scrapings in the county'.[16] According to Denison, the system did have a few advantages in that the employer got the work done quickly and cheaply, the gangmaster gained a certain local power and prestige, not to mention a living, while those employed did at least obtain work of a kind; but these advantages were outweighed by the many disadvantages. It was really a means of getting the maximum work for minimum pay, for payment was by the piece. The employment of such young children at laborious work debarred them from attendance at school. All sorts of unsavoury characters were mixed up in the gangs – according to one overseer, 'I believe that owing to ganging, 70 out of 100 girls are very imprudent girls – prostitutes'.

One major objection to the system was that the place of work was often at a distance, requiring a walk of perhaps five miles there, and then five miles back. If the work was completely rained off, no payment would be made, and no alternative work was available in the barn or yard. The distance might even be as far as ten miles away, when the gangmaster would be obliged to provide transport in the form of carts, making an overnight stay necessary. Generally speaking, gangmasters were severe taskmasters – according to Denison, if the gangmaster was 'a low, hard man', it illustrated the proverb that no tyranny was so grinding as that of 'a poor man who oppresseth the poor'. All in all, Denison had no doubts at all about the evils of ganging: 'I can come to no other conclusion than that it is a very pernicious system'.[17]

The modern reader of his report can hardly fail to reach the same conclusion. It was not that the work required from the children was very different from other kinds of field work, but rather that their age, the long journey before work began and the harshness of the work discipline all combined to make the day's work peculiarly laborious. How far children were affected by the immorality said to characterise the women employed is hard to say. Presumably there was little time for immoral behaviour in itself, though language might be lewd if not positively obscene, as it could be in the fields at any time. Nevertheless, the suggestion that many of the women were actually prostitutes (or became prostitutes) seems far-fetched; an earthy familiarity with the opposite sex is another matter. Of course, the Victorians were always highly sensitive to the risk of improper behaviour whenever men and women, particularly young girls, worked in close proximity. The really damaging effects of the gang system for children were the distances walked to and from work, and the sustained hard work imposed by the gangmaster. It was these characteristics which distinguished child labour in gangs from other forms of agricultural employment.

During the twenty years or so following the 1843 report, few changes seem to have taken place in the nature of child labour in agriculture. The same kinds of jobs were undertaken, dependent on the physical development of the children, and technological improvements such as the increased use of the scythe instead of the sickle, the introduction of the mechanised reaper and binder, and of steam ploughing, affected very few young children. However, a further report on ganging by the commissioners of the Children's Employment Commission, appointed in 1862, resulted in the prohibition of public gangs by the Agricultural Gangs Act, 1867. Meanwhile, the migration of young people from the countryside into the towns continued apace. Though agriculture was still the largest single occupation in 1851, it accounted for only 1.79 million out of a total population in Britain of 21.0 million; by this time there were four times as many industrial workers as agricultural workers. Ten years later, in 1861, the numbers employed in outdoor agricultural labour had shrunk still further:

Males		*Females*	
5–10	6,996	5–10	256
10–12	32,576	10–12	1,264
	39,572		1,520

Total: 41,092[18]

Thus the number of the youngest children (under ten) was really quite small. But by now, half a century of factory legislation was beginning to have obvious implications for the employment of children in agriculture. This was not so much because of fears that the labour was too hard, but rather because of the effect of child labour on their education. This aspect had not been completely ignored in the 1843 report – in Yorkshire it was said, 'school, as might be supposed, is invariably sacrificed to work' – but in 1867 a Commission was appointed specifically to enquire 'to what extent the principles of the Factory Acts could be applied in agriculture, especially with a view to the better education of children'. Closely associated with the subject of education was the problem posed by the need for children to earn money to supplement the family income.

The two reports of the 1867 Commission cover a much wider area than their predecessors in 1843. Generally speaking, they provide the same kind of information as before as regards working ages, hours, and tasks. Children began work at seven or eight, the employment of the youngest in Norfolk, Essex, Sussex, and Gloucestershire being said to be 'precarious, occasional, and fluctuating', but then 'of constant use' from the age of ten.[19] This was usually so in other counties as well, the principal exception being Northumberland, where children were kept in school until they were twelve or even fourteen.[20] On the whole, the commissioners had little to say on the severity or otherwise of the children's labours, although it was stated that boys were sometimes employed with horses at too early an age. However, according to the commissioner, Mr Tufnell, 'there is an almost total lack of proof that any cruelty exists'. The major concern of the assistant commissioners was with the often expressed need of the children to work in order to augment the family income. Inevitably this interfered with schooling, especially after the age of nine. The point was made most forcibly by Mr Culley, reporting on Bedfordshire and Buckinghamshire; according to him, the earnings of the agricultural labourer were so small that his children's labours were of great importance. As a consequence he dealt at length in his report with ways in which the labourer's wages might be supplemented by providing him with cottage gardens or field allotments.

There seems no doubt that the importance of children's earnings was not exaggerated in the 1843 and 1867 reports. Generally they would depend on the age and capacity of the child, ranging from 3*d* or 4*d* a day upwards. The income of any one family obviously varied with its size. While in one part of Suffolk in 1843 women and children constituted only a seventh to a twelfth of the whole labour force,[21] in another part (the Woodbridge to Ipswich area) women and children formed as much as a third to a sixth of all labour employed.[22] All in all, according to Professor Armstrong, the contributions to family income by both women and children 'must be judged considerable and usually indispensable'. In extreme cases, Professor Armstrong estimates such earnings at up to half the total family income.[23] Hence the problem as it seemed to the commissioners of the 1867 enquiry: to keep a child in school meant not only the forefeiting of wages otherwise earned in the fields, but also the payment of school fees – a double penalty, in fact. How was this difficulty to be resolved?

In their first report, the commissioners were divided in their views. Some suggested the prohibition of work altogether at the earlier ages, while others recommended compulsory schooling up to the age of ten or eleven. This division of opinion was reflected in the two separate reports of the senior commissioners.[24] The first report, by the veteran investigator H. S. Tremenheere, acknowledged that a general opinion existed that children under ten should be excluded from work, but he took the view that this might bring privation, because there were large districts where children's earnings were very important to their parents. It is not surprising that Tremenheere should express this view, given his wide knowledge of children's earnings in industry, and his attempts to give financial assistance to parents in the mining districts who sent their children to school when they could have been earning.[25] Tremenheere rejected the view that there should be an age below which it would be unlawful to employ children in agriculture; he simply asserted that the analogy of the Factory Acts was not applicable. Instead, every child should complete 160 school attendances per year until he or she was twelve years old, starting from the date of first employment. This requirement might be lifted for any eleven-year-old, or child between eleven and twelve, who passed the fifth standard. A child of nine who passed the fourth standard could have his or her number of attendances reduced to 60 a year until reaching the age of twelve.

The second report, by Mr Tufnell, pointed out that employers were willing to prohibit the employment of children under ten years of age, and labourers mostly agreed with this. It would therefore be safe to forbid any child under the age of ten to work in agriculture, a limit which might later be extended to eleven or twelve. The great obstacle to education to be surmounted, in his opinion, was the apathy of parents. Turnell did not discuss how far this apathy might be due at least in part to the loss of earnings due to schooling. His final answer to the questions originally addressed to the Commission on its appointment was sharp and to the point; none of the principles of the Factory Acts was applicable, 'except the single one of prohibiting children working under a certain age, which age should be nine immediately, and ten at some period not exceeding two years from the passing of the Act, and this prohibition should apply to every child in the kingdom'.

The difference of opinion between Tremenheere and Tufnell is interesting, and perhaps to be explained partly by the differences in view expressed by the junior commissioners and partly by Tremenheere's awareness of the importance of children's earnings, and his own attempts in previous years to solve the problems they posed in the coalfields. Tufnell made no effort to provide an answer to the problem of lost earnings in his report. Ultimately the Government attempted to satisfy both points of view by means of the Agricultural Children Act, 1873, by which there was to be no employment in agriculture under the age of eight, while between the ages of eight and twelve a certain minimum number of school attendances would be required. According to one modern authority, Dr Pamela Horn, this act was a dead letter.[26] Eventually what happened was the Education Act, 1870 gave school boards power to require attendance, while the 1876 Education Act and Gladstone's Education Act, 1880 together made attendance compulsory in board schools and voluntary schools alike (see Chapter Five). Of course, this did not prevent children of school age continuing to work in agriculture from time to time, especially after school in summer and at harvest time. Indeed, school holidays were sometimes adjusted so as to permit children to assist with the harvest and at other times, right up to the First World War. As we shall see later in this book, schoolchildren were similarly employed part-time in both trade and industry in 1914.

To sum up, as a result of the attention fixed on child employment in factories in the early nineteenth century, little regard was paid to child labour in agriculture till the 1840s. It is easy to overlook the fact that this kind of employment was not only of very long standing but at the beginning of the century was the principal occupation for a large proportion of working children, a fact well known to all. Everyone travelling through the English countryside would be familiar with the sight of children working in the fields. It was thus taken for granted that this kind of work was in itself not objectionable; and on the whole, this belief was not challenged by the findings of the 1843 enquiry. The comfortable conclusion was reached that, generally speaking, the children were not being abused, and that the work undertaken was usually appropriate to their age and capabilities. The hours worked varied with the seasons, of course, and might be very long at harvest time; but the labourers did not complain at this, especially if part-time work for their families was involved. Thus, a Mrs Stone, a labourer's wife, testified as follows in 1843: 'I went out leasing [gleaning] this autumn for three weeks . . . I got up at 2 o'clock in the morning, and got home at 7 at night. My other girls, aged 10, 15, and 18, went with me and sometimes as far as 7 miles off. I have had 13 children, and have brought 7 up.'[27] No doubt these hours were exceptional. None of the witnesses before the 1843 enquiry complained of the hardness of the work, and one young boy said that he would rather work than play – the victuals were better when he was working. There is also the further consideration that working in the open air was far healthier than working in an urban workshop or factory. It is worth observing, too, that there was a surprising variety of jobs to be undertaken in agriculture, some of them calling for some skill and intelligence. This could be reflected in pay differentials; slower and less capable boys were paid less. For example, boys in the West Country were generally paid 1*s* 6*d* a week on starting work at the age of seven or eight. At the age of eighteen, lads were sometimes still earning only 3*s* 6*d* a week, while others of the same age might be earning a man's full wages.[28]

What does emerge from both the 1843 and 1867 commission enquiries is not so much the scandalous conditions of child labour, but evidence of particular abuses such as the exploitation of parish apprenticeship and agricultural ganging. Another significant problem raised, especially in 1867, was the wretched nature of much village housing, a subject to be dealt with in a subsequent chapter. Above all, and to a major degree in 1867, there was the problem of schooling for the child labourer. It was concern over this, rather than the harshness of the work regime, which shaped the reports of the 1867 commission and finally resulted in legislation. Few of the criticisms levelled at child labour in the factories can be made of child agricultural labour. Work discipline was often a family matter, and varied with the age of the child, the task, the time of the year, and so on, the exception here being gang work which, as we have seen, was commonly regarded as slave labour and universally condemned.

A last point worth touching on here is that child labour must have made a significant contribution to agricultural production in the first half of the nineteenth century. It is true that the relative physical weakness of small children set limits to the kind of jobs on which they could usefully be employed, and that in any case they might need to be supervised by adults. This obviously limited the net financial gains of their labour. Nevertheless, at a time when agricultural production was so heavily labour-intensive, their input must still have been important in the mid-nineteenth century. Even after the coming of compulsory education, children could still make a useful contribution on the family farm both before and after school, as indeed is still sometimes the case today.

To turn to workshop employment, it has already been pointed out that before the coming of the factory system the workshop was the standard mode of manufacturing production, save where the nature of the work processes made this inappropriate, as for example in the manufacture of iron pig, or plate. The workshop was the workplace of the medieval craft guild, and in its domestic form it was where the basic processes of spinning and weaving in England's premier industry, the woollen cloth industry, took place. By the beginning of the nineteenth century the cotton factory, utilising water or steam power, had established itself, but the vast majority of industrial workers were still employed in workshops using a traditional hand technology. At this time they were still less numerous than agricultural workers. An estimate of the numbers of families engaged in the main branches of the economy in 1801–03 is as follows:[29]

Commerce	205,800	
Industry & building	541,026	
Agriculture (excluding labourers)	320,000	660,000
Labourers in husbandry	340,000	

The relationships shown here changed rapidly thereafter, so that by 1831 trade, manufacture and handicraft employed half as many again as agriculture:[30]

Families in	*1811*	*1821*	*1831*
	(000s)	*(000s)*	*(000s)*
Agriculture	896	979	961
Trade, manufacture, handicraft	1,129	1,350	1,435
Others	519	612	1,018

By 1851, although agriculture was still the largest single occupation, the total of workers in industry was by then over four times as great. Nevertheless, although the factory system had made great strides in the textile industry, especially in Lancashire, it by no means predominated. In fact, it has been calculated that mechanised industry, using steam-driven machinery, employed less than a quarter of all industrial workers in 1851; and this is so even if the coal industry is counted as being mechanised, although steam power was used to only a limited extent in that industry, mainly for winding, pumping, and ventilation.[31] Thus in manufacturing industry the traditional workshop was still the typical place of work in the mid-nineteenth century. Some workshops could be large, of course, employing a hundred or even two hundred workers, but according to Professor Mathias, the average workshop in 1851 still had less than ten employees.[32] It was in this kind of workshop, large or small, but for the most part small, that the typical industrial child worker was to be found in the mid-nineteenth century.

Where were such workshops located? In the textile industry, domestic weaving lingered on into the 1840s in Lancashire, and both domestic spinning and weaving survived even longer in Yorkshire. Of greater importance for workshop production by the mid-century was the metalwork industry which was strongly represented in Birmingham, in the Black Country (to the west of Birmingham), in the Sheffield cutlery trades, in Warrington and other parts of Lancashire, and from place to place in the West Country. Workshop production was also found in the hosiery industry (Nottingham, Leicester, and Belper) in lace manufacture (Nottingham, Leicester, Derby), and in pillow lace making in parts of Buckinghamshire, Bedfordshire, Oxfordshire, and Northamptonshire.[33] A good deal of workshop manufacture was also carried out in the clothing and boot and shoe trades in London and in many other towns, both large and small.

The ages at which children were employed did not differ greatly from the ages of agricultural child workers. Once again, a minimum amount of both physical strength and understanding was required, so that regular employment would generally begin between seven and eight; but children might be found at work at much earlier ages than this, as early as three and four. In one exceptional instance, an infant under two years old was discovered in regular employment in 1843, in the domestic machine lace industry, urged on by frequent admonitions from the mother to 'Mind your work'.[34]

As for hours of work, there was naturally some variation from industry to industry, but a twelve-hour day was common enough, sometimes including meals, sometimes not. Mealtimes seem normally to have amounted to one and a half hours, an hour being given for midday dinner. The working hours in Birmingham seem to have been shorter than in some places elsewhere; ten hours, excluding mealtimes, was usual. According to one of the visiting sub-commissioners of the Children's Employment Commission of 1843, R. D. Grainger, the hours are generally moderate in Birmingham, the common hours being 12, out of which 2 are usually deducted for meals, so the actual time of labour is 10 hours; this may be considered the rule. In some manufactories 13 hours are the regular time . . . on the whole, it may be stated that the hours of labour are probably shorter and less fatiguing than in any other manufacturing town in the kingdom.[35]

However, hours of this moderation were not always observed in practice. Sometimes they could be considerably longer, and if there was a rush of work, children might be working for 15, 16 or even 18 hours consecutively. The most extreme case of long hours encountered by the commissioners of the 1840 enquiry was in London, where young dressmakers were apprenticed at the age of twelve, beginning paid work at fourteen. Their regular hours in the busy four months of the London season were 15, and in an emergency, 18 hours or even more. It was said that during the season these young women would never get more than six, often not more than four, and occasionally not more than two hours for rest and sleep out of the twenty-four. Such hours may appear unbelievably long today, but were confirmed by one witness, a Mr Devonald, a surgeon, who said he was convinced that 'in no trade or manufactory whatsoever is the labour to be compared with that of the young dressmakers'.[36]

To put the whole matter of working hours into perspective, it must be observed that in the first half of the nineteenth century work was often held up by slumps in trade or by other causes, such as the failure of raw materials to be delivered on time. Before the coming of the railways, transport delivery times were often unreliable, especially in winter, when bad road conditions and frozen rivers and canals would cause great delays. Variations in trade were a very real problem, too, as any reading of local newspapers in industrial areas will confirm. In 1830 the Select Committee on Manufacturers' Employment, reporting in a year which was a bad one for trade, stated in their report that 'fluctuations in employment frequently occur in manufacturing districts, [and are] productive of great distress'.[37] Their remedy for this was to suggest the setting-up of employment fund societies, into which all workmen would be required to pay regularly, so they could be helped when trade was bad. This suggestion was based, of course, on the existing practice of skilled workmen of making contributions to friendly societies so that they could draw relief when out of work or on short time. To recommend that this should be extended to all workmen seems a remarkable proposal for the time, and in fact no such scheme was put into effect until the passing of the National Insurance Act, 1911. However, the simple fact that the idea was put forward gives a clear indication of the increasing middle-class awareness that the interruptions in trade which often occurred could and did have serious consequences for industrial workpeople.

Another more regular break in the routine of work resulted from the eighteenth-century practice of not working on Monday (and sometimes not on Tuesday, either). The keeping of St Monday was not confined to workshop industry, and might be observed even in larger workplaces, and down the mines. It was certainly widespread throughout industry, but was especially deep-rooted in Birmingham and the Black Country (in Birmingham it died away in the second half of the nineteenth century, but lingered on in the Black Country up to the outbreak of the First World War).[38] Thus the working week began for many not on Monday, but on Tuesday, and continued until work was broken off late on Saturday afternoon. In this way, most workers would have two days off at the weekend, Sunday and Monday. Further, since payment by the piece was very common, it was often the practice for workers to take things easy at the beginning of the week, and to work much harder towards the weekend, sometimes working all night on Friday, in order to complete enough work for payment on the Saturday.

Another break in the work routine was provided by the occasional holiday. Larger workshops in Birmingham might close for a week or so at Christmas in order to take stock; one or two days might be taken off at Easter and Whitsun, and workshops often closed when local fairs or wakes were held.[39] In addition, in some parts of the Black Country it was customary for working holidays to be taken in the summer. In the mid-years of the nineteenth century, nailers would strike bargains with local farmers for a week or fortnight's work on the harvest. The nailers would then set off to help with the reaping, or pick apples or hops, returning in procession, according to one observer, singing hymns or (as he put it) 'other, more dubious songs'. Their home-coming he described in picturesque terms:

> Anon, the work being completed, and an almost incredible quantity of cider consumed, and after sleeping almost promiscuously together in barns and such places, they return pretty much as they went, but with the addition (among others) of bags of apples, carried on almost every head, and with long strings of the same fruit arranged around the necks of the females, like monster coral necklaces.[40]

It would be wrong, therefore, to suppose that the work routine of the traditional workshop followed closely the harsh and unrelenting discipline of the textile factory with its steam-driven machinery. Nevertheless, on the whole, the hours were often very long, and the working environment usually dirty, ill-lit, and badly ventilated. The commissioners of the 1840 commission concluded that the places of work were 'in general, lamentably defective in drainage, ventilation, and due regulation of temperature, and cleanliness'. There was scarcely any accommodation for washing at mealtimes, or for preparing or warming up food. Usually there were no separate privies for men or women, or boys and girls, and the privies were 'commonly in a disgusting state of filth'. Only the more recently erected buildings were in a somewhat better state.[41]

In fact, having criticised the workshops in this way, the commissioners had relatively little to say about their use of tools, machinery, and so on. In practice, workshops varied considerably from one to another, the equipment depending on the product manufactured. In the decaying domestic textile industry, the workshop would simply be a room in a cottage containing the spinning jenny or hand loom. In metalware, there would be a separate one-storey brick building or shack, furnished with work-benches and appropriate tools. Nailing, for example, required work-benches, usually round the walls, a central hearth burning breeze (small cinders), a bellows, commonly fixed in the rafters, and a few hand tools, the most important in the Black Country being the famous nailer's 'ommer'. The only machine tool (if it can be so called) was the oliver, a spring-loaded, treadle-operated hammer used with thicker rod. Both boys and girls worked at the bench, while girls operated the overhead bellows. In the Birmingham metal trades, a relatively sophisticated hand technology was employed, utilising the stamp, the press, the drawbench, and the lathe. Small children were invaluable in assisting in the operation of these tools, for example, in arranging buttons into *rouleaux* for stamping (called 'cobbing'). In lacemaking, up to three lacemaking machines could be operated in the home, with greater numbers in workshops and factories. There were still more hand machines than powered machines in lacemaking in the early 1840s. Children worked principally on the machines in winding bobbins, or in threading. Simple lace-finishing processes needed only a needle, of course, ('drawing'), not a machine, and could be carried out at home by a very young child. In the cutlery trades, children worked at the bench as hefters (putting different parts of knives together, polishing and finishing them), or as grinders, crouching over the grindstones in a cramped position and freely inhaling the stone dust in what was considered the unhealthiest job of all in the trade.[42]

A more important issue, perhaps, than environmental health hazards was the treatment the child industrial worker received at the hands of his or her master or of the adult workers in the workshop. We have already seen that the evidence for ill-treatment of child agricultural workers is limited. How far can the same be said of their counterparts in the industrial workshop? The 1842 commissioners were very cautious in drawing conclusions on this matter in their general report. They remark that in too many cases the child is the servant of the workman, and entirely under his control, the proprietor himself knowing nothing of how the child is treated, and being wholly indifferent to it. In these circumstances, they considered that the child was often severely and sometimes cruelly used, while in one district visited, the treatment was 'oppressive and brutal to the last degree'.[43]

Reference to the detailed reports of sub-commissioners and to depositions bear out these comments, sometimes in a quite horrifying way. In some areas, treatment was not particularly objectionable; in Sheffield, for instance, the children were not generally ill-used, except by the small cutlers, and the evidence of children themselves did not contain any serious complaints of ill-treatment. Again, in Lancashire, the children were beaten at times, but seldom severely. In the west of England, the treatment was generally mild, without improper punishment or striking.[44] But it was otherwise in the Black Country, where the worst cruelty was to be found, especially in the Wolverhampton area, where punishments were not only harsh and cruel but 'in some cases can only be described as ferocious'. In Willenhall, according to the sub-commissioners, 'the children are shamefully and most cruelly beaten with a horsewhip, strap, stick, hammer-handle, file, or whatever tool is nearest to hand, or are struck with the clenched fist or kicked.'[45] The opportunities for practising cruel punishments when working at the forge were numerous. In Sedgley, near Wolverhampton, children were sometimes struck with a red-hot iron, thus being burnt and bruised simultaneously. One favourite trick was to send them a 'flash of lightning':

> When a bar of iron is drawn white-hot from the forge it emits fiery particles which a man commonly flings in a shower upon the ground by a swing of his arm before placing the bar upon the anvil. This shower is sometimes directed at the boy. It may come over his hand and face, his naked arms, or on his breast. If his shirt be open at the front, which is usually the case, the red-hot particles are

lodged therein, and he has to shake them out as fast as he can.[46]

But much worse treatment was inflicted on apprentices, who were the most abused and oppressed of all children. Graphic evidence was given by apprentices in the Willenhall district of Wolverhampton.[47]

Aged 13 His master often beats him with a whip with four lashes to it, and tied in knots: his master beats him for not doing enough work, and he could not do more – not able to do more –
Aged 15 The neighbours who live agen the shop will say how his master beats him; beats him with a strap, and sometimes a nut-stick; sometimes the weals remain on him for a week; his master once cut his eye-lid open, cut a hole in it, and it bled all over his files that he was working with.
Aged 16 He has been beaten at that time with a whip-handle – it made weals all down his arms and back and all; everybody he shows it to said it was scandalous. Wishes he could be released from his master . . . never has enough to eat at no time: ax him for more, he won't gie me.
Aged nearly 17 Is beaten every day; last time his master give it him he went up the garden and fetched two sticks down, and when he once begins he hardly ever knows when to leave off; he brought two sticks to use, one when the other wore out with beating him; the sticks are ashen plant.[47]

Although the sub-commissioners drew particular attention to Willenhall, examples of cruelty were to be found elsewhere in the West Midlands, even in Birmingham, where they considered that on the whole the children were not ill-treated. Such examples were to be found in the large pin workshops, where the pin-headers were children who came from the very poorest homes. Here was the same story of children being struck with any weapon which came to hand, and of one girl who had a long pin shank driven into her skin so deeply that pincers had to be used to extract it.[48]

As for apprenticeship generally, it appears that it existed in two forms in industry in the first half of the nineteenth century: one was apprenticeship of the traditional kind, with a premium paid and indentures signed before magistrates, the apprentice then living in with his master; the other form was of an informal nature, with or without a written agreement, and often made with a workman (that is, an employee) rather than the proprietor of the firm. Industrial apprenticeship was not confined to children from the workhouse, as in agriculture, and a boy properly apprenticed to a skilled trade such as that of flint-glass making could look forward eventually to a well-paid job as a member of the labour aristocracy. It was the other, informal kind of apprenticeship (including poor law apprentices) which was subject to abuses, and was really a very debased form of juvenile employment. As such, employers in Birmingham frowned on it; one even stated that no respectable employer would trouble himself about apprenticeship, while parents would not bind their children because they hoped that they would gain a man's wages before the expiry of their indentures.[49] The situation in Birmingham might have been exceptional to some degree, of course, because there was no tradition of craft guilds there. On the other hand, there were many skilled trades, and certainly apprenticeship of the more traditional kind persisted in some of the older crafts, such as that of goldsmithing.

In the Black Country, and among the lockmakers of Willenhall, it was very different. Here the more degraded form of apprenticeship existed widely, and a large proportion of the apprentices consisted of orphans, the children of widows, or were from the very poorest families. Frequently they were apprenticed by the board of guardians. Such children were sometimes apprenticed from the age of seven, and frequently suffered great hardship and ill-usage of the kind just described. Apart from these unfortunates, and those undergoing apprenticeship of the more respectable and worthy kind, it would appear that most children simply picked up whatever workshop skills were required as they went along. Of course, many were employed in domestic workshops and worked as members of the family. This was commonly the case in the lace, hosiery and glove trades, and in metalwork trades such as nailing and chainmaking.[50]

Other aspects of life for child workers in the workshops may now be considered. As nearly all the machinery employed in the small workshop was hand-operated, the risk of injury was much less than on the factory floor with its steam-driven machinery operated by overhead bands. Consequently really serious accidents were relatively rare, though minor mishaps were frequent. These often took the form of injuries to fingers and hands, sprains and contusions, wounds and burns and scalds. Probably the workshop environment itself was a greater danger to children's health than the work processes in themselves. As already noted, premises were commonly very dirty, often lacking both heating and proper ventilation, and frequently foul-smelling, due to the proximity of neglected privies. The commissioners discovered one nailing workshop in the Black Country where the nailers stood upon duckboards, this being made necessary by the overflow from a nearby cesspool. In Birmingham, the workshops were considered on the whole to be 'less unwholesome' than the large factories in Lancashire, yet the buildings in which they were housed were strongly criticised:

> In general, the buildings are very old, and many of them are in a dilapidated, ruinous, and even dangerous condition. Nothing is more common than to find many of the windows broken . . . great and just complaint is made upon this point by those employed. The shops are often dark and narrow; many of them, expecially those used for stamping, are from 4 to 7 feet below the level of the ground: these latter, which are cold and damp, are justly complained of by the workers. From defective construction, all these old shops are liable to become suffocatingly hot in summer (and also at night when the gas is lighted), and very cold in winter.[51]

It is interesting that the commissioners should be so forthright in condemning the workshops they inspected, making exceptions only of the newer workshops they saw. No doubt they were shocked by the wretchedness of many premises, so different from their own lawyers' chambers in London. Nevertheless, the sights they encountered could not have been so very unexpected, for they must have been aware that industry had been expanding for over half a century, and buildings were often adapted in a rough and ready fashion for industrial use. This was especially so in the metalware industries, where a minimum of equipment was required to set up in business. How far the quality of workshop provision had declined since the beginning of the nineteenth century is impossible to say, though it is known that much of the building during the wars against France was of poor quality, due to shortage of building materials, particularly of timber. The reports of 1842 give little or no indication of this. A reasonable guess might be that there had not been much noticeable change since 1800, but that older premises naturally continued to deteriorate in the almost complete absence of any controlling health or safety regulations. Of course, it might be that an increasing sensitivity to the effects of an unhealthy environment, itself the product of the public health movement of the time, sharpened the response of the commissioners to what they saw. At all events, their reaction to the working conditions of the 1840s was remarkably robust.

Further light was thrown on working conditions in the 1860s with the appointment of a second Children's Employment Commission in 1862. This time the commissioners were specifically directed to enquire into industries where legislation was already favoured by both employers and employees, industries which had grown in importance since 1842, or industries which the previous commissioners had shown to have a great need for legislative protection.[52] As a result, attention was paid to some workshop industries, such as lace manufacture, hosiery, straw plaiting, and dressmaking, while other industries were ignored. The reports of the commission yield some useful figures; for example, that there were still about 2,000 children under ten at work in Birmingham, a quarter of these being under eight;[53] but unfortunately the national figures given, though making it clear that milliners and dressmakers constituted the largest groups investigated, are in some cases contradictory and unreliable. It is probably better to take figures from a more modern source[54] to indicate the numbers of younger children still at work:

Number of children under ten recorded as occupied in census returns

	1851	*1861*	*1871*
Males	26,492	22,755	11,592
Females	15,434	13,760	10,244
	41,926	36,515	21,836

Given the fact that the UK population increased from 27.39 million in 1851 to 31.56 million in 1871, it is clear that on these figures, at least, there was a significant reduction in the number of the youngest children at work. It is likely that this was due to a number of causes; for example, the relative prosperity of the decades after 1851, which made it less necessary for the youngest to go out to work so soon, the increasing belief that children should have some schooling, and so on.

Whatever the causes may be, the 1862 commissioners drew attention in their fifth report to some of the improvements which had taken place since 1840. Significantly enough, their first point was that the age of the youngest children sent to work was now 'a little advanced': formerly it was sometimes as early as three or four, and not infrequently five, or between five and six. By the mid-1860s employment below the age of six had become comparatively rare, except in the straw plaiting schools (really workshops rather than schools in the ordinary sense of the word) where three-, or three-and-a-half-year-old children were still set to work. Further, the treatment of children had improved and instances of cruelty or severity appeared to be few, while apparent suffering from insufficient food and clothing had diminished. Moreover, complaints arising out of apprenticeship had become rare, employers' sense of responsibility had greatly improved, efforts 'directed to the moral and intellectual improvement of the work people' were more widespread, and the means of secular and religious instruction were 'immensely increased, and greatly more efficient'.[55] All this may seem to present a somewhat rosy view of what had happened in the previous twenty years, but certainly the economic situation had improved greatly since the depressed early years of the 1840s, a fact to which the decline of Chartism and advances in the friendly society movement, the co-operative movement, and trade unionism all bear witness (the grant of the franchise to working-class householders in the towns in 1867, the famous 'leap in the dark', is also not without significance). Certainly the 1850s and 1860s saw an easing of the social tensions which characterised the late 1830s and early 1840s – the change to what Professor W. L. Burn called the 'age of equipoise'. Thus it is not unreasonable to suppose that conditions for child workers had improved, though the workshop itself was beginning to be affected by the increasing use of powered machinery. As an example of this, while hosiery was almost entirely domestic in manufacture in the 1840s, by the 1860s it was more and more to be found in factories.[56]

At this point it becomes possible to view some of the matters discussed so far in this chapter in a longer perspective. One question in particular regarding the working lives of children has still to be answered: did working conditions get better or worse as the pace of industrialisation increased? So far as the agricultural children were concerned, there is little to show any marked change either way. Technological innovation hardly altered the basic work routines of the children, and their mode of work remained much the same over the whole period from 1800 to the 1870s.[57] It was assumed throughout that there was nothing inherently harmful in the nature of the work, or indeed in the treatment of the children. The major difference in attitude between these two dates came from the realisation that if children were to receive an adequate education, the younger children must not be sent out to work at so early an age. Apart from this, as we have seen, the only truly harmful aspects of children's employment in agriculture were thought to be poor law apprenticeship and the gang system.

The position of child industrial workers is more complex and harder to assess. Perhaps the best-known social consequence of industrialisation was the employment of children in textile factories (a subject to be dealt with in a subsequent chapter). The ill-treatment of these children is so familiar that it has helped to obscure the fact that the majority of child workers did not work in factories at all, but were mostly (though by no means exclusively) employed in workshops. The question then arises: did working conditions deteriorate for them, as so obviously they did for the factory children? It is often taken for granted that this must be so, and eminent historians have commented on the hardships suffered by *all* industrial workers as the change to an industry-based economy intensified in the early nineteenth century.[58] Yet more recent research emphasises again and again that economic change at this time took place at a far slower pace than was previously assumed.[59] Consequently, the pace of social change is likely to have been less dramatic than was thought earlier. Further, there are few indications that the pace of work in the workshop accelerated, or that hours were lengthened, or that children were employed at an even younger age. As one might expect, eighteenth-century work routines continued into the nineteenth century. The increase in demand for manufactured goods other than textiles was met by an increase in the number of traditional work units and of industrial workers, not by a great spurt in productivity, which was already high in some industries, such as the Birmingham metalware industry with its high-level hand technology and its division of labour.[60]

However, it must be said that it is difficult to reach positive conclusions on this subject. One obvious line of enquiry is to investigate the number of hours worked, together with the nature of the work discipline which was enforced. Although there is plenty of evidence available regarding the length of the working day, the vicissitudes of trade, combined with self-imposed variations in working hours make it virtually impossible to establish long-term patterns of the working day with any certainty. All that can be said in general terms is that nominal hours of work show little variation from the eighteenth century to the early nineteenth century.[61] Moreover, workshop workers clung tenaciously to St Monday and even St Tuesday, paying for their easier time at the beginning of the week by working extremely long hours at the end of it. As for work discipline, though efforts were certainly made by some employers to foster belief in the virtues of hard work and regular hours,[62] there is no evidence to show that workshop employees were everywhere being driven harder than they had been previously. When strikes occurred, for the most part they were over pay and conditions, rather than over the lengthening of the working day or the result of the slave-driving tactics of the employer. None of the commissioners of the 1840 enquiry, although condemning cruelty to the children when they encountered it, remarked on the severity of the new work discipline resulting from the expansion of industry; nor did witnesses, child or adult, ever refer to this. After all, workshop industry had been laborious enough in the eighteenth century. It remained so in the first half of the nineteenth century, and child workers continued to work as hard as ever – but not noticeably more so than before.

The one clear case of domestic workshop workers affected directly and adversely by technological change after 1830 is provided by the hand loom weavers in Lancashire who fought a losing battle against factory production. Their plight was such that they were the subject of a special government enquiry in 1840. However, it has been argued that by 1815 most of these weavers were part-time workers and women, most male weavers having found alternative jobs.[63] It may be, of course, that with the overall increase in trade during the first half of the century the more sustained demand for products meant that there were fewer interruptions in workshop routines, less time idled away between deliveries of raw materials, and so on. This may conceivably be so, but signs that the working day in the small workshop was beginning to resemble the working day in the factory with its non-stop, steam-driven machines, are singularly absent. The working children still kept St Monday, and worked longer hours towards the end of the week along with the adults. Thus there is little to show that workshop children were subjected on the whole to longer hours, or to a harsher work discipline, as the nineteenth century progressed.

Another striking and somewhat curious aspect of the employment of child workers in both agriculture and in the workshops in the first half of the nineteenth century is the ready acceptance of child employment by middle-class observers. Clearly they did not find the employing of children objectionable in itself, except when it was of very young children or was accompanied by obvious cruelty. As we have seen, the nature of agricultural work was not thought to be injurious, and it was actually described as 'conducive to health' in one of the 1843 reports. Similarly, in the same year the second report of the Children's Employment Commission expressed the opinion that, with few exceptions, nothing in the nature of the children's industrial work was directly injurious to health; but the demands made on the strength of the children by early labour and long hours of work were 'not generally sustained by wholesome and sufficient food'. Nor were the children usually protected by warm and comfortable clothing. Indeed, although some children were robust, active, and healthy, many were pale, weak and sickly.

The report concludes that many in pin-making, nailmaking, lacemaking, and the hosiery trades were underfed and ill-clothed; great numbers said they had seldom or never enough to eat, and many of them were in rags. Finally it was said that these children for the most part were stunted in growth, and 'they present altogether the appearance of a race which has suffered general physical deterioration'.[64]

It is true that this severe judgement on the general state of the children in certain trades is toned down at a later date in the conclusions of the fifth report of 1866 of the commission appointed in 1862, where it is said that the apparent suffering from insufficient food and clothing in the earlier period had diminished. It is also true that in 1843 the commissioners were aware that the fact that a large number of the Birmingham children were in a deplorable state might be explained by the bad condition of trade at the time.[65] Yet the overall impression left on the commissioners in 1843 was that the industrial children were in a far worse physical condition than the agricultural children. Why this should be is not discussed, other than by the reference to the poor state of trade, a comment which was fully justified given the acute depression in trade at the time. Presumably the implied criticism was not of the harmful nature of the work, but of the standard of living which it conferred; either because the wages of the parents were relatively low, or because of parental indifference and neglect, or perhaps because of a combination of both these factors. It must not be forgotten, of course, that the major reason why young children went to work is that without their earnings their parents would have found it hard to feed them, or so it was frequently alleged. Children's wages early on in the century ranged from 2*s* to 3*s* a week, rising from the age of thirteen to 4*s* to 10*s* per week.[66] These wages were usually handed over to parents, and were an important contribution to the family income. However, not all observers thought that children's earnings were always essential to the family economy. Some argued that the extra money simply went to pay for the father's beer.[67] Clearly all would depend on the circumstances of the individual family. In the second half of the nineteenth century, the increasing acceptance of the idea that all working-class children should have some form of schooling became economically feasible as the loss of their labour was compensated for by more mechanical production and increased productivity. Moreover, the loss of their earnings was offset by the improvement in real wages in the last quarter of the century. In these ways, it is suggested, the economic and social problems posed by the employment of young children were at last solved.

Lastly, there is the question of the extent of cruelty to children which was revealed by the reports of both the 1840s and the 1860s, especially since it has been argued that greater sensitivity was being shown at this time to children and their needs. One simple explanation of this apparent paradox, of course, is that the increasing sensitivity was manifested among the middle classes rather than the working classes, as was demonstrated in the Prologue. Middle-class reformers were quick to blame the degrading effect of the urban industrial environment on the working classes. Thus Southwood Smith, the public health reformer, testified to this in a striking statement in his evidence before the Health of Towns Commission in 1844:

> In the filthy and crowded streets of our large towns and cities you see human faces retrograding, sinking down to the level of brute tribes, and you find manners appropriate to the degradation. Can anyone wonder that there is among these classes of the people so little intelligence, so slight an approach to humanity, so total an absence of domestic affection, and of moral and religious feeling? . . . if from early infancy, you allow human beings to live like brutes, you can degrade them down to their level.[68]

This is certainly the classic environmental explanation of uncouth and brutal behaviour; it was rooted in what one commentator called 'a low and grovelling mode of living'. It finds expression again in the opinions voiced in the second report of the 1840 enquiry, regarding the cruelty inflicted on the apprentices in Willenhall. Many of the small masters, it was said, treated the apprentices

> not so much with neglect and harshness, as with ferocious violence, the result of unbridled passions, excited often by ardent spirits, acting on bodies exhausted by overwork, and on minds which have never received the slightest moral or religious culture, and which never exercise the slightest moral or religious restraint.[69]

One is tempted to ask how the commissioner could be so sure in his judgement of the causes of the violence inflicted on the children. The fact that the worst sufferers were apprentices, frequently from the workhouse, is surely of some significance; since pauper children usually have no parents to protect them, and were often illigitmate – in other words, fair game. Nevertheless, the contemporary verdict is clear enough: the violence was due to outbursts of temper, to drink, overwork, and the complete lack of religious or moral belief.

How far modern observers would agree with this diagnosis is another matter. Even if it is true that middle-class attitudes to children were becoming more enlightened in the eighteenth and early nineteenth centuries, it is not possible to say whether working-class adults were treating children in a more kindly fashion than before, or whether their treatment actually grew harsher. The existence of cruelty to children in the early Victorian period was an undoubted fact, as indeed it is to some extent today in late twentieth-century England in the forms of physical and sexual abuse. There was nothing new about it in the first half of the 19th century, and so far as the workshop is concerned, it would be unwise to treat it as a consequence of the new industrialism. However, middle-class reaction may owe something to the new sensitivity, and to other reforms, such as the abolition of slavery, the campaign to abolish cruel sports, and the prevention of cruelty to animals. A more direct and immediate influence, perhaps, came from the revelations regarding the treatment of factory children, and also of the working conditions of children down the mines (the first report of the 1840 commissioners on the latter produced such a dramatic effect on middle-class opinion that legislation was immediately introduced). A fair summing-up might be that however striking the cruelty practised on factory children, the treatment of workshop children, and especially apprenticed labour, might be equally harsh at times. The point was well put by Professor J. H. Plumb more than forty years ago, but has not received the emphasis it deserves: 'The worst conditions, long hours, irregular payment of wages, truck, gross exploitation of female and child labour were to be found in small-scale and domestic industry.'[70]

By way of final comment on the subject matter of this chapter, it may be observed that centuries-old practices in agriculture and in workshop industry for the first time came under systematic review by middle-class reformers. Presumably most of the commissioners saw and heard what they expected to see and hear, with the important qualification that it was judged in the light of the newer sensibility informed by newly-acquired knowledge of the horrors of the factory system. This knowledge, it is suggested, set new standards by which working conditions and treatment of working children might be assessed. There was the further belief that education (mostly of a religious and moral nature) was necessary if the ever-growing numbers of boys and girls were to be disciplined and turned into conforming members of the new urban society. There is little or no evidence that there was much fundamental change in working conditions for child workers in the first half of the nineteenth century in either agriculture or workshop industry, or anything to show that cruelty had increased as industralisation intensified;

but a new kind of industrial society was developing, and by the more humane standards of the day and in the interests of shaping a more civilised community, increased regulation appeared necessary. Hence the extension of government control of child labour in and after 1867. Fortunately this was to come when the increasing wealth and economic capacity of the nation would allow it to be imposed, and indeed it was predicated upon economic growth. Keynes is supposed to have said that England had Shakespeare when she could afford him. This was a provocative and over-simplified way of putting it, of course, but it might equally well be argued that England abolished child labour when it became economically possible to do so. To say this is not to imply that there was any direct and immediate connection between the growth of prosperity and the ending of child labour, but merely to observe that whatever the contribution to the economy made by child labour earlier in the century, by the 1870s it could increasingly be dispensed with as productivity grew. Curiously enough, the importance of a trained juvenile labour force was to become a subject of increasing discussion at the end of the century, as will be seen in Part IV of this book.

References

1 François Crouzet, *The Victorian Economy*, 1982, p. 67.

2 For general accounts of children working in agriculture, see R. Samuel (ed.), *Village Life and Labour*, 1975; G. E. Mingay, *Rural Life in Victorian England*, 1977, *The Victorian Countryside*, I & II, 1981, and (ed.), *The Agrarian History of England and Wales*, Vol. VI, 1750–1850, 1989; P. E. Razell and W. R. Wainwright, *The Victorian Working Class*, 1973; Pamela Horn, *The Victorian Country Child*, 1974, *Labouring Life in the Victorian Countryside*, 1976, and *The Changing Countryside in Victorian and Edwardian England and Wales*, 1984.

3 See the reports of the Special Assistant Poor Law Commissioners of the *Commission on the Employment of Women and Children in Agriculture*, 1843, especially on pp. 28, 184 and in the detailed reports on individual areas.

4 *Ibid.*, p. 31.

5 The great variety of jobs is well set out in the reports of 1843 mentioned above, though it should be noted that the scope of their enquiries was limited to twelve counties.

6 *Report*, 1843, p. 30.

7 *Ibid.*, p. 31.

8 *Ibid.*, p. 72.

9 *Ibid.*, p 209.

10 Mingay (ed.), *Agrarian History*, p. 644.

11 E. H. Hunt, *British Labour History 1815–1914*, 1981, p. 140.

12 *Report*, 1843, p. 95.

13 *Ibid.*, pp. 98, 105, 108, 112.

14 *Ibid.*, pp. 52, 46, 55.

15 *Ibid.*, p. 55.

16 *Ibid.*, (Denison's Report), pp. 223–6.

17 *Ibid.* p. 225.

18 *Commission on the Employment of Children, Young Persons, and Women in Agriculture*, 1867, Second Report, p. xliii, quoting the 1861 Census Returns.

19 *Ibid.*, p. ix.

20 *Ibid.*, p. xiv.

21 *Report*, 1843, p. 231.

22 Mingay (ed.), *Agrarian History*, p. 687.

23 *Ibid.*, p. 716.

24 The separate reports of the two men are in the Second Report of the Commission, pp. viii–lxxiii.

25 Eric Hopkins, 'Tremenheere's Prize Schemes in the Mining Districts, 1851–1859', *History of Education Society Bulletin*, No. 15, Spring, 1975.

26 Pamela Horn, *The Changing Countryside in Victorian and Edwardian England and Wales*, 1984, p. 164.

27 *Report*, 1843, p. 65.

28 *Ibid.* p. 31.

29 B. R. Mitchell, *British Historical Statistics*, 1988, p. 102.

30 *Ibid.*, p. 103.

31 J. D. Chambers, *The Workshop of the World*, 1961, pp. 21–2.

32 Peter Mathias, *The First Industrial Nation*, 2nd edn, 1983, p. 247.

33 For the best contemporary general survey of children's employment in workshop industry, see the Second Report, 1843, of the *Children's Employment Commission*, 1840, also named the *Commission on Trades and Manufactures*. For a good modern account of industry in the nineteenth century see A. E. Musson, *The Growth of British Industry*, 1977.

34 *Report*, 1843, pp. 195, 10.

35 *Ibid.*, Appendix to Second Report, Grainger's Report, at fos 17 and 18.

36 *Ibid.*, p. 116.

37 Report from the *Select Committee on Manufacturers' Employment*, 1830.

38 Douglas A. Read, 'The Decline of St Monday, 1776–1867', *Past & Present*, 71, 1976; Eric Hopkins, 'Working Hours and Conditions during the Industrial Revolution: A Reappraisal', *Economic History Review*, XXXV, No. 1, Feb. 1982; *Children's Employment Commission*, 1862, Third Report, p. xi, and J. E. White's Report, p. 57.

39 Eric Hopkins, *Birmingham: the First Manufacturing Town in the World 1760–1840*, 1989, p. 111.

40 J. Noake, *The Rambler*, 1854.

41 *Children's Employment Commission*, 1840 (hereafter *CEC*, 1840), Second Report, 1843, p. 32.

42 For the nailing workshop, see E. I. Davies, 'The Hand-made Nail Trade of Birmingham and District', Birmingham M.A. thesis, 1933, and A. F. Moseley, 'The Nailmakers', in *West Midland Studies*, II, 1968. For Birmingham metal trades, see William Hawkes Smith, *Birmingham and its Vicinity*, 1836, Pt III, p. 16, and Hopkins, *Birmingham*, pp. 7–10. For lacemaking and the Sheffield trades, see *CEC*, 1840, Second Report, 1843, Grainger's Report, F1 to F4, and E1 to E5.

43 *CEC*, 1840, Second Report, 1843, p. 79.

44 *Ibid.*, pp. 84, 85.

45 *Ibid.*, p. 80.

46 *Ibid.*

47 *Ibid.*, pp. 81–2.

48 Hopkins, *Birmingham*, pp. 104, 106–8.

49 *CEC*, 1840, Appendix to Second Report, Report on apprentices, fos 170 and 171.

50 An up-to-date book on apprenticeship in the nineteenth century has yet to be written. The basic books are still Jocelyn Dunlop, *Apprenticeship and Child Labour*, 1912, and S. and B. Webb, *Industrial Democracy*, 1902 edn. However, see William Knox, 'British Apprenticeship 1800–1914', Edinburgh Ph.D. thesis, 1980, and his article, 'Apprenticeship and De-Skilling in Britain, 1850–1914', *International Review of Social History*, XXXI, 1986. There are also informative passages (discussed in Chapter Eight) in Charles More, *Skill and the English Working Class 1870–1914*, 1980. For Birmingham, see Hopkins, *Birmingham*, pp. 58–60, and on the Black Country, his 'Were the Webbs wrong about Apprenticeship in the Black Country?', *West Midland Studies*, Vol. 6, 1973.

51 *CEC*, 1840, Second Report, Grainger's Report, fo. 20.

52 *Children's Employment Commission*, 1862 (hereafter *CEC*, 1862), First Report, p. 7.

53 *Ibid.*, Third Report, Mr White's Report, p. x.

54 B. R. Mitchell, *British Historical Statistics*, 1988.

55 *CEC*, 1862, Fifth Report, 1866, p. xxvi.

56 *Ibid.*, First Report, p. lxxx.

57 Some historians, espcially those on the Left, would question this. For example, E. P. Thompson claims that agricultural labour discipline increased at the end of the eighteenth century: see his 'Time, Work-Discipline and Industrial Capitalism', *Past & Present*, 38, 1967. This is in line with the pessimistic view of the results of the development of industrial capitalism, but it is difficult to see how and why this happened, or to find supporting evidence for it.

58 For example, Professor J. D. Chambers stated that the labour force in the Industrial Revolution was not only very much larger, but was worked very much harder: *Population, Economy and Society in Pre-Industrial England*, 1972, p. 149. Professor Pollard put the same point when he said that the modern industrial proletariat was 'not allowed to grow in a sunny garden: it was forged, over a fire, by the powerful blows of a hammer'; S. Pollard, *Genesis of Modern*

Management, 1965, p. 207. These views are disputed by the present author in the article referred to in note 38 above.

59 See generally A. E. Wrigley, *Continuity, Chance and Change*, 1988. See also N. F. R. Crafts and C. K. Harley, 'Output Growth and The British Industrial Revolution: a re-statement of the Crafts-Harley view', *Economic History Review*, XLV, No. 4, November, 1992.

60 For Birmingham productive methods, see Hopkins, *Birmingham*, pp. 6–9.

61 Variations are discussed in M. A. Bienefeld, *Working Hours in British Industry: An Economic History*, 1972.

62 Thompson gives good examples in his 'Time, Work-Discipline, and Industrial Capitalism', *Past & Present*, 38, 1967.

63 Peter Mathias, *First Industrial Nation*, p. 185; D. Bythell, *The Handloom Weavers*, 1968.

64 *CEC* (1840), Second Report, pp. 100, 198, 199.

65 *Ibid.*, Appendix, at F23.

66 *Ibid.*, Second Report, p. 93.

67 *The Times* for 20 October 1865 reported a debate in Sheffield Town Council, where a leading councillor, a Mr Harvey, declared 'Away with the nonsense about the wages of the child being necessary for the support of the family. The men drink the wages of the boys (hear, hear)'.

68 *Health of Towns Commission*, 1844, 1845. First Report, pp. 82–3. Southwood Smith also commented that sanitary conditions were so bad in some parts of London that 'the result is the same if twenty or thirty thousand of these people were annually taken out of their wretched dwellings, and put to death', p. 69.

69 *CEC*, 1840, Second Report, pp. 80–1.

70 J. H. Plumb, *England in the Eighteenth Century*, Harmondsworth, 1950, p. 88. For a recent survey of workshop industry in the earlier period, see Maxine Berg, *The Age of Manufactures 1700–1820*, 1985, who asserts that the intensive exploitation of labour, particularly that of women and children, was at least equal to that suffered under the factory system (p. 19), thus echoing Plumb's earlier verdict.

Chapter Two

Iron manufacture, mining, and other industries

If the employment of children in agriculture and in workshop manufacture was already well established in the eighteenth century before the Industrial Revolution, the same might be said of child employment in ironworks and down the mines. The iron industry has a long history in this country, and it entered into a new phase of expansion in the Tudor period with the introduction of the blast furnace from Belgium around the beginning of the sixteenth century. A hundred years or so later a further technological innovation in the form of the slitting and rolling mill came into England from Flanders, and was widely adopted in the West Midlands. By the early eighteenth century, the iron industry had spread from its original home on the Weald to the Forest of Dean, the West Midlands, south Wales, north Wales and Cheshire, and to parts of Lancashire and Yorkshire. At this time the industry was still dependent on supplies of charcoal for fuel in the blast furnace, and also on water power for operating the bellows for blast and for driving hammers in the forge train. Children were employed on a variety of tasks in the ironworks of the time, but the opportunities for employment were greatly increased by further technological advances which led to a massive development of the iron industry towards the end of the eighteenth century.[1]

The first of these advances was the substitution of coke for charcoal in the blast furnace, by Abraham Darby in 1709. This use of mineral fuel took time to spread throughout the industry, but became widely known and adopted by the mid-eighteenth century. A further advance came in 1783 with the invention by Henry Cort of the puddling and rolling process for the better converting of pig iron into wrought iron. Lastly, in the last quarter of the eighteenth century, the use of the Boulton and Watt steam engine instead of water power greatly improved the efficient provision of blast for the blast furnaces, and of power for rolling machinery and hammers.[2] These technological changes set the scene for an impressive expansion of the industry, especially in those areas where coal was readily available for conversion into coke and also as fuel for steam engines. For these reasons the iron industry became a great source of employment for both adults and children in south Wales and in the Black Country, two regions in which supplies of coal, ironstone, and limestone were ample at the beginning of the nineteenth century. The 1840 Children's Employment Commission paid particular attention to conditions of child labour in the ironworks of south Wales, which included some of the largest ironworks in the country. They also investigated child employment in some of the local tinplate and copper works.

A feature of child labour found in the south Wales ironworks but not in the West Midlands was the employment of girls as well as boys on the blast furnaces. One explanation given for this at the time was that many of the ironworks were situated in relatively remote parts of the valleys where there was a shortage of labour. Another reason could have been that the employment of girls down the local pits (a practice not followed on the South Staffordshire coalfield) encouraged their use in the ironworks close at hand. As happened in other occupations, of course, the tasks given to children were commensurate with their age and physical strength. The age of starting work seems to have varied from place to place – sometimes from the age of six or seven for both girls and boys, sometimes a little later. In the Pontypool area, they were set to work from about nine, the greatest number of children at work being aged between ten and thirteen years of age.[3]

All the jobs at which the children were engaged took the form of assisting the adult workers in the various work processes. Some were simply employed in the adjoining fields, building up the heaps of coal which were to be turned into coke, or heaping up ironstone, or breaking up the limestone which was used as flux in the blast furnaces. Others worked more directly on the blast furnaces, filling boxes with coke or calcinated (roasted) ironstone, or riddling fine ironstone from dirt and dust. Still others helped on the puddling furnaces; *pullers-up* opened the furnace doors when required by operating a lever and chain arrangement. Children played an important part as well in operating the rollers. *Hookers-on* helped the iron into the rolling machine; they were described as standing by the rolls (i.e. rollers) 'with a suspended lever to support the bar of iron before it enters the groove'. *Catchers* caught the bar of iron once it had gone through the rolls. *Tip girls* removed cinders from the furnaces. Girls might also act as *pilers* – piling up bars after they had been cut by shears worked by water or steam power, and before they were put through the rolls again.

Other jobs required rather more strength. For this reason, children on these jobs were rarely under twelve; they included *straighteners, roughers, iron-fillers,* and *water carriers*. In the tin and copper works, there were other, more specialised jobs. For example, in the tinworks with their plating processes, there were *pickle and scale boys, cold rollers, grease boys, rubbers, gate-boys,* and *plate openers*.[4]

The hours worked by these children were the same as those of the adults, that is, twelve-hour shifts, one week on days, and the next on nights. One vexed problem was that of Sunday working, for the furnaces had to be kept working continuously through the whole week. Hence the need for the 'double turn', from 6 a.m. on Sunday morning to 6 a.m. on Monday. Some employers tried to avoid this by allowing the furnaces to stand for several hours during Sunday. About one third of the furnaces in south Wales were allowed to stand in this way in 1842. They included those of the Dowlais Iron Works (proprietors, Sir John Guest & Co.), the largest ironworks in the United Kingdom. In Staffordshire, about the same proportion of furnaces were similarly left to stand. In Shropshire, the furnaces stood from ten to four o'clock on Sundays at the famous Coalbrookdale works. The nearby Madeley Wood Iron Works also stood idle for six to eight hours. A partner of the works, Mr John Anstice, remarked to a sub-commissioner, 'The stand takes place during the double turn, which is a geat relief, as there are only 16 or 18 hours' labour instead of 24'. Those employers who enforced the full double turn claimed that to stop the furnaces usually meant a loss of iron, and difficulty in getting the furnace back to normal operation. In all 12 hour turns, there were commonly two breaks for meals.[5] In the copper works, 24-hour shifts sometimes occurred during the week. Boys in the calcining process worked 24 hours non-stop, then rested for 24 hours. At the Margam Copper Works, James Phillips, aged 14, a sheet dryer (he was described as a short, delicate, intelligent little boy), gave evidence. He had been at the works for four years, having worked previously down the pit. He was reported as follows: 'Prefers this to tramming in the coal-pit, but doesn't like such long hours, although better paid. Works usually 13 hours, and three times a week, 24 hours. The work is very wet and hot.'[6]

As for working conditions generally, the ironworks were usually open, but were roofed over so as to give protection from the rain. In most cases the floor was paved. For the visitor, the outstanding characteristic of the working conditions was the extreme heat, with a consequent great drop in temperature when the ironworker left work. The result was alleged to be the frequent occurrence of 'diseases of the respiratory organs' and of 'febrile and inflammatory disease'. The children were just as subject to this change in temperature as the men. In addition, it was said that children at the Cyfarthfa iron works were badly affected by the fumes from the calcining furnaces: 'When children are brought early, as they too frequently are, the sulphurous vapour arising from the calcinators injures them, and keeps them down in size and strength.'[7] In the copper works, it was observed that the smoke form the chimneys killed the surrounding vegetation; though rather surprisingly the fumes were not thought to be injurous to human health.[8]

The other great characteristic of work in the ironworks was the risk of accidents and injuries. Molten metal was constantly on the move, either on the casting floor or in ladles. Rolls were unfenced. Burns were commonplace, and many witnesses referred to this fact. For example, David Evans, aged ten, who had started work at eight, said 'I do not like night work; have often been burned, as most boys are when first at work; the work is very hard for boys as well as men, and we are kept well at it; no-one ever falls asleep.'[9] As for accidents, the employers in south Wales were said to be unwilling to give evidence on this subject, and no statistics were supplied by them. Nevertheless, the 1842 report voiced a popular opinion when it referred to 'a population so exposed to frightful accidents as those engaged in the ironworks'.[10] Rhys William Jones, reporting on the Pontypool district, estimated that one in a thousand accidents a year was fatal, and one in 500 accidents was serious. This might well be something of an understatement. One youth, Thomas George, who had worked at the rolls, reported at some length to Mr Jones:

> About a year ago I lost my left arm above the elbow; I slipped my foot and fell down, and my arm got into the rolls. I was only saved from going through by being caught hold of by the men; my arm was crushed to pieces, and was 10 minutes in that state before they could stop the mill and raise the rolls. It was cut off in about two hours after they took me home . . . While I was at the Dowlais forge there were two men killed by the rolls and the wheels, and two boys lost their left leg in the rolls and by the locomotive engine.[11]

Accidents also occurred, of course, in the copper works and the tin works. Thomas Smith, a greaser, aged twelve, at the Mellagriffith Tin Works, said that he had been at the works three years. He was a lusterer, and had to dip the plates in the metal. He had lost the tips of his fingers on his right hand, the result of passing the plates too quickly through the shears.[12]

How hard was the work required of the children? They were generally under the control of the adults who paid them, usually by the piece. Often they worked under their fathers, or otherwise under overmen or agents. According to the first report of the Children's Employment Commission, 1840, the work was not necessarily laborious or exhausting; but several of the young witnesses said they thought the work was hard. Breaking up limestone was very severe labour – some of the young women engaged in it actually worked for twelve hours a day, seven days a week.[13] Other tasks were less continuous and more intermittent in nature. For example, once blast furnaces were duly charged, they needed merely maintenance (including recharging, of course) until they were tapped. Similarly, puddling furnaces had to be maintained at the right heat until the iron had 'come to nature', that is, until the desired chemical changes had occurred (denoted by particular flames known as 'puddlers' candles'), when the iron was ready to be extracted. This process could not be hurried, and would depend on the skill of the master puddler and his knowledge of the furnace and the metal. His assistant would have to conform to the timetable he followed. According to the sub-commissioner Rhys William Jones, there would be periods of an hour, or half an hour, of very hard work, followed by an interval ('a period of cessation') of fifteen or twenty minutes. These cessations would occur seven or eight times in the twelve hours.[14]

How exhausting the work really was for the children is difficult to estimate. Clearly some found it harder than others, depending on their physical development and stamina. One furnace agent, Thomas Price, said in evidence that the boys were not generally overworked, but that coke-filling was the hardest task. In the copper works, boys of thirteen to sixteen on their twenty-four-hour turns could sleep for an hour or so, two or three times in the night, as the furnaces needed tending every two hours. The next hardest work was wheeling ashes and coal to and from the furnaces; this work was carried out by girls of thirteen and above.[15] Surprisingly enough, some of the boy witnesses said that they played after work. One said they then washed before going to bed, as their mothers wouldn't allow them to go filthy to rest. A medical man in Pontypool confirmed that children would play after work: 'On summer evenings, the young of all ages may be seen in great numbers eagerly engaged in amusements and games requiring considerable exertion and activity, quite incompatible with their previous exhaustion.'[16] It may be that this was to paint too rosy a picture. It is hard to say, but the youngest children must have found the day very long. More typical of their experience, perhaps, was the testimony of David Williams, an eight-year-old plate carrier at the Aberdulais Iron and Tin Plate Works:

I have been carrying the plates to the men half a year, and do so every day from 6 in the morning to 8 at night: feels very tired when work is over. Mother washes my face after work; sometimes I wash my feet. Runs home to meals; stays a quarter of an hour to each. Never got burned; gets the toes cut sometimes. Never been to school.[17]

So much for the fourteen-hour working day of this young boy who had started work at the age of seven and a half. He was by no means exceptional.

None of the witnesses before the Commission complained of cruel treatment by the men, and the horrific stories of cruelty practised, for example, on the workshop apprentices of Willenhall are noticeably absent from their evidence. It was said that there was 'a great spirit of emulation' among the boys, so that their labours were seldom enforced by punishment, nor was corporal punishment employed; misbehaviour was usually punished by fines – 2*s* 6*d* for drunkenness, fighting, or neglect of work, with more serious offences attracting fines of 5*s* or 10*s*. Thomas Griffith, an agent, said that boys were never beaten; if they misbehaved, they were simply dismissed. One twelve-year-old boy confirmed this, saying that 'nobody beats the boys here', but it is difficult to believe that children were never struck at all. Another boy, George Haddock, aged fourteen years, four months, was the only boy to claim that he had been beaten many times by the men, 'but they did not hurt me very bad'. It might be, of course, that these child witnesses thought it better not to complain of ill-treatment, but the general impression given is that they spoke up freely enough. One sixteen-year-old girl, Sarah Jones, certainly spoke up for herself: 'Why do you ask me my age? . . . I have heard that you want the boys to go for soldiers . . . that you want to take us all away.'[18] She was described, somewhat stiffly one might think, by Mr Jones as 'totally uneducated'; but she was clearly prepared to ask questions, nevertheless.

All in all, it is clear enough that work for children in the ironworks was hard and strenuous, and the hours were long. Overtime was imposed from time to time, and there were few holidays; work stopped for most only on Sundays, on Christmas Day, Good Friday, and Easter Monday.[19] Inevitably there were times when trade was slack, and the pressure to produce was lessened, but on the whole, the first half of the nineteenth century was a period of expansion for the iron industry; and even during the French wars at the beginning of the century the demands of war production kept the industry busy at a time when other industries were badly affected by the interruption of trade with Europe. It is difficult to assess the appeal of work in the industry to young children. For some, starting work must have been the beginning of growing up, a matter of joining adult society. At least one witness preferred it to school, and said that though his father wanted him to go to school, he ran away because he liked cleaning the ashpit better than learning his letters. An older witness, aged sixteen, had spent five years in farming, where he said all he earned was his victuals; as a smith, he earned 12*s* per week – 'Striking iron is much harder than farm work, but you see, I get more money and liberty.' Presumably he had been a poor law apprentice. At his age, he might well be retaining some, if not all, of his wages, though younger children, as already noted, would hand them over to their parents. The usual earnings for boys (girls were paid less) in the Pontypool district were 3*s* to 4*s* 6*d* between the ages of seven and ten, 5*s* to 12*s* for the ten- to fifteen-year-olds, and 12*s* to 18*s* a week for fifteen- to eighteen-year-olds.[20]

In the twenty years or so following the reports of the Children's Employment Commission, 1840, little basic change took place in the employment of children in ironworks. Certainly the reports did not lead to any legislation on the subject, though textile factory legislation was extended, and children's work in mines was regulated by the Mines Act, 1842. It appears that child employment in the iron industry was not thought sufficiently objectionable to warrant immediate legislation. When the second Children's Employment Commission was appointed in 1862, ironworks were inspected in Yorkshire, Durham, Northumberland, Scotland, north and south Wales, and Staffordshire and Shropshire. Only Staffordshire was reported on in full, it being stated that the mode of work and the working hours in all the other areas were the same as in Staffordshire.[21] By 1863, the numbers of children employed in the West Midlands iron industry in Staffordshire and Worcestershire were relatively small. The total number of blast furnaces in blast was 110, and they employed only 200 boys under 13 (youths from 13 to 18 numbered 400). The total of mills and forges in operation was 100, and these employed 1,000 boys under 13, and 2,000 youths aged from 13 to 18.[22]

The age at which boys started work in the 1860s was about eight, and the jobs they were employed on remained more or less the same as in the 1840s. The youngest were 'door drawers' on the furnaces, or scrap carriers, helping the shearers in carrying and cutting up scrap iron. From the age of nine, the majority of young boys helped on the rolls, where it was said a great rapidity of movement was required, and a great amount of labour. They ran 11 miles at each turn. At the age of 14, boys might become underhands on the puddling furnaces or on the rolls. The turn was still usually of 12 hours, with 1½ hours off for meals. Nightwork continued, of course, and Sunday work was still performed on two thirds of the blast furnaces. No girls were employed in Staffordshire, but 200 women worked on the blast furnaces, presumably in barrowing limestone or ashes.[23]

General conditions remained as they had been in the earlier period. The great heat was remarked upon, and the violent exertion of the child workers who, it was said, 'very rarely got through many turns without burns of a more or less serious nature'. Sometimes there was dense, heavy smoke, described as 'a most unpleasant, suffocating exhalation from the scraps of incinerating iron ore near the blast furnaces'. Puddlers were said not to be unhealthy, but retired early, being prematurely worn out by reason of hard work, thereafter becoming labourers at a much reduced wage. Yet the general condition of the boys seemed to be healthy and strong; many were sons of workmen in the same works, and nearly all (it was claimed) had a certain prospect of employment for life.[24] In one large works where evidence was taken, that of Bradley & Co. in Stourbridge, a printed list of rules was supplied to workmen, with specified fines for breach of each rule. Workmen losing their copy could be supplied with another at a charge of 6*d*. On leaving the firm's employ, they were supposed to write the reason for leaving on the back of their copy of the regulations.[25] Nevertheless, labour relations at this works appear to have been good. In 1856 the proprietor, Mr W. O. Foster, was asked by the workmen for permission to use part of the grounds of the works as a cricket field. Not only did he give this permission, but he also met the cost of the necessary bats, balls, stumps, and so on. This firm also provided a reading room, and later in the century, some company housing and pensions for retired workmen.[26]

The third report of the commissioners appointed in 1862 failed to condemn the employment of child workers as such in the ironworks, but did comment adversely on several aspects. As far as blast furnaces were concerned, they drew attention to two points 'especially requiring legislative interposition'. The first was the employment of children under thirteen years of age on night shifts, the second the employment of children, young persons, and women on Sundays. In iron mills and forges, they considered that the employing of young boys on night turns and the consequent obstruction of their education justified the application of the Factory Acts.[27] The result was the Factory Act, 1867, which redefined factories so as to include ironworks and other large places of work, generally allowing only part-time work and no night work at all for children up to eleven or twelve. One inspector's report subsequently recorded that as a result, half-time boys were 'practically expelled' from the forges because they could not work at night.

It seems strange that standard works dealing with the employment of children in the first half of the nineteenth century rarely comment on children's working lives in the iron industry.[28] Perhaps this is because there are fewer quotable examples in the reports of the kind of cruelty which was uncovered in the accounts of work in the textile mills and down the mines. Yet there can be no doubt that the work was physically exhausting, the hours were long, and the risk of injury, especially of burns or mutilation, was always present. Moreover, there was no St Monday, and for some, not even Sunday off. How far did the great expansion of the iron industry bring with it an actual worsening of working conditions for the children? Did work discipline intensify as the works grew larger? There are some indications that suggest that this might have happened. The switch to mineral fuel meant that blast furnaces could be much larger. Further, the replacement of water power by steam power resulted in much more continuous working of the furnace, and campaigns which might last for years before the furnace was finally allowed to go out. Steam power similarly permitted the non-stop operation of rolls and hammers. In works of increasing size, sometimes employing hundreds and even thousands of men, where working operations could inflict death or injury, it was obviously necessary to impose strict rules and regulations, not only regarding the working of the furnaces and machinery, but also regarding general conduct about the works, for example, the theft of equipment or material, drunkenness, fighting, and absenteeism. All this suggests that work practices became more strictly supervised and controlled in the larger ironworks of the early nineteenth century than in the smaller works of the preceding century.

However, it would be wrong to suppose that work discipline in the large ironworks came in time to resemble the discipline of the cotton mill. In the first place, it is clear that some rules were both necessary and unavoidable where work processes were potentially so dangerous; new workers, young and old, had to be trained in simple safety precautions. Secondly, some operations had to go at their own pace, dependent on the chemical changes taking place. This is particularly true of the right time to tap a furnace, or to begin puddling. An example has already been given of this: it was impossible to hurry a heat at the puddling furnace, where all would depend on the skill and judgement of the puddler. Thirdly, as a consequence of this, the work often took the form of violent exertion followed by intervals of rest. For all these reasons, it would be a mistake to think that the work discipline in an ironworks was similar to that in a textile factory with its steam-driven machinery. It is true that furnaces needed attention night and day, but their operation was very different from that of power-driven mules or automatic looms. Lastly, lack of evidence makes it difficult to demonstrate any lengthening of the shift or turn in the early nineteenth century. What little evidence there is for the eighteenth century is of turns of about 12 hours, which made for a convenient division of the 24 hours into day and night shifts of equal length.[29] So there is nothing very definite to be said about changes in working hours in the iron industry as industrialisation intensified; and indeed even in the early nineteenth century, in some works the children worked shorter hours than the full 12-hour turn.

Coalmining, like the iron industry, was well established in Britain at the beginning of the nineteenth century. It also had begun to expand as an industry in the Tudor period, having been regarded earlier on as merely a branch of agriculture; but in the early eighteenth century it was still no more than a part-time occupation except in the north-east of England.[30] The coming of the Industrial Revolution brought great changes, not because of technological innovation – it has been said that coalmining did not pass through an industrial revolution[31] – but because of the greatly increased demand for coal, both for industry and for domestic consumption. The only technological advance below ground in the eighteenth century was the invention by John Curr of four-wheeled corves or carriages which could be pushed by boys along tramways of cast-iron rails. If the height of the passageway permitted, horses or donkeys, instead of children, could be used to draw the carriages. Above ground, the Newcomen steam engine was employed for pumping and drainage purposes from the early eighteenth century onwards, but in most pits winding was accomplished by a simple windlass, or by the more elaborate horse-drawn whimsey. Most small pits were very primitive in nature at the beginning of the nineteenth century, sometimes having only a single shaft. By the 1840s, however, steam engines were more commonly used for winding, ventilation was improved by the use of separate down shafts and up shafts, trapdoors were used to control currents of air round the passageways, and larger mines might even employ mechanical fans for ventilation purposes. The much more efficient Boulton & Watt engines replaced the Newcomen atmospheric engine for pumping, and guide rails and cages for winding came into use. The invention of the Davy and Stephenson safety lamps, about 1816, also gave additional warning of dangerous gases below.[32]

These improvements still left the basic work processes down the pit unchanged. The cutting of the coal by the collier (known variously as the holer, pikeman, or hewer) was still accomplished entirely by hand, and was physically beyond the strength of young children. They were employed principally in transporting the coal from the coalface to the pit bottom, but they were also used for trapping, for driving horses, and for baling water.[33] Women and young girls were employed underground only in a limited number of coalfields – in Yorkshire, north Lancashire, south Wales, and the eastern Scottish coalfields.[34] However, the introduction of carriages on iron tramways in the eighteenth century increased the demand for child labour, and so did the improvements in ventilation; even small children could be used as trappers. Hence by the early nineteenth century the employment of boys and girls in the mines had very probably increased, not only absolutely, but relatively to that of adults; and there was a growing tendency to put very young children to work.[35]

Certainly the employment of young children had become widespread by the early 1840s. The first report of the Children's Employment Commission, 1840, was published in 1842, and was devoted to mines; its early pages provide an exhaustive survey of the ages of all children working down the mines.[36] From this it appears that ages varied from coalfield to coalfield. The very youngest were only three or four, but this was exceptional. Generally speaking, the youngest children were to be found in the south Wales pits. Overall, the commonest age for starting work was six or seven, but five-year-olds were not unusual in Derbyshire, the West Riding, and around Oldham.

The publication of this report caused a great stir, not only because of the revelations regarding the ages of the child workers but also because of the nature of their work. The report was well illustrated by drawings of children pushing or drawing loaded carriages, of women carrying baskets of coal on their backs, and of workers being wound up and down the shaft. Two forms of employment attracted particular attention and censure: trapping by very young children was criticised severely by the commissioners, who were of the opinion that were it not for the passing and repassing of the coal carriages, it 'would amount to solitary confinement of the worst kind'.[37] This entrusting of the air doors to very young children, they added, was a frequent cause of fatal accidents.[38] Sometimes the child had a candle, sometimes not. Thus John Smith, a seven-year-old in the Soap Pit, Sheffield, said in evidence: 'I stand and open and shut the door. I'm generally in the dark, and sit me down against the door; I stop 12 hours in the pit; I never see daylight now except on Sundays; I fell asleep one day, and a corve ran over my leg and made it smart.'[39]

The other task which was much criticised was transporting the coal in carriages from the coalface to the pit bottom. Sometimes this took the form of simply pushing the carriages, often up considerable inclines. At other times, the children, both boys and girls, were harnessed to the carriage. William Tranter, the ground bailiff at Coalbrookdale, put it clearly: 'A girdle is put round the naked waist, to which a chain from the carriage is hooked and passed between the legs, and the boys crawl on their hands and knees.'[40] Drawing by girdle and chain was much disliked by the children. James Pearce, aged twelve, spoke of his experiences in a Shropshire pit:

> About a year and a half ago, I took to the girdle and chain; I do not like it; it hurts me, it rubs my skin off. I often feel pain. I have often had blisters on my side . . . I crawl on my hands and feet. I have often knocked my back against the top of the pit, and it hurt very sore. The legs ached badly.[41]

The terse description by the commissioners of these unfortunate children is well known, and needs no further elaboration: 'Chained, belted, harnessed like dogs in a go-cart, black, saturated with wet, and more than half-naked – crawling upon their hands and feet – they present an appearance indescribably disgusting and unnatural.'[42] Women were also employed in drawing with the girdle (sometimes known as the dog-collar) and chain, and Betty Harris, a Lancashire married woman of thirty-seven described her experiences graphically, claiming that she had drawn 'till the skin was off me', and that 'the belt and chain is worse when we are in the family way'.[43] In Scotland, women and girls were employed to carry coal in baskets on their backs. The baskets or creels held up to three hundredweight. It was estimated that one girl of twelve carried her load up four ladders and along passageways for a distance greater than the height of St Paul's cathedral.[44]

These accounts of the heavy and indeed degrading work undertaken by boys, girls, and young women are well known, and understandably upset the early Victorians, but it is likely that equally shocking were the references in the reports to the limited or even complete lack of clothing among adults and children alike when working down the mines. Since it was always comfortably warm in the pits, it is not surprising that miners wore the minimum of clothing when at work, sometimes working completely naked (though sometimes an otherwise naked man would wear a cap). In the West Riding, girl hurriers, aged between seven and twenty-one, usually worked naked to the waist, as did the boys. The girls who drew with the girdle and chain were similarly half-naked, and their breeches became ragged and torn. Thus, according to Ebenezer Healey, aged thirteen, in a West Riding pit, 'Our breeches are often torn between the legs with the chain. The girls' breeches are torn as often as ours; they are torn many a time, and when they are going along we can see all between the legs, naked; I have, often.'[45] The sub-commissioner J. C. Symons commented very strongly on this.

> In two other pits in the Huddersfield Union I have seen the same sight. In one, near New Mills, the chain, passing high up between the legs of two of these girls, had worn large holes in their trousers, and any sight more disgustingly indecent or revolting can scarcely be imagined than these girls at work. No brothel can beat it.[46]

One is tempted to comment that Mr Symons obviously had very little experience of brothels. Nevertheless, the extent of nakedness was of great concern to the sub-commissioners, and it was freely alleged by witnesses that sexual intercourse took place down the pit, and bastards were common. The conclusions to the report declared that 'all classes of witnesses bear testimony to the demoralising influence of the employment of females underground.'[47]

Undoubtedly the lurid details of working conditions and of sexual activities in the mines attracted much public attention, but other basic aspects of mining life such as working hours, night work, and holidays must also be noted. Once more it must be said that conditions varied from one coalfield to another. Working hours were usually about twelve, though they could be only eight or nine, as in Halifax, or ten to eleven, as in Bradford; in Derbyshire, the children and young persons worked fourteen to fourteen and a half hours (sixteen hours door to door).[48] These hours require further interpretation in that in some areas, for example in south Staffordshire, St Monday was kept, especially the Monday after the fortnightly pay-day. On this coalfield, a system of stints operated, and once a miner had completed his stint he was free to leave the pit, so that a good, strong man could complete his day's work in six or seven hours.[49] On the Durham and Northumberland coalfield, miners worked in pairs, known as 'marrers', sharing the twelve-hour shift between them.[50] Thus it is difficult to generalise about the length of the turn, and Professor Michael Flinn has remarked that by the standards of working hours in other industries at the time, miners enjoyed a comparatively short working day, even when they worked a twelve-hour shift, and an unusually short day when working only eight hours.[51] This may well be so, but children's hours were not necessarily the same as the men's. Since the operation of the trapdoors was essential to the working of the pit, trappers were usually the first to start work and the last to leave. They were, of course, the youngest of all the children employed.

As for night work, this was part of the ordinary system, though the extent to which it was used depended on the current demand for coal. In the summer-time, miners were often on short time as the demand slackened. In a few districts, there was no night work at all – in north and south Staffordshire, Shropshire, Leicestershire, most of the West Riding, north Somerset, and the west of Scotland.[52] Holidays were limited to the customary days off at Christmas, Good Friday, and Whitsun, with additional days off for local wakes, and for St Monday, where it was observed. Again, it must be remembered that not only summer-time but also trade recession could bring short-time working. Whether hours actually grew longer overall as the industry expanded in the first half of the nineteenth century is impossible to say in the light of all these variables. The problems of determining the length of the working day in the Black Country, for example, given the system of stints, seasonal variations in employment, trade fluctuations, and St Monday, really make precise calculation impossible. Looking at the industry as a whole, Flinn has suggested that 'In the absence of specific comment on this subject during the early nineteenth century, it is unlikely that there was any marked trend one way or the other.'[53]

One well-known aspect of work down the pits in the first half of the nineteenth century was the risk of accidents, many of them fatal. The introduction of the Davy lamp in 1816 seemed at first to promise a reduction of casualties, but the Select Committee of the House of Commons on Mining Accidents, 1835, found that this was not so. In the eighteen years before 1816, 447 miners were killed in the Durham and Northumberland pits; in the eighteen years after, 538. The committee thought this increase due to more coal being raised, more dangerous seams being worked with the lamp, and less care being taken when the lamp was introduced.[54] It should be mentioned that in some coalfields the light given by the Davy lamp was so feeble that it was a common practice to accompany it with a candle. As one collier witness said in 1842, 'It is a life of great danger for both man and child: a collier is never safe after he is swung off to be let down the pit.'[55] Perhaps the easiest way of summarising the various causes of accidents in the mines is to reproduce the table given in the first report, 1842, of deaths in the mines and on pit banks for the year 1838:

Deaths in mines and on pit banks, 1838

Cause	*Under 13*	*13–18*	*18 and over*
Fell down shafts	13	16	31
do. (rope breaking)	1	–	2
Fell out when ascending	–	–	3
Drawn over pulley	3	–	3
Fall of stone out of skip	1	–	3
Drowned in the mines	3	4	15
Fall of coal, stones, rubbish	14	14	69
Injuries (unspecified)	6	3	32
Crushed in coalpits	–	1	1
Explosions of gas	13	18	49
Suffocated by choke damp	–	2	6
Explosion of gunpowder	–	1	3
By tram waggons	4	5	12
Totals	58	64	229

One of the most dangerous coalfields of all was the South Staffordshire and East Worcestershire field in the Black Country. On this coalfield alone there were seventy-eight deaths in 1838, not far off a quarter of the national total. One sub-commissioner remarked that to judge from the conversation of people 'we might consider the whole population to be engaged in a campaign'. Later on, in 1854, the local mines inspector, Mr Wynn, referred to 'this monstrous wrong' done to the mining population.[57] In Lancashire, the Chief Constable of Oldham commented caustically on public attitudes to death in the pits –[58]

There are so many killed that it becomes quite customary to expect such things. The chiefest talk is just at the moment, until the body gets home, and then there is no more talk about it. People generally feel, 'Oh, it's only a collier!' There would be more feeling a hundred times if a policeman were to kill a dog on the street.[58]

In addition to the risk of death or injury from a multitude of causes, many children had cause to fear ill-treatment at the hands of the men. Casual blows and brutality were common enough, but once more their incidence seemed to vary from coalfield to coalfield.[59] In the Durham and Northumberland mines, no kind of corporal punishment was permitted, any boy who misbehaved being dismissed. In the Bradford and Leeds areas, it was said that the parents would remove their children if they were ill-treated. The worst treatment seems to have been in Derbyshire and in the Halifax pits. In Derbyshire, the children were often assaulted by the corporals or butties for not getting the donkeys to move fast enough. One adult witness confirmed the complaints of the children:

No rewards excepting the stick, that's all the rewards in pits for little lads. Has within three months seen a boy of nine beaten by a butty until he wetted his breeches because he had not come the day before. He has often seen them beat so that they were black and blue; and if the parents were by, they dare not say anything, or they would be turned off the ground directly.[60]

These parents seem to have been more cowed than the parents in Leeds and Bradford, but all would depend on the local supply of juvenile labour. In Halifax the children received much harsher treatment than in other parts of the West Riding. It was here that the notorious incident was recorded of the sub-commissioner meeting a child crying and bleeding from a face wound. The overlooker explained that the boy was one of the slow ones who would only move if he saw blood, and by throwing a piece of coal at him the overlooker had achieved his purpose.[61]

As for apprenticeship, it was still common in Yorkshire, Lancashire, the west of Scotland and most of all in south Staffordshire. Once more there were stories of cruelty to the apprentices, all of whom came from the workhouse. One boy, an illegitimate child, said he had run away from his master because he had lost the boy's indentures, and had treated him badly; he had twice stuck a pick into his bottom (the boy showed the scars). In Lancashire, an overseer had an appalling story to tell of parish boys being punished for allegedly stealing other boys' dinners. One of the biggest boys, or a young man, got a boy's head between his legs, and each of the eighteen to twenty boys in the pit inflicted twelve strokes on the boy's rump and loins. According to the overseer, he had never seen such a sight in his life: 'the flesh of the rump and loins was beaten to a jelly'. The doctor said the boy could not live, though in fact he survived. Any boy who refused to give his strokes would be given the same punishment himself.[62]

What had a boy to look forward to if he survived the harsh conditions of life in the pit? The children's wages started from about 6*d* or 8*d* a day. In some places their wages were better than in other occupations. For instance, in the south Staffordshire mines the boys were said to be in 'a very far superior condition' to children in the manufacturing districts and in workshops in their own area, earning nearly three times as much. This permitted them to have substantial food and other comforts.[63] Tremenheere, the mines inspector, commented very strongly on the 'sensuality' and 'extravagance' of the miner's mode of life when he was in funds. On the other hand, the nature of the work inevitably took its toll on the adult collier. Although in some coalfields it was said that his physical condition was good (in Warwickshire, the miners were said to be a tall, athletic, powerful race of men 'having all their lives lived like fighting cocks'), in other areas, such as Lancashire, the men were said to be thin and gaunt, with a shambling gait. In the West Riding, a contrast was drawn between the swarthy collier 'all grime and muscle', and 'the puny, pallid, starveling little weaver, with his dirty-white apron and feminine look'. Nevertheless, there was general agreement that most colliers were stunted in growth, except in Warwickshire and Leicestershire, and that in many places they suffered premature ageing and death.[64]

The condition of the children themselves seemed surprisingly good. This was reported to be so in most coalfields, the main exceptions being in Lancashire and Cheshire, and also among particular groups of children, such as those drawing with the chain and girdle in the West Riding. In Halifax, a witness said that it was the practice of parents of children with chest complaints to send them into the pits for a change of air, which did many of them good. As for the strain of the work, this obviously varied with the age and strength of the child, and the nature of the task. In the Forest of Dean, hardship was suffered by 'lads of more delicate fibre, and active intellect', who found the work 'decidedly irksome'. Some child witnesses said they were very tired after work. Yet this was not always so; in south Durham after their day's work they appeared 'as playful as schoolboys come out of school'. In north Wales, the underground bailiff at Ruabon, James Jones, when asked whether the children were so tired that they couldn't enjoy recreation when work was over, replied (in Welsh), 'No, they bound like young goats from their work to their play', and this remarkable statement was confirmed by the sub-commissioner. Perhaps alongside this opinion should be placed the comment of another sub-commissioner, J. C. Symons, who described the evidence given by some witnesses, that the children were cheerful when they got out of the pit, 'as somewhat akin to evidence that people are cheerful when they get out of prison'. He did add, however, that it was a remarkable fact that except in cases of extreme labour, cheerfulness was a characteristic of collier children.[65]

In surveying the evidence presented in the first report of the Children's Employment Commission, 1840, attention has always been focused on the most striking aspects, the drawing by girdle and chain, and the manipulation of the trapdoors. No doubt the illustrations helped to concentrate interest on these activities. However, it must not be forgotten that many children were engaged on other tasks – for example as skip loaders, pitchers, pushers, and drivers of horses or asses. Above ground, boys were employed as horse drivers on gins, or even, in Lancashire, put in charge of the steam engine for winding. This last practice led to the danger of overwinding, which could and did cause fatal accidents, and was strongly criticised by the commissioners.

In their conclusions the commissioners appear to have concentrated mostly on two matters – not, as one might have expected, on the intrinsically degrading and unsuitable nature of the children's work, but rather on the young age at which it was undertaken, and on the demoralising effect of women and girls working underground. As for the first point, trapping as such was obviously not unhealthy, but long hours in the dark in a solitary state were very hard on young children. Similarly, pushing loaded carriages was not in itself a danger to health 'except that physical injuries produced by it are due to the early age at which it begins, and the length of time continued'. Thus it was the age of starting work that was criticised, not the nature of the work itself. As for the second point, much could be said about the attitude of the early Victorians to what they considered to be sexual impropriety. Twentieth-century commentators have been prone to exaggeration on this subject,[66] but there can be no doubt about the concern expressed by the commissioners in their conclusions that 'the boys and girls, and the young men and young women, and even married women with child, commonly work almost naked, and the men, in many mines, quite naked'.[67]

It seems to have been taken for granted that men and women working together in close proximity, even above ground, would be sexually attracted to each other, and that this attraction would naturally be increased when clothing was discarded in the warmth below ground. The modern reader can only be puzzled at the practical difficuties of sexual intercourse in the dark, surrounded by seams of coal, and often in wet and cramped conditions. There is also the simple fact that work was paid by the piece, and it was necessary to keep working to make a living wage. Presumably it was reckoned that lust would overcome all problems of this kind. No doubt some sexual activity did occur, but the opportunities for it must have been limited. One of the passages in the report which caused most offence was that provided by Betty Harris, quoted previously, who said that working with the chain and girdle was worst when women were in the family way. This must have been particularly offensive to Victorian ideals of motherhood. Yet some years after and in reply to a question, a pit-brow woman in St Helens said, 'No, the chain never galled me between my legs, nor when I was in't family way, for I used to leave off at five months.' The same woman admitted that she had been harnessed like a horse or dog, but she claimed that surface work was harder, and 'we were warm in't pit'. She added, 'I only wish I was at it again.' Other women present supported this view; one said of working down below 'she liked it reet well – would like well to work below again – used to draw with belt and chain – liked it better than working up here.'[68]

This evidence is not to suggest that the hardships of women toiling underground were exaggerated in the report, or misrepresented to any degree, but that different women accommodated themselves in different ways to their working conditions, and in consequence not all of them disliked the job. At both St Helens and Wigan there were women who professed an actual liking for underground work, and in St Helens an overseer drew attention to the financial losses suffered as a result of women being prohibited from working down the mines by the act of 1842. Nevertheless, the shock to Victorian sensibility given by the evidence regarding semi-naked and naked working had an immediate effect. The Mines Act was passed in the same year as the report was published, a striking contrast to the time taken to achieve effective factory legislation. The act forbade all female labour below ground, and prohibited the employment of all boys below the age of ten (originally as noted later in this chapter the age limit was to have been twelve, but the House of Lords reduced the starting age to ten). Government inspectors were appointed under the act, and in 1872 the age was raised to twelve for underground working. In this way the evils of too youthful employment, and of alleged sexual malpractices in the mines were dealt with directly.

It remains to say something regarding the employment of children in larger places of work other than the textile factories which will be discussed in the next chapter. Quite large work units were to be found in a variety of trades, ranging from silk and cotton printing works, dye works, and chemical works to potteries, paper works, brickyards, glasshouses, and rope-walks. Child employment in such places might be considerable, while in naval dockyards the total number of workers could run into thousands. To describe working conditions in all those industries which were carried on in larger places of work would be both tedious and unhelpful; instead, it is proposed to deal with three industries which together give some indication of the varying conditions for child workers in larger establishments – earthenware, brickmaking, and glassmaking.[69]

The major centre for earthenware manufacture was the Staffordshire potteries, which were visted by the Children's Employment Commission in 1843 and again in 1863. In the 1840s the largest class of pottery works employed from 50 to as many as 800 hands. The workshops were often small, low, damp, close, and dirty. Two aspects of the work of the children were especially objectionable: the first was the carrying of excessive loads by young boys, often throughout a very lengthy day. Thus, jiggers and mould runners began work at half-past five or six in the morning, sometimes working on to eight, nine, or even ten o'clock at night. During the nominal day of twelve hours they carried loads totalling up to 3,840 lbs, usually in temperatures of between 100 and 120 degrees. In this time they would walk nearly eight miles. Secondly, they would go directly from the heat into the cold outside, and as a result (or so it was said) they were noticeably subject to pulmonary diseases.[70]

In the following twenty years little change seems to have taken place. Mr Long reported that there had been no increase in the age at which children started work, that is, about seven. The total number of boys employed was about 2,800 and of youths about 3,500, making 6,300 in all. Girls and young women, employed as painters, numbered some 4,700. Of the grand total of about 11,000 children and young persons, about 2,500 were jigger turners (turning potters' wheels), and mould runners (carrying ware on moulds into the stove-rooms, and bringing articles out). These were the hardest jobs of all because of the great heat in the stoves and the dust in the air. Their hours were normally from about 6.30 a.m. to 6.30 p.m., but overtime was common, and sometimes night work as well.[71] J. Murray, aged twelve, described his work: 'I turn jigger and run moulds. I come at 6; sometimes I come at 4. I worked all night last night, till 6 this morning. I have not been in bed since the night before last. There were 8 or 9 boys working last night . . . I have worked five times in my life all night. I worked two nights last week.'[72]

Apprenticeship appears to have been common from the age of thirteen, but not only of workhouse children. The form of apprenticeship was of a loose and casual nature, and not really binding, since the indentures were rarely stamped. Moreover, after three years the boys were usually earning half-wages, so that it seems that an apprenticeship of this kind was of a very limited value. It was strongly (and somewhat unexpectedly) attacked by the commissioner, Mr Scriven, not because of its injustice, but because of its lack of discipline, and the way the boys left home after a while, and did as they pleased. His view was that the stamp duty on indentures should be reduced, and indentures properly enforced.[73]

Working life in the potteries did not lend itself to sexual impropriety as did life in the mines, but there are still one or two references in the 1842 report to sexual activities at work. In some rooms, for example, there were only two persons, a man and a women working on their own, and such workshops were referred to in the report as 'emporiums of profligacy'. It was also stated that sexual intercourse was very common in such places, and that 'bastardy was very lightly thought of'.[74] Once more, one can only marvel at the extreme sensitivity of the age, among the middle classes at least, to the slightest hint of sexual misbehaviour. A more serious threat, perhaps, to the well-being of the children, was brutality and physical ill-treatment by their masters. Curiously enough, there are no references to cruelty to pottery children in either the 1842 or the 1863 reports. The later report actually records one manager as saying that as a rule the boys were not ill-used by the workmen, and anything of the kind would be stopped.[75]

The major feature of child employment in the potteries was therefore not the physical ill-treatment of the children but rather the nature of their employment and the excessive length of the working day. Hence the central point at issue was that of the hours worked rather than anything else; it was not thought necessary subsequently to attempt any exclusion of feminine labour, and nothing could be done about the sudden changes of temperature when leaving work – after all, this applied to a number of industries other than earthenware manufacture. In 1864 a further Factory Act brought six industries, including the manufacture of pottery, within the scope of the existing Factory Acts. Further, employers were required to make special rules for the observance of cleanliness and ventilation.[76]

Working life for children in the brickyards seems to have varied from place to place, depending on the kind of brick manufactured. In any case, it must be remembered that sub-commissioners reacted in their own individual ways to what they saw. This is true particularly of the reports on brickyards. When in 1843 the sub-commissioner visited the five large fireclay brickworks near Stourbridge, he was very impressed by the condition of the young girl workers. They worked as pages to the women moulders who fashioned the bricks on large moulding tables, and were paid by them. The girls brought the tempered wet clay to the moulders, then carried the finished bricks off to be fired. It was very hard work. Yet the girls were reported to be in excellent condition, and the sub-commissioner said that he had seen no children looking so happy, or so well-made in person as these girls. Their dress, he thought, was very picturesque; they were like girls in Persian costume, straight and healthy. When one considers that they worked in the roughest of working clothes, often saturated with the water from the dripping clay and bricks, this description seems a little surprising, to say the least. Mr White, visiting the same works in the 1860s, seems to have been impressed rather more by the heavy labour of the girls. Each moulder had a stint of 1,000 bricks to make in the twelve-hour day, and these bricks were carried off by her pages, six bricks at a time. It is understandable that one employer said that he would employ no girl under twelve, for the common firebrick weighed 9 lbs wet, 7¼ lbs dry. For this work, the moulders were paid 2*s* 2*d* a day, with 9*d* of this going to the girl pages. One girl witness, Sarah Ann Smith, aged sixteen, a moulder, had started at eleven as a page, when she said she once carried 1,550 bricks in one day, wet, two at a time. She wore no shoes or socks and claimed that she could write, but could hardly spell.[77]

Conditions in red-brick making appear to have been somewhat different. Here employment seems to have started as early as the age of four, and visitors who came to inspect the children under both employment commissions were struck by the degraded appearance of the girls. In 1866 it was said that:

> The evil of the system of employing young girls at this work consists in binding them from their infancy, as a general rule, to the most degraded lot in after life. They become rough, foul-mouthed boys before nature has taught them they are women. Clad in a few dirty rags, their bare legs exposed far above the knees, their hair and faces covered with mud, they learn to treat with contempt all feelings of modesty and decency.[78]

In 1865 similar comments were made about the appearance of both girls and women: 'sparsely clad, up to the bare knees in clay splashes, and evidently without a vestige of womanly delicacy'.[79] Clearly, these sub-commissioners were shocked in particular by the sight of so many bare female legs, and unimpressed by the children's costume, Persian or otherwise.

On the whole, it seems likely that it was the harshness of the working conditions in the red-brick yards which made such an unfavourable impression both in 1841 and in 1864, rather than any cruel treatment meted out to the children. The larger brickyards, that is, those with more than fifty workpeople, were brought within the scope of the Factory Acts by the Factory Act, 1867, while the 1871 Factory Act forbade the employment of any female under the age of sixteen.

Lastly, the glass industry: in this industry, work routines depended on the type of glass manufactured. If it was flint glass tableware, the glassmakers worked in teams of four, known as a 'chair', with a boy as a fourth member of the team, called the 'taker-in', because he carried the finished glass articles into the lehr (the annealing oven). Boys started work between nine and ten.[80] The turn or shift lasted only six hours, but glassmakers worked six hours on, and six hours off throughout the week, usually with Monday off.[81] Glass-cutters, on the other hand, worked the usual twelve-hour day shifts, the boys starting work at the age of twelve. In making plate, sheet, or crown glass, however, the basic unit of work was the *journey*, which covered the using-up of one furnace of molten glass. A journey lasted from ten to sixteen hours, and there were usually three journeys in a week.[82] The flint glass trade was the most prestigious trade in the glass industry, and apprenticeship was the norm among both makers and cutters. Flint glass makers were aristocrats of labour, and the full seven years' apprenticeship was insisted upon. Nevertheless, pay was poor at the lower end of the chair, and it was only the head of the chair (the 'workman' or 'gaffer') who was really well paid.

The glass industry was smaller and more specialised than many other industries, and the flint glass industry was unique in its organisation and work routines. So far as the employment of children was concerned, boys and not girls worked at the furnaces and in the engraving or cutting section. They do not seem to have been ill-treated by the men, but the work was strenuous enough, boys reputedly walking fifteen or sixteen miles per turn; and the shortness of the shift was offset by the fact that the interval between turns was only six hours. Nevertheless, the trade was held in high esteem, and if only a boy could survive his apprenticeship, and finally head a chair, he would have a well-paid job with a fair degree of job security. Working conditions were not especially dangerous, though the proximity of the furnace always brought the risk of burns, and the atmosphere was naturally very hot. Perhaps this explains the glassmakers' reputation for being heavy drinkers. The sub-commissioner who reported on the glass industry in 1865, Mr J. E. White, said that he was repeatedly asked for money for drink when visiting glasshouses: 'I have been followed and importuned for it'. This had never happened, he said, in works of other kinds. One wonders whether harassing a visitor in this way was the glassmakers' idea of a joke, for many other industrial establishments utilised furnaces where working conditions were equally hot.[83]

All the industries discussed in this chapter were in existence before the coming of the Industrial Revolution, and there is nothing to show any great change in working conditions in them when industry expanded. However, in one there could have been an extension of child employment as industry began to predominate in the economy – in the mining industry, as we have seen, the introduction of skips or carriages moving on cast-iron rails may have increased the employment of both women and children. In the iron industry, the use of boys and girls as ancillary workers continued as before. The only significant change here is that there might possibly have been some tightening of work discipline as the size of the works increased, and the need for a well-regulated regime became more necessary. With these two exceptions, there is nothing to show that the Industrial Revolution brought a distinct worsening of the working conditions of children, other than those in the textile factories (see the next chapter).

In view of this, it is interesting to consider why the reports of both Children's Employment Commissions should have stirred up such controversy at the time. One obvious cause has already been suggested, namely, that the earlier revelations of conditions in the textile mills had increased middle-class sensitivity to the ill-treatment of children employed in other parts of industry, and even in agriculture. Further, these disclosures came at a time when humanitarian attitudes were gaining ground, and had been successful in achieving the abolition of slavery in 1833. The humanitarian movement in itself owed much to evangelicalism. But some reaction was rather more critical. Some observers, commenting on the earlier reports of the Children's Employment Commission, 1840, considered that the roots of all social evils were to be found in the lack of education of the parents, who misused their children, and in the lack of employment, all occupations (they claimed) being overstocked, with a consequent deterioration in working conditions and in wages; and it was argued that only free trade would solve this problem. Critics who took this line were quite capable of arguing in addition that the Mines Act was really beside the point, in that it was quite likely to drive both women and children into worse privation and misery.[84]

Indeed, the passing of the first Mines Act in 1842 provides some interesting indications of attitudes to reform at the time. The bill passed the Commons 'at railway speed', but took far longer to pass the House of Lords, where the mineowner Lord Londonderry fought a long and increasingly desperate battle against it. This noble lord even alleged on one occasion that some coal seams could be worked only with the help of women; he was interrupted by a questioner who asked, what seams? How could it be that men's superior strength could not replace that of women? Londonderry did not answer, though he was supported by others in the Upper House on such matters as the loss of wages which would be suffered by women if they were prevented from working in the mines. According to the Duke of Hamilton, 'The poor females so employed did not desire to be relieved from it. It was sweet to them, because by it they were enabled to maintain themselves, or perhaps a parent or children, or perhaps all three'.[85] Towards the end of the debates, Londonderry was reduced to attacking the integrity of the sub-commissioners, who unlike the four commissioners, could not take evidence under oath. He also picked on one sub-commissioner for having failed twice in business as a hatter in London. However, he did succeed in forcing Ashley to give ground on the age at which boys might begin work underground, this being lowered from twelve to ten years of age.

Nevertheless, in both Houses the majority opinion was in favour of reform, though the focus of protest was as much as anything on the employment of women rather than on the work performed by children. In the Commons, for example, Mr Lampton, commenting on Ashley's speech, said that he had listened to all of it with the profoundest attention, but

> that part which excited his feelings the most was where he exposed the manner in which females were employed in the mines. He had listened to that part with feelings of disgust, indignation, and shame that in this enlightened country, in the middle of the nineteenth century, such a savage state of things should be found to exist.[86]

He was followed by Lord Egerton, who said it was a monstrous thing that the female sex should continue to be so employed.[87] In the Upper House, most critics of the bill emphasised the potential loss of earnings by both women and children, rather than the nature of the work they were required to perform. Few of the peers, in fact, dwelt on the sufferings of the children. Indeed, Lord Londonderry actually presented a petition from mineowners in Durham and Northumberland protesting against exaggerations in the report, claiming that the employment of the trapper was neither cheerless, dull, nor stupefying; nor was he kept in solitude and darkness all the time: 'The trapper is generally cheerful and contented, and to be found, like children of his age, occupied with some childish amusement – as cutting sticks, making models of windmills, waggons, etc., and frequently in drawing figures with chalk on his door, modelling figures of men and animals in clay, etc.'[88] All this may have had some truth, since conditions in this coalfield, where there were no women underground, and no apprenticeship, may well have been better for the children than elsewhere, but it by no means disproves the truth of statements regarding working conditions in other coalfields.

In summing up comments on the reports of the 1840s, it is clear that the opinions expressed were very varied in nature, and by no means all in favour of reform. Moreover, in spite of all the arguments which had raged in the 1820s and 1830s regarding child factory workers and child labour in general, no immediate action was taken in the 1840s to regulate the work of the many thousands of children covered by the reports, the one exception being work in the mines. Even here, the factory acts were not applied directly to the mines. Undoubtedly the most significant aspect of the Mines Act was the forbidding of female labour below ground. Such a sweeping prohibition naturally attracted much comment and criticism, but it was the most straightforward way of ending the sexual antics which allegedly occurred in the mines. This was evidently a matter of major concern. Some members of the Lords even found the illustrations of half-naked women in the 1842 report (by today's standards, the very reverse of erotic) both disgusting and obscene. One powerful impetus in the direction of reform – indeed, it might have been the most powerful influence – was, therefore, the early Victorian fear of sexual impropriety. Otherwise, in spite of references in the reports to the unseemly use of privies by both sexes, and to men and women working together, in the potteries, for example, nothing further was done to regulate working conditions till the 1860s. For children to go to work in the 1840s was in general terms still quite acceptable to public opinion. Only the employment of the very young, or the possibility of sexual malpractice, or downright and undeniable cruelty provoked unfavourable comment at the time; and only in the special circumstances of work in the mines was any governmental action taken. The extension of the factory acts to other places of employment had to wait till the 1860s.

However, by then the reports of the next Children's Employment Commission, appointed in 1862, cetainly had an effect. The Factory Act, 1864 regulated hours and conditions in several industries, including earthenware and match manufacture, where a report had shown how the phosphorus used took deadly effect on the jaws and lungs of the workers. In 1867 a further Factory Act brought larger places of work (that is, with more than fifty workers) within the scope of the existing factory legislation. Only part-time work and no night work was permitted in these places below the age of twelve. In the same year the Workshop Regulation Act was passed, defining a workshop, and providing that no child might be employed under eight; between eight and thirteen there was to be only part-time work, and women and young persons (between thirteen and eighteen) were not to work more than twelve hours. Thus at last the small domestic workshop was to be brought under legislative control.[89]

Unfortunately, the error was made at first of appointing local inspectors of workshops, and the system of inspection worked very imperfectly until the local inspectors were replaced by the national Factory Inspectorate in 1871. Even then, there were great problems of enforcement for some time; in 1876 a Black Country inspector claimed that he had 10,000 workshops to inspect, and an average of three and a half persons in each workshop.[90] Again, there was the difficulty of checking ages in both large and small establishments. One inspector reported that just when he had rounded up the children for questioning, the gas lighting went out. When it was restored, the children had disappeared.[91] Nevertheless, 1867 is really the turning-point in the regulation of working hours and conditions for children, for in that year for the first time both workshop children and children in many of the larger workplaces outside the textile industry (already under the Factory Acts) came under statutory regulation. Henceforth government intervention in the working hours of child workers became an accepted principle.

References

1 Books and ariticles on the early history of the iron industry are numerous. There is now a very useful introduction to the history of the industry up to 1850: J. R. Harris, *The British Iron Industry 1700–1850*, 1988. See also H. R. Schubert, *History of the British Iron and Steel Industry from c.450* BC *to* AD *1775*, 1957; H. Cleere and D. Crossley, *The Iron Industry of the Weald*, 1985; W. K. V. Gale, *The British Iron and Steel Industry, A Technical History*, 1967, and *The Black Country Iron Industry: A Technical History*, 1979. Relevant articles are listed in Harris, *The British Iron Industry*.

2 For the iron industry in the eighteenth century, see Harris, *The British Iron Industry*. See also T. S. Ashton, *Iron and Steel in the Industrial Revolution*, 2nd edn, 1951; A. Birch, *The Economic History of the British Iron and Steel Industry 1784–1879*, 1967; C. K. Hyde, *Technological Change and the British Iron Industry 1700–1870*, 1977; and A. Raistrick, *Dynasty of Ironfounders: The Darbys and Coalbrookdale*, 1953. The literature is rich in learned articles supplying interpretations of the development of the industry. These articles are in Harris's bibliography.

3 *Children's Employment Commission*, 1840: Appendix to First Report, p. 582.

4 *Ibid.*, 1st Report, pp. 200, 478, 479.

5 *Ibid.*, pp. 200–2, 480, 481.

6 *Ibid.*, p. 559.

7 *Ibid.*, p. 485.

8 *Ibid.*, p. 679.

9 *Ibid.*, p. 504.

10 *Ibid.*, p. 486.

11 *Ibid.*, p. 641.

12 *Ibid.*, p. 522.
13 *Ibid.*, pp. 200, 278.
14 *Ibid.*, p. 582.
15 *Ibid.*, pp. 596, 683.
16 *Ibid.*, pp. 504, 622.
17 *Ibid.*, p. 569.
18 *Ibid.*, pp. 586, 598, 599, 605.
19 *Ibid.*, p. 584.
20 *Ibid.*, pp. 560, 530, 584.
21 *Children's Employment Commission*, 1862, Third Report, p. xxvi.
22 *Ibid.*, p. iv.
23 *Ibid.*
24 *Ibid.*, pp. 2–4.
25 Copy in the possession of the author.
26 *Worcestershire Chronicle*, 2 July 1856 and 10 August 1856.
27 *Children's Employment Commission*, 1862, Third Report, 1864, pp. xxii, xxiii.

28 For example, Ivy Pinchbeck and Margaret Hewitt, *Children in English Society*, Vol. II, 1973; ignore child ironworkers in their chapter on children as wage earners in early industrialism.

29 The working day in the eighteenth century at the famous Ambrose Crowley works outside Newcastle, which specialised in forge works, was from 5 a.m. to 8 p.m., that is, 15 hours less 1½ hours off for meals. At Coalbrookdale towards the end of the century, the hours in the Ironbridge ironworks for the *turn* were 6 a.m. to 6 p.m., less meals. One must always remember that where water power was employed, there could be long interruptions of work when the water was too low in summer for efficient operation, or when the mill was undegoing repairs. Matthew Boulton in Birmingham refers more than once to this kind of difficulty in his papers of 1765: 'No water, no polishing'. When the mill was temporarily dismantled, he comments, 'The millwright tells us that it will be next Wed or Thurs before it will be set to rights'; Eric Hopkins, *Birmingham: The First Manufacturing Town in the World 1760–1840*, 1989, p. 188.

30 A. R. Griffin, *Coalmining*, 1971, p. 130.

31 T. S. Ashton and J. Sykes, *The Coal Industry of the Eighteenth Century*, 1929, p. 174.

32 There are many books on the history of the coal industry. Among the most recent are Michael W. Flinn, *The History of the British Coal Industry, Vol. 2, 1700–1830: the Industrial Revolution*, 1984; and Roy Church, *The History of the British Coal Industry, Vol. 3, 1830–1913*, 1986.

33 Flinn, *The History of the British Coal Industry*, Vol. 2, pp. 336–7.
34 *Ibid.*, p. 333.
35 Ashton and Sykes, *The Coal Industry of the Eighteenth Century*, pp. 172–4.
36 *Children's Employment Commission*, 1840, First Report, Mines, pp. 9–23.

37 *Ibid.*, pp. 255–6.
38 *Ibid.*, p. 257.
39 *Ibid.*, p. 71.
40 *Ibid.*, p. 67.
41 *Ibid.*, p. 68.
42 *Ibid.*, p. 75.
43 *Ibid.*, p. 84.
44 *Ibid.*, p. 92.
45 *Ibid.*, p. 77.
46 *Ibid.*, p. 76.
47 *Ibid.*, p. 256.
48 *Ibid.*, pp. 106–13.
49 T. E. Lones, *History of Coal Mining in the Black Country*, 1898, p. 60. For a discussion of the problems of determining hours of work in the Black Country mining industry, see Eric Hopkins, 'Working Hours and Conditions during the Industrial Revolution: A Re-Appraisal', *Economic History Review*, 2nd series, XXXV, No. 1, February, 1982.
50 *CEC*, 1840, First Report, p. 122. See also R. L. Galloway, *Annals of Coal mining and the Coal Trade*, 2nd series, 1904, Vol. 2, p. 357.
51 Flinn, *The History of the British Coal Industry, Vol. 2*, p. 373.
52 *CEC*, 1840, First Report, pp. 113, 118.
53 Flinn, *The History of the British Coal Industry, Vol. 2*, p. 369.
54 *CEC*, 1840, First Report, p. 135.
55 *Ibid.*.
56 *Ibid.*, p. 136.
57 'No other District shows such a melancholy list of human sacrifices such as this exhibits, for in no other light can I view this monstrous wrong to which the mining population are daily exposed': *Reports of Inspectors of Coal Mines*, 1854.
58 *CEC*, 1840, First Report, p. 144.
59 *Ibid.*, pp. 125–34.
60 *Ibid.*, p. 128.
61 *Ibid.*, p. 130.
62 *Ibid.*, pp. 41, 43–4.
63 *Ibid.*, Appendix to First Report, p. 28.
64 On the physical condition of the mining population generally, see *CEC*, 1840, First Report, pp. 161–72, and on the effects of coalmining on the miners' physical condition, pp. 174–91.
65 *Ibid.*, pp. 162–71, and p. 123.
66 For a recent helpful survey, see Gertrude Himmelfarb, *Marriage and Morals among the Victorians*, 1986; see also the balanced discussion in Walter E. Houghton, *The Victorian Frame of Mind 1830–1870*, 1957, chapters 13 and 14.
67 *CEC*, 1840, First Report, p. 256.
68 Derek Hudson, *Munby: Man of Two Worlds*, 1972, p. 75.
69 The Second Report of the *CEC*, 1840 deals with eleven miscellaneous

industries ranging from metalwares to tobacco manufacture.

70 *CEC*, 1840, Second Report, at C5 and C6.

71 *Ibid.*, pp. xi–xii, xxviii.

72 *Ibid.*, p. xxix.

73 *Ibid.*, at C7.

74 *Ibid.*.

75 *Ibid.*, p. 11.

76 B. L. Hutchins and A. Harrison, *A History of Factory Legislation*, 1911, p. 155.

77 *CEC*, 1840, Second Report, Appendix Pt II, at Q89; *CEC*, 1862, Third Report, pp. 140–1.

78 *CEC*, 1862, Fifth Report, p. 152.

79 *Reports of Inspectors of Factories*, 1 January 1865, Report by HMI Robert Baker.

80 *CEC*, 1862, Fourth Report, pp. 181 ff.

81 *Ibid.* See also *Flint Glass Makers Magazine*, II, 1854, p. 1.

82 *CEC*, 1862, Fourth Report, pp. 181 ff.

83 *Ibid.*, p. 200; on employment generally in the Stourbridge glass industry, see T. Matsumura, *The Labour Aristocracy Revisited: the Victorian Flint Glass Makers 1850–80*, 1983.

84 *Edinburgh Review*, LXXIX, No. CLIX, 1844, pp. 151–3.

85 *Parliamentary Reports* (Hansard), Third series, Vol. 65, p. 316.

86 *Ibid.*, Vol. 63, p. 1351.

87 *Ibid.*, p. 1355.

88 *Ibid.*, Vol. 64, pp. 538–46.

89 There is a useful summary of the law relating to employment in factories and workshops in the mid-1870s in the *Report of the Commissioners appointed to enquire into the Working of the Factories and Workshops Acts*, 1876, Vol. I, pp. xii–xiv; and see also Hutchins and Harrison, *A History of Factory Legislation*, Chapter VIII.

90 *Report of the Commissioners appointed to inquire into the Working of the Factory and Workshops Acts*, 1876, Vol. II, p. 323.

91 Although the civil registration of births and deaths began in 1837, it was not compulsory, and there were difficulties even then in checking the ages of working children. Baptismal certificates were often produced, but they could be forged, or simply borrowed from an older child. Sometimes inspectors would resort to estimating ages from an inspection of the children's teeth. Compulsory registration did not come until 1874; see Chapter Seven.

Chapter Three

The factory system and the mid-century work situation reviewed

The last two chapters were concerned with life at work for children in some of the oldest forms of child employment in the country. All the occupations discussed were in existence long before the coming of the Industrial Revolution. In this chapter a new kind of employment is examined, and one which is often thought to be of the very essence of the revolutionary change which began in industry from about the mid-eighteenth century onwards. In the course of the following hundred years it became the largest single industrial occupation of all. It has an unenviable reputation; work in the textile factories is often represented as the worst and most notorious kind of labour in the early nineteenth century, so much so that its evils are generally familiar to all even today. Yet this familiarity can make for a false historical perspective, and the erroneous impression is often gained that most of the nation's children worked in factories before the passing of the factory acts; and those who were not in the factories, it is often thought, were either down the mines or up the chimneys. In fact, as already emphasised in Chapter Two, in 1851 mechanised industry using steam power employed less than a quarter of all industrial workers. Earlier on, in 1830, less than 10 per cent of industrial workers had any experience of factories, that is, only about 3 per cent of the working population as a whole. The typical place of work in industry in the first half of the nineteenth century was still the workshop, not the factory. As for the number of children in the factories, in 1830 those under fourteen comprised about 13 per cent of all factory workers, about 26,000 in all. It follows quite clearly then that the factory children formed only a small proportion of the total work force in the factories, and only a minute proportion of the sum total of all children at work.[1] As we shall see later, the significance of the story of these children is not to be found in the great numbers of children employed in the factories; rather it lies in the peculiarly harmful nature of their long hours of work, in the reform movement which sprang up, and in the repercussions for other forms of child labour (and adult labour, too) of the success of that movement.

Firstly, for those unfamiliar with the course of events, it may be as well to outline as briefly as possible the history of factory reform in the first half of the nineteenth century before discussing the nature of factory work for children.[2] It is a well-known story: as early as the 1780s some anxiety was being expressed by doctors in the Manchester area about the employment of young children in newly-erected factories. These factories were often quite small, and were usually located in the countryside because of the need for water power; steam power did not become predominant until the 1830s. Their location often meant that there were difficulties in obtaining labour in the immediate neighbourhood. To remedy this shortage of labour, parties of poor law children were brought up from London and other parts of the south of England, and then apprenticed to the mill-owners. Lodged in apprentice houses near the mills, these small children spent their lives either in the mill or in the apprentice house. Their condition was such that in 1784 the Manchester magistrates agreed not to permit apprenticeship of any children in factories where they worked more than ten hours a day, or at night. In 1802 the first factory act, the Health and Morals of Apprentices Act, was passed, having been introduced by Robert Peel Sr, a Bury factory owner. This limited the working day for apprentices to twelve hours, exclusive of meals, and forbade night work, but provided for enforcement by local officials only. Another act introduced by Peel in 1819 limited the employment of children in cotton mills, whether apprenticed or free, to those of nine years of age and above, and fixed a maximum of twelve hours daily for children between nine and sixteen. Like its predecessor, this act was poorly enforced, and the same may be said of further acts in 1825, 1830 and 1831, which altered the law in detail but made little difference to existing hours of work.

Why was the law so ineffective and reform so slow? This is an interesting question, given the fact that working conditions were becoming increasingly notorious by 1831. At first this was not the case, as so many of the early mills were hidden away in the countryside; but by the 1830s there were many town mills using steam power, and often employing 200 or more workers. By then, it was not ignorance of what went on, or even the opposition of the factory owners themselves (some actually supported the cause of reform) which made for such slow progress. It was, rather, opposition in principle to regulating hours which was a major stumbling block. There was no historical precedent for it, and since regulating the hours of children would ultimately affect those of adults, this was thought grossly improper, for men must be left to choose their own hours, and work for as long or as short at time as they pleased – a belief reinforced by the increasing support for *laissez-faire* ideas. Those opposed to legislation agreed with Francis Place, the well-known working-class leader, who declared that 'All legislative interference must be pernicious. Men must be left to make their own bargains.'

There were other arguments, of course. Some were of a somewhat theoretical nature, such as the belief expressed by the Rev. Thomas Malthus in his famous *Essay on Population* (1798), that population grew at a geometical ratio, while food supply increased only at an arithmetical ratio. Consequently, population always tended to outstrip subsistence, and it was only famine, war, and voluntary self-restraint in procreation which together kept population growth and the food supply in balance. If life was made easier for working people, they would have larger families, place greater strain on food supplies, drive up food prices, and so make the situation as bad as before. Other views hostile to legislation stressed the fall in earnings which would result from reduced hours, the loss of export trade to foreign competitors, the fact that all right-minded employers treated their workpeople well, because otherwise their work would decline in quality, and – a most impressive argument from the famous economist, Nassau Senior – the belief that 'the whole profit is derived in the last half hour'. As Senior put it, basing his argument on what appeared to be a simple arithmetical example, 'if the hours of working were reduced by one hour per day (prices remaining the same), net profit would be destroyed; if they were reduced by an hour and a half, even gross profit would be destroyed.'[3] Fortunately for the reformers, flaws in Senior's calculation were attacked in the press, and in particular in a long and critical article in the *Spectator*. The gloomy science of economics had failed to convince.

From 1830 onwards the factory reformers concentrated on a campaign to reduce the working day to ten hours – the Ten Hours Movement. Short Time Committees were set up, especially in the West Riding of Yorkshire, where up to 1833 there was no restrictive legislation affecting woollen mills (as opposed to cotton mills) at all. It was in 1830 that Richard Oastler, the real founder of the Factory Movement, wrote his letter of protest to the *Leeds Mercury* on 'Yorkshire Slavery', comparing child workers to slaves. This letter is so famous (and deservedly so) that it is worth quoting again:

> Thousands of little children, both male and female, but *principally female*, from seven to 14 years of age, are daily *compelled to labour* from six o'clock in the morning to seven in the evening, with only – Britons, blush while you read it! – with only *30 minutes allowed for eating and recreation*. Poor infants! Ye are indeed sacrificed at the shrine of avarice, *without even the solace of the negro slave*; ye are no more than he is, *free agents*; but ye are compelled to work as long as the *necessity* of your needy parents may require, or the cold-blooded avarice of your worse than barbarian masters *may demand*! Ye live in the boasted land of freedom, and *feel* and mourn that *ye are slaves*, and slaves without the only comfort which the negro has. He knows that it is his sordid, mercenary master's interest that he should *live*, and be *strong*, and *healthy*. Not so with you.[4]

In 1831, Michael Sadler, Tory MP for Leeds, introduced a Ten Hours Bill into the Commons in a three-hour speech in which again a comparison was made with slavery (which in fact was abolished in the British Empire in 1833):

> Sir, children are beaten with thongs, prepared with that purpose. Yes, the females of this country, no matter whether children or grown-up – I hardly know which is the more disgusting outrage – are beaten upon the face, arms, and bosom – beaten in your free market, as you term it, like slaves. These are the instruments [*Here the honourable member exhibited some black, heavy, leathern thongs, one of them fixed in a sort of handle, the smack of which, when struck upon the table, resounded through the House*]. They are quite equal to breaking an arm, but the bones of the young are, as I have said before, pliant. The marks, however, of the thong are long visible.[5]

His bill was referred to a committee of enquiry (Sadler's Committee) which produced strong criticisms of the treatment of the children; but by then the Reform Act, 1832, had been passed, and Sadler lost his seat in the general election which followed. Ashley (later Lord Shaftesbury) took his place and reintroduced the Ten Hours Bill in 1833, but even then the Whig government insisted on a Royal Commission on factory conditions. Its report was in favour of reform, whereupon the Government brought in its own bill, introduced by Lord Althorp. This became the Factory Act, 1833. It applied to all textile mills, except silk mills, and restricted hours of work to eight between the ages of nine and twelve, and to twelve hours between thirteen and eighteen. Children were to receive two hours' education daily, and night work was forbidden under the age of eighteen. In addition, four government inspectors were to enforce the act. Thus, although the Ten Hour Day had not been achieved, the 1833 act was a definite step forward, especially the provision of government inspectors instead of the local inspectors who were too often under the influence of the millowners.

It was another fourteen years before a Ten Hours Bill was passed. There were unsuccessful attempts to pass further factory bills in 1838, 1839 and 1841. In this last year, the Tories came to power under Sir Robert Peel, but it was not until 1843 that another factory bill was introduced by the Home Secretary, Sir James Graham. This bill proposed to raise the educational provision to three hours daily, and this led to such protests that the bill was dropped. In 1844 another bill was drafted, leaving the existing educational requirements unchanged, but limiting the hours of work of eight to thirteen year-olds to six and a half, and fixing a maximum of twelve hours for all women as well as for young people up to the age of eighteen. An important additional clause required dangerous machinery to be fenced. Ashley attempted but failed to have the twelve-hour limitation reduced to ten hours, but nevertheless the Factory Act, 1844, represented real progress. Finally, in 1846, John Fielden, the radical MP for Oldham, and himself a leading cotton manufacturer, introduced a bill (drafted by Ashley) which was only very narrowly defeated in the Commons. It was reintroduced in 1847, when because of trade depression many factories were working for only ten hours a day. This helped the bill to succeed, and it at last fixed a maximum of ten hours a day for all young persons, and for women. The Ten Hour Movement had at last triumphed. Its victory was a little soured when it was realised that children could still be worked in relays so as to stretch the working day for men to beyond ten hours. This was stopped by Grey's Factory Act, 1850 (amended by the Factory Act, 1853) whereby the maximum was increased to ten and a half hours in return for the fixing of the normal working day as between 6 a.m. and 6 p.m. It is noteworthy that it took all these years of struggle for the gaining of a ten and a half hour day which, in the form of the twelve-hour day, less one and a half hours for meals, had been the accepted working day for many years in the workshops of Birmingham and the Black Country. Textile factories had at last been made to conform to existing workshop practice in the West Midlands.

To return to the question as to why reform had taken so long. Some of the reasons were touched on earlier in this chapter; again, some were of an abstract nature, others were more practical. Of the former, some of the more intellectual members of the House of Commons continued to argue against legislation as a matter of principle. Even Macaulay, who later became converted to the cause of reform, argued in 1833 that the free man could not be forced to ruin his health; if he worked long hours, it was by his own choice that he did so. The law should not protect him, for he could protect himself. In the House of Lords, Brougham, the Lord Chancellor, took the same line: 'Every man has a Ten Hour Bill already. No man need work longer than he pleases.' These arguments seem to show an extraordinary ignorance of the realities of contemporary working-class life. However, early in the present century the pioneer historians of factory legislation, Hutchins and Harrison, suggested that by the 1830s the main line of opposition had little to do with abstract ideas of freedom or the philosophy of *laissez-faire*, but rather with the notion that shorter hours would mean reduced profits, and that the alleged overworking of children was grossly exaggerated by the reformers. The suggestion that the evidence presented by the reformers and investigators was misleading will be considered in some detail a little later in this chapter; as for the commercial argument, it is worth repeating that though this obviously weighed heavily with the manufacturers, some factory-owners, like John Fielden, actually supported reform. This was partly out of humanitarian considerations, and partly out of a desire to restrict the competition created by unscrupulous employers imposing hours as long as they could. It should also be mentioned that fears that shorter working hours would reduce profits proved unwarranted in the long run, mainly because excessive hours often led to tired workers making serious and costly mistakes. Again, it was sometimes argued that restrictions on children's hours would lead to a shortage of labour; but Leonard Horner, one of the inspectors appointed under the 1833 act, claimed that not a single mill throughout the United Kingdom stopped for a day for want of hands because of the act.[6]

The allegations that children were ill-treated in the factories came from a variety of sources. The principal and most reliable official sources are the minutes of Peel's select committee in 1816, and the evidence presented before the Factories Inquiry Commission, 1833. There is also the evidence given before Sadler's committee in 1831. The witnesses before Peel's committee were mostly factory-owners, together with a number of medical practitioners and businessmen; there were no child witnesses. Sadler's committee did call child witnesses, but the evidence given has often been attacked as being too biased in favour of reform. Manufacturers also complained that they had not been given a fair chance to present their side of the case. The Reports and Examinations of the 1833 commission certainly give the impression of being rather more balanced. Child witnesses were again called, together with numerous older factory workers, factory owners, and medical men. The hearing of oral evidence was preceded by the sending out of questionnaires in the major factory districts. Thus, the proceedings of the 1833 commission seem to have been both systematic and orderly, though it must be remarked that the evidence against the Ten Hours Bill is rather stronger than one might expect. On the other hand, the adverse conclusions drawn in the first report concerning the physical results of factory work are more severe than the medical evidence given appears to warrant. In addition to these official reports, there is a wealth of further evidence contained in speeches in the House of Commons, and in contemporary books and pamphlets such as the sensational *Memoir* of Robert Blincoe, published in 1832. From all these sources, it is easy to select passages to illustrate the cruelty inflicted on child workers. For example, child piecers, whose job it was to mend broken threads, were often beaten by the spinners in many mills. An eleven-year-old girl piecer, Mary F. (anonymity was granted to witnesses if requested; they were on oath) testified in Manchester as follows: 'Hears other spinners swear very bad at their piecers; sees 'em lick 'em sometimes, some licks 'em with a strap, some licks 'em with hand; some straps is as long as your arm; some is not that long . . . some is very thick, and somes thin, a quarter of an inch thick.'[7] Another witness, a boy aged fifteen, also told of beatings:

> You have had 8 masters and two mistresses: which did you like working with best? – The women.
> Why better than with men? – Because the men licked me.
> What for? – For having my ends drawn, and for being late.
> Did they hurt you much? – They licked me for 5 minutes at a time sometimes, with a strap, and a cane sometimes.
> Did you ever work for a master who did not lick you? – No, sir.
> How often is a piecer licked in a week? – Sometimes 6 and 8 times in a week.[8]

Among the many descriptions of extreme ill-treatment in Robert Blincoe's *Memoir* (written up by a journalist, John Brown) is an account of how one overseer used to punish Blincoe when he could not or did not keep pace with the machinery: according to Blincoe, this man used

> to tie him up by the wrists to a cross-beam and keep him suspended over the machinery till his agony was extreme. To avoid the machinery, he had to draw up his legs every time it came round or returned. If he did not lift them up, he was

cruelly beaten over the shins, which were bare; nor was he released till growing black in the face, and his head falling over his shoulder, the wretch thought his victim near expiring.[9]

Blincoe repeated this story of being tied to the cross-beam to the Factory Inquiry Commission of 1833.[10]

Yet it was not direct, physical cruelty to the children which was the central issue in the enquiries, but rather the length of the working day, the age of staring work, the physical strain of the work, and the resulting tiredness which precluded any real attempt at education after the day's work. As for working hours, in the north-east areas, the regular hours in the early 1830s were not more than eleven; in Leicester and Nottingham, they were not less than twelve, and it was the same in Leeds and Manchester. Children usually started work at the age of nine, but a few began at the age of five or six, and there were many who began at seven or eight. In 1816 Robert Owen claimed that to his knowledge, children of four were employed in Stockport. Some efforts were made both in 1816 and in 1833 to determine how far the work had long-term effects on the health of the children, and there was a good deal of evidence that children were very tired at the end of the day. It was sometimes necessary to prevent them from falling asleep by getting them to sing hymns, or by use of the iron or wooden rod known as the billy-roller, or simply by blows to the head or body. One overseer testified to this effect in 1833:

I found that when I was an overlooker, that after the children from 8 to 12 years had worked 8 or 9 or 10 hours, they were nearly ready to faint; some were asleep; some were only kept awake by being spoken to, or by a little chastisement to make them jump up. I was sometimes obliged to chastise them when they were almost fainting, and it hurt my feelings; but the last 2 or 3 hours were my hardest work, for they got so exhausted.[11]

Other aspects of employment to take into account were the heat of the rooms, the dust in the air, the lack of proper cooking facilities, and the filthy state of many of the privies. It must be remembered, too, that recruitment to the new factories brought in a very mixed labour force. In some mills the adult females were free in their favours and coarse in their speech. It was sometimes alleged that most of the young girls had lost their virginity at an early age. A Manchester witness in 1833, one Simeon Cundy, claimed that three-quarters of factory girls between the ages of fourteen and twenty were unchaste (as he put it).[12] As for foul conversation, this was common enough; there is an informative passage on this in the Manchester evidence:

Do the boys ever say anything naughty or pert? – Yes, sir; some boys are always doing it.
Do the girls care about it? – Some doesn't like it; some don't mind it.
Some lasses is almost as bad as the boys themselves, with being used to work among such boys.
Is this the case in all spinning mills that you have ever been in? – Yes, sir, all spinning mills go that way. Some spinners never minds it; some don't allow it.
Do they use gross, dirty words? – Yes, sir, a good deal.
Very bad words? – Yes, in all kinds as one may think on a'most; the big ones will set the little ones on it.[13]

In their first report, the commissioners passed rather lightly over the immorality of factory girls, remarking that there was no evidence to show that vice and immorality were more prevalent in the factories than elsewhere; but though they rejected the proposed Ten Hours Bill, they recommended some restrictions in hours, and emphasised that the children's labour resulted in many cases in a permanent deterioration of their physical condition, in the production of diseases 'often wholly irremediable', and in an exclusion from education because of the children's fatigue. Nor had children any choice in the matter; they were not free agents, but were sent to work by their parents who took their wages.[14]

The case which was made in 1833 for the reduction in hours and for excluding very young children seems overwhelming today, yet the problem remains as to how far the undoubted evils were really widespread. There is a surprisingly long list of qualifications which may be made to some of the evidence regarding the ill-treatment of children. In the first place, it must be said that there were some well-run mills where conditions appear to have been far above average. Robert Owen's mills at New Lanark employed up to 1,700 workers, young and old; there were no children under ten, and the daily hours of work were ten and three quarter hours.[15] Mills such as this were highly exceptional, of course, and children in them might still be punished for misdemeanours by dunce's caps, notices hung round the neck, and so on. One woman witness who had left the mills for a post elsewhere said in evidence that at New Lanark the dancing was more exhausting than the actual work. Other good employers included Richard Arkwright at Cromford, and the Strutts at Belper. Generally speaking, the newer mills were much larger than the old, and provided a better working environment, being properly heated and ventilated, and often being fireproofed, with tiled instead of boarded floors. As the first report put it, 'the large factories have a prodigious advantage over the old and small mills'.[16]

The work undertaken by the children was not in itself particularly exhausting. According to one contemporary writer, Edward Baines, 'it is scarcely possible for any employment to be lighter'.[17] A mill-owner said the same in 1816 in reply to a question as to whether the employment was laborious: 'Not at all, it is more a matter of attention than of labour.' Another owner was asked whether he knew of any employment that was so little laborious for children as that in the cotton factories. He replied, 'None whatever'. A third witness, Kinder Wood, an Oldham surgeon, having the same question put to him, was perhaps more perceptive: 'Not in actual labour; I believe the labour of it is very light; it is the incessancy that I speak of. I believe the labour in itself is slight.'[18] This would certainly apply to piecers, who were constantly on the go. In other rooms, the pressure was less intense, and it was alleged that in the Manchester district children in the card room sometimes brought a book to read in the intervals of work. Dr Ure's evidence takes some believing today, but he claimed to have visited many factories over a period of several months, and said that he had never seen children in an ill-humour:

> They seemed to be always cheerful and alert, taking pleasure in the light play of their muscles – enjoying the mobility natural to their age. The scene of industry, so far from exciting sad emotions in my mind, was always exhilarating . . . The work of these lively elves seemed to resemble a sport, in which habit gave them a pleasing dexterity. Conscious of their skill, they were delighted to show it off to any stranger.[19]

Dr Ure also stated that during his visits he would enter the spinning rooms unexpectedly and often alone, at different times of the day, and yet he had never seen a single instance of corporal punishement inflicted on a child. This seems an extraordinary statement, unless it was that he visited only the best-regulated mills; it is also possible that in any case the presence of a stranger inhibited the customary practices of the spinners. Nevertheless, it must be said that there were witnesses in Lancashire who said that they, too, had never seen a child ill-treated, and had never heard children crying; in their experience, if children were beaten, the perpetrator would be dismissed.[20] Other witnesses did not deny that children were subjected to physical correction, but said that children were treated worse at school, or in the home, or in collieries, or in handloom weaving.[21] The first report of the commissioners in 1833 gave examples of ill-treatment of children, the worst occurring in Scotland and in Yorkshire, but they thought the greatest number of bad cases were to be found in the 'small, obscure mills belonging to the smallest proprietors', and the bad treatment was inflicted not by the mill-owners, but by 'violent and dissipated workmen'.[22]

One test of how far children suffered from their employment in the mills was, of course, whether their physical condition was noticeably inferior to that of children employed elsewhere. On this, opinions varied among medical men. Some were prepared to submit medical certificates testifying to the good health of apprentices. Others were more critical, both in the 1816 committee minutes and in the second report of the 1833 commissioners. This last criticism must have influenced them in their condemnation of child labour in the first report which, they said (as we noticed earlier) resulted in many cases in 'a permanent deterioration in the children's physical condition'. Even then, evidence is not completely lacking to show that children's health was unaffected by their work, and there is testimony to show that some children, at least, were not too tired to play after the day's work. Further, for all the alleged degradation of the young girls at work, it was also argued that factory girls could make good wives.

It may be instructive to examine two or three of the most notorious cases of cruel treatment, and to try to put them into some sort of perspective. Probably the most striking testimony before Peel's 1816 committee was provided by Mr Moss, the governor of the Preston workhouse, who had previously been in charge of the apprentice house at the mill in Backbarrow in Lancashire. He was paid £80 per annum for just over a year's employment, and was actually offered £100 a year before he left for Preston, where he was paid only 50 guineas a year, together with 5 guineas for his wife. His evidence as to the hardships suffered by the apprentices was very striking. The hours of work were from five in the morning till eight at night, with half an hour off for breakfast, and half an hour for dinner. Thus, they actually worked fourteen hours in the day. Hours were even longer when overtime had to be worked:

When making up lost time, how long did they continue working at night? – Till 9 o'clock, and sometimes later; sometimes ten.

Was this before the Apprentices Bill or after? – It was last year, and is in practice now.

How long were they making up lost time? – I have known them to be three weeks

or more making up lost time.
Did any children work on the Sundays as cleaners of the machinery? – Yes.
Did they do this regularly? – Regularly every Sunday: I do not know that ever I missed one Sunday while I was there.
Through the year? – Yes.
How many hours did they work on a Sunday? – Their orders were from 6 to 12.[23]

Mr Moss also explained that the apprentice house was about a hundred yards away from the mill, and that he got the children up at half-past four so that they could start work at five. He also inspected the beds since there were always some missing, some had run away, and so on. Mr Moss said that he had never heard of the Apprentices Act, 1802.

This was remarkable evidence, made more striking as Mr Moss voluntarily left his post to take up another at a lower salary, refusing a rise of £20 before going to Preston. Efforts appear to have been made to discredit him. A local doctor provided a certificate stating that the children were particularly healthy, and their treatment very good in all respects. A local minister also certified that the children were neat and clean, and attended church regularly. Moreover, a witness appeared who had been an overseer in the mill, one William Travers. He declared that the children were in a good condition, and that Mr Moss had been too free with them, taking a stick and putting it to the girls' petticoats, and heaving them up a little, and saying, 'let's see what sort of legs you've got'. As for Mrs Moss, she was too high for her situation, on one occasion referring to the girls as 'a parcel of bitches'. The commissioner was careful to check that the proprietors of the mill had sent this witness to give evidence, and that he expected to have his expenses paid. Under questioning, Travers also admitted that Mr Moss seemed a very decent sort of man, and that he had never heard anything against him; he had seen him take liberties only once, and no child had ever complained to him of Mr Moss's being too free.[24] The committee were obviously suspicious of Travers, and do not seem to have taken his charge of sexual harassment very seriously, nor did they comment on the evidence provided by the doctor and the parson. In this case, the evidence of the principal witness, Mr Moss, still stands up strongly.

Another kind of evidence of cruelty in the mills is contained in Robert Blincoe's *Memoir*, noted earlier in this chapter. It was published in book form in 1832, having been written up some years previously by a journalist, John Brown, who committed suicide in 1825. It consists of a catalogue of horrors inflicted on the apprentice Blincoe which are still sickening to read today. In recent times its authenticity has been disputed, in particular by Dr S. Chapman, who has thrown doubt on a number of aspects of Blincoe's story, and has described its author as a 'gullible sensationalist, whose statements must be treated with the utmost caution'.[25] Professor Pollard's view is that the treatment of apprentices described in the *Memoir* was not common to all mills, and that 'Robert Blincoe's sadistic master was untypical'.[26] However, not all historians today would go as far as Dr Chapman in his criticisms, and he has been taken to task by Professor A. E. Musson for going too far.[27] In fact, particular incidents set out in the book are not at all worse in kind than the many instances of cruelty practised in domestic workshops, as can be seen by the examples given in the preceding chapter of this book. It is rather that the various forms of ill-treatment meted out to the unfortunate Blincoe are presented in vivid detail and in a work running to ninety or so pages, so that the cumulative effect is certainly both impressive and disturbing to the reader. The *Memoir* can hardly be held to portray life in the typical mill of the time, but the individual acts of cruelty are by no means inconceivable.

A further example of the need to treat evidence with some caution is provided by the so-called Wigan Case of 1833. This concerned a certain young girl, Ellen Hooton, of Wigan. It was alleged that she had in effect been put in chains at her place of work, so that the comparison with slave labour could readily be made. No doubt rumour embroidered the tale. The girl herself, her mother, the overseer concerned, and the works manager were all examined by the 1833 commission, and it emerged that the original evidence of the girl and of her mother was both confused and unreliable. Under pressure, the girl admitted to lying and stealing. There was no question of her being made to work in chains – no chains had been employed at all. Instead, she had been 'weighted' – that is, weights had been placed on her shoulders by the overseer by way of punishment, and she was then left to roam about the factory floor. It was thought by some that this weighting was the equivalent of being made to work in chains. The punishment was reprehensible enough, but was freely admitted by the overseer; it was not entirely unknown in other mills. The final comments of the commissioner, Mr Cowell, are of some interest:

> I have to remark . . . that the girl is entirely a bad, lying girl. I hardly know what to say of the mother. Swanton [the overseer] I believe meant no harm, and the weighting of the girl gave no pain. It was an ignorant, stupid device of his to cure the girl of running away but not cruelly intended. The story of her being

compelled to work is not only a gross exaggeration, but any man who is a spinner must know the absolute impossibility of a girl working at throstle-spinning with a weight on her back.[28]

Lastly, the evidence of one Joseph Hebergam of Bradford as to excessive hours and punishments in a Bradford mill was strongly contradicted by some of his fellow-workers as well as by the owner of the mill, who sent several of them to give evidence. As a result of the conflict of evidence, Hebergam was recalled and re-examined, and admitted he had been wrong in some instances, but not in all. Finally, the central board of the commission decided to disallow his evidence altogether. The whole episode is an interesting example of a case in which the commission suspected exaggeration, though it is true that the factory owner himself took care to preserve his own good name by sending employees to discredit a hostile witness.[29]

In summing up, there seems little doubt that there was a good deal of cruelty in the factories, but precisely how much it is obviously impossible to say. Although a great mass of evidence was collected by the 1833 commission, there is no way of knowing how unbiased the evidence really was – how far the witnesses in each district represented a fair cross-section of opinion, how far they had been primed by employers as to what to say, and so on. Clearly, some of the witnesses who spoke in favour of the Ten Hours Bill, and expressed criticisms of the factory system as they had known it, may have been exaggerating. On the other hand, there was a surprising and perhaps somewhat suspicious unanimity among some groups of witnesses who thought that children could work twelve hours a day without harm, and were not ill-treated at any time, and so on.[30] In attempting to assess the reliability of witnesses before the 1833 commission, it must be taken into account that most witnesses gave evidence under oath, a proceeding taken more seriously then than at the present time. Moreover, they could speak anonymously, if they so wished. On balance then, local opinion probably came through reasonably well. Certainly, the criticisms of the factory system as it then operated were taken seriously by the commission, as can be seen by the fact that they reported unequivocally in favour of reform of children's working hours.

Was there *more* cruelty in the factories than in other workplaces? Several points may be made here. The first is that attention was focused on the factories because they provided a new and different form of employment, and one of a highly visible nature; no one in the neighbourhood could fail to notice the streams of children entering and leaving the new buildings, and many would have kith and kin working there. Even if the factory was one of the early mills in the countryside, the use of pauper children in considerable numbers and without parents to look after them would in time attract attention. As Sir John Clapham put it, 'Children were being overworked in a new and obvious way in new and unusually obvious institutions.'[31] Small domestic workshops were far less subject to public scrutiny. In consequence, factory working conditions became increasingly well known, especially with the development of the Ten Hours Movement from 1830 onwards. Further, with the Whigs in power, factory reform became a favourite weapon of the landowning Tories with which to attack a Government which represented the commercial and industrial middle classes. In this way, political motives helped to keep the spotlight on the factories, even though only a small minority of working children were employed in them, and cruelties on a far wider scale were practiced in other sectors of industry. Evidence of this did not become widely known until revealed in the reports of the Children's Employment Commission, 1840; but even in 1833 there was an awareness that children were being ill-treated in other industrial occupations. Mr Tufnell, commissioner for the Manchester district, provides a striking indication of this. He was certainly prone to exaggeration at times, but he made a fair point about what he called 'instances of ill-usage' in the factories: 'It would be the grossest injustice to assert that they equal in amount one quarter of the cruelties which children have to endure in the glasshouse, pin-heading, and colliery trades.'[32] His choice of glasshouses, and his failure to mention domestic workshops, are rather odd in this context. Nevertheless, the short answer to the question of whether there was more cruelty in the factories than elsewhere, is that this was not necessarily so. As bad, if not worse cruelty occurred in other sectors of industry.

It should also be emphasised again that humane factory owners did exist, and it was often pointed out that many factory owners had little to do with the day-to-day running of their factories, and that the ill-treatment suffered by the children was inflicted by their own fellow-workers, principally by spinners and overseers. A certain amount of physical chastisement was only to be expected, of course, given the customary practices of the age, but it could be that there was an additional temptation to discipline the children physically, since there was the need to ensure continuous production from steam-driven machinery. In order to maximise production, punctuality in attendance and concentration on the task in hand were essential. Both adult and child from the countryside had to be trained in a new work discipline, which became a feature of the factories. Fines were sometimes levied on both the adult operatives and on the children for any breach of the factory rules. Thus strict work routines became essential, with a new importance attached to achieving the best possible output in a given time (it has been argued that this involved a change from a so-called task-orientated approach to work to a time-orientated discipline, but in fact payment was still usually by the piece, so that task-orientation was still essential within the time set by the working day). At all events, children had to be kept hard at work, and this inevitably led to problems, not only during the course of the day, because of the need to curb their natural tendency to play, but also at the end of the day, through their sheer tiredness.

In concluding this section, it may be as well to point out that whether the ill-treatment suffered by the children was exaggerated at the time or not, the first report of the 1833 commission stated categorically that the children's physical condition was being adversely affected, and they were being deprived of education. This view was very largely accepted by the Government, who brought in Althorp's bill, which became the Factory Act, 1833. In other words, educated middle- and upper-class opinion was at last persuaded that further substantial reform was necessary, even if the Ten Hour Bill had to wait till 1847. This is perhaps the most convincing proof that reform really was required in the textile factories. It is worth repeating that Richard Oastler put the point very simply in 1833: 'Any old washerwoman could tell you that ten hours a day is too long for any child to labour.'

Not everyone agreed with him, even then, and there were still opponents who fought a rearguard action against those reformers they termed 'humanity-mongers'. Ashley himself was attacked for devoting himself so exclusively to the sufferings of the factory children, when just as bad examples of ill-treatment were to be found in other branches of industry (a criticism he rebutted by pointing out the impossibility of remedying all the evils of child employment at once). There was also considerable opposition to the Ten Hour Bill by workmen witnesses before the 1833 commission who understandably feared a loss of wages if hours were curtailed. Further, there was the loss of earnings by the children themselves to be considered. Rather remarkably, Mr Tufnell wrote very strongly against *all* factory legislation in his report – a surprising outburst from one who should have been an impartial observer: 'The true interests of humanity, of justice, and of morality, require that not only no new factory bill should be passed, but that every former one should be instantly repealed.'[33] Yet paradoxically he still supported Ashley's factory bill, giving his approval as an *education* bill. Even in the twentieth century there were one or two historians who thought that the whole agitation over working conditions was misplaced. In an article republished in 1954, W. H. Hutt suggested that the apparent benefits of the early factory acts were largely illusory, since there had been considerable and steady improvements in conditions before 1833. Factory legislation was not essential, he argued, to the ultimate disappearance of whatever evils existed in child employment.[34] Other historians (including the present writer) would disagree with this verdict, and would point out the value of the factory acts not only in improving conditions in the factories but in drawing attention to child employment in other sectors of industry, as evidenced in the appointment of Children's Employment Commissions in 1840 and 1862. This was a most valuable consequence of the factory reform movement which will be touched upon a little later.

In the final analysis, the question must be asked, how did children respond to life in the factories? Is it at all possible to see conditions through their eyes? Few if any children of the time recorded their attitude generally to factory life. It is all too easy, of course, to dwell upon the horrors. Although it is really beyond dispute that hours were long, the labour sustained, and that in some cases the children were ill-treated, yet some children appeared not to dislike the work. Starting work, after all, was a rite of passage, the beginning of an entry into a more adult world, and as the children grew older, they would keep part of their earnings. Indeed, several young witnesses referred to 'liking the money' when working long hours. As for the working environment, in the smaller mills it could be very bad – overheated, dirty, smelly, and at times dangerous. But again, larger and more modern mills were much better than this. Presumably Tufnell had these mills in mind when he reported on working conditions in his customary forceful manner: 'It would be an outrageous falsehood to assert that any part of a cotton mill is one-tenth as crowded, or the air one-tenth as impure, as the House of Commons with a moderate attendance of members.'[35] This at first sounds rather like Dr Ure, until one remembers that the Chamber was very small, and members of parliament not particularly noted for their personal hygiene or abstinence from alcohol and tobacco; but of course they were free to come and go as they pleased, or simply to go to sleep.

Nevertheless, the more modern mills were certainly better to work in than the smaller and older mills. As for initiation into adult attitudes and practices, swearing and foul talk were commonplace, as in many workplaces today, so that the children had to get used to this, if they were not already accustomed to it at home. Promiscuity does not seem to have been unusual, so that some children had their first sexual experience as a result of working in the factory. According to one not altogether reliable witness in 1833 in the Leicester area, sexual activity never took place to his knowledge in the factory itself, but in the adjoining fields (he said he himself had had two bastards sworn to him).[36] Once more, there can be exaggeration here, and as already noted, the 1833 commission concluded that there was no evidence to show that vice and immorality were more prevalent in the factories than elsewhere. This is a significant conclusion, given the strength of the evangelical revival of the time, and the keen interest shown by middle-class reformers in any examples of sexual dalliance which they might uncover among the working classes. In short, one may surmise that for many children, beginning factory work, in spite of all its hardships, meant a not unwelcome entry into the world of work, new relationships with adults, new companionships, new experiences. This is not in any way to deny the all too prevalent cruelty, especially the strain of over-long hours, but it would be wrong to represent it all without qualification as simply hell on earth.

Finally then, to return to the consequences of factory legislation, the working lives of factory children were transformed by the Factory Acts, espcially from 1833 onwards. This had important consequences for working children in other areas of industry; the voluminous reports of the Children's Commissions of 1840 and 1862 prompted further reform, leading first to legislation on bleach and dye works, and then to the passing of the Factory Act, 1867, extending regulations beyond the textile factories to other large places of work. The Workshops Act of the same year at last imposed restrictions on children's employment in domestic industry. Legislation of this kind inevitably affected the working hours of adults, as the reformers had intended, of course. Moreover, one important result of factory reform was that young children now had more time to go to school, and by the acts of 1876 and 1880 attendance at school became compulsory. The factory reform movement therefore had profund consequences for working children in the nineteenth century. On the one hand, it progressively removed them from the workplace – not all at once, and at first, to only a limited degree; the progress was slow, but it was irreversible. On the other hand, it sent the children to school, an equally important and even revolutionary development, as will be seen in Chapter Four.

At this point it becomes possible to take into account the principal features of the developments outlined in this and the preceding two chapters, and in this way to obtain some kind of overarching view of child employment before 1867. Naturally, the survey of work in agriculture and industry which has been undertaken does not include the wide spectrum of jobs of a miscellaneous kind, and something must be said of these occupations here. Of all such occupations, that of the climbing boys – the child chimney-sweeps – is perhaps the most notorious, if only because of Charles Kingsley's *The Water Babies* (1863). In fact, the numbers employed were never more than three or four thousand, there being less than 400 in London in 1841,[37] but it took more than a century for legislation to become effective. The first regulating act was passed in 1788, but the *Committee on the Employment of Boys in Sweeping Chiminies* (*sic*) (1817) reported that the law was widely ignored in what it called 'this painful and degrading trade'. Further legislation was equally ineffective. Small boys were still driven up chimneys by force, by lighting fires beneath them, by having pins stuck in the soles of their feet, and so on. By the mid-nineteenth century, they were still getting stuck in the chimneys and sometimes asphyxiated, and were still contracting sweeps' cancer from the soot. It was not until 1875 that the last of a series of acts finally placed the enforcement of the law in the hands of the police, who were henceforth to issue licences to sweeps annually.

Far larger numbers of boys were engaged in navigation and the docks. In 1851, about 46,000 boys under fifteen years of age were so employed; this would include work not only in shipping but on the still busy canals.[38] They comprised 10.9 per cent of the occupied age group of boys, and there were 9,000 more of them than the total number of boys down the mines. A surprisingly large number of boys under fifteen were in the dress and garment trade (23,000), more than in general labouring (15,000), dealing (including lodging and coffee-houses) (12,000), building (11,000), and domestic service (9,000). Somewhere among these categories would be the myriads of stable-boys, pedlars, pot-boys, messenger- and errand-boys, boots, street entertainers, and all the others encountered so frequently in the pages of Dickens and of other Victorian writers. As for the girls, the largest occupation of girls under fifteen at work was employment in textiles, followed by domestic service. Next, and equally to be expected, came the 32,000 in the dress trade.

There were 4,000 girls in navigation and docks, and 2,000 in dealing, that is, retailing. All in all, the main occupations of boys and girls under fifteen in Britain in 1851 may be summarised as follows:

Principal occupations of boys and girls under fifteen in Britain, 1851

Boys	*(000s)*	*Girls*	*(000s)*
Agriculture	120	Agriculture	17
Textiles	82	Textiles	98
Navigation & docks	46	Navigation & docks	4
Mines	37	Metalwork	4
Metalwork	26	Earthenware	3
Earthenware	6	Dress	32
Dress	23	Dealing	2
General labour	15	Domestic service	71
Dealing	12	Miscellaneous	6
Building	11		
Domestic service	9		
Miscellaneous	36		
	423		237

From this it is clear that among the boys agricultural employment was still important, but that it employed many less than industry and transport (navigation and docks) put together. If industry and agriculture are added together, they constitute about two-thirds of all employment for boys. Among the girls, textiles employed the largest number, but domestic service was not far behind, followed by dress. The numbers in the first two occupations add up to more than half all the occupations for girls.

A further and important qualification must be made to all this: although figures are not available earlier in the century of a kind which would make detailed comparisons possible, it seems that child employment actually declined in the first half of the nineteenth century. This was due partly to restrictive legislation, but it was also due (probably to a greater extent) to more parents sending their children to school, and for longer periods (see Chapter Four). this was probably because more parents came to realise the value of education, and was also perhaps the consequence of an easing of the financial strain which had made it necessary for them to send their children out to work. Whatever the causes, the number of smaller children in employment, (that is, those between five and nine), has been calculated to have been only 85,000 in 1851, or 3.5 per cent of all children between those ages.[39] At first sight, this seems remarkably small, but quite apart from the possibility of under-recording in the census returns, it must be remembered that most children had never started work till eight or nine, which would obviously reduce the proportion of the age-range at work. Further, of the total number of five to nine-year-olds, calculated at 2.2 million, there would be children in middle- and upper-class homes who certainly would not begin work until they were much older (if at all). The low figure of 3.5 per cent must therefore be seen in this context; but it is a salutary reminder that by 1851 child labour by very young children, in spite of the emphasis given to it by the reports in the 1840s of the Children's Employment Commission, appears to have been reduced considerably.

When child employment in all its forms in the period from 1800 to 1870 is seen in perspective, the reality remains much the same – long hours, often under wretched conditions, and accompanied from time to time by ill-treatment. This applies whether the child worked in agriculture, industry, trade, or the service industries. It is still possible, all the same, that the average child of the time, boy or girl, is unlikely to have seen it in that way, or to have thought of himself or herself as a member of an exploited underclass. They were born into the work situation, and work and its rewards were often essential to the survival of the family. Work was the central fact of ordinary people's lives, occupying most of their waking hours during the week. For some children, even Sunday was not a day of rest, but a busy day with attendance at church or chapel and Sunday school. It is not easy for the modern observer at the end of the twentieth century to grasp the widely accepted nature of child employment in the early nineteenth century, and the extent to which it dominated many youthful lives. It was not something which generally came at the end of a lengthy period of schooling. Once embarked on, work continued for the same daily hours as for adults till old age and infirmity brought it to an end.

Yet it would be wrong to look upon child employment as simply the beginning of a long period of servitude experienced by those born into the working classes, the price paid for being born unprivileged and without influence in the world. It was the essential preliminary to having a trade as an adult, and to the increase in independence and status which went with adulthood, limited though that might be. Moreover, it was during the childhood years at work that character was formed and lifelong habits acquired. Lack of evidence makes it unsafe to generalise too widely about the formative effects of work experience on young children in the early nineteenth century, but it would be wrong to dwell too exclusively on the long hours and the beatings, the staple fare of many social histories of this period. Much would depend on the good nature or otherwise of the overseer, on the temper of the adult workers, on the kindness (or cruelty) of a parent close at hand, and on the friendliness or hostility of other child workers. Relationships were formed, sometimes for life, gossip exchanged, stories told, vocabulary extended (sometimes by 'gross, dirty words'), and as puberty approached, the mysteries of sexuality would begin to manifest themselves. All this is the stuff of growing up, even today, though in the early nineteenth century it all took place in a predominantly adult work situation rather than in school or college. Thus for the majority of children the universe of work was the context in which maturation began, and too narrow a concentration on the grimmer aspects of life at work would be both misplaced and anachronistic. Even in the most adverse circumstances, most young children will try to make the best of it, and high spirits will seek an outlet. One thinks of some of the childish pranks at the Strutts' factory, and of the girl fined for calling through the window to the soldiers.[40] Tears were sometimes shed in the mill or workshop, but laughter was not entirely excluded. It should also be remembered that there were breaks in the routine of work from time to time, sometimes in the form of local wakes, sometimes because of short-time working. The more enlightened mill-owners, such as the Ashworths, allowed unpaid holidays of a week or more, while the child workers aged nine to thirteen in the Ashworth mills could take a month's holiday in the summer. It would be quite wrong to suppose that work went on relentlessly throughout the week and for fifty-two weeks in the year.[41]

Lastly, it may be said that the period from 1800 to 1870 brought changes in the employment of child labour which were of great significance. At the beginning of the century, child labour was an acknowledged fact of childhood, and universally accepted. By 1870 it was viewed with reserve, and was subject to substantial restrictions in industry and even in agriculture. Two major factors appear to have brought this about: the first was the development of the humanitarian movement, seen most clearly in the abolition of slavery in 1833, and also in the factory reform movement, which in turn was the consequence of the new work discipline in the factories. The second factor was the increasing concern for the education of the masses, something viewed much more at first as a necessary civilising influence in the new industrial towns than as something of value in itself, let alone a right of the individual child. The combined effect of these two changes in outlook led not only to factory reform, but also to reform in other branches of industry and later in agriculture; and of course it was reform which affected both child and adult workers. Thus the limitations placed on child labour had remarkable and far-reaching effects on the employment of children and ultimately on employment as a whole.

References

1 F. M. L. Thompson, *The Rise of Respectable Society: A Social History of Victorian Britain, 1830–1900*, 1988, pp. 25, 23.

2 B. L. Hutchins and A. Harrison, *A History of Factory Legislation*, 2nd edn, 1911, still provides a sound factual account of the subject. See also M. W. Thomas, *Young People in Industry 1750–1945*, 1945 and *The Early Factory Legislation*, 1948; J. T. Ward, *The Factory Movement 1830–1855*, 1962 and *The Factory System*, 1970; U. R. Q. Henriques, *The Early Factory Acts and their Enforcement*, 1971.

3 Nassau Senior, *Letters on the Factory Act*, 1837, pp. 11–16.

4 *Leeds Mercury*, 16 October 1830.

5 *Memoirs of the Life and Writings of Michael Thomas Sadler*, 1842, pp. 337–79.

6 Leonard Horner, *On the Employment of Children in Factories and other Works in the UK, and in some Foreign Countries*, 1840, pp. 15–16.

7 *Factory Enquiry Commission*, 1833, Examinations, D1, p. 33.

8 *Ibid.*, D1, p. 78.

9 John Brown, *A Memoir of Robert Blincoe*, 1832, Caliban Books edn, 1977, p. 56.

10 *Factory Inquiry Commission*, 1833, Second Report, D3, pp. 17–18.

11 *Ibid.*, First Report, p. 27.

12 *Ibid.*, D1, p. 57.

13 *Ibid.*, D1, pp. 76–7.

14 *Ibid.*, pp. 31–2, 33–4, 52.

15 *Select Committee on Manufactures*, 1816, p. 20.

16 *Factory Inquiry Commission*, 1833, First Report, p. 16. For conditions in the mills of two model employers see R. S. Fitton and A. P. Wadsworth, *The Strutts and the Arkwrights 1758–1830*, 1958 and Rhodes Boyson, *The Ashworth Cotton Enterprise: the Rise and Fall of a Family Firm*, 1970. In the Ashworth factories, tubs of hot and cold water and soap and towels were provided for the workers (p. 91).

17 Edward Baines, *History of the Cotton Manufacture in Great Britain*, 1836,

p. 456.

18 *Select Committee on Manufactures*, 1816, p. 116.

19 Andrew Ure, *The Philosophy of Manufactures*, 1835, p. 301.

20 See, for example, *Factory Inquiry Commission*, 1833, First Report, D1, pp. 58–63, 98–100.

21 *Ibid.*, D1, pp. 58–63 (evidence of six adult witnesses with long experience in mills).

22 *Ibid.*, pp. 19–20.

23 *Select Committee on Manufactures*, 1816, pp. 178–85.

24 *Ibid.*, pp. 288–93.

25 S. D. Chapman, *The Early Factory Masters*, 1967, pp. 208–9.

26 S. Pollard, *The Genesis of Modern Management*, 1965, p. 186.

27 A. E. Musson, 'Robert Blincoe and the Early Factory System', in A. E. Musson (ed), *Trade Union and Social History*, 1974, pp. 195–207. For a recent treatment of the *Memoir*, which seems disinclined to reassess it critically, see John Rule, *The Labouring Classes in Early Industrial England, 1750–1850*, 1986, pp. 147–9.

28 *Factory Inquiry Commission*, 1833, First Report, pp. 103–15.

29 *Ibid.*, Bradford evidence, C1, p. 134.

30 *Ibid.*, D1, pp. 98–100, 128–31.

31 Quoted in E. H. Hunt, *British Labour History 1815–1914*, 1981, p. 12.

32 *Factory Inquiry Commission*, 1833, Second Report, p. 194.

33 *Ibid.*, p. 226.

34 W. H. Hutt, 'The Factory System of the Early Nineteenth Century', in F. A. Hayek (ed), *Capitalism and the Historians*, 1954.

35 *Factory Inquiry Commission*, 1833, Second Report, D2, p. 200.

36 *Ibid.*, First Report, C1, p. 20.

37 G. L. Phillips, *England's Climbing Boys*, 1949, p. 3.

38 For all the figures quoted in this paragraph, and also the tables which follow, see Booth, *Journal of the Royal Statistical Society*, XLIV, 1886, quoted in Hunt, *British Labour History*, p. 14. It will be noted that the figures given here for textiles are much larger than the figures given for factory children under fourteen in 1830 at the beginning of this chapter. This is because in 1830 the factory system was still on a small scale, being confined very largely to the spinning side of the industry. Weaving had yet to go over to factory production. Further, the 1851 figures include all branches of textile manufacture, in the factory or otherwise, whereas the 1830 figure is limited to factory production. It should also be observed that in 1830 the ages of the children were up to fourteen, while they were up to fifteen in 1851. Lastly, after the end of the French wars in 1815 the cotton industry expanded at a phenomenal rate, far faster than any other industry, other than iron and steel; the rate of growth between 1814 and 1846 was 6.6 per cent *per annum* (see Francois Crouzet, *The Victorian Economy*, 1982, p. 196).

39 P. E. H. Hair, 'Children in Society 1850–1980', in Theo Barker and

Michael Drake (eds), *Population and Society in Britain 1850–1980*, 1982, p. 47. Hunt, *British Labour History*, p. 343, gives an even lower estimate, of 42,000 children employed under ten, and this figure is also given in B. R. Mitchell, *British Historical Statistics*, 1988, p. 103. Only Lionel Rose, *The Erosion of Childhood: Child Oppression in Britain 1860–1918*, 1991 suggests a higher figure, of about a *third* of boys aged 5–9, and rather more of girls, being employed in *1861* (p. 3). However, this figure appears to be a miscalculation based on the printed census occupational tables for 1861.

40 Fitton and Wadsworth, *The Strutts and the Arkwrights*, p. 235. Other misdemeanours punished by the Strutts by fines included riding on each other's back; dancing in the room; making T. Ride's nose bleed on the hanks; terrifying S. Pearson with her ugly face; throwing water on Ann Gregory very frequently; and throwing tea on Josh Bridworth (*ibid.*, p. 236).

41 It has recently been suggested that the extent of underemployment and unemployment in the eighteenth and early nineteenth centuries has been greatly underestimated. See Hugh Cunningham, 'The Employment and Unemployment of Children in England *c.*1680–1851', *Past & Present*, no. 126, Feb. 1990, in which it is argued that in most rural areas children were unemployed, and that in most towns throughout the period, and in agricultural areas particularly in the late eighteenth and early nineteenth centuries, underemployment and unemployment were the norm. Further, wages were not paid to younger children in agriculture. Although it is helpful for attention to be drawn to the frequently intermittent nature of employment, these views are difficult to reconcile with the evidence presented in Chapter One for children's paid employment in agriculture and in domestic industry, to say the least. See the 'Conclusions and observations' for a further discussion of this matter.

Part II

Home, school and church before 1867

Chapter Four

Children at home

It is well known that in the first half of the nineteenth century families were substantially larger than they are at the present day. As a result, the working-class child was commonly a member of a small community of brothers and sisters, and grew up subject to both parental authority and sibling influence, both of which might be profound. The actual size of any one family obviously changed over time as the parents produced more offspring, but of married women born between 1771 and 1831 the number of children born to them peaked at between 5.7 and 6.2 – in round figures, the typical family contained about six children.[1] However, this figure could be misleading, in that it does not indicate the size of families at any one specific time, nor is family size the same as the size of the household, clearly a bigger unit than the family. On the first point, the composition of families was constantly changing not only as babies came into the family, but also as older children left home. Further, babies and very young children were particularly susceptible to illness and death in the early nineteenth century. In the worst districts in the largest towns two out of ten babies would not live to see their first birthday, while one in four babies would not survive to the age of five.[2] Life expectancy in the countryside and in market towns, not surprisingly, was better than in the great industrial towns and ports; a baby born in Liverpool in 1861 had a life expectancy of only 26 years, while one born in Okehampton in Devon might expect to live to 57 years (the national average for England and Wales was about 40 in the mid-nineteenth century).[3]

When considerations of this kind are taken into account, it follows that any study of particular families in particular trades can reveal rather smaller families than at first might be anticipated; for instance, an analysis of Black Country nailing families in two nailing villages in 1851 has produced average family sizes of 4.6 and 4.9 persons, including parents.[4] It is wrong, therefore, to suppose that the young worker always grew up surrounded in all the early stages of his or her life by a milling crowd of brothers and sisters. In fact, as he or she grew older, in addition to the loss of brothers and sisters, death might also remove one or both parents far more frequently than happens today. According to Professor Anderson, very large numbers of children lived through much of their childhood having lost at least one parent; for example, of boys born in 1861, by the age of ten, 11 per cent, on average, had lost their father, and 11 per cent their mothers. By the age of fifteen, 17 per cent of boys had lost fathers, and 17 per cent mothers.[5]

As for the second point raised above, household sizes naturally varied, but when they were larger than the basic conjugal (or nuclear) family, in most cases this was not because the family had been extended because of the presence of grandparents. On the contrary, the three generation family was comparatively rare in the mid-nineteenth century; only 10 per cent of families contained related persons spanning either three or four generations. Thus the extended family in its classical form was in quite a small minority.[6] At the same time, the conjugal family living alone was also in a minority; in 1851, only 36 per cent of families consisted solely of a married couple with children. The majority of households were made up of conjugal families plus a variety of outsiders. These might be lodgers, distant relatives, apprentices, or even servants. Lodgers were probably the largest group; they were to be found in one in nine households of skilled workers, nearly one in five of semi-skilled households, and one in seven of unskilled households. Lodgers contributed to the family income, and certainly helped to pay the rent. Surprisingly enough, servants were to be found even in working-class households. About 2 per cent of working-class families had living-in servants, though these might be farm servants or other employees of the head of household.[7] All in all, the working-class child must have been accustomed to frequent changes of face among members of the household, and not least to sudden disappearances resulting from the onset of illness and death. The literature of the time is full of dramatic and sometimes macabre references to the death of children:

> Remember Kate Morris – poor dear little girl –
> So merry, so active and bright;
> So happy and full of gay spirits one morn,
> A scorched, blackened corpse the same night.[8]

Nor would the sight of a corpse be unfamiliar to many children. They might have to share the same room with the departed, who would be laid out on a stripped bed, or if a child, on a table. From early years on, children grew up in the awareness of death, faced as they so often were by the death of a parent, brother, sister, or other relation and the hearse with its black-plumed horses waiting for the coffin at the door. Death had its familiar rituals.

How many working-class children had mothers at home during the day? Or, to put the question another way, how often were mothers employed away from home? As we have already noted in previous chapters, the subject of working wives, and especially working mothers, caused great concern in the early Victorian period. At a time when work was increasingly separated from the home, the middle-class wife was accustomed to seeing her husband depart each morning on his way to the works, factory, or office, while she remained at home to supervise the household duties of the servants, and to delegate the care of the children to nanny and governess. Women's place was clearly in the home, or so it was thought, and for working-class mothers to go out to work was decidedly improper, leading to neglect of both father and children. This middle-class view appears time and again in the nineteenth century. For example, in Chadwick's 1842 Report on Sanitary Conditions, the Committee of Physicians and Surgeons reporting on Birmingham gravely remark:

> The habit of a manufacturing life being once established in a woman, she continues it and leaves her home and children to the care of a neighbour, or of a hired child, whose services cost her probably as much as she obtains by her labour. To this neglect on the part of their parents is to be traced the death of many children; they are left in the house with a fire before they are old enough to know the danger to which they are exposed, and are often dreadfully burnt . . . To the habit of married women working in manufactories may also often be traced those jealousies and heart-burnings, those quarrels and that discontent which embitter the home of the poor man.[9]

Nor was this exclusively a middle-class, sexist attitude. It could also be encountered among working men, too, partly because it seemed natural to them for wives and mothers to stay at home, and partly perhaps through fear of competition in the job market. One Birmingham mechanic, giving evidence before the Children's Employment Commission of 1840, blamed all the unhappiness of his childhood (he was one of eleven children in all) on his mother's going out to work as a girl, and as a result never gaining any domestic knowledge at all. She continued to work, even with this large family: 'My mother's ignorance of household duties; my father's consequent irritability and intemperance; the frightful poverty; the constant quarelling; the pernicious example to my brothers and sisters . . . cold and hunger and the innumerable sufferings of my childhood, crowd upon my mind and overpower me.'[10] One cannot help wondering whether in this case it was masculine resentment at not having a woman ready to serve meals and to wait upon the family that was the real cause of the trouble. Presumably the poverty would have been even worse if the mother had not had a job.

In actual fact, only a minority of married women went out to work, and only a minority of these women had children at home. Thus in 1851 in the mill town of Preston (enshrined in literature as Coketown by Dickens in *Hard Times*, 1854), 26 per cent of married women living with their husbands were out at work, but probably only 15 per cent of wives with children worked away from home for most of the day. The figures might be higher elsewhere; for example, in Oldham and in Northampton it has been estimated that over a third of mothers with children aged eleven or under went out to work.[11] A recent summing-up of this subject has it that in the cotton industry, which was the largest employer of women outside the home, no more than a quarter of the female workers were married women; of these, many were childless, or had only one child. Probably only about one tenth of wives in a mid-century Lancashire mill town (presumably Preston) went out to work in the mills; nearly four fifths were plain wives and mothers undistracted by any paid work.[12]

So while the composition of the household was in many cases constantly changing as the child grew up, most children at least had a mother at home to look after them, always providing that she did not succumb to an early death. In the mid-nineteenth century female mortality rates were higher than male mortality rates, possibly because females took a smaller share of the food than men, sometimes died in childbirth, had less access to clothes and washing, and spent more time indoors, sometimes nursing the sick.[13] Not only were women second-class citizens in the home, but their health suffered from poor feeding and their home environment. There is a further point that in addition to care of the children, household duties and cooking, many women also had part-time employment such as taking in washing, or going out to clean in middle-class homes and offices.

Just what home meant to the myriads of working-class children in the early nineteenth century (in 1826, nearly 40 per cent of the nation were under fifteen[14]) is difficult to say. Memories of childhood are usually fleeting and episodic; the visual memory of a small child is often limited to images of mother at work in the home, the gleam of a lively fire, a candle to light the way to bed, and so on. The wider environment only becomes known with a growing awareness of surroudings as the child matures. One thing is tolerably certain, however, and that is that most working-class homes in the first half of the nineteenth century were small and poorly furnished. The playroom would be the kitchen, and the bedroom (and the bed itself) in most cases would be shared with parents and or other children. Bed-sharing was commonplace, and in some areas, quite usual. An instance of this is provided by conditions in Preston in 1844, where investigators reported that:

The streets, courts and yards examined contained about 422 dwellings, inhabited at the time of the enquiry by 2,400 persons sleeping in 852 beds, i.e. an average of 5.68 inhabitants to each house, and 2.8 persons to each bed.

Persons sleeping in one bed

Persons	*Occurrences*
4	84
5	13
7	3
8	1[15]

As for the bed itself, bedding was often both scanty and meagre. The Birmingham committee referred to earlier in this chapter mentioned that bedding in working-class homes was often very limited, 'consisting only of a small quantity of flock or feathers, the place of which would be better and more cheaply supplied by a liberal quantity of oat-chaff or straw.'

Other furnishing was likely to be of a rough and ready nature. Downstairs in the kitchen there would be a table with a few chairs, stools or benches. Cooking would be on an open fire, with water brought in from outside, either from a pump or purchased by the pail. The shared earth privy was in the yard or court. Such features of the working-class home of the time are likely to be familiar to most readers; what is less well known is the variety of furnishings to be found, depending on the occupation and income of the principal breadwinner. On the one hand, there were the abodes of the very poorest, often overcrowded, dirty, verminous, noisome, with only a few sticks of furniture, sometimes broken, and little else save piles of rubbish. This kind of home was described in detail by Engels, and by the commissioners of the public health reports of the 1840s. Their descriptions have been the stock-in-trade of social historians ever since. On the other hand, and at the other extreme, were the homes of the best-paid workers. The homes of the longest serving employees of the Ashworths may serve as an example. The beds in these homes had sheets, blankets, and quilts. Many bedrooms had bed and window curtains, together with strips of carpet. Some had mahogany chests. Books, Bibles, and clocks were all prominent. The inside walls were papered, while the outside walls were whitewashed every year, and the woodwork painted every two years.[17]

It goes without saying that all this was highly exceptional, but there certainly were marked differences between the homes of the skilled workmen and those of the unskilled, labouring classes (who, of course, were more numerous than the so-called aristocracy of labour). Somewhere in between were the homes of the semi-skilled and of those unskilled workers who managed to keep themselves in more or less regular employment. Generally speaking, most mothers did their best for their children in the home, and it was taken for granted that it was the mother's job to keep both the house and the children clean and tidy. Here is a decription from 1842 of a 'respectable house', where the housewife was a 'very decent woman', being the wife of a mechanic (a pearl button maker), earning a moderate wage of 18*s* a week: 'Her house is neat and tidy . . . this house is well-furnished, and has altogether a comfortable appearance. There are sufficient kitchen utensils, candlesticks, and spoons; a metal soup ladle was on the table for dinner, which consisted of meat, potatoes and bread.'[18] Here there was only one child, a grown-up daughter, who must have profited from this and from the fact that her father had a steady though not particularly well-paid job. Neither she nor her mother went out to work. The adjective 'respectable' may be applied to many working-class households in the first half of the nineteenth century, and many working-class mothers were 'very decent women'. There was no lack of homes which were kept remarkably clean and tidy, polish being applied liberally, especially in the parlour or front room (where it existed), while doorsteps were hearthstoned and scrubbed. It is wrong to suppose that the wretched home conditions in the worst slums were typical of all working-class homes, and indeed it is insulting to the millions of working-class mothers who toiled ceaselessly to keep their homes clean and decent, often in the very adverse conditions of smoky industrial towns with their muddy roadways, filthy communal privies, and water for cleaning in short supply.

If, then, there were wide variations in the nature and quality of home furnishings, the same applies to working-class housing.[19] Again, readers will no doubt be aware of the pestilential conditions of the worst slum housing in the early nineteenth century, the consequence partly of the great urban expansion of the time and partly of the primitive sanitary amenities that were provided in the form of the shared earth privies, without any form of underground drainage or piped water supply. It is arguable that it was the lack of proper sanitation and of an adequate and pure water supply which contributed as much as the poor quality of some urban building to the high death rates of the new industrial towns. Nevertheless, it is necessary to keep a sense of perspective; although attention is customarily focused on the expanding towns of the early nineteenth century, large numbers of the working classes still worked on the land and were housed in agricultural cottages. Their cottages were of very poor quality and the accommodation was very limited – often having no more than one room up and one room down, with an earthen or flagged floor, wattle-and-daub walls (often verminous), and leaky thatched roofs.[20] Whatever may be said about the horrors of urban housing, many working-class children grew up in cramped, damp, insanitary rural hovels, and if they failed to join the exodus to the towns, went on living as adults in the most wretched housing conditions. As noted in Chapter One, there are a number of references in the 1843 report on agriculture to the poor state of agricultural workers' housing. In fact, Professor Burnett has suggested that the agricultural worker was almost certainly the worst-housed among fully employed workers.[21] His children suffered accordingly, and probably only a life lived in the fresh air away from home prevented rural death rates from rivalling the urban rates.

In the towns, housing varied considerably in the quality and extent of accommodation offered. One of the best-known types of housing was the back-to-back terraced house, often (but by no means invariably) with only one room on the ground floor, and one bedroom above, accessible by stairs or ladder. They were very common in the large industrial towns such as Leeds and Birmingham (but not, curiously enough, in London). The child's perception of home, limited in his or her early days to its floors, skirting boards, doors, doorways and stairs, all the things familiar to the young child at eye level, would have depended on the kind of house he or she lived in, which in turn would depend on the fortunes of the family, in particular on the employment of the head of the family. If he was a skilled worker, and had a steady job, he would usually live in a better house than an unskilled labourer. It has been observed that in London the worst housing was occupied by the worst-paid and the most irregularly employed; the amount of living room available increased roughly in step with money wages and security of employment.[22] Thus there might be considerable variation in working-class housing in any one town. In Birmingham, for example, housing ranged from the most primitive (and often squalid), with only one room up and one down, to much more 'respectable' houses with five rooms or more arranged on three floors. In Leeds, on the other hand, one up and one down, back-to-back housing (each room measuring 15 ft × 15 ft) was almost universal. Further, workers liked to live near their work, so that workmen in the same occupation tended to live in the same area, and their children would play in the street together.[23]

For the young child, it may be assumed that the care and attention of the mother and the physical environment of the home would loom large in their perception of home. Perhaps of equal importance would be food, for both babies and young children. For babies, breast-feeding was the rule – it was cheap and natural, and might be continued for a year or more, especially as it was believed that pregnancy could not occur while a mother was still breast feeding. The only alternative was to use the services of a wet-nurse, which would have to be paid for, or to feed the baby with some form of milk substitute, usually a preparation of bread and water, coloured withh a little milk, and sweetened with sugar. This pap was often kept warm all day on the hob. There were no baby-powders or manufactured milk substitutes before the mid-century, and in any case they, like feeding bottles, would have been too expensive for working-class mothers; the baby simply took the food from a spoon. Fractious babies would be soothed by a dose of Godfrey's Cordial, Atkinson's Infant Preservative, or Street's Infant Quietness.[24] Such medicaments were usually highly efficacious – not surprisingly, as they all contained laudanum, and were easily (and legally) obtainable. In 1842 the commissioners of the Children's Employment Commission encountered two girls, both aged ten, at Lye in the Black Country, who claimed to be 'nurses', that is, they nursed babies at home. Both gave their babies a spoonful of Godfrey's three times a day (the common practice of the time). One said she thought it was made of tea with brown sugar in it; it made the baby sleep quietly during the day. She took it herself, too.[25]

Older children naturally needed something more substantial than bread and water. What they got would depend on the circumstances of each individual family and its total income. As might be expected, children in the homes of skilled workers in the towns ate better than the children of rural labourers. In fact, it might be said as a broad generalisation that working-class diets in the countryside were poor for most of the first half of the nineteenth century.[26] This was due to the relatively high price of foodstuffs until the 1830s, when prices began to fall, coupled with low agricultural wages. Both baking and brewing at home declined markedly, especially in the south of England, where fuel prices were higher than in the Midlands and the North. Tea was drunk more and more in place of beer, though sometimes even tea could not be afforded. One witness in Wiltshire in 1843 said that their common drink was burnt crust tea. The basic food of most families was bread and weak tea, supplemented by cheese, beer and meat, when they could be afforded; but meat was a luxury item, not be be eaten every day. James Hunter, writing of his rural childhood in Northamptonshire in the 1830s and 1840s said that 'with respect to a bit of meat, I never see any the first ten years of my life, only on a Sunday'.[27] Additional items included potatoes, sugar, fats and milk. Several witnesses to the agricultural enquiry of 1843 commented on the poor diet of rural labourers in the southern counties. For example, Dr Greenup observed that their food was insufficient, while Theo King, a surgeon, remarked that if the women and boys suffered in health, it was not due to their work, but was the result of want of food.[28] Of course, as in all working families, the male head of the household had the best of what food was available, and the biggest helpings. This was not just sexism, but a recognition of the fact that the most important wage-earner in the family had to be fed adequately if he was to do his work and bring home his wages. It was essential to keep up his physical strength, for the sake of all the family.

All in all, times were hardest for agricultural families living in the South, where labour was plentiful and there was no competition for labour from the factories to push up wages. In these counties, the diet was monotonous, and limited to the basic bread, potatoes, root vegetables, and weak tea. Fresh meat was certainly rare – salt pork or bacon might be enjoyed once a week. Things were a little better in other agricultural areas; in Yorkshire and Northumberland, in addition to bread, potatoes and tea, milk and broth, oatmeal porridge, hasty pudding, and pies and bacon were much more frequent than in the South.[29] One advantage which the village labourer had over his town counterpart was that he usually had a patch on which to grow vegetables. He might also enliven the family diet by poaching a rabbit or two, but poaching was severely punished, and a risky business. The weekly budget of a rural family from Lavenham, Suffolk, in 1843 gives an indication of household expenses as a whole:

Name	*Age*	*Earnings* (*s*)	(*d*)	*Expenditure*	(*s*)	(*d*)
Robert Crick	42	9	0	Bread	9	0
Wife	40		9	Potatoes	1	0
Boy	12	2	0	Rent	1	2
Boy	11	1	0	Tea		2
Boy	8	1	0	Sugar		3½
Girl	6			Soap		3
Boy	4			Blue		0½
		13	9	Thread, etc.		2
				Candles		3
				Salt		0½
				Coal and wood		9
				Butter		4½
				Cheese		3
					13	9[30]

It will be noted that the man's wages alone were only enough to keep the family in bread, and that potatoes were the next most important foodstuff, even though presumably he could dig some of his own. After bread, potatoes, and rent the most expensive item was fuel for cooking and keeping warm. Admittedly 1843 was a hard year, but even in better times this family's food intake must have been severely limited when divided among two adults and five children, three of them working boys with hearty appetites. What kind of home life did they all have?

The diet of town dwellers in the first half of the nineteenth century was not altogether dissimilar from that of agricultural labourers in its reliance on the basic foods of bread, potatoes, water and tea, and it similarly depended on the size of the family; but in the towns there was more variety in the food consumed. Urban rents varied from town to town, and, in particular, high rents in London reduced the proportion of wages available for food. Further, the large towns contained different classes of workers, ranging from the skilled man on high wages to the unskilled and poorly-paid labourer. Most important of all, perhaps, was the fact that the industrial towns were subject to the swings of the trade cycle, sometimes busy and prosperous with work for all, at other times with trade depressed, and short-time working and unemployment rife. Another factor to take into account is that in the large towns the male worker might also take his midday meal or dinner at the local pie shop or pub, thus limiting his meals at home (though not, of course, his spending from the family budget). For her part, the housewife in the towns had a wider choice of shopping than her rural counterpart, but at the same time she might be open to exploitation by unscrupulous shopkeepers. This seems to have been so in Birmingham, on the whole a prosperous town with a wide range of skilled tradesmen, many of whom ate well when trade was good. According to Chadwick's Report, 1842

> Tea, coffee, sugar, butter, cheese, bacon (of which a great deal is consumed in this town) and other articles, the working people purchase in small quantities from the hucksters, who charge an enormous profit on them, being, as they state, compelled to do so to cover the losses which they frequently sustain for bad debts. Huckster dealing is a most extravagant mode of dealing; there were in this town, in 1834, 717 of these shops, and the number has greatly increased since that time.[31]

Meat seems to have been much in favour with the better-off workman in Birmingham. Again, according to the committee of medical men reporting to Chadwick in 1842

> The working men generally contrive to have a good joint of meat upon the Sunday: the dinner on the other days of the week is made from steak or chops, which is the most extravagant mode either of purchasing or cooking meat . . . when trade is good, the working people will always purchase the best joints and most delicate meats . . . the mechanic of this town will not put up with . . . inferior parts, and the butcher generally sells this kind of meat to the country people, or to the lowest description of labourers.[32]

After describing the food available in Birmingham's ninety-five cookshops, and in pubs – roast meat, potatoes, bread, stew, and soup – Chadwick's report at length moves on to the diet of the women and the children. They 'dine principally on bacon and potatoes'; the more careful housewife was said to buy bits of meat at 5*d* a pound, which she stewed with potatoes and onions, thus forming a wholesome and nutritious meal for herself and her children.[33]

All this may represent too rosy a picture of better-off town families, of course, but undoubtedly the children of skilled and well-paid workers would eat better than children in labourers' families. In times of depression, it would be down to bread, potatoes, and weak tea even for the better-off families, and near starvation for poorer children. In the course of the first half of the century, however, town diets were beginning to improve, very gradually. Potatoes were eaten everywhere by the mid-nineteenth century, meat consumption was creeping up, and the use of sugar was increasing noticeably.[34] Although the average diet in towns at this time was still very starchy, bread and potatoes figuring prominently, by the prosperous 1860s less bread was eaten and more meat consumed, a trend which accelerated from the 1870s onwards.

Although the natural tendency in surveying working-class diets in the early years of the nineteenth century is to emphasis the paucity and poor quality of the food compared with modern diets, it must always be remembered that everything turned on the income of the family; and this depended on the occupation of the head of the family, as we have seen, together with the number of children working, and so on. Families themselves went through well attested periods of poverty and prosperity – poor when the children were too young to work, better-off when they were bringing home a wage, poor again in old age. In investigating the mining districts of south Staffordshire in 1850, H. S. Tremenheere had some interesting comments to make on the ups and downs of family life. Clearly he regarded the miners as a rough, undisciplined lot, though he was not unsympathetic to their grievances against their masters. Their children, he thought, were not subject to parental control. They simply ran wild, going to school when they liked, and leaving when they liked. They were treated with a mixture of over-indulgence (the mother often being out to work all day) and of violence and anger (this has quite a modern ring about it). As for diet, Tremenheere was scandalised at the sensuality and extravagance, as he put it, of the miners when trade was good; a miner on the thick seam might earn up to 30*s* a week, and his family could bring in 20*s* more each week. This could result in great splurges on food and drink. Tremenheere describes this in a splendid passage which deserves to be better known:

> Poultry, especially geese and ducks; the earliest and choicest vegetables (e.g. asparagus, green peas, and new potatoes when they first appear on the Market); occasionally even port-wine, drunk out of tumblers and basins; beer and spirits in great quantities; meat in abundance, extravagantly cooked; excursions in carts and cars are the well-known objects on which their money is squandered.[35]

He thought there might have been a slight improvement 'in recent years', but this was due more to cholera and comparatively low wages than anything else (one cannot help observing in passing that

Tremenheere must have been somewhat disturbed in his retirement to hear in 1874 that a miner elected by this turbulent community in Staffordshire had taken his seat in the Commons as one of the first working-class MPs).

To turn from diet to sickness: they are closely connected, of course, for poorly-nourished children are less likely to resist illness than better-fed children. In fact, given the low level of nutrition and the dirt and general squalor in many working-class homes, it is remarkable that children survived their early years in such great numbers. It was noted previously in the chapter that death was no stranger in working-class households of the first half of the nineteenth century, and that the deaths were often those of the children themselves. At the mid-century, a quarter of all deaths in England and Wales were of infants under one year of age; and infants under the age of five accounted for nearly half of all deaths.[36] Babies were peculiarly susceptible to infection resulting from contaminated food and personal dirtiness. Diarrhoea was common, and could kill in 48 hours. Other killing illnesses for infants under two were whooping cough, croup, measles, and smallpox. Whooping cough could be deadly, and in the mid-century years it killed more females than males. In London it was responsible for about one in thirty deaths, and almost as many deaths as measles and smallpox combined. There was no known cure, and parents would resort to superstitious practices derived from folk medicine in their efforts to relieve the sufferings of their infants, such as taking them to ride on donkeys (associated with Christ), or having frogs breathe into their mouths.[37] (The author, when recovering from whooping cough, was taken to breathe the fumes from a tar-boiler.) Another illness affecting small babies was croup, but it was not a major killer, and it disappeared when teething began.

Among older children, the principal deadly diseases were scarlet fever, measles, diphtheria, and smallpox. Scarlet fever became more virulent from the 1840s to the 1870s, when it assumed a milder form. Mortality was highest in the immediate post-natal period, but the death rate was still 27 per cent between two and four years of age. Children over ten suffered a much lower death rate of 5 per cent. There were severe local outbreaks in 1863 in Worcester, St Austell, and Oxford. It was thought erroneously that scarlet fever affected middle-class children more than children of the working classes – this was not so, though working-class parents objected to the policy of isolating children which was adopted in the middle years of the century.[38] At the end of the 1860s the virulence of the disease decreased sharply, partly due to a decrease in the potency of the streptococcus, and partly due to notification and isolation of the sufferers. Nevertheless, over the century as a whole, scarlet fever was the main cause of childhood death, with 95 per cent of all cases being under the age of ten.[39]

Measles, like scarlet fever, was highly contagious, being spread by touch or by droplet infection. It was a major killer, and in peak years was more fatal than scarlet fever; throughout the nineteenth century at least 7,000 persons died from it in Great Britain every year. For example, in 1868 there were 11,630 deaths, and in 1874, 12,235 deaths.[40] Diphtheria was another serious disease, manifesting itself suddenly in 1855. From then until 1869 it claimed 61,000 deaths in England and Wales, half of the victims being under five years old, with four fifths of the fatalities being in the age-range five to thirteen. The death rates were highest in the north Midlands and the south-east and south-west counties, and lowest in London, the north-west and northern counties. Rural areas seemed to suffer more than towns.[41] Lastly, smallpox became less of a killer than in the eighteenth century, principally due to vaccination, though working-class parents were hostile to having their children vaccinated (mostly by Poor Law doctors), and it became regarded as a disease of the poorest classes. The first vaccination act was passed in 1840, while the 1853 act made vaccination compulsory before the age of three months. The 1871 act imposed a 25*s* fine or imprisonment on parents refusing to have their infants vaccinated.[42]

Just what the reaction of children was to these various illnesses from 1800 up to the 1870s can only be guessed at. Presumably they were no more aware of the implications of their condition than are young children at the present day. Undoubtedly the very early years were the dangerous years, when mortal illness was the most likely. A baby of good weight born of a healthy mother was more likely to survive the first few years – something which applied *mutatis mutandis* even in the mid-twentieth century (in 1956 an old Shropshire farmer remarked of the author's eldest daughter, then a healthy-looking baby in arms, 'I think you'll rear her'; she did in fact survive). Older children might be more aware of the dangers of their condition, and might even be consoled by religious parents by the reminder when they were near to death that Heaven and all its angels awaited them. Not much could be done for working-class children of any age who fell ill. Homely and often herbal remedies could be applied, but doctors were a last and expensive resort. Working-class parents in the early nineteenth century did not have a great deal of faith in them, especially when it came to the care of babies. In the villages, the local wise woman would be asked for advice before a physician. In towns, pharmacists would be consulted before doctors, and even in smaller towns there was usually a free dispensary available for both medicine and advice by the mid-century; though quite often free help would be forthcoming only if the applicant had a ticket for free treatment obtainable from some middle-class well-wisher. Help was also forthcoming in poor law infirmaries and the out-patient departments of the voluntary hospitals. On the whole, working-class parents dealt with everyday illnesses, at least, by themselves.[43]

In the first half of the 19th century, there were no children's hospitals as such, Great Ormond Street Hospital for Children in London not opening till 1853. Very few general hospitals admitted children at all; in 1843, there was a total of only 136 patients under ten years old in all the London hospitals, at a time when the average yearly deaths under ten in London were about 25,000. Even when Great Ormond Street was opened, only the first treatment was free; subsequent treatment had to be paid for. It was not until the late 1860s that two further London hospitals were opened for children, the Evelina Hospital for Sick Children, and the East London Hospital, the latter being the first hospital to admit children under two. Elsewhere in the country there were no hospitals at all specialising in the care of sick children.[44]

The attitude of working-class parents to sickness in their children seems to have been very much what one might expect – a mixture of anxiety and yet of some degree of resignation, because they knew that little could be done medically to effect a cure. It must be remembered that it was not until the 1860s that the transmission of disease by germs became understood, it being thought that illness could be caught through mysterious miasmas; at least this theory identified the source of disease as decaying and putrifying matter – Chadwick claimed that 'all smell is, if it be intense, immediate acute disease'. What was not understood was the way in which diseases like cholera and typhoid could be transmitted through water supplies or through infected milk. Not until the 1870s were the importance of sterilisation and the use of antiseptics accepted, as the result of Lister's pioneering work (surgeons operated in bloodstained frock-coats, without anaesthetics, let alone gowns, masks, gloves and sterilised instruments). In these circumstances, medical and surgical knowledge were still rudimentary, and parents could do little but watch and pray. It is sometimes said that parents could be indifferent to the fate of their children in Victorian times, for so many of them died at an early age, but there is really little evidence of this. There is no reason to suppose that most parents did not have a natural love for their children, and grieved over them when they died.[45] But since death was so common a happening, and medical aid so limited, it is not surprising that parents felt they could do little except administer the 'tender, loving care' traditional in the nursing profession. According to Dr Ramsey, giving evidence before the Select Committee on Medical Poor Relief, 1844:

> A sort of fatalism is very prevalent among the poor: they have . . . far less reliance on medical care than the upper classes. Some appear careless and apathetic; some resign themselves to the event; but from one or other of these causes, not a few of the poorest and most degraded allow their diseases to take their course.[46]

One might guess it was not only the poorest and most degraded who experienced a sense of helplessness when faced by the serious illness of their children. Well might they think that the Lord giveth, and the Lord taketh away.

At this point it is perhaps appropriate to go back to the nature of family life, having sketched in the background of housing, home furnishing, diet, sickness and death. If all these aspects of life at home provide an important backcloth to the daily routine, at the heart of life in the home were familial relationships. These were necessarily close, both literally and metaphorically. Large families in small habitations meant that life was lived cheek by jowl, and discipline had to be maintained. Older authorities tend to emphasise the harsh punishments inflicted on children by working-class parents in the early nineteenth century. Pinchbeck and Hewitt describe children of the time as being without rights or protection.[47] They were not protected by law against cruelty until later in the century, and children were legally the property of their parents, being regarded as personal or family assets. They could be sold as climbing boys, or into prostitution, and if convicted of a crime, children could be hanged or transported from the age of seven. The justification for all this, it is said, was the belief that children were evil by nature, and their wicked propensities had to be checked. To interfere with parental authority would be to undermine family stability, and indeed to oppose the will of God. So the cruelty in the factories was only a reflection of the brutality of life outside, both generally and in the home.[48]

More recently historians have begun to modify this picture of the savage treatment of working-class children in the home. Linda Pollock has written strongly on this, and her views were discussed in the Prologue. As we have seen, she takes the view that the majority of children were *not* subjected to brutality, though she does concede that there was an intensification of adult demands for obedience and conformity in the early nineteenth century, especially in the schools.[49] Professor John Burnett has also argued against the notion that brutality and indifference to children persisted longest among the lower classes; the evidence of working-class autobiographies is that concern for children was present to a varying degree in all classes, as far as economic circumstances permitted.[50] Again, Professor Thompson has emphasised that there is plenty of evidence of parents showing solicitude for their children's well-being, even though there might not have been much open demonstration of warmth and tenderness between parents and children, though plenty between siblings.[51]

In seeking a fair and balanced assessment of the treatment of children by their working-class parents, it is necessary to weigh up a wealth of evidence, some of it self-contradictory. On the one hand, there is the evidence of the treatment of children at work, not only in the factories and mines, but also in the workshops, many of them domestic. If children could be treated in this way by members of their own class, it seems unlikely that they were never subjected to physical violence in the home. On the other hand, there is a great deal of difference beween a casual clip round the ear and a prolonged beating. Correction by stick or belt could be administered as a short, sharp shock, or laid on with sadistic zeal. There is really no doubt that physical chastisement was common, but few writers of childhood memoirs recall savage beatings when they were young. They seemed prepared to accept some degree of physical punishment as fair and just, and part of the everyday life of childhood.

Any conclusion on this aspect of childhood can only be tentative, but it is clear enough that a certain degree of physical correction was generally accepted in a world in which the savage flogging of convicts, seamen, and public school boys was still practised. Brutal and cruel treatment of working-class children in the home was a different matter; when it occurred, it was likely to be in the homes of the more degraded and sometimes drunken parents. In the majority of families, however, punishment was limited to what was deemed necessary to maintain order in what was often a large family living in cramped conditions. In these circumstances, some kind of routine was essential, and children had to conform. As soon as they were big enough, they were expected to help with household tasks – the girls in the kitchen helping to prepare food, or taking part in the cleaning or sewing, the boys assisting in the heavier tasks of fetching coal or water. There were plenty of other tasks, too, for small children in households almost completely lacking in labour-saving devices – washing up, mangling, hanging out the washing, chopping wood, making beds, and so on. Both boys and girls would start as soon as possible in the family workshop, though a girl might remain behind in the house to look after the baby if its mother was occupied in the workshop. Once full-time work was begun, household tasks were necessarily reduced, though not entirely remitted, and children would usually (though not invariably) remain at home until marriage was undertaken in the mid-twenties.

The relatively advanced age of marriage, and the overcrowded nature of some working-class accommodation, especially in the towns, with much sharing of bedrooms and of beds, naturally led to a measure of sexual misconduct and abuse, especially incest. That incest occurred is not in doubt, as Dr Pollock has shown by reference to cases reported in *The Times*, and although it was a taboo subject, there were public references to it from time to time, even as early as in Gaskell's *The Manufacturing Population of England* (1833). Gaskell remarks on the overcrowding which resulted in the sexes 'mingling in wild carouse, and crimes of all shades are perpetuated, blasphemy, fornication, adultery, incest, child-murder'.[52] Towards the end of the nineteenth century references become more frequent; Andrew Mearns, the author of *The Bitter Cry of Outcast London* (1883), referred to the fact that 'incest is common', and not much later (in 1890) General Booth of the Salvation Army claimed that 'incest is so familiar as hardly to call for remark'. In her autobiography, Beatrice Webb recorded her shocked reaction on hearing references to incest in the conversation of her workmates during her brief experience of working in the East End of London in the 1890s:

> The fact that some of my workmates – young girls, who were in no way mentally defective, who were, on the contrary, just as keen-witted and generous-hearted as my own circle of friends – could chaff each other about having babies by their fathers and brothers, was a gruesome example of the debased social environment on personal character and family life . . . the violation of little children was another not infrequent result.[53]

It appears quite indisputable that incest took place, but on what scale it is very difficult, if not impossible, to determine. It was not until 1908 that incest became a criminal act, and before this date offences of this kind had to be prosecuted as rapes or as offences against minors. According to Professor Wohl, it can be assumed that incest was much more common among young children and young adults than between drunken fathers and daughters, and that it was generally casual and temporary rather than long-term.[54] This can be only speculation, of course, and it might be remarked in passing that a significant proportion of child sexual abuse in the 1990s appears to be long-term rather than short-term.

Similar problems of quantification occur when investigating the prevalence of other forms of sexual abuse of children in the first half of the nineteenth century; they certainly took place, but to what extent will never be known. As this book is concerned with children up to the age of fourteen, or thereabouts, it is unnecessary to consider at any length the related subject of pre-marital intercouse and sexual promiscuity, but it should be noted that pre-marital sexual activity was not at all uncommon, and not particularly something to be ashamed of, provided the couple married in the event of pregnancy. Again, common-law marriages took place without the official sanction of a church wedding, older forms of informal alliances sometimes being based on ancient rituals, such as jumping over a broomstick in the presence of witnesses.[55] Prostitution was scarcely a feature of normal working-class home life, but juvenile prostitution was widespread in the towns. In Birmingham, for instance, there were many young girl prostitutes.[56] More recent research has shown that many of their customers were working-class, and not middle-class. In Birmingham at the end of the eighteenth century apprentices might end an evening's revelry at the inn with a little vandalism, such as smashing a street lamp, with a fight with the Watch, and then with a visit to a brothel:

> And if a Watchman interrupt the deed,
> He beats him if he can – then flees with speed,
> By mad intoxication led astray
> In a vile brothel to complete the day.[57]

It need hardly be said that a knowledge of sex was something children would pick up from older siblings, from friends, and at school. Not all children were interested, of course. It was a forbidden subject, viewed by many no doubt with a mixture of fear and fascination – the 'dirty little secret', as Lawrence called it.

What was the daily routine of the working-class child, given all the varied aspects which have been discussed? Granted that it would depend on a great many variables, it may be said that childhood itself could be seen to experience three major states of development. The first stage was that of the very early years of babyhood, of sitting up, learning to walk, learning to talk, and so on, followed by a period of active play, mostly in mother's presence, lasting into the fifth year and beyond. During this period, girls and boys dressed in frocks, though male infants seem to have gone into breeches between the ages of two and three. Frequently their clothes would subsequently be in the form of cast-offs. This first stage was the classic stage of childhood fears and fantasies, often to do with death and its manifestations in the world around them. From the age of six or seven, there was the matter of starting work – that is, apart from the customary helping with household tasks. It is clear from the evidence reviewed in the first three chapters of this book that work could start at a very early age. Below five was exceptional, of course, if only because of physical incapacity to do a proper job; but as we have seen, children of five or thereabouts could help in the fields or in the family workshop. By the 1840s, however, work started more usually around seven or eight, with restrictions on the age of beginning work in the factory or mine. For many children, therefore, from the age of five (or even sometimes from four) there began a second stage, of attendance at school, as described in the next chapter. Such attendance might well be intermittent and indeed spasmodic. It was supplemented very often (or simply replaced on starting work) by attendance at Sunday School. This period of schooling constituted a second period of development in the home life of most children, a period which was to assume greater and greater importance as the years went by; by the middle of the century, going to school was becoming a central feature of working-class childhood, and we shall return to this fact a little later in this chapter. The third stage of development began with the start of regular work, and at an age which depended on a number of factors – physical capacity, financial need, and availability of jobs.

What all this meant in the context of the typical working-class family in the home was that during the working week children might be encountered in any one of the three stages – early childhood, at school, or at work. Babies, toddlers, and older infants were often to be found at mother's apron strings. Children of school age might also be found at home, either because it was a school holiday, or because they had been kept at home for some particular purpose, not least to help in the family workshop, or because they or a parent were ill. Children who had started work full-time would be absent, of course, during working hours, though these varied with the season and the amount of work available. Some also came home for midday dinner, and all would be home after the day's work. In areas of traditional domestic workshop industry, St Monday might well find all the children in or around the home. Monday was also the traditional washing day, with clouds of steam and the rumbling of the mangle as the washing was wrung out ready for pegging on the line. Saturdays and Sundays were also days with a difference. On Saturdays there was normally no school, and work usually stopped early in the afternoon, and was followed by going to market or to the shops. Sunday was the special day of the week, when father and all the children would be at home. It was the day for a lie-in (at least, for non-agricultural children), although church- and chapel-goers had to be up betimes. For many children, it was Sunday School Day. It was also the day, if the family funds ran to it, of the best meal of the week – the Sunday roast. Thus, each day of the week had its own characteristics, and children would have their own expectations of what it would bring.

It remains to sum up, if indeed it is at all possible to summarise the living conditions and familial relationships of some millions of children at a time of great social change stretching over a period of seventy years. As Professor Thompson has wisely remarked, no simple generalisations about working-class childhood are likely to be correct.[58] There are so many variables to be taken into account: where do the children live, in town or country? In new industrial town, old market town, industrial village? Or what age, male or female? Working full-time, or not? What is the father's occupation, skilled or unskilled, employed or unemployed? Any grand generalisation which attempts to take all these factors into account is still likely to be unsafe, to say the least, and very probably open to criticism. Nevertheless, of the variables mentioned (and this is by no means an exhaustive list, of course), perhaps the most significant is the occupation of the father, for the family income was the biggest single determinant of the family's life-style. If he was skilled, and in receipt of good money, this could see the family through even the harder times when the children were young and had not begun work, or when work was hard to find in times of depression. Even when unemployed, the skilled worker could fall back on his friendly society for out-of-work and also sickness pay. Family income was all-important. It determined the kind of house the family lived in, its furnishing, and the kind of food eaten.

Of course, all this was subject to further variation conditional on the tone set by the father, whether strict or indulgent, religious or otherwise, drunk or usually sober; and also on the incidence of sickness. Family discipline clearly depended on the attitude of both father and mother, and for the most part children were expected to take a subordinate place, to behave themselves, to be respectful, and to keep neat and tidy. By and large, they did as they were told. Nevertheless, all this must be seen against the background of the affluence or otherwise of the family, and the general state of its fortunes. Social historians in the past have emphasised the squalor and hardship of much working-class life in the towns in the mid-nineteenth century, and the evidence for this is clear enough in the reports of the various enquiries of the early 1840s; but less attention has been paid to the conditions of the better-off working classes, living in superior housing, with better furnishing. Some of their housing survives even today, refurbished and now with modern plumbing, an inviting prospect to first-time buyers. One comes back again to the difference between the living conditions of the respectable working classes and of the lumpenproletariat, those whom Engels described in Manchester in 1844 as 'a hoard of ragged women and children [who] swarm about, as filthy as the swine that thrive upon the garbage heaps and in the puddles'. Obviously enough, life in the slums was very different from life in the houses of better-paid workers.

Next, what were the most prominent changes in working-class family life at home in the period from 1800 to 1870? Once more, the difficulties of generalisation are immense. The older approach would perhaps stress the disruption caused by the transition to work in the factories. Certainly, where this took place, principally in Lancashire and in the West Riding of Yorkshire, there could be substantial changes in the family routine, especially if it was from the spasmodic kind of work which characterised domestic industry to the more regular mode of work in the mill. Indeed, one of the criticisms made of the factory system is that it 'broke up' the family. Yet in practice this was hardly so; the family still lived in the same home, while in the factory itself mule spinners customarily employed their own children as doffers and piecers, at least until they were too old for the job; and as we have already seen, most mothers with children in mill towns stayed at home rather than work in the mill. Further, a point strongly stressed in this book, factory workers were still in a minority among industrial workers as a whole in 1851. Older views on the disruption of the family and of home life are hardly tenable today, even though it would be wrong to disregard localised distress caused by the coming of the factory, as suffered by handloom weavers in parts of Lancashire.[59]

What changes, then, can be discerned in the home lives of child workers taken as a whole? One must be the gradual improvement in the standard of living over these seventy years. Controversies over the standard of living during the Industrial Revolution have died down during recent years,[60] and there is some agreement that conditions improved for the working classes by the 1850s and 1860s as the benefits of industrialisation made themselves felt. Before then it is clear that the agricultural labourer's home remained wretchedly poor, and industrial workers certainly suffered impoverishment and hardship after the end of the French Wars in 1815, again in the mid-1820s and early 1830s, and above all in the early 1840s. By the 1860s the economy was in a buoyant mood, and it is possible that better real wages meant a marginally improved standard of living in the home, that is, a moderately improved diet; though even here there are exceptions – certainly the diet of Lancashire cotton workers did not improve during the American Civil War and the resulting cotton famine in the mill districts.

One approach to the question of change in the home life of children has been to suggest that the only change which can be discerned with any confidence is a trend to less frequent and harsh punishments in the course of the century, together with the greater use of verbal correction.[61] Of relevance here is the fact that the reports of the Children's Employment Commission, 1862, appear on the whole to contain rather fewer horror stories of ill-treatment of child workers than the reports of the earlier commission, appointed in 1840. This suggestion may have some force, but it is not easy to see it taking effect in the home situation of the working classes before 1870. Otherwise there are no very marked changes in other aspects which have been surveyed in this chapter. The size of the family remains the same, and the high infant mortality figures change little between 1839 and 1871, after which date there is a slight fall. However, death rates for the ten to fourteen year age group do show an improvement between 1838 and 1872: the death rate for boys per 1,000 declined from 5.8 in 1838 to 4.1 in 1872, while the rate for girls went down from 5.8 to 4.0 between the same dates. The last national cholera epidemic in 1866 killed only half the numbers dying in 1853–54.[62] So the health of young children, if not of babies, improved somewhat, though the improvement is not striking. There is really no other aspect of home life described in the preceding pages which can be said to exhibit any striking change over the period. Yet there is one significant development in the home life of working-class children which has only been touched on here, and is discussed in detail in the next chapter. This is attendance at school.

The justification for suggesting that this is important is simply that in spite of the continued opposition of some parents, school attendance appears to have increased in the 1850s and 1860s. Whereas attendance was intermittent and of short duration in the early years of the century, after 1850 it improved considerably. Why it did so is perhaps the consequence of a combination of favourable circumstances: as prosperity increased, school fees could be afforded more easily, and children's earnings were of less importance. Middle-class public opinion also seemed to be swinging more and more in support of schooling for working-class children – we have already seen that the need for working-class education was referred to time and again in the reports of the Children's Employment Commission, 1862. The Sunday School movement was still doing valuable work in the middle years of the nineteenth century. By the 1860s it appears that going to school had become normal practice for the children of the respectable working classes, and by 1870 the proportion of children of school age on the registers was probably between two-thirds and three-quarters. The time was obviously drawing near when those children still outside school would be brought into the system.

What this means is that at the mid-century childhood was slowly being transformed from a limited period in the home followed by starting work to a life based in the home but after the age of five (or earlier) dominated by attendance at school. This indeed is the theme of this book: the lives of working-class children were slowly changed in the course of the nineteenth century by two compelling developments – one the increasing restrictions placed on child labour, especially as regards factories after 1833, and as regards factories, workshops, and other places of work after 1867; and the other the spread of popular education, leading to the Education Act, 1870, followed by compulsory and free schooling. In conclusion, it can be said that at the beginning of the century school was only a minor aspect of the lives of working-class children. By 1870, great changes had taken place, and from then on it was to become normal to expect children to be absent from home between the ages of five and ten not because they were in paid employment, but because they were at school.

References

1 Michael Anderson, 'The social implications of demographic change', in F. M. L. Thompson, (ed.), *The Cambridge Social History of Britain 1750–1950*, Vol. 2, 1990, p. 39. This article provides a very helpful survey of its subject. For the standard work on the nineteenth-century industrial family, see M. Anderson, *Family Structure in Nineteenth Century Lancashire*, 1971. See also E. A. Wrigley and R. S. Schofield, *The Population of England 1541–1871: A Reconstruction*, 1981; P. Laslett, *Household and Family in Past Time*, 1972; and N. L. Tranter, *Population and Society 1750–1940*, 1985.

2 F. M. L. Thompson, *The Rise of Respectable Society: A Social History of Victorian Britain*, 1830–1900, 1988, p. 124.

3 Thompson, *Cambridge Social History of Britain*, Vol. 2, pp. 15, 20.

4 Eric Hopkins, 'The Decline of the Family Work Unit in Black Country Nailing', *International Review of Social History*, XXII, Part 2, 1977.

5 Thompson, *Cambridge Social History of Britain*, Vol. 2, pp. 48, 49.

6 *Ibid.*, p. 60.

7 *Ibid.*, pp. 63, 65.

8 James Walvin, *A Child's World: A Social History of Children, 1800–1914*, 1982, p. 31. The quotation is from *The Children's Friend*, May, 1865.

9 *Report on the Sanitary Condition of the Labouring Poor* (Chadwick's Report), 1842, p. 211.

10 *Children's Employment Commission*, 1840, Vol. XIV, Report by R. D. Grainger, at fo. 131.

11 Anderson, *Family Structure*, p. 71; John Foster, *Class Struggle in the Industrial Revolution*, 1974, pp. 96–7; for older views see Ivy Pinchbeck, *Women Workers and the Industrial Revolution, 1750–1850*, 1930, pp. 197–9 and Margaret Hewitt, *Wives and Mothers in Victorian England*, 1958, p. 290.

12 Thompson, *Rise of Respectable Society*, pp. 118–19.

13 Thompson, *Cambridge Social History of Britain*, Vol. 2, pp. 18, 19.

14 *Ibid.*, p. 47.

15 *Commission on the State of Large Towns and Populous Districts*, 1844, First Report, p. 45.

16 Chadwick's Report, p. 213.

17 Rhodes Boyson, *The Ashworth Cotton Enterprise: The Rise and Fall of a Family Firm*, 1970, pp. 118, 125.

18 *Children's Employment Commission*, 1840, Grainger's Report, 1843, fos 140–1.

19 The best general account of working-class housing in the nineteenth century is in J. Burnett, *A Social History of Housing, 1815–1970*, 1978. See also S. D. Chapman, (ed.), *The History of Working Class Housing*, 1971; J. N. Tarn, *Five Per Cent Philanthropy: An Account of Housing in Urban Areas between 1840 and 1914*, 1973; E. Gauldie, *Cruel Habitations: A History of Working Class Housing 1780–1918*, 1974; A. S. Wohl, *The Eternal Slum: Housing and Social Policy in*

Victorian London, 1977; M. J. Daunton, *House and Home in the Victorian City: Working Class Housing 1850–1914*, 1983; D. Fraser and A. Sutcliffe (eds), *The Pursuit of Urban History*, 1983; R. Dennis, *English Industrial Cities of the Nineteenth Century*, 1984. Among the numerous local studies, see the author's 'Working Class Housing in the Smaller Industrial Town of the Nineteenth Century: Stourbridge – a Case Study', *Midland History*, IV, Nos. 3 & 4, 1978, and 'Working Class Housing in Birmingham during the Industrial Revolution', *International Review of Social History*, XXXI, 1986, Pt I.

20 See Burnett, *Social History of Housing*, chapter 2, for rural housing.

21 *Ibid.*, p. 31.

22 H. J. Dyos and Michael Wolf (eds), *The Victorian City: Images and Realities*, 1973, p. 367.

23 For Stourbridge and Birmingham, see Hopkins, 'Working Class Housing'. See also J. E. Vance, Jr, 'Housing the Worker: Determinative and Contingent Ties in Nineteenth Century Birmingham', *Economic Geography*, XLIII, 1967.

24 There is a useful account of the feeding of babies in Thompson, *The Rise of Respectable Society*, pp. 121–2.

25 *Children's Employment Commission*, 1840, Appendix to Second Report, Pt II, q. 74–80.

26 For a good survey of rural diets, see D. J. Oddy, 'Food, drink, and nutrition' in Thompson, *Cambridge Social History of Britain*, Vol. 2, chapter 5.

27 *Ibid.*, p. 272.

28 *Reports of Special Assistant Poor Law Commissioners on the Employment of Women and Children in Agriculture*, 1843, pp. 59, 61.

29 John Burnett, *Plenty and Want*, 1966, p. 27.

30 *Commission on the Employment of Women and Children in Agriculture*, 1843, p. 233.

31 Chadwick's Report, p. 221.

32 *Ibid.*, p. 212.

33 *Ibid.*

34 See Oddy in Thompson, *Cambridge Social History of Britain*, pp. 269–70.

35 Tremenheere's *Report on the Mining Districts in South Staffs*, 1850, pp. 9–10, 26–7.

36 F. B. Smith, *The People's Health 1830–1910*, 1979, p. 65.

37 *Ibid.*, pp. 105–10.

38 *Ibid.*, pp. 136–42.

39 Virginia Berridge, 'Health and Medicine', in Thompson, *Cambridge Social History of Britain*, Vol. 3, p. 200.

40 Smith, *The People's Health*, pp. 142, 144, 145.

41 *Ibid.*, pp. 149–50.

42 *Ibid.*, pp. 156, 157, 161.

43 Thompson, *Cambridge Social History of Britain*, Vol. 3, p. 186.

44 Smith, *The People's Health*, pp. 152, 153, 155.

45 See Thompson, *The Rise of Respectable Society*, pp. 123–4; and Michael Anderson, 'New Insights into the History of the Family in Britain', *Refresh*, 9, Autumn, 1989.

46 Quoted in Smith, *The People's Health*, p. 157.

47 Ivy Pinchbeck and Margaret Hewitt, *Children in English Society*, Vol. II, 1973. The first chapter in this volume is entitled 'Childhood without Rights or Protection'.

48 *Ibid.*, pp. 348, 351–2, 359–60.

49 Linda A. Pollock, *Forgotten Children: Parent–Child Relationships from 1500 to 1900*, 1983, p. 269. Dr Pollock also argues strongly against the view of Pinchbeck and Hewitt that cases of child abuse were not reported in the press till late in the nineteenth century. She has discovered 385 cases of child neglect and sexual abuse (19 cases were of incest) reported in *The Times* for 1785–1860, and she gives details of 14 of these cases, pp. 91–5.

50 John Burnett (ed.), *Destiny Obscure: Autobiographies of Childhood, Education and Family from the 1820s to the 1920s*, 1982, p. 53.

51 Thompson, *The Rise of Respectable Society*, p. 128.

52 Quoted in Anthony S. Wohl (ed.), *The Victorian Family*, 1978, p. 205.

53 *Ibid.*, pp. 207, 209–10, 203.

54 *Ibid.*, p. 212.

55 Leonore Davidoff, 'The Family in Britain', in Thompson, *Cambridge Social History of Britain*, Vol. 2, p. 90.

56 *Children's Employment Commission*, 1840, Grainger's Report, 1843, fo. 172. See also Chapter Seven for the extent of prostitution in Birmingham in the 1840s.

57 George Davis, *Saint Monday, or Scenes from Low Life*, 1790.

58 Thompson, *The Rise of Respectable Society*, p. 133.

59 For the Lancashire handloom weavers, see D. Bythell, *The Handloom Weavers*, 1968.

60 P. H. Lindert and J. G. Williamson, 'English Workers' Living Standards during the Industrial Revolution', *Economic History Review*, 2nd series, 36, 1983 is a recent attempt at an overall assessment.

61 Thompson, *The Rise of Respectable Society*, p. 134.

62 Smith, *The People's Health*, p. 196, 230.

Chapter Five

Education and religious observance

In the preceding chapters there have been frequent references to middle-class views as to the desirability of working-class children attending school, and at the same time to the only very limited school attendance possible when children started work so young, and worked such long hours. It should be repeated that it would be wrong to conclude from this that there was any general agreement in the early nineteenth century that all children were entitled to a substantial period of education, or even that education for the working classes was in itself a good thing. On the contrary, there were those who thought that education would make the working classes discontented with their lot, and hence a source of unrest. Such views were strengthened by the outbreak of the French Revolution and the subsequent successes of the French armies. By the end of the eighteenth century the newly-established Sunday School movement, which aimed principally at teaching children to read the Bible, came under strong attack. Rather remarkably, William Pitt seriously considered introducing a bill to suppress Sunday Schools,[1] and in 1800 the Bishop of Rochester launched a fierce attack on them:

> The Jacobins of this country are I very much fear making a tool of Methodism . . . schools of Jacobinical rebellion and Jacobinical politics . . . schools of atheism and disloyalty abound in this country; schools in the shape and disguise of Charity schools and Sunday Schools, in which the minds of the children of the very lowest order are enlightened – that is to say, taught to despise religion and laws and all subordination.[2]

It is hard to see how teaching children to read the Bible on their day off work could have such striking consequences, and there is no record of any wholesale closure of Sunday Schools or charity schools following this outburst. It is also difficult to say how widespread beliefs of this kind really were, though the idea that education for the working classes would not be for their benefit was not uncommon among the middle classes, and it found expression in a speech by Davies Giddy in 1807 in the House of Commons which subsequently became well known:

> Giving education to the labouring classes of the poor . . . would be prejudicial to their morals and happiness; it would teach them to despise their lot in life, instead of making them good servants in agriculture and other laborious employments. Instead of teaching them subordination, it would render them fractious and refractory.[3]

Fortunately for future generations of working-class children, there was an opposing view. This was not that children as such had any right to education – that idea had yet to make much headway – but rather that education could play an important part in teaching working-class children their proper station in life, and in this way promote social harmony and quell unrest. Education could thus become a valuable means of securing co-operation between classes and avoiding class conflict – in other words, it could act as a major instrument of social control of the masses. Moreover, it was taken for granted that any education for the children of the poor should be within a religious framework, which would allow them to be taught the due subordination of the working classes in the divine order of things, and that their reward was to be in heaven rather than here on earth.

From the middle-class point of view, it was urgent that these ideas should be transmitted to the lower orders at a time of such great social change; the possibilities of unrest were becoming alarmingly apparent. The population had grown by 50 per cent in the second half of the eighteenth century, and was to double in the first half of the nineteenth century. Much of this increase took place in the towns, especially in the new industrial towns of the Midlands and the North, where working and living conditions were producing great social strains. Most of these new towns had severe public health problems, and many had yet to develop local governing bodies. They also lacked police forces and the threat of civil disorder was, therefore, very real and pressing. Moreover, to these adverse conditions was added all the political unrest generated by the French Revolution and by political thinkers such as Thomas Paine and William Godwin.[4] In the period of disturbances after Waterloo episodes such as the Pentrich rising in Derbyshire in 1817, the march of the Blanketeers in the same year and Peterloo in 1819 all provided clear and ominous signs of working-class discontent. The short-term answer of the authorities to such disturbances was simply repression, coupled with a willingness to let minor discontent die down thereafter; but one long-term answer was an extension of working-class education within the limits just described, reinforced by the provision of more churches in the new urban areas. Education was thus to be applied as a social emollient, not so much perhaps as the result of cold-blooded calculation, but rather as a common-sense and practical way of dealing with new social problems, and with the minimum of government intervention and expenditure. Both measures, it was thought, would also help to reduce crime and the cost of the prisons.[5]

There were already plenty of schools for working-class children in existence, their drawback being that schooling was not compulsory, and was rarely free. Two types of such schools have already been mentioned earlier in this chapter, charity schools and Sunday Schools. The former were founded in the seventeenth and eithteenth centuries, being financed either by local subscription or by endowment. Sometimes they were residential schools, but more often they were day schools. Most of them were intended to give a basic education, followed by apprenticeship; some were known as 'blue coat' schools, blue coats being the traditional wear of the apprentice. These schools, which were generally free, catered for both boys and girls, and the so-called charity school movement is commonly thought to date from the founding of the Society for the Promotion of Christian Knowledge in 1698. In fact there were charity schools before this. There has also been some dispute among historians in the past about the extent of the charity school movement, and although there were about 179 charity schools in and around London in 1800, their numbers were more limited throughout the rest of the country. Some of them were very restricted in the number of school places provided, since this depended on the funds available, which might be very small.[6]

The Sunday School movement was on a much larger scale. Starting in the 1780s in Gloucestershire on the initiative of Robert Raikes, a newspaper owner, the movement grew from 2,290 schools in 1801 to 23,135 schools in 1851. The numbers of children enrolled increased from 59,980 in 1788 to more than two million in 1851, at which date, according to modern calculations, three-quarters of working-class children were on their books.[7] These figures are very impressive, but the contribution of Sunday Schools to building working-class culture has been questioned, whatever their other virtues. Most of the schools taught only reading (the teaching of writing was confined for the most part to dissenting Sunday Schools) and the reading was limited to the Bible. Further, the average Sunday School day was not long, and it included prayers and hymn singing, so that the time given to reading was necessarily somewhat limited. Nevertheless, Sunday Schools must have made a considerable contribution to working-class reading skills and to familarity with biblical texts (though not necessarily to their understanding). Working-class parents must have been grateful for the chance to get the children out of the house for a while on what was for many the one day of rest; but Sunday Schools were not compulsory, attendance might be intermittent, and obviously they were no substitute for full-time school attendance throughout the week.[8]

Other types of schools for the working classes at the beginning of the nineteenth century included parish schools and private or proprietorial schools. Parish schools were not usually endowed, and were often held in the parish church, where a small group of children might be taught either by a schoolmaster paid by the parish or by the clerk to the parish, or by a curate. Private schools were run by private individuals for profit, and were of two kinds – dame schools, and common day schools. Dame schools had a bad name; they were often no more than child-minding establishments, run by elderly women in their living-rooms or kitchens, who would leave the children from time to time and get on with their housework or other business. Anyone could open a dame school, and literacy on the part of the dame was not essential. It was not always a very profitable undertaking. In Birmingham there were 267 dame schools in 1838, with an average of about 14 pupils, and an average weekly income of 4*s* 3½*d*. One dame teacher, asked why she continued to teach, replied 'Bless you, I would not continue school another day, but I can do nothing that pays me better. I am sure I have prayed every day since I began, that it may do, but it's no use. I can't get my prayers answered, instead of that it gets worse.'[9] The common day schools were for older children, and here the teacher would usually be a man who could find no better employment, through lack of skill or general ability, perhaps, or sometimes as a result of disablement. As the children were older and more unruly, the master might well have discipline problems. An inspector described one master in a school of forty-three children aged from five to fourteen, in a room twelve feet square; the master had taken off his coat because of the steaming atmosphere in the room:

In this undress he was the better able to wield the three canes, two of which, like the weapons of an old soldier, hung conspicuously on the wall, while the third was on the table ready for service. When questioned as to the necessity of this triple instrumentality, he assured us that the children were 'abrupt and rash in their tempers', that he generally reasoned with them respecting their indiscretion, but that when reasoning failed, he had recourse to a little severity.[10]

The use of the cane was not at all exceptional, of course, and later in this chapter we shall refer to the punishments common in Lancasterian schools. Not all dame schools and common day schools were badly run, and more recently it has been pointed out that, with all their deficiencies, they did at least enable substantial numbers of working-class children to acquire some rudimentary knowledge of the three Rs. It has been claimed that in 1851 there were still twice as many private schools as public day schools, and one-third of pupils were still in private schools.[11]

Other kinds of schools for the working classes deserve a brief mention. Here and there could be found trade or industrial schools in which children were taught simple trades such as straw-plaiting or pin-making, and the work produced was sold to provide income for the school. Such establishments hardly merited the name of schools, and they were not very popular with parents, who preferred to send their children directly out to work, or with manufacturers, who disliked their competition. Then again, some of the larger incorporated poor law parishes had their own schools attached to the workhouse. With the coming of factory legislation from 1802 onwards, some factories established their own schools. These varied in quality, from the well-organised school at Robert Owen's mills at New Lanark to makeshift, sham affairs, sometimes in the stoke-hole, with a completely unqualified factory worker as teacher. Such schools were set up merely to comply with the new factory law. Lastly, although the old endowed grammar schools with the classical curriculum were attended very largely by middle-class children, here and there working-class boys with skilled and better-paid parents were on the school register. For example, sons of artisans were to be found at Manchester Grammar School in the eighteenth century.[12]

From this description of schools for the children of the working classes about 1800, it is clear that education of a kind was available for those parents who wanted it and could pay for it. Working-class children were by no means totally illiterate. However, the quality of education on offer was often very poor, and there were two major obstacles to anything approaching a satisfactory elementary education. The first was the by now familiar problem of the demand for child labour and the temptation to parents to send their children out to work rather than to school, where they usually had to pay fees. The second was the growth of population, especially in towns, as described earlier in this chapter. It was this second problem, and the threat of disorder which made the ultimate provision of more schools inevitable. It was equally inevitable that any new system of schools should be under the influence of the religious bodies of the time, as indicated earlier. As Kay Shuttleworth put it later in the century: 'No plan of education ought to be encouraged in which intellectual instruction is not subordinate to the regulation of the thoughts and habits of the children by the doctrine and precepts of revealed religion.' The bigoted ultra-Tory, Sir Robert Inglis, made the same point, but rather more pithily: 'Knowledge, unless sanctified by religion, was an unmitigated evil.' Since it was so taken for granted that education ought to be influenced by religious beliefs, it is not surprising that the first moves towards a national system of elementary education took the form of the establishment of church schools.

What then might be the attitude of working-class children to schooling in the early years of the nineteenth century? Clearly enough, the average working-class boy or girl of the time would almost completely lack the modern child's acceptance of the notion that going to school was a normal part of the process of growing up. It is true that literacy rates at the begining of the nineteenth century are to some extent a subject of historical controversy, as we shall see later, but it is safe to say that nationally only about half of the men and less than half of the women could sign their own name when getting married, and these proportions were even lower in industrial areas. Given this simple fact, it is evident that neither boys nor girls were spending very long in school. Indeed, even when they did go to school, attendance was not compulsory; nor was it free. Throughout the first half of the century, educationalists are to be found lamenting the short periods of attendance in school, sometimes a matter of only a few weeks or months. Many children in the early 1800s can never have gone to school at all, and grew up completely illiterate. This being so, it is evident that for most childen at the time school must have been something alien, a somewhat forbidding place of demanding and threatening adults, armed with a cane, requiring instant obedience, and quick to punish both the slow and the recalcitrant. Of course, there were exceptions. Even in rural areas, there were rarities like John Clare, whose imagination might be caught by the magic and fascination of words. Again, one may guess that Sunday School could provide moments of illumination, wonder or joy which could make the dull routines of hymn singing and Bible reading worthwhile. But day school in the early years of the nineteenth century could hardly have held much attraction for the ordinary working-class boy or girl. It was something which might or might not be encountered before the proper business of starting work began, probably something to be avoided if possible, and certainly not thought of as an essential preliminary to earning a living. It took time for these attitudes to change in the first half of the century.

As it happened, it was the dissenters, not the Church of England, who took the initiative.[13] In 1808 they founded the Royal Lancasterian Institution (later renamed the British and Foreign Schools Society), with the aim of building schools of an non-denominational nature (in practice, they were nonconformist in approach). Shortly after this, in 1811, the Church of England set up its own National Society for Promoting the Education of the Poor in the Principles of the Established Church. Both bodies relied on the voluntary subscriptions of their supporters – there was to be no help from the Government for another twenty years or more – but the National Society was by far the bigger of the two societies, both in its resources and in the number of its schools. Both societies used the famous monitorial system of instruction, which was undoubtedly very cheap to run (something much in its favour). The British and Foreign Schools Society adopted the system pioneered by the Quaker Joseph Lancaster, who used it in the school which he opened in the Borough Road in London in 1798. The National Society preferred the system employed by Dr Andrew Bell, who had first used it in Madras in India (hence the alternative name for the National schools – Madras schools). The two systems utilised the same basic principle: the lesson was first taught to selected children known as monitors, who would then teach it to their own group of children (between ten and twenty in a group). Cards of instruction were customarily used in the course of teaching. In this way a single master might teach, through his monitors, a whole school of 200 children or more. The Borough Road had up to 1,000 children and 67 monitors. It was a kind of mass-produced learning, very crude and very cheap (Lancaster's children used no paper or ink, merely chalk and slates; Bell's used sand trays); it was also extremely noisy – visitors were usually stunned by the sheer noise – and it was no doubt exhausing for both teachers and monitors, but it was quite effective. The monitors were key figures, of course. If they got it wrong, so did their group. Monitors might have extra tuition after school, and were awarded merit badges or were given token payments of a penny or so a week. The system proved so popular that it spread to some grammar schools and even to public schools.

The church schools were certainly a valuable additional source of education for working-class children, but their establishment was only the beginning of a long struggle to provide an adequate system of popular education. As they were neither free nor compulsory, attendance was still very limited in nature. In 1818 the Select Committee on the Education of the Poor reported that only about 7 per cent of the total population of England and Wales was attending day schools, and that this attendance might be for only a few months or less. Clearly there was a need for many more school places, but the resources of the voluntary societies were limited, and when in 1820 Henry Brougham brought in a bill for financing schools out of the rates, the teachers to be members of the Church of England, he met with much opposition, and the bill was dropped. At last (in 1833) the financial needs of the societies were acknowledged by the Government by the grant of £20,000, to be divided between the societies and used only for the building of school houses, not for salaries or other expenses. Further, the societies had to raise half the cost of any new building themselves before seeking government aid. This first annual grant to education was relatively small – it is usual to point out that in the same year £50,000 was voted by the Commons for the repair of the royal stables – but it was a start, and by 1839 it had grown to an annual grant of £30,000, and in that year important additional reforms were proposed.

The most important of these was the proposal to set up a special committee of the Privy Council to administer the grant from the Treasury. Government school inspectors were to be appointed, a model school and a teachers' training college were to be set up, and government grants were to be made available to schools other than church schools. These reforms were far too radical for both the National Society and the Church of England, and a number of the proposals had to be withdrawn. Although the special committee was established, school inspectors for Anglican schools could be appointed only with the approval of the diocesan authorities, and in 1843 the Government reached a similar agreement with the British and Foreign Schools Society that no inspectors of their schools should be appointed without the society's consent. So both societies resisted strongly and successfully any increase in government control over their schools. In the same year, 1843, Graham was forced to withdraw his Factory Bill, which proposed an increase in the existing educational requirement, from two hours to three hours daily. The dissenters would not have it, because they thought it would give too much of an advantage to the National schools, which were much more numerous than theirs. In this way, vested religious interests fought off government intervention, and jealously maintained their authority over what they regarded as their own. Public secular education was still a thing of the future.

Some further developments of the 1840s must be noted before surveying the wider scene. In 1843 it was decided that the government grant could be used by the societies for furniture and apparatus as well as buildings, and money was also made available to meet the cost of building denominational training colleges. In 1846 the hard-working secretary to the Committee of the Privy Council, Dr James Kay (later Sir James Kay Shuttleworth) drew up a new scheme for training teachers. In selected schools, a pupil-teacher system was to be set up. Promising children of thirteen and older were to be apprenticed to the master for five years. They would be examined annually by the inspectors, and grants were to be paid both to the apprentices and to their masters. At the end of the five years, they would sit national examinations, and the best candidates would be given Queen's Scholarships to the training colleges. Those who failed to gain the highest marks might still gain certificates of merit, bringing their school a special annual grant to help pay their salaries.

By the mid-nineteenth century, therefore, some progress had been made in supplying additional schools for the ever-increasing numbers of working-class children who were flooding the towns. The new schools were still financed by voluntary subscriptions, though by 1860 the annual government grant to assist the societies had grown to nearly three-quarters of a million pounds – a massive increase on the original £20,000. Something approaching a national system was beginning to emerge. Moreover, a teacher training system had at last been established, and an inspectorate appointed to keep an eye on the spending of the taxpayers' money. However, the inspectors were still expected to exercise their duties with extreme care. The Minute spelling out their remit made this quite clear: 'The Inspectors will not interfere with the religious instruction, or discipline, or management of the school, it being their object to collect facts and information and report the results of their inspection to the Committee of Council.'[14]

In fact, their reports make it clear that the inspectors carried out their duties for the most part very conscientiously; and it was hard work, too, there being only two inspectors at first, though the number grew by 1852 to twenty-three, together with two assistant inspectors. On the whole, inspectors acquitted themselves very well, though by the mid-sixties it had been found necessary to dismiss three, and one, the Revd M. Mitchell, was severely rebuked, but not dismissed, in 1853:

> There cannot be two opinions upon the indecorum of the practices which you describe of wiping your hands on the pinafores of the children and of kissing them. Their Lordships are obliged to remind you of the terms in which their secretary was instructed to characterise such practices in 1848 when the managers of the Tamworth Infant School complained of similar behaviour.[15]

Mitchell, like the famous Revd Francis Kilvert in another context, seems to have had an inordinate liking for young schoolchildren.

More government money, more schools, more trained teachers, more inspectors – but what did it signify in practice to the ever-increasing numbers of working-class children at the mid-century? In the first place, some improvement in literacy might be anticipated in the first half of the century. Indeed, some historians have argued that the spread of industry increased the demand for literate men and women workers who could read notices, instructions for operating machines, and so on. The problem lies in the difficulty of obtaining satisfactory evidence of literacy, the one kind of evidence readily available being 'signature-literacy', that is, the ability to sign one's name in the marriage register, as opposed to making one's mark. On this basis, it appears that literacy actually declined in certain industrial areas during the late eighteenth and early nineteenth centuries, the reason being that the new machinery did not necessarily require a literate work force. Child doffers and piecers in cotton mills, for example, certainly did not need to be literate. At the same time, literacy seems to have risen somewhat in rural areas.[16] It is now clear enough that literacy in the simplest sense varied considerably from region to region, much depending on local conditions, such as the demand for child labour, the attitude of the local middle classes, the extent of religious enthusiasm, and so on.[17] This local diversity is confirmed by reference to the many (and often conflicting) descriptions of the furnishings of working-class homes. Some had books, some had not. The factory workers in the Ashworth cotton mills were provided with good cottages by their benevolent but autocratic employer, and in the homes of the longest-serving employees there would be as many as ten to thirty books.[18] On the other hand, an enquiry into local rural conditions in Kent after the Bossenden Wood rising in 1838 emphasised the lack of books in labouring homes. Unfortunately, there is not enough evidence of this kind to add materially to our knowledge obtained from the signature evidence in the marriage registers.[19]

The whole subject of working class literacy during the first part of the nineteenth century is really incapable of precise definition and conclusions, though from the 1840s onwards the story is different, and there seems little doubt that literacy had begun to rise nationally. According to the official figures of literacy published by the Registrar General for each census year, the percentages for literacy were as follows:

	1841	*1851*	*1861*	*1871*
Males	67.3	69.3	75.4	80.6
Females	51.1	54.8	65.3	73.2[20]

So it seems reasonable to suppose that the work of the church schools (and of private schools, as well) was taking effect. However, one simple fact must not be overlooked here, that signing with a mark did not necessarily mean complete illiteracy – the signatory might still be able to read after a fashion.[21] In the late eighteenth and early nineteenth centuries, jobs for working men were often advertised in the Birmingham press, while printed popular tales and political tracts circulated freely with considerable sales. Tom Paine's *The Rights of Man* is generally supposed to have sold 200,000 copies by the end of 1793, and Hannah More's religious tracts had a much larger sale than this. So the ability to read (rather than to write) might have been rather more widespread than might otherwise be supposed. There is also the likelihood, of course, that weak readers or non-readers would get their more literate friends to read for them, which would explain why advertising jobs in the local newspapers was an accepted means of recruiting labour.

As for the proportion of children who actually attended school in the first half of the nineteenth century, again, there are really no figures reliable enough to give an accurate picture, and even if there were, it would be necessary to know how long they stayed at school. Earlier in this chapter, it was noted that in 1818 only about 7 per cent of the population of England and Wales were estimated to be on school registers. Another estimate, in the *Abstract of Educational Returns*, 1833, gives a figure of 11 per cent. When a further survey was made in 1851, it was calculated that the proportion attending school was still about 11 per cent.[22] All these figures must be seen against the fact that the proportion of children between the ages of five and twelve accounted for nearly 17 per cent of the total population; but again we are not told how long children stayed at school. In 1857 it was stated at a conference on school attendance that of the two million children registered as school pupils, as many as 42 per cent attended for less than a year, and only 22 per cent – about one in five – for between one and two years.[23] Naturally enough, the children who did attend were usually very young and less ready to go to work than others. In the mid-1860s, in an average county such as Kent, only 30 per cent of the school children were aged ten or above. In an industrial county such as Staffordshire, the figure was only 25 per cent.[24] It is clear then that school attendance in the mid-nineteenth century still varied from area to area, and was often of short duration.

What the children found awaiting them when they did go to school was not likely to encourage regular attendance. Schools using the monitorial system in the earlier part of the century often consisted of one large hall in which the whole school assembled for instruction. As we have seen, the outstanding characteristic of such schools was the noise of the oral teaching which was the principal method employed. With the adoption of the pupil teaching system, instruction in smaller classes became more usual, but the early reports of the school inspectors are witness to the fact that both the teaching and the buildings were often highly unsatisfactory. It seems extraordinary, but not all the teachers of the time were even able to write; over 700 teachers were said to have signed the 1851 educational returns with a mark.[25] As for the buildings, they were frequently dark, damp, and ill-ventilated. Among the worst schools were some schools of the British and Foreign Schools Society, which were situated in the basements of chapels, and conseqently badly lit and poorly ventilated. It was not unusual for the stench from the necessaries (privies) to pervade the air, the sanitary accommodation being simply in the form of buckets.

As for the keeping of order, it was remarked in Chapter One that the ill-treatment of workshop children was said to be little different from the punishment inflicted on children in school. This is probably an exaggeration, but corporal punishment was taken for granted. Thus, the striking and caning of children was commonplace, and expected by them. Even in relatively humane regimes, such as that in Robert Owen's school, children wore dunce's caps or had placards round their necks. In his book, published in 1806, Joseph Lancaster himself listed punishments imposed in his Borough Road School. They included a wooden log fastened round the neck; shackling the child's legs and making him or her walk round the room until tired; yoking offenders together by the neck; tying the elbows together behind the back; keeping children in after school, tied to the desk, so that the teacher did not need to stay behind as well; and hoisting offenders to the ceiling in a basket – a punishment much disliked by the children.[26] However harsh these methods may appear today, it must be remembered that they were thought entirely normal by most people, and, moreover, were not confined to working-class children. In the public schools of the time, there was a good deal of brutality. Boys were beaten by both prefects and masters. In 1832, Dr Keate, the famous flogging headmaster at Eton, flogged eighty boys in a single session. (He was also accustomed to taking the whole of the Upper School (198 boys) at once.) Readers of *Tom Brown's Schooldays* will recall the violence among the boys themselves, including the roasting of Tom Brown before the fire.

If teaching methods were primitive and school buildings inadequate, it must be stressed that the middle classes of the early Victorian period were seeking to provide education as cheaply as possible, and on a severely limited scale. Moreover, this was to be education for the poor, not necessarily for the working classes as a whole, for the better-off among them would send their children (it was thought) to private schools. This very limited conception of what kind of education should be provided by the church schools makes itself obvious time and time again. For example, it is true that the system of pupil-teaching opened up a new career to the working classes. A male schoolteacher could earn £90 a year, with a rent-free house, and additional payments if he had pupil-teachers. But this new occupation was really intended only for the working classes; as Kay Shuttleworth put it, 'it cannot be expected that members of the middle class of society will to any extent choose the vocation of teachers of the poor', but he did think that the profession of schoolmaster would be popular among the lower orders. Again, in 1861 the Revd James Fraser made it abundantly clear that what was on offer in the church schools was in educational terms very elementary indeed:

> Even if it were possible, I doubt whether it would be desirable, with a view to the real interests of the peasant boy, to keep him at school till he was 14 or 15 years of age. But it is not possible. We must make up our minds to see the last of him, so far as the day school is concerned, at 10 or 11.[27]

The reference to the 'peasant boy', and the general patronising tone of this passage are very noticeable. Fraser went on to list the essentials of the education of such a boy: the ability to spell, to read a common narrative (for example, in a newspaper), to write a letter home, to add up a shop bill and to have some knowledge of the whereabouts of foreign countries; but as a basic essential, he must be able to understand a plain sermon, and to know his duty towards his Maker and fellow man. In short, working-class children were to be given just enough education to make them useful to their employers and others, and to know their subordinate position in society. The agents recruited to bring this about, the new pupil-teachers, were themselves to come from the working classes, and to remain within their class. Real education would continue to be the preserve of the middle and upper classes.

Just what working-class parents of the time made of all this is not easy to say. It is likely that many had no great interest in the subject. Some undoubtedly did think that a good education was a desirable thing, but were put off by the form in which it was available, that is, by schools which were under the close control of the churches and subject to middle-class patronage.[28] Other parents, particularly fathers engaged in skilled trades, and with a higher standard of living, were more strongly in favour of education. This is true, for example, of glassmakers; there is the famous exhortation in the opening address of the first issue of the *Flint Glass Makers Magazine* (1851): 'Get intelligence instead of alcohol . . . get knowledge, and in getting knowledge, you get power.' But in the industrial areas, as has been amply demonstrated in the preceding chapters, children were sent out to work as soon as they were capable of earning a few pence. If they went to school at all, parents would ask the teachers to 'finish them off quickly' – meaning that the children should be given the elements of the three Rs as soon as possible so that they could then leave school. At the Lye National School in the Black Country, the superintendent of the girls' department said that the early leaving of the children was very disheartening, but the parents were dreadfully ignorant; not one of them in twenty could read or write, and they cared nothing for the education of their children.[29] This is probably true enough, for the principal local occupation was nailing, and traditionally children went into the family workshop as soon as they were strong enough to take part in the work. A local parson commented on this employment of young children: 'A man with a large family therefore finds it necessary to do so, and education, religion, and all moral culture is abandoned to procure the bread which perisheth.'[30]

Certainly H. S. Tremenheere, the mines inspector, who had

previously been one of the first two inspectors of schools, took this problem of children's earnings very seriously. In the first place, he thought it hard to know how to convince uneducated parents of the value of education when a certain amount of education was needed to appreciate its advantages. This was especially so when education of their children meant the sacrifice of the children's wages and the payment of school pence. Tremenheere's solution was to establish prize schemes in the mining districts, whereby cash prizes would be awarded to children who stayed on at school, so as to compensate parents for the loss of earnings from their offspring. In the end, some twenty-three schemes were established by 1859, and prizes duly awarded. However, the schemes were not very successful, and on the whole it was only the better-paid parents who could afford to keep their children on at school anyway who really benefited; but the whole idea shows the difficulty of persuading even well-intentioned parents to forgo their children's wages.[31]

It must also be said that the number of working-class parents who were either indifferent or positively hostile to education at the mid-century was probably still quite large. In the industrial areas, particularly in the Black Country, education was simply not thought to be of much concern to ordinary working folk. It seemed natural that children should go to work when strong enough; to keep them at home was to encourage idleness, and to make 'rodneys' of them (that is, softies).[32] Education was not thought necessary for success in life. It was argued that people who read and kept books were not always more prosperous than those who remained illiterate. Learning might even be a drawback; in the Black Country, there was a well-known saying: 'The father went to the pit and made a fortune; the son went to school and lost it.' It was easy for the more feckless parent to adopt such views, and school inspectors commented time and again on the indifference and apathy of parents. One assistant commissioner in 1861 commented that in Dudley some of the best nailers, themselves illiterate, owned valuable breeds of pigeons costing 4*s* to 5*s* a week in barley and peas. They betted heavily on the birds' performance, yet they could not afford 2*d* or 3*d* a week for school fees.[33] Their order of priorities was clear: racing pigeons came before schooling.

If it is difficult to generalise about working-class parents' attitudes to education, it is equally difficult to describe children's attitudes to the schooling they received. As is still the case today, those who did best at school probably liked it better than those who found it hard going. But even those who took to it sufficiently to learn to read and write well, and afterwards wrote of their experiences, do not appear to have remembered school with much affection. School was too often thought of as a place of frightening teachers and harsh punishments, and even in the better-run church schools, children would sometimes rebel against their teachers, kicking and struggling when beaten.[34] Rebellions were not confined to public schools in the first half or so of the nineteenth century: on 21 September 1854, nearly half the school, amounting to forty-three boys, ran away from a residential charity school, Old Swinford Hospital in Stourbridge, complaining of severe and cruel treatment by the master, of being struck by the porter with a cane, and of insufficient food.[35]

Nevertheless, by the 1850s more and more children were attending school, and government expenditure on the church schools was growing year by year. The idea of supporting schools financially through the rates was again mooted, but a bill introduced by Lord Russell in 1853 to allow larger towns to assist church schools in this way was rejected. Finally, in 1858, the Newcastle Commission was appointed to enquire into the state of popular education, and to report on any measures thought necessary to extend 'sound and cheap elementary education to all classes of people' (the word 'cheap' will not go unnoticed). In 1861 the commission issued its report. It estimated that just under one in eight was attending school in 1858, and declared that the commission had not come across any large number of children who did not go to school at some time in their lives (in fact, this was a somewhat optimistic conclusion). All the same, it was recommended that the cost of local schooling should be met through a county education rate. Further, teachers were not spending enough time teaching the three Rs, and this should be remedied by making grants to schools dependent on annual examinations by special county inspectors. The first suggestion regarding aid from the rates was ignored by the Government – there were too many objections to this from the non conformists. The second suggestion was adopted by Robert Lowe, vice-president of the Committee of Council for Education. A revised code of regulations for the schools was drawn up, making the annual grant dependent on examinations conducted by the school inspectors. Payment by Results depended not only on the examination results but on regular attendance as well. The new system perpetuated one important aspect of the old monitorial system – instruction was to be given as cheaply as possible. Robert Lowe summed up his view of Payment by Results in a famous if rather strange claim in the House of Commons: 'If it is not cheap, it shall be efficient: if it is not efficient, it shall be cheap.' However the matter is viewed, cheapness was obviously to be a guiding consideration.

So by the mid-sixties, with the emergence of something beginning to approach a universal system of education for working-class children in England and Wales, a renewed emphasis was placed on saving money. It is true that for a time this aim was achieved, and the national grant was reduced. In 1862 this was £840,000, while in 1864 it had dropped to £705,000. Again, Payment by Results may have produced more efficient teaching of the basics in some instances, but undoubtedly it also had adverse effects. Great emphasis was placed on registration of attendance ('getting your mark'), and children were expected to attend school even if ill. Teachers were constantly worried by low attendance caused it might be by a local epidemic, or by harvesting in the summer. Since examination results were all-important, children were drilled remorselessly, and the actual examination day was an anxious time for all, including the teachers, whose salaries might be affected by the results. Payment by Results was probably not entirely deleterious in its consequences, and indeed may have administered a beneficial shock to the whole system. Some historians more recently have emphasised that the revised code was not all bad, nor were Lowe's intentions. Nevertheless, the overall effect was illiberal and restrictionist, and it was some time before the code was relaxed and a less narrow approach adopted.

How then may the state of working-class education in the mid-sixties be assessed? Undoubtedly more children went to school, and for longer periods, than at the beginning of the century. Literacy was rising, and so was the publication of cheap and popular reading matter. Clearly, and for the first time, elementary education had become a reality for many working-class children, even though it was still neither compulsory nor free. Gradually the balance was turning towards schooling, rather than the world of work, as the expected activity and experience of the young child. Slowly childhood was being transformed for the majority of the child population, at least. But two important qualifications must still be made. Throughout the first half of the century, the churches, both Anglican and nonconformist, exercised a strong control over the growing school system. Rivalry between them, and their dislike of government interference, were at times a positive barrier to advance. As Graham said in connection with the opposition to the 1843 bill, 'Religion, the keystone of education is in this country, the bar to progress.' One argument which can be made in favour of the revised code is that it placed a new emphasis on the secular as opposed to the religious elements in the curriculum. At last the iron grip of the churches over the curriculum was being loosened, but it had taken over half a century for this to happen.[36]

The second qualification is that even if working-class education was perhaps becoming more secularised, it was still conceived of as a very limited form of education. This was so at the beginning of the century and was still so in the 1860s (witness the views expressed by the Rev Fraser in 1861, quoted earlier in this chapter). The boy or girl was still to be given only the minimum skills thought necessary to earn a living, and then at the least cost to the taxpayer. Lowe made this clear yet again in the House of Commons:

> We propose to give no grant for the attendance of children at school unless they can read, write and cipher; but we do not say they should not learn more. We do not object to any amount of learning; the only question is how much of that knowledge we ought to pay for . . . We do not propose to give these children an education that will raise them above their station and business in life.[37]

Here the beliefs of Kay Shuttleworth and others earlier in the century can be heard again. It was to be many years before the idea of *secondary* education for working-class children took hold – elementary education was all that was required, or so it was thought in the 1860s. Nevertheless, the financial problems of the church societies, faced with an ever-increased school population, were becoming more pressing, and as will be seen in Chapter Eight, they forced the Government to introduce a new type of elementary school in 1870.

If the church societies had such influence over the Government in the first half of the nineteenth century, this in itself gives some indication of the importance of religion in society at this time. It had not always been so, and in the eighteenth century the Church of England was noted for its general laxity and complacency. Pluralism was rife, and so was absenteeism, and abuses of this kind continued into the early decades of the nineteenth century. There were examples of conscientious parish priests, and indeed of caring bishops, but there were plenty of clerks in holy orders who took the easy way out of pastoral care. In Birmingham, for instance, the rector of St Philip's was only occasionally in the town itself, spending his time in London or at livings in the country; while the rector of the other Anglican church, St Martin's, lived some miles away in Solihull until his death in 1829.[38] Nevertheless, by this time at least the evangelical movement within the Church of England was making itself felt, while nonconformity, especially new dissent in the form of methodism, was growing ever stronger. In 1818 Parliament voted a million pounds and in 1824 another half million for church building; by 1833 about six million pounds had been raised for this purpose from all sources. In 1836 the Church of England was given a powerful administrative shake-up by the Whig Government, and in the 1840s the Church was subject to much doctrinal dispute because of the development within its ranks of the Oxford Movement. By the middle years of the century, religion was as powerful an influence in society as it had been since the seventeenth century. In particular, evangelicalism, with its great emphasis on the importance of the Bible, had made the English, as R.C.K. Ensor put it, 'people of a book', rather as devout Moslems are people of the Koran, but as few other Europeans of the time were.[39]

If this is so, the question naturally arises as to how far the working classes were religious in outlook, and how far childhood itself was influenced by religious beliefs. These are immensely difficult questions, and a historian of religion has recently begun a study of religion and the working classes in the nineteenth century by observing that there seems to be almost complete disagreement among historians on this subject.[40] This, perhaps, is to go rather too far; but there are certainly substantial difficulties in interpreting the evidence. Not only are there problems of ascertaining to what extent working people attended church or chapel, and of the significance of what attendance figures are available, but also there is the problem of how far religion entered into daily life and thought, irrespective of formal attendance at worship. Only when these matters have been surveyed and assessed will it be at all possible to comment in any way on the effect of religion on children's lives. Much of what is said later on is therefore speculative in nature, but this is inevitable, given the nature of the subject. Some degree of historical guesswork is perhaps better than blank historical agnosticism.

In the first place, and against a background of hectic church- and chapel-building in the first half of the nineteenth century, designed to accommodate the increase in population, attendance at church and chapel must be examined. The first difficulty to be encountered here is that there was only one national census of church attendance in the nineteenth century (though there were some local censuses in the 1880s). The 1851 census of attendance was voluntary in nature, and was based on returns made by individual incumbents, the results being analysed and published by the principal organiser of the 1851 population census, Horace Mann. Most historians seem agreed that the returns were reasonably accurate, and there is little evidence to show any massaging of the figures to boost morale.[41] In fact, the results were a deep disappointment to contemporaries, as it appeared that even if allowance was made for people unable to attend by reason of age, sickness, or employment, only about one in two adults free to attend church or chapel nationally actually did so. Moreover, attendance by the working classes in the larger towns and cities was remarkably low. More than anything, it seems, it was this that led Mann to say that the proportion of artisans in the congregations was 'absolutely insignificant', and that 'the masses of our working population . . . are never or but seldom seen in our religious congregations'.[42] This merely echoes Engels's trenchant words earlier in 1844, based on his observations in Manchester:

> All bourgeois writers agree that the workers have no religion and do not go to church. Exceptions to this are the Irish, a few of the older workers, and those wage-earners who have a foot in the middle-class camp – overlookers, foremen, and so on. Among the mass of the working class population, however, one nearly always find an utter indifference to religion – the mere cry, 'He's a parson', is often enough to force a clergyman off the platform at a public meeting.[43]

Subsequent to Mann's report on his findings, other leading Victorians joined in the general lamentations at the godlessness of the working classes. In 1860 the famous evangelical, Lord Shaftesbury, said that not 2 per cent of the working men in London attended church.

This gloomy picture of working-class attendance remained unquestioned in the first half of the twentieth century. The author of a standard and respected textbook published in 1938, Professor E. L. Woodward, merely remarks on this subject, 'The poor, at least in the great towns, were largely pagan, with a veneer of religious observance and much hidden superstition.'[44] So much for the pagan working classes. Even after the Second World War, historians clung to the same interpretation. Bishop Wickham declared that in Sheffield in 1843 the general view was that not one family of artisans in twenty attended church or chapel. Dr K. S. Inglis asserted that even in the northern and midland towns, the majority of workers did not attend worship; popular abstinence from worship (as he put it) had become an inherited custom. Professor Perkin took the same line.[45]

What seems to have escaped the attention of all these commentators is that if nationally about one in two of all classes attended worship in

1851, and the working classes were probably (according to Mann) some four-fifths of the nation, then those who did attend could not have been all middle- and upper-class, for these classes constituted only about one-fifth of the entire population. There simply must have been a substantial working-class attendance somewhere to bring the national average up to one in two. Moreover, on inspection of the county figures for Bedfordshire, Buckinghamshire, Cambridgeshire, Huntingdonshire, Northamptonshire, Suffolk and Wiltshire, the attendance as a percentage of total population was in every case over 80 per cent (uncorrected for non-availability or multiple attendance).[46] It is quite clear that there was an impressive working-class attendance in these rural counties, and even in some industrial areas of traditional domestic industry, such as the Black Country, there was similarly a very respectable attendance.[47]

Thus it can be shown that *nationally* working-class attendance was far greater in the countryside than in the larger centres of population where, for a variety of reasons, attendance might be very limited. In some instances it could be that church- and chapel-building had simply failed to keep up with an expanding population, so that there was a shortage of seats. More commonly a newly settled working population from the countryside had failed to reassume the habits of churchgoing in their native villages, which had been under the watchful eye of the parson and squire. Some of the poorest-paid were reluctant to attend when they could not afford respectable clothes – it was widely held that suitable clothing was necessary for church or chapel, and some churches even advertised the fact that worshippers were welcome in their working clothes. Pew rents were another obstacle – they were charged even in the chapels – and though there were some free seats even in Anglican churches, to use them was to emphasise the social gulf between those who could afford to pay for their pews and those who could not. Illiteracy could also be a barrier for those who could not read the Prayer Book or hymnal. Then again, towns could supply alternative, though limited forms of amusement on a Sunday; the pubs were open, although usually for fewer hours than on a weekday. In some of the Birmingham pubs no dramatic entertainment was allowed on Sundays, though hymns and psalms might be sung, accompanied by drinking and smoking. In the same city the efforts of missionaries often seem to have been counter-productive, for generally they were thought patronising and interfering.[48]

For all these reasons, attendance at church or chapel in the large towns might be much lower than in the village or small industrial community. It was likely to be higher, too, in the chapel rather than in the Anglican church, which was attended by the employer class and was very much the church of established authority. Working men and women and their children were likely to feel much more at ease in the homelier surroundings of the chapel, especially the chapel of the Primitive Methodists, whose preachers were well-known for their simple, direct and emotional appeal – their 'rantin' and roarin', as it was termed at the time. For many chapels, of course, attendance was not merely a Sunday duty; the chapel was also a social centre, with plenty of activities during the week, such as Bible classes, mothers' meetings, tea gatherings, musical evenings, choir practices, and so on. For its members, the mid-nineteenth-century chapel was something of a home from home. For Roman Catholics, too, the church was an important centre of their lives, and one where the priest exercised a strong personal discipline through the confessional.

However, for the children the Sunday School may really have been the most important activity on a Sunday. It is true that the influence of these schools may have been exaggerated in some ways, but, as indicated earlier in this chapter, very considerable numbers did attend them, and did learn to read there. As the primary purpose of the Sunday School was to teach children to read the Bible, many could not avoid picking up the fundamentals of the Christian religion, however ill-taught by volunteer, often middle-class teachers. Some of the teaching was of a lurid kind, especially on the subject of hell. One ex-pupil recalled how in the 1840s she learned by heart

There is a dreadful hell,
And everlasting pains,
Where sinners must with devils dwell
In darkness, fire, and chains.[49]

Nevertheless, most writers of working-class biographies seemed to have enjoyed attending Sunday School, one writing in 1851, 'I can truly say I loved my school – no crying when Sunday came round.'[50] For many children, the whole of Sunday might be taken up by visits to church or chapel and to Sunday School. It must also be remembered that there was a social side to Sunday School, too, which added to its attractions – the occasional lantern-slide show, the annual outing, and the processions, such as the Whitsun Walks.

So far, attention has been concentrated on the institutional aspects of religion, the churches, chapels, and Sunday Schools. There are other, related matters to be considered; indeed, it would be wrong to concentrate too narrowly on the facts and figures of religious observance. For example, no major efforts appear to have been made to whip up attendance on Census Sunday, so there must have been some believers not included then who attended only occasionally, perhaps at Easter or Christmas, so that the census figures do not tell the whole story. Again, there were others of little faith or none who obtained help from church soup kitchens, or were given bread or gifts of blankets or clothing when times were bad. Even non-attenders could hardly have been totally ignorant of the physical presence of the churches and chapels, and of their social activities, even though they might actually resent having to take charity from them when driven to it (others, of course, were cynically prepared to accept aid in return for a little hymn-singing, as Shaw brings out later in the century in the Salvation Army citadel scene in *Major Barbara*). So even for those who attended church only occasionally, or not all, there must have been an awareness of the presence of the churches and chapels, especially in the smaller communities.

In most working-class homes, of course, there was a much greater consciousness among both young and old of the uncertainties of life, and of the realities of death than at the present day, when death is hardly a popular subject, except at a safe instance on the TV screen. With such high mortality rates in the early nineteenth century, sickness and death were commonplace occurrences. Families were large, but many children died young. Cholera epidemics took their thousands, and were accompanied by national days of prayer and repentance. Mortality at work could be high, too, especially in industrial areas where there were mines and ironworks. Funerals were a sight familiar to children, who might have shared bedrooms with the deceased. For grown-ups and children alike, therefore, religious beliefs, however ill-formed and incoherent, could provide some sort of explanation and consolation in times of grief and stress. The dead were not lost, it was said, but 'gone before'. It is impossible to quantify all this, but it is a reasonable assumption that many working-class children who might not even attend Sunday School would still have learned something at their mother's knee about the Deity and about the hoped-for life hereafter. Such children would learn through personal experience about the misfortunes and tragedies of life. Many not especially religious homes had a family Bible, and very few could have been unaware of the special nature of Sundays, given the Sabbatarianism of the time. Quite apart, therefore, from the acquisition of religious beliefs at church or chapel, in Sunday School, or in church schools, it may be supposed that many children (though not all) learned the rudiments of Christian belief in the home through an informal transmission of ideas. The attendance figures of Census Sunday, 30 March, 1851, tell only part of the story.

At this point it might be helpful to the reader if the threads of this discussion are drawn together. In the first place, whether children had any knowledge of the principles of Christianity or not might depend to some extent on where they lived – in rural areas or in industrial areas, in small industrial villages or in great towns or cities.[51] By and large, their parents were more likely to be church- or chapel-goers if they lived in the countryside and in small communities, or in long-established non-industrial towns in the provinces; and less likely to be so if they lived in large industrial towns, including London. Regular worshippers would naturally take their children to church or chapel. Next, many working-class children would be more familiar with chapel than with church, for in the first half of the nineteenth century methodism had a strong appeal to the working classes. Although it is true that skilled workmen in regular employment might be attracted to either Anglicanism or methodism, the semi-skilled and the unskilled were much more to be found among the congregations of the Primitive Methodists.[52] Pew rents in their chapels were lower than elsewhere, and employers were not often to be encountered in them, at least before the mid-century. Trustees of Primitive Methodist chapels were often working men themselves, and the social life of the chapel catered for respectable working-class taste rather than middle-class predilections.

As for knowledge of the Scriptures, it was probably gained mostly by attendance at Sunday School, or at church schools, rather than in adult company in church. Further, some instruction undoubtedly took place in the home, either from parents or from other members of the family. Once again, it is worth observing that the transmission of ideas within the home must have been important for the reception by children of Christian principles; and the learning of simple prayers and the saying of grace, for example, would play a significant part in this process.

To sum up: how important was religious belief in the lives of working-class children in the first half of the nineteenth century? Although it is impossible to answer this question with any degree of precision, it is evident enough that Horace Mann and his contemporaries failed to see the 1851 attendance figures in national perspective, and even modern historians in the 1960s appear to have been unduly influenced by mid-nineteenth-century views. Admittedly, attendance was poor in the great new industrial conurbations, but there were exceptions even to this. Merthyr Tydfil, for instance, which was the largest town in Wales in 1851, had the astonishing attendance figure of 88.5 per cent of the population, about a third of the worshippers attending Baptist chapels.[53] This was highly exceptional, of course, and there is no doubt that attendance was generally poor in London and the large industrial towns in England, this being balanced to some extent by the relatively high attendance in the smaller towns, industrial villages and agricultural areas. Once more, as Dr Coleman has put it, the study of religion at this time requires 'some sense of social geography, of region and of locality, and of the various forces operating upon people's behaviour in each'.[54]

When we move beyond the attendance figures to consider the individual child, it is not possible to do more than speak in general terms about family circumstances and the influence of Sunday Schools and church schools. All these together must have had a considerable effect on many working-class children.[55] It is probable that only a minority grew up totally and completely ignorant of the simplest religious beliefs, but the 1862 commissioners did report striking examples of both general ignorance and lack of religious knowledge. Thus William Favell, aged fourteen, a foreman in a spade works in Lye in the Black Country, said he had never been to day school, but went on Sundays, and to chapel 'when I got some clothes'. He thought (but wasn't sure) that Birmingham was a town, but had never heard of London; he had heard of the Queen. The sea, he thought, was made of land, not of water. A violet was a pretty bird. The commissioner who interviewed this young man actually encountered another boy who claimed that 'Christ was a wicked man', and that 'The devil is a good person' (he had clearly confused the two names). The commissioner commented that the state of mind in the area regarding the simplest facts of religion was incredible.[56] Yet chapel attendance in Lye was remarkably good in 1851. The New Connexion chapel was nearly full in the afternoon, and full up in the evening, with forty-four standing; while in the Primitive Methodist chapel on Lye Waste, four-fifths of the seats were occupied in the afternoon, and every seat occupied in the evening. The Independent (Congregational) chapel in the High Street, founded by the local paternalistic manufacturers, Wood Brothers (William Favell's employers), who are buried there, did less well, but still had a congregation of 150 in the afternoon (it is now a mosque; the worship of Allah has replaced Christian worship).[57]

Finally, to suggest that religion had significance for many working boys and girls at the mid-century in spite of the evidence of low attendance in large towns (especially, but not exclusively, industrial towns) is not to be perverse. It is merely to draw attention to areas where attendance was better, and also to the influence of Sunday Schools, church schools, and the home environment. For one small section of the population, the Irish immigrants, religious observance, of course, was a powerful means of enforcing social solidarity, for the influence of the Roman Catholic priest on his flock was known to be strong. But the Protestant communities themselves formed part of a society in which religious belief was all-pervasive. Clergy would be present at all public occasions, and the Church of England still exercised power on the government of the day through the House of Lords. Mid-Victorian society was a religious society; though there may well have been a good deal of disbelief and a fair amount of hypocrisy, it was highly impolitic to reveal religious scepticism in public. Darwin's *Origin of Species* was not published till 1859, and the great debate over evolution did not begin till the 1860s, nor the rationalist arguments over the existence of hell and the need for personal salvation. Thus at the mid-century religious ideas were predominant, and the very fact that the revelation in 1851 that only one in two attended church or chapel should have caused such dismay and led to such discussion and a flurry of missionary work in the towns illustrates the point very clearly.

It follows that in such a society it was inevitable that working-class families should be affected by religious thinking. In the expanding towns the new redbrick churches and chapels, soon to become grimy and blackened from smoke and soot, were permanent reminders of institutional religion. The same may be said of many of the new church schools. One way and other, working-class children could only with difficulty escape some acquaintanceship, at least, with the basic tenets of the Christian religion.

References

1 Harold Silver, *The Concept of Popular Education*, 1965, p. 17.

2 Quoted in Guy Kendall, *Robert Raikes, A Critical Study*, 1939, p. 122.

3 Harold Silver, *The Concept of Popular Education*, p. 23.

4 For a helpful recent account of radical movements in Britain at the end of the eighteenth century, see H. T. Dickinson, *British Radicalism and the French Revolution 1789–1815*, 1985, and on the influence of Thomas Paine see the same author's 'Thomas Paine's "Rights of Man 1791–92": a bi-centenary assessment', *The Historian*, no. 32, Autumn, 1991.

5 In the early nineteenth century, the Prime Minister, Lord Liverpool, like many other politicians, considered that government intervention to remedy social distress was a waste of time; he took the view that most miseries of mankind were beyond the reach of legislation. On the whole, the best policy therefore was to quell immediate disorder, then to wait for the gradual restoration of calm. Education was best left to the churches and their school societies.

6 M. G. Jones, *The Charity School Movement in the Eighteenth Century*, 1938, is still the standard work, but it is not entirely reliable in detail. See also Joan Simon, 'Was there a Charity School Movement? The Leicestershire Evidence' in Brian Simon (ed.), *Education in Leicestershire 1640–1940*, 1968. There are few studies of the working of such schools in the nineteenth century, but see Eric Hopkins, 'A Charity School in the 19th Century: Old Swinford Hospital School, 1815–1914', *British Journal of Educational Studies*, XVII, No. 2, June 1969.

7 The standard work here is Thomas W. Lacqueur, *Religion and Respectability, Sunday Schools and Working Class Culture 1780–1850*, 1976.

8 For a criticism of Lacqueur's views, see Malcolm Dick, 'The Myth of the Working-Class Sunday School', *History of Education*, Vol. 9, 1, 1980. For a brief survey of the shortcomings of Birmingham's Sunday Schools, see Eric Hopkins, *Birmingham: The First Manufacturing Town in the World 1760–1840*, 1989, p. 159.

9 Hopkins, *Birmingham*, p. 160.

10 Mary Sturt, *The Education of the People*, 1967, p. 40.

11 T. W. Lacqueur, 'Working Class Demand and the Growth of English Elementary Education 1750–1850', in L. Stone (ed.), *Schooling and Society*, 1976.

12 Michael Sanderson, 'The Grammar School and the Education of the Poor', *British Journal of Educational Studies*, XI, 1962.

13 The account given in this and succeeding paragraphs of the development of popular education in the first half of the nineteenth century follows the conventional pattern. The best general account is still Mary Sturt, *The Education of the People*, but see also J. M. Goldstrom, *The Social Content of Education 1808–1870*, 1972; D. G. Paz, *The Politics of Working Class Education 1830–50*, 1980, G. Sutherland, *Elementary Education in the 19th Century*, 1971; J. S. Hurt, *Education in Evolution*, 1971; R. W. Musgrave, *Society and Education since 1800*, 1968; D. Wardle, *English Popular Education, 1780–1970*, 1970; Gillian Sutherland, 'Education', in F. M. L. Thompson (ed.), *The Cambridge Social History of Britain 1750–1950*, 1990, Vol. 3, and Michael Sanderson, *Education, Economic Change and Society in England 1780–1870*, 2nd edn, 1991.

14 Quoted in Sturt, *The Education of the People*, p. 96. See also pp. 97–8 for further details of duties.

15 Quoted in Hurt, *Education in Evolution*, p. 56.

16 The controversy is reviewed in Sanderson, *Education, Economic Change and Society*, Section I, 'Literacy and Mass Elementary Education'. A formidable survey of the subject is provided by W. B. Stephens, *Education, Literacy and Society 1830–70: The Geography of Diversity in Provincial England*, 1987.

17 Stephens, *Education, Literacy and Society*, pp. 264–5.

18 Rhodes Boyson, *The Ashworth Cotton enterprise: the Rise and Fall of a Family Firm*, 1970, p. 125.

19 Barry Reay, 'The Context and Meaning of Popular Literacy: Some evidence from rural England', *Past & Present*, no. 131, May 1991.

20 Sanderson, *Education, Economic Change and Society*, p. 19.

21 Reay, 'Context and Meaning', makes much of this.

22 *Census of Great Britain, 1851: Education, England and Wales, Report and Tables*, 1854, pp. xxvi and xxxvi.

23 C. Birchenough, *History of Elementary Education in England and Wales*, 1914, p. 92. See also M. Sturt, *The Education of The People*, chapter 13, especially p. 270, on problems of attendance at this time.

24 Minutes of the Committee of Council on Education, 1863–64.

25 Stephens, *Education, Literacy and Society*, p. 267.

26 These methods of punishment are listed in Silver, *The Concept of Popular Education*, p. 50.

27 *Enquiry into the State of Popular Education in England*, 1861, Vol. I, p. 243.

28 See Richard Johnson, 'Education Policy and Social Control in Early Victorian England', *Past & Present*, No. 49, November, 1970.

29 *Children's Employment Commission*, 1840, Second Report, Appendix, Part II, under 'Stourbridge.'

30 *Ibid.*, evidence of R. J. Mason.

31 For the details of the schemes, see Eric Hopkins, 'Tremenheere's Prize Schemes in the Mining Districts 1851–1859', *History of Education Society Bulletin*, no. 15, Spring, 1975.

32 *Reports of Inspectors of Factories*, October, 1875.

33 *Enquiry in to the State of Popular Education in England*, 1861, Vol. II, Report of Assistant Commissioner George Coote, p. 250.

34 See the interesting section on Education in John Burnett, *Destiny Obscure*, 1982.

35 Hopkins, 'Old Swinford Hospital School', p. 184.

36 Hurt, *Education in Evolution*, pp. 202–4. It should also be mentioned that just over 30 per cent of the two million schoolchildren in 1851 were in private schools, not church schools, though Sunday schools were still flourishing in 1851, with 75.4 per cent of working-class children attending them (Anne Digby and Peter Searby, *School and Society in Nineteenth-Century England*, 1981, pp. 5, 29).

37 Hurt, *Education in Evolution*, p. 208.

38 David E. Mole, 'Challenge to the Church: Birmingham 1815–65', in H. J. Dyos and Michael Wolff, *The Victorian City: Images and Realities*, Vol. II, 1973, p. 822.

39 R. C. K. Ensor, *England 1870–1914*, 1936, p. 137.

40 Hugh McLeod, *Religion and the Working Class in Nineteenth Century Britain*, 1984, p. 9.

41 On the accuracy of the religious census, see K. S. Inglis, 'Patterns of Worship in 1851', *Journal of Ecclesiastical History*, XI, 1950; W. S. Pickering, 'The 1851 religious census – a useless experiment?', *British Journal of Sociology*, XVIII, 1967 and D. M. Thompson, 'The 1851 religious census: problems and possibilities', *Victorian Studies*, XI, 1967–8.

42 Horace Mann, *Religious Worship in England and Wales*, 1854, p. 93.

43 F. Engels, *The Condition of the Working Class in England* (ed. W. O. Henderson and W. H. Chaloner), 1958, p. 141.

44 E. L. Woodward, *The Age of Reform 1815–1870*, 1938, p. 483.

45 E. R. Wickham, *Church and People in an Industrial City*, 1957, p. 92; K. S. Inglis, *Churches and the Working Classes in Victorian England*, 1963, p. 323; Harold Perkin, *The Origins of Modern English Society, 1780–1880*, 1969, Chapters IV and IX.

46 These arguments are set out in my 'Religious Dissent in Black Country Industrial Villages in the First Half of the Nineteenth Century', *Journal of Ecclesiastical History*, Vol. 34, No. 3, July, 1983.

47 Hopkins, '*Religious Dissent*'; G. Robson, 'Between Church and Country: Contrasting Patterns of Churchgoing in the early Victorian Black Country', in D. Baker (ed.), *The Church in Town and Country*, Studies in Church History, XVI, 1979.

48 Hopkins, *Birmingham*, pp. 168, 163–4.

49 Burnett, John, (ed.), *Destiny Obscure: Autobiographies of Childhood, Education and Family from the 1820s to the 1920s*, 1982, p. 142.

50 *Ibid.* This book has a most helpful section on Sunday Schools, (pp. 140–2).

51 Estimated attendance in 1851 in the thirty-four towns with a population of between 20,000 and 30,000 was 39.5 per cent, as compared with 27.2 per cent in towns over 100,000 and 25.4 per cent in London. Perkin, *The Origins of Modern English Society*, p. 201.

52 R. F. Wearmouth, *Methodism and the Struggle of the Working Classes 1850–1900*, 1953, p. 105; Inglis, *Churches and The Working Classes*, p. 12; S. Mayor, *The Churches and the Labour Movement*, 1967, p. 15; A. D. Gilbert, *Religion and Society in Industrial England: church, chapel, and social change 1740–1914*, 1976, p. 65; McLeod, *Religion and the Working Class*, p. 26.

53 B. I. Coleman, *The Church of England in the Mid-Nineteenth Century: A Social Geography* (Historical Association pamphlet no. 98, 1980), p. 41.

54 *Ibid.*, p. 39.

55 It may be noted that Professor Burnett considers that for a high proportion of children, the church or chapel was a dominant influence on their childhood (*Destiny Obscure*, p. 37).

56 *Children's Employment Commission*, 1862, Third Report, pp. xvi–xvii.

57 *Home Office Papers*, *Census Papers*, *Ecclesiastical Returns* (HO129), for the Stourbridge Union. Full attendance figures for the district are given in the article referred to in note 46.

Part III

Deprived children 1800–1914

Chapter Six

Children and the Poor Law

There are two main reasons why the Poor Law was of such importance in the history of working-class children in the nineteenth century: the first is that throughout the century social services of the modern kind were almost entirely absent, so that the parent of any child in need would have to turn to the only official welfare agency of the time, the poor law authorities. Secondly, it is well-known that the nineteenth century saw enormous and unprecedented social changes. Population grew at a previously unparalleled rate, doubling in the first half of the century, and nearly doubling again in the second half. The result was a predominantly youthful society, and great floods of children; children under the age of fourteen constituted at least a third of the total population, and for most of the period nearly 40 per cent.[1] Moreover, society was in a highly volatile state, being transformed from a mainly agricultural community in 1800 to one based on industry and commerce by 1900, as the great industrial towns developed in the Midlands and the North. It was an age of extraordinary change, all based on Britain's industrial supremacy – as Kinglake's Turkish pasha puts it in *Eothen* (1844), 'Whirr, whirr! All by wheels! Whiz! Whiz! All by steam!'[2] – and inevitably the growth of an industrial capitalist economy was accompanied by booms and slumps, some of the latter being severe and prolonged, as in the early 1840s. Nor was economic depression confined to industry, for agriculture was in a depressed state for most of the period between the end of the French Wars in 1815 and the mid-century. So the working classes suffered during slumps, and so did their children. The history of working-class children in the nineteenth century cannot be written without reference to the Poor Law, and in particular to the workhouse.

At the beginning of the century, the care of the poor was administered under a system of relief dating back to the end of the sixteenth century, and commonly referred to as the Elizabethan Poor Law, or simply the Old Poor Law.[3] This provided for the care of the poor in each parish by elected officials known as overseers, the cost of the system being met by a poor rate levied on all householders in the parish. There were four major classes of paupers: the able-bodied, who in return for relief were supposed to work in the workhouse; the sick and aged, who could be relieved in the workhouse itself, or in almshouses, or in their own homes; the children, who were apprenticed at a suitable age; and the idle, or beggars, who were to receive punishment in a house of correction, usually the same building as the workhouse. In practice, a good deal of outdoor relief was given, usually because it was cheaper and easier to administer than taking the applicant into the workhouse. This parish-based method of relieving the poor was well suited to the needs of an agricultural population and served its purpose reasonably well throughout the seventeenth century, though in the eighteenth century certain administrative changes took place. In the early part of the century there was a growing tendency to incorporate groups of parishes by local act of parliament, thereby permitting the setting-up of a larger workhouse serving a wider area. At the same time, attempts were made to restrict relief to indoor relief in the workhouse. By 1834 (a turning point in the history of the Poor Law, as will be seen later), there were about 125 incorporations of this kind.

Towards the end of the eighteenth century Gilbert's Act, 1782 made it easier to establish unions of workhouses without the aid of a special local act, and at the same time it encouraged a return to outdoor relief. An additional number of about 67 unions resulted from this act, covering 924 parishes. Another important development a few years later (in 1795) was an extension of the existing practice of supplementing inadequate wages, named after its place of origin in Berkshire, the Speenhamland system. This was intended to make low wages up to a tolerable living wage, dependent on the size of a man's family and the price of bread. As such, it was a specialised form of outdoor relief, and was employed widely in agricultural districts, especially during the French Wars (1793–1815). If we pause and sum up at this point, we find that at the beginning of the nineteenth century working-class children might be relieved through the Poor Law in several different ways. Outside the workhouse, their parents might obtain help, dependent on the policy of the local overseers, in the form of small cash doles (or payments in kind). These doles might be in the form of supplementary additions to wages varying with the size of the family, or they might even be simple child allowances, usually paid for the third child onwards. Inside the workhouse, there were always numerous children; some were there because their parents had become destitute, and there was nowhere else for them to go. Others were orphans, or children deserted by their parents, or bastards taken into the house by the overseers. All these children might equally well be boarded out. One last and separate class of workhouse children were those who were apprenticed at the age of seven or eight.

What were conditions like for children in the workhouse under the Old Poor Law, which remained in force until 1834? Two preliminary points should perhaps be made: the first is that not all parishes had workhouses. The population of a rural parish might be so small that it was not worthwhile erecting a workhouse. Applicants for relief needing accommodation might be put into rented cottages, while others were simply relieved in their own homes. The other point is that there were more than 15,000 parishes responsible for administering the Old Poor Law, and in consequence there was great variation from parish to parish both in the size of the workhouse and in the way it was administered. In fact, to use the words of one of the earliest modern historians of the Old Poor Law, a national Poor Law existed only on paper. Some workhouses were very large – Liverpool's house, for example, contained between 900 and 1,200 inmates in the period 1782–94,[4] while others were much smaller, with only a few hundred inmates. Still others accommodated a mere handful. Generally speaking, the largest workhouses were incorporated, and served a large area. The House of Industry at Gressinghall in Lincolnshire, which was opened in 1777, served fifty parishes. Whatever the size of the workhouse, children were likely to constitute a significant proportion of the total number of paupers – usually up to a half, and more than half in Gressinghall, where their numbers included about a hundred bastards.[5] Clearly, the numbers in any one workhouse would depend on a variety of factors, such as whether outdoor relief was given or not, the state of local agriculture and industry, and so on. In some places, relief was given partly in the workhouse, and partly at home. Birmingham, having a large incorporated workhouse, is an interesting example of this, with children continually coming and going in the workhouse. Thus births and deaths for the Birmingham workhouse at the end of the eighteenth century were as follows:

Year	*Births*				*Deaths*				
	Average No. in House	*Boys*	*Girls*	*Total*	*Men*	*Women*	*Boys*	*Girls*	*Total*
1794	640	43	20	63	41	57	40	24	162
1795	500	25	36	61	28	57	18	18	121
1796	464	25	16	41	27	39	8	8	82

But in addition to these children, parish pay was also given outside the workhouse to support 143 bastard children and 1,522 legitimate children. Children at nurse were also supported, paid for at 2*s* a week or if at home 1*s* 6*d* a week (further sums of outdoor relief were given in addition to 684 old and infirm widows, 550 soldiers' wives, and some wives of the militia).[6]

If the size of the workhouse varied from place to place, so did its condition. Some workhouses were dirty, infested, and badly run, for instance, one of the two houses at Bristol (the other was clean and comfortable), and the Oxford workhouse, though this was later reformed. The Wolverhampton workhouse may serve here as an example of the less salubrious workhouses at the beginning of the nineteenth century. Eden describes it as follows:

> The workhouse is an inconvenient building, with small windows, low rooms and dark staircases. It is surrounded by a high wall, that gives it the appearance of a prison, and prevents free circulation of air. There are 8 or 10 beds in each room, chiefly of flocks, and consequently retentive of all scents and very productive of vermin. The passages are in great want of whitewashing. No regular account is kept of births and deaths, but when smallpox, measles or malignant fevers make their appearance in the house, the mortality is very great. Of 131 inmates in the house, 60 are children.[7]

Other houses were much better than this. Newark workhouse was said to be one of the very best in England, with 'a degree of comfort and cleanliness which is seldom met with'. At Bradford (Wilts) the house had been much improved, and 'the apartments are now exceedingly neat and comfortable: the poor are kept clean and well-fed, but are made to work, or are punished'. Sometimes the running of the house was let out or farmed (in the jargon of the present day, 'privatised'), but although contractors were popularly supposed to run things on the cheap, this was not always so: St Albans was a farmed house, but was considered by Eden to be in good condition.

The workhouse at Shrewsbury was an example of one of the newer, incorporated workhouses.[8] It was first opened in 1784, and was based on an incorporation of six parishes. It contained 389 inmates when visited by Eden, and as it dispensed only very limited outdoor relief, in his words 'the number of young and stout is, as might be expected, very considerable'. As in the case of the other inmates, the boys' coats and waistcoats and all the girls' clothes were manufactured in the house. The children were taught to read and 'other useful branches', and were to have their hands and faces washed, and their hair combed every morning (we are not told when soap and water reached other parts of their bodies). During the first three and a half years after opening, 60 babies were admitted to the house, as well as 52 infants under two years of age and 356 children aged between two and fifteen. These together constituted about half the total admissions. In the same period, 42 babies were sent out to nurse, 61 children were apprenticed, and 78 sent into service; 38 children under fifteen years of age died. Clearly, a substantial part of the daily routine of the workhouse would be taken up with the care of the children. Although we are not told how far the older children were put to work, it seems likely that in a well-ordered workhouse of this kind they would have taken part in the spinning and weaving which was the work given to most of the adults.

What the food and discipline were like for children in the early nineteenth-century workhouses it is difficult to say. Ideas today about the treatment of workhouse children are too often coloured by literary memories of Oliver Twist and his experiences in the workhouse. As far as food is concerned, again it obviously varied from place to place, and would hardly be expected to be ample. Yet especially in times of scarcity, the food in the workhouse would usually be better than that eaten by the average, half-starved labourer. In most of the workhouses reported on in 1797, meat was served on two or three (or even more) days a week. At Newark, 'at dinner, all have as much bread and meat as they can eat, but are not allowed to take any away'; at Melton in Suffolk, where of the 289 inmates the majority were children, 'Children receive as much victuals as they can eat.' At Kingston upon Hull, the children's diet was as follows:

Breakfast milk and oatmeal, 5oz bread
Dinner Sunday and Thursday, 7oz meat, 5oz bread and potatoes
Monday, pease soup
Tuesday and Friday, 8oz flour, made into cakes or dumplings
Wednesday, hasty pudding, 2 oz treacle, 10 oz butter
Saturday, milk and oatmeal, barley made into frumenty

Supper Sunday, Thursday, broth, and 5oz bread
Monday, Wednesday, Saturday, bread and milk
Tuesday and Friday, milk and oatmeal, 5 oz bread[9]

The hasty pudding referred to here was made of oatmeal, water and salt, about 13 oz of meal to a quart of water. This was thought sufficient for two labourers. It was eaten with a little milk or beer poured on it, or with a little butter or treacle in the middle. Frumenty or furmenty was barley milk, made from barley with the husk taken off, boiled in water, and mixed with skimmed milk.[10]

As for discipline, it may be supposed that it was stricter in the larger, incorporated workhouses – the pauper palaces, as George Crabbe the poet called them in the late eighteenth century – than in the smaller, parish workhouses where the inmates might be well known to the staff. In some of these, the atmosphere might be very relaxed and even disorderly: in the Hampton workhouse in Middlesex, Eden reported

> Meat is served every day, with vegetables from the garden. The female paupers are not content with the ample allowance of food, and would be riotous without tea every morning. This is not allowed by the master, but they contrive to get tea and sugar, cups and teapots . . . the children are taught to read and say their prayers, but no kind of work seems going forward.[11]

Much would depend on the attitude of the overseers (or directors or guardians in incorporated workhouses) and of the workhouse master or governor. Presumably, too, the extent to which children would be kept at work was an important consideration. Most work schemes do not seem to have been taken very seriously, following the failure of plans earlier in the eighteenth century to make the workhouses financially self-supporting through the sale of goods manufactured in the house; but in 1800 able-bodied paupers were still supposed to do some work, and children were employed at knitting and spinning, or sent outside to work on farms or in local manufactories. Most work inside the house appears to have concentrated on the making of articles for use in the house itself, such as clothing for the paupers, as at Shrewsbury. In some places, the Elizabethan practice of badging the poor was still kept up, and even in the less rigorous regime in the Hampton workhouse inmates wore a red badge on their shoulders, marked PH (Parish of Hampton). Paupers were also badged at Newark, at Melton (Suffolk), and at Bradford (Wilts).[12]

From the age of seven or even earlier, children might be apprenticed until they were twenty-one, either within the parish to ratepayers, or at a distance beyond the parish. If within the parish, ratepayers were compelled to accept pauper apprentices but could avoid liability by payment of a fine. If outside the parish, the overseers enjoyed the advantage that such apprenticeship gave settlement under the Act of Settlement, that is, conferred the right to poor relief, thus shifting the burden of relief to the overseers where the apprenticeship was served. The more formal apprenticeship required the payment of a premium of £5 or so, and its terms were set out in indentures sworn before the magistrates, which would include provisions for a set of clothes when the apprenticeship was completed; but many apprenticeships were less formal than this, and were a convenient way for the parish authorities to shift responsibility for maintenance of the child to its new master (because apprentices commonly lived in, of course). Many workhouse children in country areas were apprenticed either to husbandry or housewifery, while in the towns they might be apprenticed to small masters in domestic workshops. Whatever the kind of apprenticeship, it was too often a kind of slave labour until the age of twenty-one, or in the case of females, until marriage or attaining the age of twenty-one.[13]

The treatment of the more unfortunate apprentices in agriculture and in workshop industry has been described and discussed in Chapter One, and it is not proposed to go over this ground again here. It is sufficient to say that although agricultural apprenticeship might not be so subject to abuse as industrial apprenticeship, it had its critics, and after lingering on in the West Country, disappeared altogether after the mid-nineteenth century. Workshop apprenticeship could result in much greater ill-treatment and cruelty, of a kind comparable to that inflicted in the new cotton factories. The children were often bastards, and had no parents to keep an eye on them; nor did the overseers supervise their apprenticeships. They were left to fend for themselves, and were fair game for cruel and sadistic masters. The worst and most notorious treatment was accorded the factory apprentices, as described in Chapter Three, and this led to the campaigns for factory reform. Altogether this aspect of the operation of the Old Poor Law is perhaps the most to be criticised, whatever the final verdict on the achievements and shortcomings of the old system might be.

What then can be said in summing up about the care of children as a whole under the Old Poor Law – that is, up to its abolition in the mid-1830s? Undoubtedly outdoor relief could be a lifeline to poor parents in times of hardship. Admittedly, the relief given was very limited, and applicants were at the mercy of the overseers, whose attitude could vary from benevolence to simple indifference or even worse. Yet the poor and their children could be and were in fact helped in a variety of ways, from the supplementing of wages, to child allowances, grants for medicine and appliances and payments in kind such as coal, clothing and blankets. There are many recent local studies – for example, for south Staffordshire, Worcestershire, and the North Riding of Yorkshire – which support the view that the Old Poor Law was often administered in a humane way, by overseers who were part of the local community and understood the needs of the poor, whether destitute, sick, aged or young.[14] Nor was the help available regarded by the poor as humiliating or shameful; it was thought to be a proper contribution by the more affluent members of the community to those who had fallen on hard times. Indeed, the poor law commissioners appointed under the Royal Commission on the Poor Laws, 1832, found that many of the paupers they questioned regarded their relief as a right, and produced scraps of paper certifying payment of relief as evidence of this right. According to William Cobbett, the general view of the Old Poor Law in the 1820s and early 1830s was that it was part of the Englishman's birthright. Thus there was little shame in accepting relief, and Professor F. M. L. Thompson goes so far as to refer to the popular attitude to the Old Poor Law as one of affectionate attachment.[15]

This did not apply, however, to attitudes to the larger workhouses. Here there is no doubt that the large-scale incorporated workhouse was greatly disliked as being too much like a prison. As Crabbe put it

That large loud clock, which tolls each dreaded hour,
Those gates and locks and all those signs of power,
It is a prison with a milder name,
Which few inhabit without dread and shame.[16]

So it is necessary to distinguish between the Old Poor Law in its small-scale local form, relieving more in their own homes than in the workhouse, and the forbidding district workhouse accommodating several hundred paupers drawn from a wide area, and often severely limiting outdoor relief. Such Bastilles were harbingers of the new regime to be set up after the passing of the Poor Law Amendment Act, 1834.

On the whole, the Old Poor Law probably served the majority of its claimants well by the standards of the day, and of these claimants, children constituted a substantial proportion. To judge from the workhouses described by Eden in 1797, as we have seen, children numbered up to half of their inmates. According to Professor Mark Blaug, the Old Poor Law, at its best, provided a welfare state in miniature. This may be to overstate the case, and so far as children are concerned, the policy of apprenticeship as it worked in practice makes the statement questionable. Nevertheless, there is plenty of evidence to show humane treatment of the various classes of paupers. The problem was that, as will be seen in the next section, increasing doubts arose in the first decades of the nineteenth century as to the working of the system as a whole. It came to be believed that not only was there too much outdoor relief but that the workhouse itself lacked discipline and provided far too high a standard of living for its inmates. In contrast to all that Eden had to say about the workhouses, it is instructive to see what the Poor Law Report of 1834 said about indoor relief. It is clear that the report as a whole was heavily biased against the Old Poor Law system. The wilfulness of workhouse children is stressed in the evidence of Mr W. Lee, the master of the large St Pancras workhouse with more than a thousand inmates:

> There are 300 children; if we get them places, they throw them up, or misconduct themselves so as to lose them, and return to the workhouse as a matter of course because they prefer the security and certainty of that mode of life to the slightest exercise of forebearance or diligence. As little or no classification can take place, the younger soon acquire all the bad habits of the older, and become for the most part as vitiated.[17]

Then as to the condition of the workhouses generally, the report sums up

> But in the greater number of cases, it is a large almshouse, in which the young are trained in idleness, ignorance, and vice; the able-bodied maintained in sluggish sensual ignorance; the aged and respectable exposed to all the misery that is incident to dwelling in such a society, without government or classification; and the whole body of inmates subsidised on food far exceeding both in kind and amount, not merely the diet of the independent labourer, but that of the majority of the persons who contribute to their support.[18]

This was a gross exaggeration, of course, but it is clear that if the authors of the report had their way, the old Poor Law system was doomed, and along with it the care of the children as it had been practised and developed over the previous 230-odd years.

What had brought about such hostility to the whole of the Poor Law since Eden had reported in 1797? It is not the purpose of this chapter to give a general account of the operation of the Poor Laws in the nineteenth century, but some explanation of the reasons why the Poor Law Amendment Act was passed in 1834 is necessary if the nature of the New Poor Law is to be understood. Briefly, the rising cost of poor relief during and after the Napoleonic Wars led to the appointment of a Select Committee which published a critical report in 1817. This was followed by Sturges Bourne's Act, 1819, by which minor administrative reforms in granting relief might be instituted. In 1824, another select committee reported, again adversely, drawing attention once more to the subsidising of agricultural wages, these wages having dropped to remarkably low levels, especially in the south of England. By 1826 the cost of poor relief began to rise again, and by 1831 was over £7 million annually. But it was not merely the ever-increasing cost of maintaining the poor which aroused middle-class protest: the whole system of paying relief was thought to be wrong, for it was alleged that subsidising wages simply demoralised the labourer, who was thus given no incentive to work. What was wanted was an end to all such forms of allowances, and for relief to be provided only in a strictly-run workhouse. With ideas of this kind in mind, and spurred on by the outbreak of agricultural riots in Kent (the Swing Riots) in 1830, the Government appointed a Royal Commission on the Poor Laws in February, 1832. This produced a remarkable report based on extensive enquiries which was published in 1834. This famous report was followed by the passing of the Poor Law Amendment Act in the same year.

Historians have argued at great length over the findings of the Poor Law Commission, from Sidney and Beatrice Webb (writing in the 1920s) onwards. In 1926 Professor Tawney called their report 'brilliant, influential and wildly unhistorical'; Professor Blaug has described it as 'wildly unstatistical'. The substance of their criticism is simply that the authors of the report ignored the great mass of evidence collected, and their report was based on their own preconceived ideas and prejudices. Since Professor Blaug's pioneering work, much further research has largely confirmed such criticisms of the report.[19] Nevertheless, the Poor Law Amendment Act, 1834, followed its recommendations in setting up a new central authority – three Poor Law Commissioners – while locally parishes were grouped into unions, each managed by a Board of Guardians assisted by salaried officials. The new principles of administration were quite clear. With certain minor exceptions, all outdoor relief should end – 'all relief whatever to able-bodied persons or to their families otherwise than in well-regulated workhouses . . . should be declared unlawful, and shall cease'.[20] Secondly, life in the workhouse should be made deliberately harsh as a deterrent. The report puts this rather delicately in one place – 'that the condition of the pauper should in no case be so eligible as the condition of persons of the lowest class subsisting on the fruits of their own industry'.[21] In another place, it is spelt out more brutally – 'that his situation should not be made really or apparently so eligible as the situation of the independent labourer of the lowest class . . . every penny bestowed that tends to render the condition of the pauper more eligible than that of the independent labourer, is a bounty on indolence and vice'.[22] Thus the New Poor Law was to be based on the two administrative maxims of the 'Workhouse Test' (relief only in the workhouse), and 'Less Eligibility' (a deterrent workhouse).

How were the children hitherto cared for under the Old Poor Law affected by all this? In fact, the report had little to say about children in general, such was its preoccupation with outdoor relief and the able-bodied labourer. Its authors did not seem to be very much concerned with the treatment of children in the workhouse, and the only extensive reference to them is in the passage quoted above regarding the children in the St Pancras workhouse. Otherwise, the children were mentioned only occasionally, as when it is stated that nailing families in Old Swinford in the West Midlands believed that large families, whether legitimate or illegitimate, were an advantage (as it happens, research has shown that nailing families in this parish were no larger than other families); and again it is said that in Suffolk the desertion of children was encouraged because the parish would always support them.[23] Apprenticeship is mentioned, but only to say that the commissioners had received less information on this subject than on any other; the Central Board was to make regulations regarding apprenticeship, and later on enquire into their effectiveness.[24] The only lengthy section regarding children relates to bastardy. Here it was proposed that the law should be reformed since it operated unjustly as far as putative fathers were concerned, and in some cases higher allowances were paid for illegitimate children than for legitimate ones. Some women were quite brazen about claiming relief for bastards. The clerk to the magistrates at Swaffham, Suffolk reported that 'A woman of Swaffham was reproached by the magistrate, Mr Young, with the burdens she brought upon the parish upon the occasion of her appearing before him with her seventh bastard. She replied, "I am not going to be disappointed in my company with men to save the parish." '[25] In theory, children were not directly and immediately affected by the New Poor Law. In the workhouse, for example, 'less eligibility' was supposed to be applied to the able-bodied adult, and not to the young, the sick or the aged; but in practice it might well be otherwise. Outside the workhouse, children were affected by the determination to restrict outdoor relief, especially the subsidising of wages, though no immediate changes were proposed in the apprenticing of pauper children. So as far as children are concerned, therefore, the early years of the New Poor Law saw no radical changes in their treatment, but a tightening-up of discipline in the new union workhouses was only to be expected.

In fact, generalisation about the treatment of pauper children during the first few years after the 1834 Act is difficult; the one certainty is that it often varied from union to union. The commissioners were faced with the immense task of converting a system based on 4,000 or so parish poor houses or workhouses (some of them already incorporated by local act of parliament) into a system based on about 600 union workhouses, all of them administered by Boards of Guardians applying the 'less eligibility' and 'workhouse test' rules. This took years to accomplish, and some of the new union workhouses were not built till the mid-century. There were still several unions without workhouses even in 1868.[26] The 1834 Act was enforced without much difficulty in the south of England, but in the North it was a different matter. Here the Old Poor Law had operated without many of the abuses alleged to exist in the southern counties. Speenhamland was not widespread, and outdoor relief was often employed to help industrial workers thrown temporarily out of work in large numbers during trade depressions. The attempt to replace a system which already seems to have worked adequately enough, and in particular the attempt to abolish outdoor relief, provoked rioting and a massive anti-poor law campaign run by the Anti-Poor Law Association. Stories of ill-treatment of workhouse inmates under the new 'less eligibility' regime circulated widely, many of the more sensational being quite untrue. On the other hand, there is no doubt that some paupers, including children, were treated cruelly, though not necessarily because of the attempt to enforce 'less eligibility'. For example, according to *The Times* in 1840, reporting on conditions in the Rochester workhouse

> On Sunday, the Master flogged little Jemmy [a pauper's illegitimate child, then two years of age] with a birch rod, so that the *child carried the marks a month*, because it cried for its mother, who was gone to church, and for its little brother, who was that day put into breeches, and taken away from the children's ward.[27]

The master was later prosecuted, and found guilty of assault.

Generally speaking, it proved impossible in practice to enforce the two administrative principles encouraged by the Poor Law Report, 1834. Attempts were certainly made to impose the workhouse test, and restrict relief to those so desperate that they were prepared to enter the house, but it was simply not possible to accommodate all within the workhouse in times of local mass unemployment, so that outdoor relief continued to be given in return for a task of work, usually of a monotonous and distasteful nature, such as stone-breaking or oakum-picking. There is the further point that maintaining paupers on outdoor relief was distinctly cheaper than providing for them in the workhouse. Thus many pauper children continued to be supported on outdoor relief, as will be seen later. As for conditions within the workhouse, it was similarly not a practical proposition to deter applicants for relief by providing a standard of living below that of the worst-off independent labourer, simply because his standard of living was already at near-starvation level. In reality, however spartan a diet adopted in the new workhouses, it was usually better than that eaten by most of the inmates before entering the workhouse; and this was largely true both before and after 1834. The real deterrent in the union workhouse was not so much the food, but the discipline imposed, the workhouse uniform and the prison-like haircuts, which made the workhouse and indeed the whole Poor Law apparatus so disliked and feared by the working classes – a remarkable example of the conditioning of public attitudes by the Government of the day.

Of course, as we have seen, 'less eligibility' was supposed to apply only to the able-bodied (whose numbers were certainly reduced in the workhouse), and not to the children or the sick, infirm and aged. But in some of the older workhouses conditions were very lax, so that the new discipline must have come as a shock. In the Deptford workhouse before 1834 we are told that when any discipline was applied 'the boys were broken-spirited, cringing and deceitful'; when there was less physical correction, 'the girls were refractory, obstinate and insolent . . . both boys and girls were equally addicted to lying, swearing and petty thieving.'[28] After 1834 discipline was tightened up, and during the early years under the central direction of the Poor Law Commissioners (1834–47) a stream of orders sought to impose a strict uniformity on children and adults alike. All who were aged seven and over, save the aged, sick and infirm, were to rise at 5 a.m. in the summer and 7 a.m. in the winter; all were to work ten hours a day in summer, and nine in winter. Education for the children was very limited – a teacher (who might be the matron, porter or an aged pauper) could be appointed if the Board of Guardians thought fit. According to the Webbs, all had to suffer a uniform regime, including of course the children, and in spite of the intentions of the report, there was no segregation of the children at first, so that they were in the same building as lunatics, vagrants, nursing mothers and criminals.[29]

These impressions of a worsening of conditions for children in the new workhouses were strengthened at the time by the propaganda of the Anti-Poor Law Association, and by the fiction of the day, notably by Dickens's *Oliver Twist*, which was published in 1837 at the height of the agitation against the New Poor Law. In 1845 there was the notorious scandal over the administration of the Andover workhouse, where paupers fought over scraps of meat adhering to the bones which they had been set to grind – an ugly episode leading to a Select Committee of Enquiry, and to the replacement of the Poor Law Commissioners by a new central Poor Law Board in 1847. Further incidents occurred from time to time which caused concern about conditions in the workhouses of the new unions. As late as 1855 the children in the Bakewell workhouse were in such a poor state of health due to the literal application of instructions from London that the inspector protested and recommended a more nourishing diet and outdoor exercise.[30]

In the light of all this, there is no difficulty in presenting a very bleak picture of life for workhouse children under the New Poor Law. Yet it is clear enough that in the nature of things there was considerable variation in conditions from one workhouse to another, and that in some areas there were positive attempts to provide a good environment for the children. In Norfolk and Suffolk the local authorities already had experience of large incorporated workhouses, and lengthy accounts of these workhouses were given in 1837–38 by the assistant commissioner, Dr James Kay (later Sir James Kay-Shuttleworth), a great believer in the value of working-class education, and later secretary to the Committee of Council for Education. According to Kay, 1,906 children between the ages of two and sixteen were maintained and educated in the 35 unions of Norfolk and Suffolk. More specifically, in December, 1837, there were the following categories of pauper children: 443 bastards, 382 orphans, 279 deserted by their fathers, 54 deserted by both parents, 171 with fathers in prison, 116 children of persons on relief on account of mental or bodily infirmity, 144 of able-bodied widows in the workhouse, 36 of able-bodied widowers also resident, and 122 of large families, admitted to relieve the parents. Some stayed for only short periods of time. Of those aged two to sixteen, 193 stayed for less than a fortnight, 223 for a fortnight to a month, 548 for between one month and three months, 307 for three months, 275 for six months but less than a year, and 474 for more than a year. This analysis gives a good idea of the transient nature of the child pauper population in the East Anglian workhouses in the late 1830s. The long-stay children – obviously a special category – were composed of bastards, orphans, children deserted by their parents, or children with parents on relief because of mental or bodily infirmity.[31]

In the matter of discipline, Kay declared that in the workhouse schools in Norfolk and Suffolk discipline was in every respect milder than in any parish school. He was then asked about the strictness of the workhouse regime as it affected the children:

> Are not the children subject to the restraint and discipline which the adults are subject to? – They are not.
> What is the difference? – They are allowed to walk in the garden. Sometimes they walk out with the teacher to take exercise. Sometimes they attend the parish church. They are furnished with the means to amuse themselves in the yards: the whole discipline is not intended in the slightest respect to be a discipline of restraint, but simply one which will tend to their moral and general improvement.
> And are they never whipped? – I will not say they are never whipped . . .
> Do you think that under any system of training you can make the children love the workhouse better than the cottage of their parents? – It would be most injurious if this occurred as the extinction of all the natural affection between parents and children.[32]

The last two questions suggest, perhaps, that the committee thought that Kay was painting too glowing a picture – the modern reader might also be inclined to take his evidence with a pinch of salt; but even when allowance is made for his enthusiasm, it still seems that some attempts were being made to treat the children considerately and also to give them some schooling. Although in the early days there might be little or no instruction of the children, workhouse schools were not confined to Norfolk and Suffolk. For example, in the Nottingham Union the British and Foreign system was used, and in particular, 200 children of widows were fed as well as educated. They had breakfast at eight o'clock, dined at twelve or one o'clock, had supper at five o'clock, and then went home. In the Westhampnett Union in Sussex the boys went into school after breakfast at about 8.30 or 9.00 till 11.30 a.m., when they played till dinner. After dinner, the young ones returned to school, while the older children worked in the garden or with the carpenter, shoemakers or the tailor. These children were taught writing as well as reading and arithmetic.[33]

One charge levelled at the New Poor Law was that it broke up families who were driven into the new union workhouse, and there separated. In fact, and contrary to the recommendations of the Report, workhouses continued to be mixed, though, as might be expected, there was segregation of the sexes. Certainly families were not permitted to live together as families, but neither was this usual under the Old Poor Law. In Bradford in 1837 the widows were separated from their children when the latter were five or six years old, but were said to be able to see them whenever they pleased. In Droxford, the man was separated from his wife, but the children stayed with the mother, and he had access to them 'at all reasonable hours of the day'. At Farnham, mothers had access to children 'at the proper hours', and were always permitted to nurse them when they were unwell.[34] In the Norfolk and Suffolk workhouses, we are told, the mothers could see the girls at breakfast, dinner and supper, and the fathers could see the boys at the same meals. Whenever a parent wished to see a child, he or she could do so, if application was made at reasonable hours, and it did not interfere with the management of the house. Children under two were always with their mothers at night, and infants were never separated from their mothers.[35] What is not clear is how far seeing children at mealtimes included talking to them; and the general impression given by the evidence is that access was often limited, though not actually forbidden. Families were not really broken up by the New Poor Law, and if the figures given by Dr Kay were at all typical, the majority of children stayed in the workhouse for only three months or less; but the segregation of the sexes and the operation of institutional rules made easy access difficult, and emphasised the prison-like atmosphere of the workhouses.

So much for workhouse conditions in the earlier days of the New Poor Law. Before moving on to the mid-years of the century, a word must be said about pauper children on outdoor relief. They constituted by far the largest category of pauper children – four-fifths of all destitute children were relieved outside the workhouse, and on any one day during the whole period from 1834 to 1909, their numbers rarely fell below 200,000 and in some years exceeded 300,000.[36] So although attention is understandably concentrated on the workhouse children, in fact far more children were subject to the working of the poor law outside the workhouse than inside. On the whole, the central records of the poor law are of little use in describing the condition of these children. The Webbs go so far as to claim that there is a complete lack of information on this subject. Of course, it was not the duty of the Guardians to enquire in detail into home conditions, but simply to grant relief when sufficient cause was shown. So outdoor children appear only infrequently in the national records, as, for example, when the Poor Law Board at first refused to permit the payment of school fees for these children, but later had to allow it under Denison's Act, 1855. Forster's Act in 1870 confirmed this, and made school attendance a condition of relief. Otherwise it must be assumed that as the standard of living of labourers even when in work was very low, when out of work and on outdoor relief it must have approached starvation levels. There is no doubt that any allowances given in respect of children were very meagre, but it was not until the beginning of the next century, as will be seen later, that there was any investigation into the state of children on outdoor relief.

To turn now to workhouse conditions for children in the middle decades of the nineteenth century and under the authority of the Poor Law Board from 1847 to 1871: during these years the principal development was the improvement in education of the children. In 1848 the Poor Law (Schools) Act permitted unions to combine together to set up district schools in the form of large boarding schools. Such schools were to have the advantage of removing the children from the harmful influence of adults in the mixed workhouse, and also of establishing schools of sufficient size to allow efficient and economic administration. They contained up to a thousand children (sometimes even more), and became known as 'barrack' schools. They were built most rapidly in London, and by 1856 78 per cent of London's workhouse children were in separate schools. A model for these schools had been provided by two large private pauper schools in London – Mr Aubin's school in Norwood, and Mr Drouet's school at Tooting, which housed 1,394 pauper children from all over London. District schools were also to be found in the larger provincial towns, though by no means universally, and also in some rural areas as well. Smaller unions were usually discouraged by the expense of building district schools, and preferred to retain their own schools on the existing workhouse site.

This development was clearly an advance, and it parallels the spread of schooling in the middle years of the nineteenth century, described in the previous chapter. However, it was patchy in nature, and in hundreds of unions the children were still taught and housed in the workhouse itself. Two comments are appropriate here: the first is that the idea persisted of education as a means to a social end, not as something of worth in itself, or as the right of the children. Education of pauper children in district schools was thought to be the best way of protecting them from the malign influence of adult paupers and of making sure that when they grew up they could earn their own living and not be a burden on the poor rates. The Poor Law Inspector E. C. Tufnell, himself an advocate of district schools, put it succinctly in his report for 1868 on the Home District:

> This is a pleasing contrast with the system of workhouse schools, whence of all the children launched into the world after their so-called education, two-thirds turn out badly . . . The main secret for destroying hereditary pauperism . . . is to well-educate the children apart from adult paupers, and then to send them into the world, as far removed as possible from their own miserable relations and parishes, where they have known nothing than vice and misery.[37]

This statement of opinion explains clearly enough why Tufnell considered careers in the navy, army and the merchant service so peculiarly suitable for this class of children.

The second comment is that although there were complaints that pauper children were being given advantages in education over those of children of the independent labourer, in practice only half of the school day was given to academic work, the other half being given to so-called industrial training. This might take the form of workshop training, for example in shoemaking, or consist of agricultural work. The Quatt workhouse (part of the Bridgnorth Union in Shropshire) was often praised for the employment of boys on its farm, as was the Atcham Union, near Shrewsbury, where the farm was run by an elderly farm labourer.[38] The Wokingham District School received a glowing report in the tenth annual report of the Poor Law Board.[39] It was said that this school of sixty-nine boys and eighty-six girls improved yearly in efficiency:

> The girls perform all the household duties, laundry work, etc.; and a certain number are regularly employed in the kitchen and dairy. For the boys, the Guardians occupy ten acres of land, which are wholly cultivated by them; and they keep thereon four cows and a number of pigs. The net profit on these ten acres for the year ending Lady Day, 1857 (after deducting £4 an acre for the rent and the rates and taxes) was £182 15*s*, or £18 5*s* 6*d* per acre.

No doubt training of this kind was helpful in obtaining jobs subsequently, and it was stated that academic work did not suffer from the physical labour – it was actually improved by it, it was said, notwithstanding the reduction of hours devoted to school instruction.[40] Mr Tufnell wrote enthusiastically of the benefits of the vocational training of pauper children:

> When I see these shoeless, half-starved Arabs turning somersaults in the streets, I long to send them to a district school where I would warrant to turn them out in two years worth at least 6*s* or 7*s* a week. The girls in these schools are all taught to wash, to sew, to cook, to clean, in short to do all that is usually required of a maid-servant; the boys are accustomed to labour, and their intellectual instruction alone is sufficient to allow them to write good hands, to keep accounts with accuracy, and they often become clerks, telegraph assistants, and many are turned out as musicians into the army and navy as previously observed.[41]

This may well have been to claim too much, though, as suggested earlier, training of some kind was of use afterwards when the children left the workhouse and sought employment. In spite of Tufnell's advocacy, the barrack schools never became very numerous, and according to the Webbs, there were only about sixty separate poor law schools in the second half of the nineteenth century, accommodating about 12,000 children. This meant that children were still in the general mixed workhouse in more than five-sixths of the unions.[42] However, it should be observed that this may be misleading, and the numbers of children still living in the workhouse at the end of the century was relatively small, as will be seen later.

One other way in which children might be helped to obtain positions on quitting the workhouse was by apprenticeship. By the mid-nineteenth century, poor law apprenticeship does not seem to have been regarded with any great favour, and in spite of the reference in the 1834 report to the need to draw up regulations, little was done for some time. In 1844, when specifying the duties of masters and other conditions of apprenticeship, the commissioners attempted to abolish premiums for children over fourteen, but had to withdraw their proposal; but in the same year, compulsory apprenticeship to householders was done away with. Thereafter no general rules or orders regulating apprenticeship were issued during the second half of the nineteenth century, and apprenticeship steadily declined under the Guardians, surviving only in certain unions such as Norwich.[43] The policy of the central authorities appears to have been not to encourage apprenticeship under the poor law, but not actually to forbid it. In 1851, the Poor Law (Apprentices)

Act was passed to prevent cruelty to apprentices; and in 1856 the Poor Law Board laid it down that no apprenticeship to domestic service was to be permitted, since this was not a 'trade or business'.[44] However, apprenticeship of boys over the age of thirteen to the merchant marine was specifically permitted by the Merchant Shipping Act, 1835.

It is not entirely clear why poor law apprenticeship was not employed more widely under the New Poor Law. It is true that the compulsory acceptance of apprentices by householders within the parish was much disliked, though fines imposed for non-acceptance were often a useful source of income for the Guardians. On the other hand, the payment of premiums could be an expense to them, and apprenticeship within the union always gave a settlement therein and a right to claim assistance. Of course, the notorious ill-treatment of poor law apprentices in both factories and workshops may have hardened attitudes to poor law apprenticeship, and the development of industrial training presumably appeared to be a more manageable and ultimately cheaper alternative at a time when apprenticeship as an institution was declining nationally. At all events, poor law apprenticeship was not seen as a major mean of settling pauper children in jobs in the second half of the nineteenth century.

In summing up the changes in the workhouse under the Poor Law Board, it is evident that by the 1860s the greatest change was in the increasing emphasis on education and the provision of district schools, though it must be emphasised that only a small proportion of unions built them. Although they attracted criticism later in the century, some of them seem to have been rather more cheerful institutions than one might expect. Dickens reported very favourably on the Manchester Board's school at Swinton.

> We went into the play-ground of the junior department, where more than a hundred and fifty children were assembled. Some were enjoying themselves in the sunshine, some were playing at marbles, others were frisking cheerfully. These children ranged from 4 to 7 years of age. There were some as young as a year and a half in the school. The greater number were congregated at one end of the yard, earnestly watching the proceedings of the master who was giving fresh water to three starlings in cages that stood on the gravel.[45]

Nevertheless, by the 1860s it was beginning to be realised that there were relatively few able-bodied adult paupers in the workhouses, and that instead they housed a variety of unfortunates to whom it made little sense to apply the 'less eligibility' rule. This was recognised by Dr

Edward Smith in his *Report on Dietaries of Inmates of Workhouses* in 1867. According to Smith

> At present, those who enjoy the advantages of these institutions are almost solely such as may fittingly receive them, viz. the aged and the infirm, the destitute sick, and children. Workhouses are now asylums and infirmaries, and not places where work is necessarily exacted in return for food, clothing, and shelter.[46]

In the light of this, increasing attention began to be paid to the different classes of inmates, not least to the children. They certainly benefited from a number of improvements recommended in Poor Law Board circulars in 1868. Where there were large numbers of children in the workhouse there were to be day-rooms, covered play-sheds in the yards and industrial work-rooms in addition to the schoolrooms. Food was also to be improved, with detailed suggestions as to actual diets, which were a marked improvement on the six specimen diets provided by the commissioners in 1836; under Diet No. 1 in 1836 there were three days of the week on which the midday meal consisted solely of 1½ pints of soup, without bread or any other supplement. In 1868 children aged nine to sixteen were to be separately dieted, if the Guardians thought fit. They were not to have rice pudding as a dinner, unless under nine. Nor were they to have tea or coffee except for supper on Sunday, but milk at breakfast and supper, and two or three ounces of bread at bedtime. How far these recommendations were carried out in practice cannot be known, but it is at least clear that real efforts were made in the late 1860s to improve conditions generally in the workhouses.[47] These efforts hardly made the workhouse less of a place to be feared by working-class children, but they do show an increasing awareness of the need to give more specialised care to the different classes of inmates, of whom children continued to form a large proportion.

To turn lastly to conditions from 1871 onwards, when the functions of the Poor Law Board were transferred to the new Local Government Board, the story here is one of further attempts to provide better care for indoor child paupers, but with little done for children on outdoor relief. This is true despite the fact that Guardians acquired more powers to protect outdoor children; for example, Guardians were directed by statute in 1868 to bring actions against parents neglecting their children, and this was confirmed by the Cruelty to Children Act, 1889. Guardians could also make orders for the supply of food under the School Meals Act, 1906. Nevertheless, their responsibilities for the well-being of children on out-relief remained very limited. Interestingly enough, the Webbs defend the Guardians against criticism of the failure to do much for this class of children by saying that they could not possibly investigate the children's condition in any depth, and had never been told to do so.[48] But they later provide some striking evidence of the state of some of these children, who still numbered as many as 157,919 (excluding boarded-out and medical cases) in England and Wales on 1 January 1907. They constituted 16 per cent of the whole pauper host, four-fifths being children of widows, and one-eighth of deserted wives or where the husband was in prison or in hospital. In less than one-sixth of the cases investigated was the husband at home. Thus overall more than five-sixths of the children were deprived of a father's care. An extensive enquiry was carried out. The investigators noted the state of rooms, buildings, street and sanitary conditions. In many cases the children were measured and weighed, and the family income ascertained. According to the principal investigator, 'The children are under-nourished, many of them poorly dressed, and many barefooted. The houses are bare of furniture, for there is not money to buy sufficient food or boots, and any extra expense has to be met by selling or pawning furniture.'[49] From this it is apparent that the funds allowed by the Guardians were insufficient. Much blame was still attached to the unfortunate mothers, many of whom obviously had to contend with adverse circumstances, with no husband to help them. The mothers were classified by the investigators as (i) good and capable – there were roughly 16,700 in this class; (ii) good but incapable – about 23,000; (iii) slovenly and slipshod – 10,300; (iv) really bad – about 6,800. This last class of 'really bad' mothers were described as follows: 'People guilty of wilful neglect, sometimes drunkards or people of immoral behaviour; no woman has been put into this class of whom it was not fairly evident that she was unfit to have charge of the children.'[50] As for the numbers of children involved in the enquiry, there were 51,000 children in the 17,100 homes where the mothers were categorised as being slovenly and slipshod, and really bad; and another 119,000 in homes where the mothers were either good and capable, or good but incapable. Yet even in these last two categories the Webbs thought that there were few who would have been considered good enough to have been entrusted with boarded-out children. (In fact, the enquiry, which had examined nearly 60,000 mothers, had been extended to include boarded-out children as well.) All in all, only just over a quarter of all the mothers were thought to be really competent – that is, good and capable.

Presumably these results did not surprise those familiar with the findings of Booth's and Rowntree's enquiries, that a third of the working classes in London and York lived in real poverty. If these findings were anywhere near the truth, it was highly likely that widows and other single mothers dependent on poor relief would have children who were undernourished, to say the least. What is noticeable is that the desire to attribute wretched home conditions to the moral failings of the mothers persists into the twentieth century. There is also a lack of any acknowledgement that some of those failings might be the result of exhaustion and malnutrition due to the continual struggle to make both ends meet.

To turn next to the far less numerous class of indoor pauper children. As indicated earlier, efforts were made to give more specialised care to them by the provision of residential schools, but by the 1870s there was some reaction against the large barrack schools which were built. This was partly because of the way in which infections spread very swiftly in them, especially ophthalmia and ringworm, and partly because of the impersonal nature of their regime, especially as it affected the girls (this was referred to as 'institutionalism'). Mrs Senior wrote strongly on the ill-effects of both workhouse and district schools on the girls, alleging that 30 per cent of them turned out badly in later life. In fact. enquiries in 1862 showed that of the more than 20,000 adult pauper inmates in London, only 2.2 per cent had been in workhouse schools, and of the London prison population only 3.2 per cent had passed through workhouse schools, nearly half of them for less than a year.[51] A partial remedy for the alleged defects of the schools was found in accommodating the children in cottage homes, which were separate villas, but all on one site. Each cottage contained fifteen to twenty children, with their own house-father and house-mother. The Webbs thought that these homes ought really to be classified with the barrack schools, of which they were an improved type, but presumably they did provide a homelier atmosphere than the large district school. In Sheffield, further attempts to give the children a better home background were made in 1893 with the 'scattered home' system. These homes were ordinary dwelling-houses scattered about the suburbs of Sheffield and within easy reach of a local board school for the children. In 1896 there were nine such homes in Sheffield, two with 15 beds, one with 16 beds, three with 17 beds, two with 21 beds, and one with 28 beds. The advantage claimed for this system was again the provision of a family group, together with attendance at local schools, so that the children gained a better acquaintance with the outside world. Renewed efforts were made to treat the children as individuals. According to the departmental report of 1896:

> In the day-rooms are pigeon holes or lockers for the children's possessions and playthings, and in the bedrooms there is a box for each child containing its clothes . . . Every effort is made to cultivate the children's individuality, and the personal attention given to them renders it possible for their natural characteristics to be studied and guided aright.[52]

Similar plans were adopted by the Whitechapel Union, by the Bath Union and by a number of other more enlightened unions, though it took time for the idea of 'scattered homes' to spread.

By the end of the century there were still substantial numbers of children under poor authority care, as opposed to being on outdoor relief. About 10,000 children were in certificated schools, that is, schools taking various classes of children on charitable grounds, such as Roman Catholic children, Wesleyan and Jewish children, and the blind, deaf, dumb and crippled. In London, following an enquiry into London's poor law schools in 1894–96, children with mental problems were transferred to the Metropolitan Asylum Board.[53] Some children, mostly orphans or who had been deserted by their parents, were put out for adoption, the procedures being regulated by legislation in 1889 and 1899. Others were boarded out with individual families – 8,781 children in 1906 – while some were still being apprenticed.[54] Boarding-out was increasingly favoured by the end of the century, but in practice the numbers of children boarded out was still limited. This was due to the difficulty of finding suitable homes and foster parents, and also of providing suitable supervision.

The two biggest categories of children still directly under care were those on poor law premises, being in ordinary union schools, and those children under school age. As for the former, there seems to have been some improvement in workhouse schools around the turn of the century, and in 1897 the Local Government Board issued an order effectively limiting the time given to industrial training. By the time the schools were investigated by the Poor Law Commission in 1906–08 there had been 'an extraordinary all-round improvement' in them, according to the Webbs.[55] As Beatrice Webb was a leading member of the Commission, this verdict deserves respect, though no doubt occasional acts of cruelty still occurred. Lionel Rose, for example, claims that workhouse and industrial school children were more vulnerable to arbitrary and excessive beatings than children in elementary schools. He cites in evidence the horrific Friday morning beatings in the Lambeth workhouse witnessed by Charlie Chaplin in 1896, and the floggings in the St Asaph workhouse experienced by Henry Morton Stanley when he was an inmate there.[56] However, even if these accounts are taken at their face value and are not exaggerated, it seems unlikely that such ill-treatment was widespread and that the Webbs were quite unaware of this. Where there was criticism in both the Majority and Minority Reports it was of the care of infants, that is, the very small children (under three or four) in the workhouses.

In the eighteenth century the London parishes were required under Hanway's Acts to transfer out of the workhouse all children between two and six, and to place out to nurse in the country all babies under two; but these acts were repealed in 1844. Subsequently infants over two were transferred to separate schools (where they existed), the age being raised to three in 1899. So at the end of the nineteenth century the workhouse was still the official residence of pauper children up to the age of three. Not till 1895 were any instructions issued for the provision of separate nurseries for infants, and they might be entrusted to any inmates at all, such as imbeciles or the feeble-minded, or to aged and infirm women. In 1897, the Medical Inspector for the rural unions strongly criticised the lack of proper care of infants in the workhouses. Two quotations from the many descriptions of infant nurseries in both reports of the Poor Law Commission may suffice. The first is from the Majority Report:

> The nursery was bad, very messy, the children looked miserable; some of the infants were being nursed by old women, some lay in cradles with wet bedding, and were provided with comforters . . . The three-year-old children were in a bare and desolate room, sitting about on the floor and on wooden benches, and in dismal workhouse dress . . . The washing arrangements are unsatisfactory; the children have no tooth-brushes, and very few hairbrushes.[57]

The Minority Report observes

> In one large workhouse, our Committee noticed that the children from perhaps about eighteen months to perhaps two and a half years of age, had a sickly appearance. These children were having their dinner, which consisted of large platefuls of potatoes and minced beef, a somewhat improper diet for children of that age, and one which may perhaps account for their pasty looks. The attendants did not know the ages of the children . . . Elsewhere we were informed that the infants weaned but unable to feed themselves, are sometimes placed in a row, and the whole row fed with one spoon from one plate of rice pudding; the spoon went in and out of the mouths all along the row.

The infant mortality rates in these circumstances were understandably high. The Minority Report claimed that it was somewhere between two and three times the national figure, especially in the first six months.[58] It seems, therefore, that whatever improvements had taken place in the conditions of the older children of school age, there remained much to be done for the babies and infants in the workhouse.

For the newcomer to the detailed study of children and the Poor Law in the nineteenth century, the obvious question which arises is, were the children really treated cruelly in the workhouse? The question is inevitable, given popular views of the workhouse derived from film and television versions of the works of Dickens. Was the treatment of Oliver Twist typical of the early Victorian workhouse? In fact, Dickens seems to have been writing of the pre-1834 workhouse, but his graphic description of conditions generally, and of the meagre fare provided, serves in the popular imagination as an image of the workhouse of the time. Dr Crowther has some wise words on this subject; she suggests that in popular history the scandals still occupy the largest space, while the academic historian tends to assume that the workhouse was cruel by accident rather than by intention. While the popular version lingers over the problems of the early years, the academic version minimises some of the evils. Some historians have taken the view that the punitive nature of workhouse discipline, which was essential if the regime was to deter, was the real cruelty of the poor law system. Crowther herself thinks that certain features of the new system, such as the officers' working conditions, made physical cruelty inevitable from time to time. She also refers to the myths of the workhouse system, some of them arising from the sensational stories put about by anti-poor law campaigners, others actually encouraged by the poor law commissioners in their attempts to strengthen the deterrent principle. The basic problem, of course, in the administration of the new law was how to reconcile the need to deter shirkers with the need to give humane treatment to genuine applicants for relief.[59]

That children were treated cruelly in the Victorian workhouse from time to time cannot be denied. It would be remarkable if they were not, if somehow they were shielded from the kind of day-to-day unthinking and often casually-inflicted cruelty suffered by children at work in the first half of the century. As we have seen in previous chapters, children in the workshops, down the mines, in the factories and elsewhere were cuffed and beaten as a matter of course, while in the schools the cane was in frequent use. What we cannot do is quantify this cruelty in any way. We cannot show statistically that there was more cruelty, say, under the New Poor Law than under the old law, or more, for example, in 1840 than in 1870. What we can say is that for various reasons children generally were treated with greater humanity towards the end of the nineteenth century than at the beginning, and in view of this it is likely that there was less physical cruelty to workhouse children by 1900 than in the early nineteenth century.

However, the fact remains that discipline was still strict even then, and the institutional atmosphere remained largely unchanged. According to Dr Crowther, it was not violence but the unrelieved tedium of institutional life which probably afflicted the inmates most. Along with this went the general detestation of the workhouse among the working classes, young and old alike. To enter the workhouse was to meet with humiliation and disgrace. The Poor Law Commissioners had succeeded too well in founding a system based not on physical cruelty but on psychological deterrence and on shame and fear.[60] These gloomy views of workhouse life are substantiated by the comments made by visitors on the condition of workhouse children in the middle years of the century. The children were often found to be apathetic and wanting in energy. In the 1870s, workhouse children did worse than elementary school children in subjects requiring independent thought. Very little recreational equipment was provided at first. In 1884, an inspector commented 'It is a lamentable thing to see children perfectly idle and listless within the four square walls of a court and, in my opinion, a false economy when the children are not allowed the use of a circular swing on the ground that it makes them wear out their boots rapidly.'[61] It was not until 1891 that an order authorised the purchase of both indoor toys and 'a reasonable amount of skipping ropes and battledores and shuttlecocks'. When girls left the workhouse to go into domestic service, employers often found them sulky and uncooperative, and many soon threw up their jobs. Of course, some had good reason to do so, given the overworking of young domestics which was common at the time. This led to the formation of care societies such as the Metropolitan Association for Befriending Young Servants and the Girls Friendly Society.

Yet the poor morale of workhouse children was only to be expected, when it is remembered that they were often orphaned or abandoned children without parents to turn to. It would be surprising if they had had the spirit and confidence of children who had parents, or of children who were used to the rough and ready security of an upbringing within the family. It must also be remembered that even then, there were noticeable improvements in the condition of workhouse children by the end of the nineteenth century, as the need to remove them from the workhouse itself became generally accepted.

By the beginning of the new century there were relatively few children left in the general mixed workhouse, though historians of the Poor Law are surprisingly divided over the precise figures concerned. In their book of 1910 the Webbs give the 1906 figure as 21,526 children under three; in their 1929 work, this figure is replaced by 14,000 under sixteen.[62] Whatever the true number, they were greatly outnumbered in 1906 by the children in district schools (12,393), in cottage and other homes (14,590), in other institutions (11,368) and of course by the children on outdoor relief (179,870). This last category included a variety of children in need – according to the Webbs, the majority (96,804) were children of widows, 72,721 had either both parents or a father living, while 10,345 had no parents at all.[63] It should be noted again that most of the children left in the workhouse attended local elementary schools by this time.

In conclusion, therefore, it can be said that substantial numbers of working-class children still came under the jurisdiction of the Poor Law at the end of the nineteenth century, but that progress had been made in giving them more specialised attention, especially in the last quarter of the century; principally by removing them from the workhouse itself and attempting to put them into something like a family situation, but also by establishing contact with the outside world through attendance at local board or church schools. Life could still be bleak and institutional for them, and the workhouse continued to symbolise failure and degradation. In 1909 the Minority report condemned the retention of children in the general mixed workhouse, commenting that 'In York certainly the children were dull and inert; they stood around like moulting crows, and did not seem able to employ themselves with any enthusiasm or vigour.'[64] The acceptance of poor relief undoubtedly continued to carry a stigma which contributed to the apathy of the children. As Professor Rose puts it succinctly, 'the lot of the workhouse child remained a dreary and disadvantaged one'.[65] But could it be otherwise? As we saw earlier in this chapter, when Dr Kay was asked in 1837 whether it was possible to make children love the workhouse better than their own cottage, he replied that if this were to happen, it was to be deplored, for it would indicate a complete absence of parental affection. It is hard to imagine how any child could be happier in the workhouse than in his or her own home, however humble and imperfect it might be. Only where home life was disfigured by drunkenness, violence, continual lack of food and the like, could life in an institution be thought at all preferable. Finally, a milestone was reached in 1913 when the Poor Law Institution Order made it illegal to retain a healthy child over three years old in a workhouse for more than six weeks.[66] The workhouse child was becoming a fast-diminishing breed.

References

1 James Walvin, *A Child's World*, 1982, p. 18.

2 Quoted in David Thomson, *England in the Nineteenth Century*, 1950, p. 41.

3 There are many books on the subject of the Old Poor Law. The best introduction is J. D. Marshall, *The Old Poor Law, 1795–1834*, 2nd edn, 1985. See also D. Marshall, *The English Poor in the Eighteenth Century*, 1926; W. E. Tate, *The English Parish Chest*, 1946; J. R. Poynter, *Society and Pauperism: English Ideas on Poor Relief, 1795–1834*, 1969; M. E. Rose, *The English Poor Law, 1780–1930*, 1971; G. W. Oxley, *Poor Relief in England and Wales, 1601–1834*, 1974 and Karel Williams, *From Pauperism to Poverty*, 1981.

4 F. M. Eden, *The State of the Poor*, 1797, abridged edn, 1928, p. 217.

5 *Ibid.*, p. 249.

6 *Ibid.*, p. 326. The children were housed in a separate Asylum for the Infant Poor. See Eric Hopkins, *Birmingham: The First Manufacturing Town in the World 1760–1840*, 1989, pp. 156–7. For further details see Mary C. McNaulty, 'Some Aspects of the History of the Administration of the Poor Laws in Birmingham between 1730 and 1834', Birmingham M.A. thesis, 1942.

7 Eden, *The State of the Poor*, pp. 190, 191–2, 310.

8 *Ibid.*, pp. 296–301. The workhouse survives as one of the principal buildings of the present Shrewsbury School.

9 *Ibid.*, pp. 357–8.

10 *Ibid.*, p. 101.

11 *Ibid.*, p. 243.

12 *Ibid.*, p. 243, 274, 314, 343.

13 For apprenticeship in the eighteenth and early nineteenth centuries, see D. Marshall, *The English Poor*, pp. 182–206.

14 Typical studies are Eric Hopkins, (ed.), *The Kinver Parish Chest*, University of Birmingham Extra-Mural Department, 1969; R. P. Hastings, *Poverty and the Poor Law in the N. Riding of Yorkshire 1780–1837*, 1982, Borthwick Papers No. 61, University of York Borthwick Institute of Historical Research, and Roy Peacock, (ed.), *Hagley, Worcestershire, from the 18th to 19th Century*, Hagley Parish Research Group, 1985. Of the earlier pioneering studies see E. M. Hampson, *The Treatment of Poverty in Cambridgeshire*, 1934.

15 F. M. L. Thompson, *The Rise of Respectable Society*, 1988, p. 355. For

basic articles on attitudes to the poor, and to the relief of the poor, see A. W. Coats, 'Changing Attitudes to Labour in the Mid-Eighteenth Century', *Economic History Review*, 11, No. 1, 1958–59, and his 'Economic Thought and Poor Law Policy in the Eighteenth Century', *Economic History Review*, 13, No. 1, 1960–1.

16 Quoted in Anne Digby, *Pauper Palaces*, 1978, p. 1. This author has also written a very helpful short account, *The Poor Law in Nineteenth Century England and Wales*, 1982.

17 S. G. & E. O. A. Checkland, (eds), *The Poor Law Report of 1834*, 1974, p. 124. This is a reprint of the 1834 report, with a lengthy introduction.

18 *Ibid.*, p. 127.

19 See J. D. Marshall, *The Old Poor Law*, for a good recent survey of new interpretations of the Old Poor Law in the early nineteenth century.

20 Checklands, *Poor Law Report of 1834*, p. 375.

21 *Ibid.*, p. 64.

22 *Ibid.*, p. 335.

23 *Ibid.*, p. 97, 133.

24 *Ibid.*, pp. 466–7.

25 *Ibid.*, p. 265.

26 *Annual report of the Poor Law Board 1868–9*, p. 94.

27 *The Times*, 26 December 1840, quoted in G. R. W. Baxter, *The Book of the Bastilles*, 1841, p. 156.

28 Sidney and Beatrice Webb, *English Poor Law History*, Part II, 'The Last 100 Years', Vol. I, 1929, p. 256 (hereafter Webbs, *History*).

29 Sidney and Beatrice Webb, *English Poor Law Policy*, 1910, new edn, 1963, pp. 72, 73, 85, 61–2 (hereafter Webbs, *Policy*).

30 Webbs, *Policy*, p. 107.

31 *Select Committee on the Administration of the Poor Law Amendment Act*, 1837–8, Qs 4392–3, 4397–8.

32 *Ibid.*, Qs 4794–7.

33 *Ibid.*, Qs 20,058, 3666–7.

34 *Ibid.*, Qs 18,307–18, 316, 3909–16, 8734.

35 *Ibid.*, Qs 18, 307–18, 316, 8734, 4941.

36 Webbs, *History*, pp. 247, 253.

37 *Twenty-First Annual Report of the Poor Law Board, 1868–9*, p. 87.

38 Webbs, *History*, p. 266.

39 *Tenth Annual Report of the Poor Law Board, 1857–8*, p. 15.

40 *Third Annual Report of the Poor Law Board, 1850*, p. 8.

41 *Twenty-First Annual Report of the Poor Law Board, 1868–9*, p. 89.

42 Webbs, *History*, pp. 244–5. For the decline in popularity of the district schools, see Francis Duke, 'Pauper Education' in Derek Fraser (ed.), *The New Poor Law in the Nineteenth Century*, 1976.

43 Webbs, *History*, pp. 294, 297, 298.

44 *Webbs, Policy*, p. 113, and see Anne Digby, *Pauper Palaces*, pp. 191–2.

45 *Household Words*, 13 July 1850, pp. 362–4.

46 Report on Dietaries, etc. in *Twentieth Annual Report of the Poor Law Board, 1867–8.*

47 Webbs, *Policy*, pp. 134–40. In 1849, an investigation into workhouse children's food in London showed wide variations in both quantity and quality. In Rotherhithe, the children lived largely on bread and milkless gruel, whereas in St George's, Hanover Square, they had a pint of milk a day, and treacle on their bread (M. A. Crowther, *The Workhouse System 1834–1929*, 1981, p. 215). The best of the diets did not compare unfavourably with diets in charity foundations or in the boarding schools investigated by the Schools Inquiry Commission, 1864–8, see Eric Hopkins, 'A Charity School in the Nineteenth Century: Old Swinford Hospital School, 1815–1914', *British Journal of Educational Studies*, XVII, no. 2, June 1969, p. 184.

48 Webbs, *History*, p. 313.

49 *Ibid.*, pp. 507–8.

50 *Ibid.*, pp. 508–9.

51 Crowther, *The Workhouse System*, p. 220.

52 Quoted in the Webbs, *History*, p. 289.

53 *Ibid.*, pp. 267–8, 290–2.

54 *Ibid.*, pp. 282, 289–9; see also I. Pinchbeck and M. Hewitt, *Children in English Society*, Vol. II, 1973, p. 353.

55 Webbs, *History*, p. 293.

56 Lionel Rose, *The Erosion of Childhood: Child Oppression in Britain 1860–1918*, 1991, p. 181.

57 Webbs, *History*, pp. 306–7, 309.

58 *Ibid.*, p. 310.

59 Crowther, *The Workhouse System*, pp. 33–4; see also D. Roberts, 'How Cruel was the Victorian Poor Law?' *Historical Journal*, VI, 1963; U. Henriques, 'How Cruel was the Victorian Poor Law?', *Historical Journal*, XI, 1968 and Derek Fraser, *The Evolution of the British Welfare State*, 2nd edn, 1984, pp. 54–5.

60 Crowther, *The Workhouse System*, pp. 270–1.

61 Quoted in Norman Longmate, *The Workhouse*, 1974, p. 183.

62 Webbs, *Policy*, p. 187; Webbs, *History*, p. 254. Longmate (*The Workhouse*, p. 192), makes the figure 16,000 for children under 16 in 1906. Rose, presumably following the Webbs, gives a figure of nearly 22,000 in 1906, (*Erosion of Childhood*, p. 256). Crowther (*The Workhouse System*, pp. 204–5), says there were only 656 children in workhouse schools in 1908. Lastly, the Majority Report (Pt. I, p. 186) states that on 1 January 1903 out of 62,426 indoor pauper children there were 16,221 indoor pauper children in the workhouse. These figures are a little perplexing, but are not incompatible, of course.

63 Webbs, *Policy*, pp. 184, 187.

64 *Minority Report*, Pt II, p. 802.

65 Michael E. Rose, *The Relief of Poverty 1834–1914*, 2nd edn, 1986, p. 37. This short book is a most helpful guide to recent research on the New Poor Law.

66 Pinchbeck and Hewitt, *Children in English Society*, Vol II, p. 541.

Chapter Seven

Street children, waifs and strays, and criminal children

Earlier in this book it was remarked that Victorian society was a very youthful society, with over a third of the population under fifteen years of age at the mid-century. Seeing that another prominent feature of that society was the remarkable growth of towns and cities, it is not surprising that children were everywhere to be seen in the urban areas. Some were going about their business on the way to and from work or school, sometimes accompanied by their parents or other members of the family, but many were simply street children, or 'street arabs', to use the contemporary term. As one of Mayhew's correspondents put it in 1864, 'Every Londoner must have seen numbers of ragged, sickly, and ill-fed children, squatting at the entrance of miserable courts, streets, and alleys, engaged in no occupation that is either creditable to themselves or useful to the community.'[1] In fact, street children were of many different kinds; some were street traders, selling a variety of small articles such as laces, matches, clothes-pegs and newspapers, especially later in the century, when more popular newspapers were on sale. Others helped with selling from market stalls or barrows, or performing services such as sweeping crossings, carrying luggage at railway stations, blacking shoes, and running errands. Girls, rather than boys, sold flowers. The line between selling and begging was a thin one, and some wares on sale were merely a front for begging; but there were many quite openly begging, sent out on to the streets by their parents to get what they could. Other children were thieves, stealing from shops and picking pockets, and there were also juvenile prostitutes, both male and female. Some children had parents, with homes (of a sort) to go to. Others had no fixed abodes, as the police put it, and were vagrants sleeping rough in doorways or under arches or stalls (properly speaking, they were waifs, or 'homeless and helpless persons', to employ a dictionary definition).

From time to time the law would descend, and street children could find themselves in prison, convicted either for vagrancy or for more serious charges. For many this could be the start of a lifetime of crime. Throughout the century street children figure prominently in the literature of the time, ranging (for example) from the Artful Dodger in *Oliver Twist* to the Baker Street Irregulars in the Sherlock Holmes stories.

The problem with dealing with so large and heterogeneous a group of children is to know how best to organise the material and how best to trace their fortunes throughout the century. The simplest way of doing this seems to be to divide them into two groups, those who on the whole managed to keep out of the hands of the police – the more or less law-abiding – and the less fortunate who became criminals. In certain respects the stories of the two groups are very similar. As we shall see, efforts to help them were largely of a voluntary nature in the first half of the century, while after 1850 more legislation was passed, setting up institutions for the rehabilitation of both delinquent and non-delinquent children, while voluntary efforts were intensified for the reclaiming and training of vagrant children in institutions such as the Dr Barnardo Homes. Finally, at the turn of the century, more protective legislation was passed, culminating in the important Children's Act, 1908.

To start with the non-delinquent children: as already noted, this is a very large and varied category. Some of the youthful street traders were accompanied by parents, and their activities could be lawful enough. They included both boys and girls, who sold simply anything which could yield even the smallest profit. According to Mayhew

> A basket of oranges or of apples is among the heaviest of all the stocks hawked by children; and in those pursuits there are certainly as many, or rather more girls than boys. Such articles as fly-papers, money-bags, tins, fuzees [matches], and Christmas [holly and evergreens at Christmas] are chiefly the boys' sale; cut-flowers, lavender, watercresses, and small wares are more within the trading of the girls.[2]

These children were everywhere to be seen in London and the other cities at the mid-century. Other children also engaged in earning a living of a kind in the streets were the crossing sweepers. Both boys and girls swept paths through the mud and horse-manure of the streets for the benefits of pedestrians. In London they combined sweeping with tumbling – turning somersaults for the odd penny or so. They usually worked in gangs, and would do anything for money, merely to please some passers-by. Mayhew gives some examples of this – knocking down a drunken man for a shilling; sweeping mud on to a woman; and even causing an uproar in a pastry shop by tumbling on the tables. Gander, the captain of the boy sweepers, had a profitable sideline. He claimed to be the first to perform ornamental work in the mud of his crossings (the boys had their own set pitches).[3]

Many of the children on the streets led wild and undisciplined lives, seeing little of their parents except late at night, and often not even then. Aged from six or seven years, their outstanding characteristics were that they were ragged, dirty, emaciated and unkempt. This is hardly surprising, given their mode of life, especially when many slept out at night, either because they had no homes or because they could not afford even a cheap doss-house for the night. In London, it was well known that there were many children in this category. In 1828 the parish constable of St Paul's, giving evidence before a select committee, confirmed that there were many boys sleeping in baskets and in the offal around Covent Garden. He was questioned further:

> Are there not certain classes of boys that have no regular lodgings, who live in the market, and who sleep in the baskets at night?
> Yes, there are, and not only at night, but in the day; we can take nearly a hundred of them, particularly at the time the oranges are about, they come there picking up the bits of oranges, both boys and girls, and there are prostitutes at 11, 12 and 13 years of age.[4]

Many children made no pretence of selling, but were simply beggars and/or thieves. Some of these would be sent out by their parents to earn what they could, either by begging or by thieving, and the more unsuccessful of these children might be too afraid to go home, and so add to the numbers sleeping in Covent Garden market, under the green stalls.[5] Other markets in London, such as the Fleet market, also had their quota of children sleeping overnight, while greater numbers slept elsewhere in any nook or cranny they could find. According to Lord Ashley, in 1848 there were about 30,000 shelterless street arabs in London, out of a total population of 2.5 million.[6]

Everywhere then in London, day and night, there were swarms of ragged children. The visitor to the capital could not fail to be aware of these children. A witness in 1828 remarked that 'It is no uncommon thing . . . to see infants of five, six, or seven years old, with a few matches in their hands, at 10, 11, or 12 o'clock at night; and upon being questioned why they do not go home, they answer that their mothers will beat them if they go home without money.'[7] Begging children were usually among the most ragged (to invoke sympathy) and might also be maimed or blind. Thieving children often specialised in picking pockets (usually for handkerchieves or purses – Dickens seems to have been quite accurate in his description of the training given to Oliver Twist), and also in shop crime. Mayhew provides plenty of examples of how shopkeepers might be robbed. Some thieves concentrated on stealing on the riverside from the ships and barges, also searching the mud for anything of value (the mudlarks).

What was done to rescue these children in the earlier decades of the nineteenth century? Of course, deserted and destitute children could turn to the poor law authorities for succour, but many preferred to take their chances on the streets, rather than go into the workhouse. Under the Vagrancy Act, 1824, begging, sleeping out, and selling without a licence were all illegal, but it was impossible for the courts to do much, if anything, for children brought up before them under the act. It was therefore left to individuals of a philanthropic turn of mind to do something for children in need of help; but although a number of societies existed for this purpose, they almost all concentrated on delinquent children, as we shall see later. In London, it was left to such bodies as the Children's Friend Society, founded in 1830, and the London City Mission (1835) to assist destitute or vagrant children. The free Ragged Schools, set up in the 1840s, were open to children of the poorest families, but they were not likely to appeal to the average street arab, living on his wits on the streets and valuing his freedom.

On the other hand, much concern was shown over the growth of juvenile delinquency in the early years of the nineteenth century, especially after the end of the French Wars in 1815. It certainly appears that crime was increasing in London and Middlesex at this time, where the population had gone up by 19 per cent in the period from 1811 to 1821, while convictions had gone up by 55 per cent.[8] The report of the Select Committee on the Police in the Metropolis, 1828, ascribed the increase in crime to several causes: the increase in population, the low price of spirits (children were said to begin drinking spirits at ten or eleven years of age), and the neglect of children by parents. This last cause was said to be 'a primary source of mischief;' and as an example of the profligate ways of youth it was pointed out that 'in the parks and outskirts of the Metropolis, principally on Sundays, but also on other days, numerous gangs or parties of young persons assemble for the express purpose of indulging in the vice of gambling.'[9] There was general agreement in the report that prison in itself was unsuitable for young offenders, because they soon became contaminated by contact with the adult convicts. Children could be sent to prison as early as seven years old, and could even be sentenced to death at that age.[10] However, children were often acquitted after being tried; of the 104 children sentenced to death at the Old Bailey between 1801 and 1836, none was executed.[11] Further, at least one London magistrate would never send children to trial for pilfering, but would remand them for a week before discharging them at the request of their parents.[12] The 1828 report concluded that what was wanted was a separate prison for young criminals, or a convict ship on the river, or training in the navy or merchant service after a spell in prison.[13]

The report is vague about the actual treatment (if any) which was to be given to young delinquents, and the oral evidence was divided on what was the most effective deterrent. According to the Keeper of Newgate prison, the boys did not dread transportation, and indeed some looked forward to it as an adventure in a sunnier clime. Flogging, he thought, was feared more than anything else, but the boys soon forgot about it. They had both public and private floggings, the boys being given about 35 lashes; men got more – the Keeper said he knew of one man receiving 280 strokes in a public flogging. He was asked, 'Does that flogging mark them for their lives?' He answered, 'As long as they live.'[14] Another witness listed the deterrents as loss of dinner, whipping and solitary confinement. Whipping merely hardened the boys, he thought – the loss of dinner was more effective. As might be expected, there was one witness who thought a major cause of crime was that the boys lacked discipline – 'The cane and the birch seem to have fallen into desuetude . . . boys are so disorderly for want of proper school discipline and correction'.[15]

Concern at the incidence of youthful crime had been rising since the eighteenth century, so that by the 1820s there was already a number of institutions for convicted juveniles. One of them was a separate prison hulk, the 'Bellerophon' at Sheerness, which accommodated about 320 boys between 1823 and 1825, after which date the boys were moved to the 'Euryalus' at Chatham. Here the discipline was harsh, and there was much ferocious bullying by the bigger boys. The regime was criticised in the 1828 report, and clearly no real efforts were made to reform the boys on the ship. The Superintendent of Hulks, giving evidence, admitted that the incarceration of boys on hulks was clearly not an effective deterrent, since eight out of ten boys who had served their sentence there had 'returned to their old courses'. This is hardly a matter for surprise, given the nature of the prison routine. The diet provided was also very frugal – on six days a week the rations consisted of 1 lb bread, 7 oz beef, ¾ lb potatoes, 6 oz oatmeal, and ½ oz salt. Saturday was a meatless day, the ration being 1 lb bread, 3 oz cheese, 6 oz oatmeal, and ½ oz salt.[16]

Other institutions were all run by voluntary bodies, and all aimed at some kind of rehabilitation, though of a rudimentary kind. One of the oldest in London was the Marine Society, which dated from the mid-eighteenth century, and provided for 'poor distressed boys' of minimum height 4ft. 9in., the point of this being that after preliminary training on the Society's ship at Greenwich, which took about a hundred boys, they were sent to sea, the captains taking them naturally preferring the taller, healthier-looking boys. Even at Greenwich there could be problems of discipline, which were tackled by flogging (six to twelve lashes), or by solitary confinement. The Philanthropic Society, founded in 1788, took about 160 children, of whom 120 were boys. Criminal boys were admitted between the ages of nine and twelve, and the sons of convicts between nine and thirteen. After training for eighteen months to two years, during which time they were taught to read and write, the boys were transferred to the manufactory and apprenticed to handicraft trades. It was claimed that relatively few reoffended. The Refuge for the Destitute was run on similar lines, mostly for criminal children, both boys and girls, from the age of twelve. They were kept for two years, taught reading and writing and then apprenticed out. Discipline could be a problem here, too, and boys causing trouble were put in solitary confinement in the dark ('black holes') for up to four days. Real fighting was said to be rare, but where boys came to blows, they were made to walk arm in arm for a day or so until they were friends – a novel form of therapy which would probably cause some comment today.[17] Lastly, the Children's Friend Society was founded by Captain Brenton, and this society set up the Brenton Asylum for boys at Hackney Wick and the Royal Victoria Asylum for girls at Chiswick during the 1820s. Flogging and blows were forbidden, and boys were admitted from the age of ten, being assisted to emigrate after six months. Between 1830 and 1834 about 278 boys and 37 girls were sent out to the colonies.[18]

All these bodies were voluntary in nature, and received no government grant. They could deal with only a small minority of juvenile offenders, and after the 1828 report (there were also reports in 1828 from a Select Committee on Criminal Commitments and Convictions) little was done for some years to improve matters, though there was general agreement that the root causes of juvenile delinquency were unemployment, drink, parental neglect and lack of training in a trade. By the mid-1830s, another House of Lords Select Committee reported on the state of the prisons, issuing five reports in all. The number of children under 21 committed in 1834 was given as 9,077. Of these, 400 were aged up to 12; 2,204 were aged between 13 and 16; the remaining 6,437 were between 17 and 21. The regime on the 'Euralyus' came in for heavy criticism, especially the extent of bullying, which actually led some boys to break their own arms in order to escape it and get into hospital. The Committee recommended that the use of hulks as prisons for boys should be discontinued, though the 'Euryalus' continued in use as a prison until 1846.[19] In the meantime, a separate prison for juvenile offenders was at last established in 1838 – Parkhurst Prison. Unfortunately, however benign the original intentions, this prison maintained a strict discipline which emphasised deterrence rather than rehabilitation. The boys worked a seven-hour day, mostly indoors, though half of this time was spent in the classroom. Parkhurst was strongly attacked by the leading advocate of reform of the treatment of juvenile offenders, Mary Carpenter. In spite of this, a further House of Lords Select Committee in 1847 actually recommended the setting-up of more prisons on Parkhurst lines (describes as 'reformatory asylums'), provoking Mary Carpenter into writing and publishing her influential book *Reformatory Schools* in 1851. In the following year she set up her own reform school at Kingswood, near Bristol.[20]

At this point it might be useful to sum up the progress made in the care of both delinquent and non-delinquent children by the mid-nineteenth century. As regards the first category, some limited progress can be seen in that the notorious 'Euryalus' had at last been closed down, and the principle of segregating convicted children from adult convicts had been put into practice with the opening of Parkhurst prison. Transportation was suspended in 1846 (it had become unusual to transport very young children, in any case), while the Juvenile Offenders Acts of 1847 and 1850 provided for trial under summary jurisdiction for most crimes under sixteen. This permitted a speedier consideration of juvenile crime than before, and had long been advocated by reformers, only to be held up by opponents who argued that trial by jury was essential in the interests of justice. Meanwhile, philanthropic societies continued to be active in their efforts to prevent juvenile delinquents from reoffending and becoming hardened criminals. The downside of all this is simply that the societies were purely voluntary and could cope with only a small minority of offenders. Further, the one prison for children which attempted to combine punishment for crime with reformatory and industrial training was still very much a prison, with armed guards accompanying working parties. As such, it was bitterly attacked by Mary Carpenter and her followers.

As for the masses of street children who kept out of the hands of the law, they still flooded the streets of the cities, and their way of life certainly became better known with the publication in 1861–62 of Henry Mayhew's *London Labour and the London Poor*, which contained a lengthy section on street children. It would be unfair to categorise all such children as neglected and deprived. Some, especially costermongers' children, were not badly looked after. Many had homes of a sort to go to. But at the other end of the scale there were the homeless sleeping rough and the itinerant population of tramps, vagrants, and gypsies. In 1868–69, there were 33,000 known tramps in England and Wales, 17 per cent of them under sixteen years of age. In the period from 1866 to 1880 the under-sixteens in the workhouse casual wards, which accommodated paupers on the tramp, numbered between one in thirteen and one in seventeen of the total.[21] The philanthropic societies could make little impact on all this, and up to the mid-century the children of the streets continued their own way of life, undisturbed for the most part except for occasional prosecutions for begging or sleeping out.

Yet a turning-point (of a sort) for both delinquent and non-delinquent children came in the mid-1850s. To take the ordinary street children first: in 1857 the Industrial Schools Act was passed to make some provision for street children of the worst condition – that is, 'vagrant, orphaned, and morally endangered children'. These were children who were not convicted of crime, but were thought to be in danger of becoming criminals since they habitually kept company with thieves or were simply running wild. The schools were to be run by voluntary agencies and aimed at moral regeneration through a combination of education and industrial training. They were variously described at the time as 'asylums for vagrants', and by the Inspector of Industrial Schools in 1870 as 'houses of correction for the young vagabonds and petty misdemeanants'.[22] It will be noted that he clearly thought that the schools should not exclude those guilty of minor offences such as vagrancy, begging and petty theft, though subsequently the original intention of not taking convicted children seems to have prevailed. By 1896 there were 141 industrial schools, all but 16 of them under voluntary management but assisted by Treasury grants, with 17,000 to 18,000 children aged between six and sixteen in them. In addition, there were truant schools and day industrial schools set up under the Education Acts.[23] By this date, the industrial schools had made some progress, particularly in giving more time to education. According to Col. Inglis, the Industrial Schools Inspector, reporting in 1895

> On the whole, the schools are going on well, and improving year by year. The progress is gradual, and it is only by looking back some 20 years that we can realise how much improvement has taken place in that period. We find that education has improved . . . less reliance is placed on corporal punishment . . . and in many schools the inmates are far better off than they used to be in regard to diet and clothing. In short, the schools have marched with the times.[24]

In theory, the industrial schools, which catered for more than three times as many children as the reformatory schools (to be described later), prided themselves that they were not for criminal children, but merely for the unfortunates of the streets (their inmates were always referred to officially as 'children', while those in reform schools were 'juvenile offenders'). In practice, as the 1896 report points out, although children in industrial schools had not been sent there on conviction, some had certainly been convicted at some time previously. All in all, the industrial schools provided a solution of sorts for children in need of care and attention and did give them some basic industrial training, but they still resembled penal institutions and were very little different in nature from the reformatory schools for delinquents which will be described later.

The institution of industrial schools did not exhaust the exercise of voluntary help for street children in the second half of the nineteenth century. On the contrary; by 1878, in London alone, there were fifty philanthropic societies for children. There were numerous missions specifically for poor children, for example, the Wesleyan National Children's Home in Lambeth; the Waifs and Strays Society (later known as the Church of England Children's Society); and the Shadwell Orphanage. Of all the homes for destitute and homeless children, the homes set up by Dr Barnardo in 1870 and 1876 are the most famous. Later in the century Dr Barnardo turned his attention to emigration for children from his homes, a way of starting a new life already explored by pioneer reformers such as Maria Rye in the 1860s and Annie

MacPherson, who trained and sent children from London to Canada. Once Dr Barnardo had himself adopted the idea of emigration, especially to Canada, his homes sent out twice the number of child emigrants as any other organisation.[25]

Other philanthropic schemes included attempts to organise street trading on a rational basis. The first scheme of this kind was devised by John MacGregor, a London barrister and ragged school teacher, who set up the London Shoeblack Society in 1851. Street boys were given regular pitches, and supplied with uniforms. A hostel was opened for them, and profits from trading went into personal savings accounts for the boys. By the mid-1850s profits of nearly £3,000 a year were being made. Similar brigades were formed elsewhere, in Glasgow by William Quarrier, and in Liverpool. By the 1890s £12,000 a year was being earned in London and nearly £76,000 nationally. Dr Barnardo set up his own brigade for boys at his Limehouse hostel. By 1904 there were brigades all round London, each with its own uniform. The Central London Society had a hostel for 44 boys, and a schoolroom for 100 pupils. Other trades were also organised; in Glasgow Quarrier went on to establish brigades for railway parcel-carriers and for newspaper boys. By the end of the century, cheaper newspapers and the increased demand for them resulted in newspaper boys becoming the largest group of street traders nationally – 23,000 of them in England and Wales in 1911. At the same time the shoeblack brigades had declined, and there were only two hostels for them in London by 1904, as compared with the nine existing in the late 1870s.[26]

Street trading by children was inevitably reduced during the last quarter of the nineteenth century as attendance at school became compulsory by 1880 and as the industrial schools increased in number, quite apart from the activities of the various homes for homeless children such as Dr Barnardo's in picking children up from the streets. By the 1880s street trading by children was prohibited by local acts in the large cities. In 1882 Manchester forbade trading by children under fourteen after dusk unless they had attained a specified standard of education (trading during the school day would obviously be illegal, of course). Birmingham and Sheffield also passed acts which limited juvenile street trading. Then in 1889 the Prevention of Cruelty to Children Act *inter alia* prohibited street trading altogether for children under ten, while for boys of ten to thirteen (and girls of ten to fifteen) trading was banned between the hours of 10 p.m. and 5 a.m. The 1894 Cruelty Act raised the minimum age for street trading to eleven.[27]

Meanwhile, public concern was being aroused at the need to protect young girls and also to put a stop to the widespread practice of baby farming. The Offences against the Person Act, 1851 made it an offence to procure the defilement of a young girl under the age of twenty-one – a provision aimed at stopping the sale of young girls to procurers – while the age of consent for girls, previously thirteen, was raised to sixteen by the Criminal Law Amendment Act, 1885. In the 1860s cruelty to babies farmed out or simply abandoned had become notorious, and in 1870 in London alone 276 babies were found dead. In 1871 the Bastardy Laws Amendment Act strengthened a mother's claim for maintenance, while a further act in the next year required all foster-mothers to register with local authorities. In 1874 the registration of births and deaths, originally begun in 1837, became compulsory.[28] About the same time, following Mrs Senior's report on the district (poor law) schools, something was done to protect young girls seeking domestic employment in London. This was the setting-up of the Metropolitan Association for Befriending Young Servants, with an additional society for the provinces, the Girls Friendly Society. By 1896 the MABYS had about a thousand lady volunteers and nearly 7,500 girls on its books in London, with lodging-houses for unemployed young female servants, and also a training home. By then it had extended its care from ex-workhouse girls to girls coming to London in search of employment and to girls from industrial schools. The Girls Friendly Society also did good work, with nearly 5,000 girls under its care. In 1887 the MABYS opened a training home for feeble-minded girls, aiming to find them situations.[29]

The increasing care for different classes of children and young persons led in 1883 to the founding in Liverpool of the first Society for the Prevention of Cruelty to Children, to be followed by the establishment of the London Society for the Prevention of Cruelty in 1884. In 1889 the National Society for the Prevention of Cruelty to Children was set up. The same year saw the passing of the Prevention of Cruelty to Children Act, the most important act in this field until the Children's Charter, the name often given to the great consolidating Children's Act, 1908. The 1889 Act provided penalties for those having custody of boys under fourteen and of girls under sixteen who wilfully ill-treated, neglected, abandoned or exposed them; it also contained provisions that children need no longer give evidence on oath, that wives could testify against their husbands and that children could be removed to a place of safety before trial. This act was followed by the Custody of Children Act, 1891, which gave the courts power to decide on custody or return to parents; and then by the Cruelty to Children Act, 1894, which redefined cruelty so as to include wilful assault and raised the maximum age for protection. Further, any child brought before a court under the Industrial Schools Act could be placed in the custody of a relative or other person instead of being sent to an industrial school.[30]

It is evident that by about 1890 a considerable body of law had been built up to protect the individual child from neglect or abuse. Moreover, there existed by this time a national body, the NSPCC, to help enforce the law; in the course of time, the inspector from the NSPCC (the 'cruelty man') became a familiar visitor in rougher working-class districts. In the period 1895–96, the NSPCC dealt with 20,739 cases, and prosecuted in 2,107. Just before the Great War, in 1913–14, the Society investigated 54,772 cases, prosecuting in 2,349 instances (a proportionate drop in prosecutions – the society always preferred to avoid prosecution and employ persuasion, whenever possible). In 1905 only 11 per cent of the cases investigated involved abuse and assault; the Society's estimate of the number of cases involving cruelty as opposed to neglect was only 0.4 per cent (though others put the figure higher).[31] The numerous laws relating to children were consolidated in the Children's Act, 1908, which advanced still further the protection of children afforded by the state: the poor law authorities were given the responsibility of supervising children at home or in care who had been the subject of cruelty proceedings; local authorities were required to inspect fostered children under the age of seven, appoint infant life protection officers, and inspect voluntary homes; and children were not permitted to enter brothels, bet in public places, smoke in public, or purchase tobacco under the age of sixteen. For children accused of criminal offences, juvenile courts were to be set up, employing deliberately less formal procedures, remand homes were to be established for offenders awaiting trial, while the first Borstals were to be provided as an alternative to prison. Imprisonment of children under the age of sixteen was at last abolished completely.[32] Taken as a whole, the act deserves its title of the Children's Charter, though of course, cases of child cruelty, some of a revolting nature, were still being disclosed by the NSPCC up to the date of the outbreak of war in 1914.

To return to street trading: in spite of its general prohibition below the age of eleven in 1894, local authorities were permitted to modify the hours specified by the act, and the legislation on the subject appears to have been largely ignored. This was due partly to difficulties of enforcement, and partly to a lingering sympathy with the child trader who might be making a useful contribution to the income of a poor family. Only in a few cities such as Manchester and Cardiff was the law enforced. Liverpool's problems with street children were notorious, though efforts were made there by a clothing association in 1895 to provide clothes for the most ragged children (some new clothes were soon pawned), while new Corporation Acts in 1898 and 1902 reinforced the main provisions regarding street trading of the 1889 act. Even then, in Liverpool in 1901, 1,144 children were picked up for trading outside the permitted hours. In London there were said still to be between 12,000 and 20,000 child traders, mostly as ragged and dirty as ever, though a big drive against illegal trading in 1911 was said to have removed 10,000 boys and 785 girls from the streets. Meanwhile, the Employment of Children Act, 1903, provided for the licensing of youths between eleven and sixteen engaged in street trading, and for stricter penalties. Enforcement still varied from place to place, and nothing further was done to restrict juvenile street trading before the Great War, though the Departmental Committee of 1910 commented on the excessive permissiveness of the 1903 act. Of the seventy-four county boroughs in England and Wales at the time, fifty had passed by-laws to control trading, but only a quarter of the smaller boroughs had done so. Even when by-laws were in place, they were not always enforced. One hopeful sign was that trading by children over the age of fourteen seemed to be declining: in England and Wales outside London in 1910 there were 15,321 holding licences under the age of fourteen, but only 6,704 aged fourteen to sixteen. Presumably this was a sign of the greater availability of jobs for the older children. However, bills attempting to provide further regulation of trading by following the recommendations of the Poor Law Commission reports in 1909 all failed to pass, partly because of opposition from newspaper interests. It was not until the passing of the Education Act, 1918 that all street trading under the age of fourteen was forbidden, and all local authorities were required to pass by-laws under the 1903 act.[33]

At this point we may return to the subject of the treatment of convicted children from the mid-century onwards. In 1847 the Select Committee of the House of Lords on the Execution of the Criminal Law, especially respecting juvenile offenders and transportation, has already been mentioned. One important witness before this committee, Matthew Davenport Hill, recorder of Birmingham since 1839, spoke strongly against the imprisonment of children. He explained how he had adopted the practice of returning convicted children to masters or friends who would take care of them, avoiding all punishment after sentence. He was asked if this procedure was legal, and assured the committee that it was. Moreover, he claimed to be achieving goods results with his method:

> You say you have the means of referring to a Record of the Results of this Mode of treating children? – I have a Record, and can product it. – Generally speaking, has it been favourable? – It has been favourable, not so much as your Lordships may perhaps expect; but what I consider favourable under all the Circumstances. The last time I saw the Account, viz. at Michaelmas last, there had been 113 Persons so disposed of. Of these, 44 were Persons who had maintained their positions without a single Relapse; 29 were doubtful cases; many of these had left the Town, and of the conduct of the whole 29, we were from one cause or other ignorant; the remaining 40 have relapsed.[34]

Davenport Hill claimed that according to the police his method produced far fewer relapses than when the children were sent to prison; and he repeated his belief that no child should be unnecessarily contaminated by being sent to prison. In spite of his evidence, the Second Report of the Committee declared that transportation could not safely be abandoned, and that further prisons on the lines of Parkhurst prison should be tried: 'reformatory asylums on the principle of Parkhurst Prison, rather than by ordinary punishment [should be tried]: the punishment in such asylums being hardly more than is implied in Confinement and Restraint, and Reformation and Industrial Training being the main Features of the Process.'[35] This suggestion of a mild prison regime was not to exclude a moderate use of corporal punishment.[36]

As we have already seen, this report brought great protests from Mary Carpenter and her supporters. Both Carpenter and Davenport Hill gave very lengthy evidence before the next enquiry, another Select Committee, this time on Criminal and Destitute Juveniles, in 1852. Davenport Hill reported further on his own procedure for dealing with juvenile delinquents, claiming that he had improved his selection of persons to be in charge of them. Having repeated his figures for 1847, he went on to give more up-to-date figures: 'a total of 66 went back to their own masters in the years 1849, 1850, and 1851, and by that table it appears that out of 66, 44 have turned out well, 11 doubtful, and 11 ill.'[37] In his own words, this was obviously 'a much more favourable result than formerly'. For her part, Carpenter hammered away at the evil results of Parkhurst: 'I consider the radical defect of Parkhurst is that it is, in fact, a juvenile prison, not as was recommended by the House of

Lords, a school; and that it acts entirely on the principle of compulsion and restraint, which is entirely fatal to any action of the will of the boy.'[38] Whether Mary Carpenter was entirely fair to the regime at Parkhurst is hard to say. The Parkhurst governor actually gave a rather mild account of the week's activities in the prison, there being two half-days in school each week, and industrial employment on the other five days. According to a report at the end of the century, extensive changes had been made in 1850, and it had become rather like a strict industrial school, the earlier practices of boys being kept in leg-irons and having armed guards outside the prison having been abandoned. However, all 578 boys there in 1852 were under sentence of transportation. A boy who was well-behaved would still be transported after two years in the prison, but would be on a 'ticket of leave', being allowed to work for a master in Australia until his sentence expired. He could not return to England till then.[39]

The evidence of the reformers at last had some effect, for in 1854 the Youthful Offenders Act (followed by a consolidating act in 1866) provided for new reformatory schools, to be set up by voluntary agencies, but with Treasury aid. Within four years of the passing of the 1854 act more than fifty reformatory schools had been established, combining schooling with industrial training. Parkhurst itself took no new inmates after 1863. No doubt the reform schools represented an advance on Parkhurst, but there was still much to criticise during the next thirty years. Their buildings were often inadequate and food and clothing were poor. In spite of all that had been said about the adverse effects of sending children to prison, they still went to prison for a short spell after conviction by way of token punishment before going on to reformatory school. It was not until Lord Leigh's Act, 1893, that this preliminary punishment became no longer obligatory, and the age limit for young offenders was reduced from twenty-one to nineteen. In the following year, of the 1,487 sent to reformatory school, 387 still suffered preliminary imprisonment.[40] Not until 1899 was this imprisonment finally abolished. Meanwhile, court procedures became rather more humane. The Summary Jurisdiction Act, 1879 permitted children to be 'admonished' instead of being sent to reform school, while the Probation of First Offenders Act, 1887 allowed probation for any offence punishable by not more than two years' imprisonment. Remarkably, no provision was made for any supervision during probation, and this did not come till the Youthful Offenders Act, 1901 and the Probation Act, 1907 which set up a recognisably more modern form of probation.

By the 1880s it was thought appropriate to appoint an enquiry into the reformatory schools – the Reformatory and Industrial Schools Commission of 1883. According to Pinchbeck and Hewitt, its report, published in 1884, was surprisingly weak and indecisive, but it did make claims for good progress by the schools:

> They are credited, we believe justly, with having broken up the gangs of young criminals in the large towns; with putting an end to the training of boys as professional thieves; and with rescuing children fallen into crime from becoming habitual or hardened offenders, while they have undoubtedly had the effect of preventing large numbers of children from entering a life of crime.[41]

The commission's report went on to claim that these conclusions were supported by the number of juveniles committed to prison in England and Wales since 1856. Commitments in 1856 numbered 13,981; in 1866, 9,356; in 1876, 7,138; and in 1881, 5,483.[42] The commission continued to support the idea of the preliminary punishment which continued till 1899, as we have seen. As an alternative to imprisonment, this could take the form of whipping in the police station for boys under fourteen. Girls could be put into solitary confinement for seven days if under twelve, or fourteen days for those above twelve.

In 1896 a further report on reformatory and industrial schools was published, this time by a Departmental Committee. Its approach was rather brisker and more businesslike than that of its predecessor, and its recommendations (many of an administrative nature) are spread out over two closely-packed pages. It reported that there were fifty reformatory schools in operation, all still under voluntary management but receiving Treasury grants amounting to about two-thirds of their income. They housed about 4,800 inmates, generally aged thirteen to nineteen years, none being admitted unless convicted and sentenced.[43] The report stresses the fact that reformatory schools and industrial schools were really very similar, even though (as pointed out earlier) managers of industrial schools were at pains to emphasise to the public that their children were not criminals. In reality, it was said, the children of the two types of school came from the same class. The difference between them was principally one of age – children in the reformatory schools were older, 'and older means more criminal'.[44] The report therefore concluded that in future the schools should be reorganised into three classes of schools – junior industrial schools, for children under ten; senior industrial schools, for children from ten to fourteen, whether charged with an offence or otherwise; and reformatories, for children from fourteen to sixteen, sent there after conviction. Nothing was done to implement these recommendations before the Great War, though the suggestion that all forms of imprisonment for children should be abolished was finally put into practice in the Children's Act, 1908. Not until 1933 was the distinction between reformatory schools and industrial schools at last brought to an end, and they were renamed approved schools.

Before summing up the treatment of criminal children throughout the nineteenth century, something should be said about child prostitution. Promiscuity from an early age seems to have been common among children of the lawless classes. An ex-prisoner of Newgate Prison claimed that most of the boys there over twelve years old, and some even younger, had mistresses. Some of these girls were only twelve or thirteen years old. The Select Committee of 1852 were told that some twelve-year olds were known to have venereal disease; representatives from the Magdalen Hospital and the London Female Penitentiary confirmed that the lowest ages of admission were eleven and twelve, though fourteen and fifteen were the more usual ages.[45] The reason for the youthfulness of these prostitutes was that young girls were in demand, being less likely to be infected than older girls; and the age of consent was still as low as twelve before 1871, when it was put up to thirteen. Child prostitution was most widespread in London, though it is impossible to give precise numbers, of course. In 1835 the London Society for the Protection of Young Females claimed that there were 400 procurers in London procuring girls between the ages of eleven and fifteen.[46]

Elsewhere the starting age seemed to vary. In Birmingham it was about fourteen. Thus Mr Benjamin Ride, superintendent of the First Division of the Birmingham Police Force, gave evidence before the Children's Employment Commission, 1840:

> Juvenile prostitution greatly prevails; the ages varying from 14 to 18. None is under 14, except in one instance, a child under 9 years. These females have principally worked in the factories of the town; most of them are notorious thieves. The men who frequent the brothels are of the age from 14 to 20. In a district which the witness could walk round in 15 minutes, there are 118 brothels, and 42 other houses of ill-fame resorted to by prostitutes. The average number of prostitutes residing in each of the 118 brothels is 3, or in the whole, 354.[47]

In Liverpool, on the other hand, the prostitutes appear to have been younger than this. A report in 1857 claimed that there were 200 regular prostitutes under the age of twelve.[48]

Only in the second half of the nineteenth century was anything very much done to attack the problem of child prostitution. Josephine Butler's campaigns against the Contagious Diseases Acts from 1869 onwards helped to draw attention to the subject, as did the revelations by W. T. Stead, editor of the *Pall Mall Gazette*, who actually procured a thirteen-year old girl for £5 and sent her off to Paris. Stead went to prison for having taken the girl without her parents' permission, but the resultant publicity (fully intended by Stead, of course) led to the Criminal Law Amendment Act, 1885, already mentioned, raising the age of consent to 16.[49] Although drug-trafficking is often associated with prostitution at the present day, it does not seem that young prostitutes in mid-Victorian times were associated with drug-dealing, perhaps because opium was freely (and legally) obtainable in chemists' shops. In Birmingham, for instance, Chadwick's Committee reported in 1842 that they had not been able to discover thirty instances of customers regularly purchasing large quantities of opium or laudanum from the local druggists.[50]

In reviewing the history of the care given to delinquent children in the nineteenth century, it is evident that, as with so many other aspects of childhood, much greater concern and understanding were displayed by the end of the century than at the beginning. This is obvious enough, of course, but it would be wrong to exaggerate the progress made, and in particular it is wrong to paint the picture in the early days in too lurid colours. It is true that children could be imprisoned at the age of seven, and even executed, but as we have seen, the death sentence was carried out on the young only very rarely. Transportation was regarded as the usual punishment for serious offences, rather than death. Sentencing policy varied from magistrate to magistrate, and some were far more humane than others. Less serious offences were often punished by relatively short periods of imprisonment which did not necessarily increase in duration with the number of offences. Dr John Tobias has provided us with the astonishing case history of one Thomas M'Nelly, aged about thirteen, which illustrates this point, and according to Dr Tobias is not untypical. M'Nelly's criminal record may be summarised as follows:

Date	*Offence*	*Sentence*
15 April 1836	Wilfully breaking glass in church	Seven days
30 April 1836	Sleeping in the open air	Discharged
29 May 1836	Stealing coal from a barge	One month
6 July 1836	Suspicion of stealing brushes	Three months
17 November 1836	Stealing two bundles of wood	Discharged
23 December 1836	Stealing carrots from a barge	Fourteen days
31 January 1837	Stealing cheese from a shop	Three months
29 April 1837	Stealing a pair of drawers	One month
2 August 1837	Stealing a silk handkerchief	Discharged
18 October 1837	Stealing a pair of trousers	Three months
23 January 1838	Suspicion of stealing three handkerchiefs	One month
23 February 1838	Suspicion of stealing some braces	Discharged
7 March 1838	(Unknown)	Three months[51]

After this, M'Nelly disappears from the criminal record. He was arrested thirteen times and given nine prison sentences, amounting to fifteen months and three weeks, in just under two years. Yet his last few sentences in no way reflect the fact that he was becoming a persistent offender. Rather they seem to show that imprisonment was hardly a deterrent to him and that he was well on the way to becoming a habitual criminal.

The lives led by many of these youthful criminals were no doubt wretched in the extreme, without parental care, and often living rough on the streets. Once convicted they were in danger not only of imprisonment but also of whipping. Although the need to keep youngsters away from the evil of adult criminals was well understood from early on (hence the continued emphasis on separating children from undesirable companions and on sending boys to sea), the idea of whipping as a punishment continued for most of the century, while imprisonment itself was still possible until 1918. Yet for some these were merely professional hazards, the rough which had to be taken with the smooth. Some clearly relished the adventure and excitement of their lives, taking a pride in knowing the tricks of the trade, and in deceiving magistrates with hard-luck stories, or even defying them with a show of knowledge of the law. Membership of a gang could be a substitute of a sort for family life, and respect would be shown to the experienced and resourceful young criminal by his fellow villains. Even Mary Carpenter admitted the attractions of the life led by young offenders. In her well-known work of 1851 on the need for reformatory schools she observed

Their present mode of life is so lucrative and so pleasant, that they will not exchange it for another apparently presenting far greater advantages. Their filth and rags are no annoyances to them, for they are the implements of their trade; the cold and hunger which they continually endure are most amply compensated by an occasional luxurious meal. The close and noisome dens in which they are stowed at night present nothing revolting to their feelings, and they prefer them to a clean abode, where they must resign their occupation and some portion of their liberty.[52]

By the end of the century much had changed. The sight of a child on the streets during term-time would naturally lead to questions as to why he or she was not at school. The reformatory schools had become more civilised and first offenders might be put on probation. Much more was known about child psychology and the need for guidance of young offenders, as exemplified by the provision of juvenile courts in and after 1908. Nevertheless, children went on committing criminal offences. Thomas Holmes, a police-court missionary and secretary of the Howard Association, in commenting on this in 1908, remarked wryly that while offences remained much the same and the ways of committing them were largely unchanged, child offenders were much better dressed, 'for civilisation cannot endure rags, and shoeless feet are an abomination'.[53] Evidently the rise in the standard of living had not in itself reduced juvenile crime, but had seen that its perpetrators were better dressed.

In conclusion, the observations made at the beginning of this chapter may perhaps bear repetition, namely, that the growth and consequent youthfulness of the population during the nineteenth century, combined with the unprecedented spread of urbanisation, meant that large numbers of children thronged the streets of city and town. During the first half of the century comparatively little was done about this, since the Victorians were only beginning to grapple with the problems of the towns in the 1840s and 1850s. In the 1860s Mayhew could still produce pages of description of London street children. Street arabs became a familiar sight, and their antics became well known. So far as criminal children were concerned, the only solution offered, as we have seen, was the deterrent of prison, flogging and transportation. The causes of juvenile criminality certainly led to much discussion and presumably were not altogether wrongly diagnosed as being lack of parental guidance and care, the corrupt influence of older criminals and the availability of cheap spirits. Given the extraordinary social strains of the first half of the nineteenth century, it is not surprising that little progress was made in getting at the roots of juvenile crime. Yet tribute should be paid to those magistrates, like Davenport Hill and the Warwickshire JPs (and also some London magistrates) who were prepared to deal leniently with selected convicted children, a procedure which foreshadowed the probation system later on.

The second half of the century was to see a gradual improvement as more legislation was passed, and in particular as a national system of education was brought into being. Above all else, this brought the myriads of street children to official attention, and willy-nilly gave them a new social role: henceforth they were to become schoolchildren, and they could trade on the streets only if they could obtain a licence. With all its imperfections, the legislative efforts of the second half-century brought results, and with this there was not only a redoubling of philanthropic endeavours to deal with street children and the waifs and strays, but also the recruitment of a new race of officials. These were the school attendance officers and later on the school medical officers and nurses, and the missioners in the crèches, all of them providing new challenges to parental authority, as will be seen in Chapter Nine. By the end of the century there were still children on the streets, but their numbers were greatly reduced and their average age was much higher. A different problem was to emerge here, that of the boys in casual urban employment, the errand boys and van boys to be described in the next chapter, but at least the ragged hordes of street children, so characteristic of the earlier period, were no longer to be seen. They were a particular feature of the growth of cities and towns and like other urban problems had been tackled with varying degrees of success by the end of the century; though the experience of the 1990s shows that homelessness on the streets is still with us. Something similar might be said about delinquent children – some progress was made, but there were substantial problems outstanding at the end of the century. Admittedly, less emphasis was given then to purely punitive methods and more was done to prevent the criminal child from developing into a criminal adult; but it is not really possible to measure the success achieved from the statistics available. It is interesting to note that while the belief in a 'short, sharp shock' as a form of treatment was still prevalent in the 1880s, a hundred years later the Home Secretary, Willie Whitelaw, used precisely the same term to designate a new, vigorous regime to be introduced for juvenile offenders. It was not long before it was regarded as a failure. It seems that the problems of the right treatment of juvenile delinquency still await solution in the last decade of the twentieth century.

Lastly, by way of supplement to all that was done in the second half of the nineteenth century to deal with street children, waifs and strays and criminal children, there was much legislative action designed to provide penalties for those guilty of offences against individual children of all kinds, while the work of the NSPCC prove invaluable in the enforcement of the laws protecting children. A hundred years later the need continues to detect and punish acts of cruelty to children of all ages.

References

1 Henry Mayhew, *London Labour and the London Poor*, 4 Vols, 1861–62 (1967), Vol. I, p. 257.

2 *Ibid.*, p. 472.

3 *Ibid.*, Vol. II, pp. 502–3, 500.

4 *Report from the Select Committee on the Police of the Metropolis*, 1828, p. 81.

5 *Ibid.*, p. 39, (evidence of the Chief Magistrate, Bow Street).

6 Lionel Rose, *The Erosion of Childhood: Child Oppression in Britain 1860–1918*, 1991, p. 80.

7 *Report.*, 1828, p. 153.

8 *Ibid.*, pp. 6–7.

9 *Ibid.*, pp. 7, 8.

10 Even at the present day, children may be convicted of a criminal offence at the age of ten if it can be shown that they knew they were doing wrong, and if found guilty of homicide may be detained for a specific period, including a life sentence, during Her Majesty's pleasure (Children's Legal Centre, reported in *The Times*, 13 November 1992).

11 James Walvin, *A Child's World: A Social History of English Childhood 1800–1914*, 1982. It was not unusual for adults sentenced to death to have their sentences commuted to transportation.

12 *Report*, 1828, p. 149.

13 *Ibid.*, p. 8.

14 *Ibid.*, pp. 54, 55.

15 *Ibid.*, pp. 106, 135. It seems that this witness simply ignored the fact that very few of the children under discussion had ever attended school.

16 Ivy Pinchbeck and Margaret Hewitt, *Children in English Society, Vol II: From the Eighteenth Century to the Children's Act, 1948*, 1973, pp. 452–3; *Report*, 1828, 103–9, where a full account of daily proceedings in the ship is given.

17 The Marine Society, Philanthropic Society, and the Refuge are all described in the 1828 *Report*, pp. 16–19, 163–5, 180–4.

18 Pinchbeck and Hewitt, *Children in English Society, Vol. II*, pp. 455–9.

19 *Ibid.*, pp. 451–4.

20 *Ibid.*, especially pp. 470–6.

21 Rose, *The Erosion of Childhood*, p. 91.

22 *Report of the Departmental Committee on Reform and Industrial Schools*, 1896, pp. 113–14.

23 *Ibid.*, pp. 9, 10.

24 *Ibid.*, p. 14.

25 Walvin, *A Child's World*, pp. 153–8. On child emigrants to Canada generally, see Joy Parr, *Labouring Children: British Immigrant Apprentices to Canada 1869–1924*, 1980.

26 Rose, *The Erosion of Childhood*, pp. 69–71.

27 *Ibid.*, p. 72.

28 Walvin, *A Child's World*, pp. 161–2.

29 Rose, *The Erosion of Childhood*, pp. 47–50.

30 *Ibid.*, pp. 238–9.

31 *Ibid.*, pp. 241–2.

32 Eric Hopkins, *A Social History of the English Working Classes, 1815–1945*, 1979, p. 185; Pat Thane, *The Foundations of the Welfare State*, 1982, pp. 78–9; Derek Fraser, *The Evolution of the British Welfare State*, 2nd Edn, 1984, p. 150, and Pinchbeck and Hewitt, *Children in English Society, Vol. II*, pp. 492–4.

33 Rose, *The Erosion of Childhood*, pp. 72–9.

34 *Select Committee of the House of Lords on the Execution of the Criminal Law, especially respecting Juvenile Offenders and Transportation*, 1847, Evidence, pp. 21–2.

35 *Ibid.*, Second Report, pp. 3, 6.

36 *Ibid.*, pp. 6, 8.

37 *Select Committee on Criminal and Destitute Juveniles*, 1852, Report, p. 33.

38 *Ibid.*, pp. 101–2.

39 *Ibid.*, pp. 259–63. See also the 1896 *Report*, p. 10.

40 1896 *Report*, p. 8.

41 Pinchbeck and Hewitt, *Children in English Society, vol. II* p. 485.

42 *Ibid.*

43 1896 *Report*, p. 8.

44 *Ibid.*, p. 13.

45 J. J. Tobias, *Crime in Industrial Society in the Nineteenth Century*, 1972, p. 101.

46 Walvin, *A Child's World*, p. 144.

47 *Children's Employment Commission*, 1840, Appendix to Second Report, Report by Mr Grainger, fo. 172.

48 Walvin, *A Child's World*, p. 144.

49 *Ibid.*, p. 146.

50 *Report on the Sanitary Condition of the Labouring Population of Great Britain*, 1842, (Chadwick's Report), p. 212.

51 Tobias, *Crime in Industrial Society*, pp. 90–1.
52 *Ibid.*, p. 102.
53 *Ibid.*, p. 94.

Part IV

Further reform, 1867–1914

Chapter Eight

Work and school after 1867

It was explained in the Prologue to this book that it is convenient to deal with the subject of children's working conditions in the nineteenth century in two sections, the first covering the ground up to 1867, and the second from 1867 to the end of the century. This is because, as we have seen, the Factory Act, 1867 extended factory legislation to many large places of work such as ironworks, while the Workshops Act, 1867 was the first measure to impose restrictions on child employment in workshops, defined as workplaces employing less than fifty persons. During the rest of the century these acts were progressively extended and refined, while at the same time the limitations placed on children's work were powerfully reinforced by educational reforms which by 1880 had made attendance at school compulsory between the ages of five and ten. In 1893 the minimum school-leaving age was raised to eleven, and it was raised again in 1899, to twelve. Of course, it took time for the legislation to become effective, especially that relating to workshops, which had first relied on a highly ineffectual system of local inspection until in 1870 the workshops were transferred to the factory inspectorate. Even then it was often difficult for inspectors to check the ages of working children who would be spirited away when the news spread of their arrival. Further, Black Country inspectors complained of children 'trooping into the workshops' to work after school hours. Undoubtedly there was a good deal of unofficial and illegal part-time work by children in domestic workshops. Nevertheless, by the end of the century, the number of children at work had diminished very noticeably; in 1851 the proportion of children aged ten to fifteen at work in England and Wales was 30 per cent. By 1911 this figure had dropped to 14 per cent;[1] and this included both full-timers from the age of thirteen and part-timers under the Factory Acts (part-timers will be discussed later in the chapter). Thus there is no doubt about the dramatic drop in child employment in the last quarter of the nineteenth century. The reader will already have noted that the subject of children's working hours and conditions in the earlier part of the century occupied three chapters. This time it will take only part of one chapter.

It is hard to say whether factory legislation or educational reform should take the greater credit for the reduction in child labour – clearly the factory acts led the way, but their effect was greatly increased by the imposition of compulsory school attendance. As regards factory legislation, it is not proposed here to trace its history in detail in and after 1867, but to give some indication of its major landmarks. Even before the 1867 legislation, the Bleach and Dye Works Act, 1860 and the Lace Act, 1861 extended the regulation of hours to industries associated with cloth production, while the Factory Act, 1864 regulated hours in a number of other industries, including the pottery industry and the manufacture of matches, which industries had been reported on unfavourably by the Children's Employment Commission, 1862. Other acts which should be mentioned are the Agricultural Gangs Act, 1868 and the 1871 Factory Act which refined the existing law and fixed the age at which girls might start work in the brickfields at sixteen. The Coal Mines Regulation Act, 1872, made twelve the minimum age for boys underground, with a maximum week of 54 hours for boys under sixteen. A further Factory Act in 1874 applied to textiles and reduced the maximum working day from 10½ hours to 10 hours, and on Saturdays from 7½ hours to 6½ hours, at the same time raising the age of starting work from eight to ten.[2]

In 1876 another commission was appointed, this time to investigate the working of the factory and workshop acts. Its report pointed out that at the time of publication there were fifteen statutes in all regulating the employment of women, young persons, and children in factories and workshops; and the tone of its introductory remarks is very different from that of some of the earlier reports of the Children's Employment Commissions:

> The improvement in the sanitary arrangements and ventilation of factories has been most marked in recent years; and the cases in which young children are employed in labour unfitted for their years, or in which young persons and women suffered physically from overwork, are now, we believe, as uncommon as formerly they were common.[3]

Be this as it may – and it could be that there is a touch of complacency in this comfortable assertion – the report goes on to set out the working hours of children and young persons firstly in workshops, then in factories in general, and finally in textile factories.[4] Basically, the working day for children under the age of thirteen was 6½ hours; children in workshops could start at eight years of age, while textile factory children could not begin work until they were ten. Young persons could still work a maximum of 12 hours a day, less 2 hours for meals in factories, and 1½ hours for meals in workshops. These differences between the rules for factories and those for workshops were (as the report put it) 'almost universally condemned', since the workshop regulations were many fewer and less binding. Factory owners actually complained of competition from workshop owners who were less bound by regulations. Moreover, the problems of inspecting the great numbers of workshops were immense. The report says plainly that the Workshop Regulation Act was difficult to enforce, 'and in many respects, as there is reason to believe, totally inoperative'.[5] Indeed, the difficulties of inspection are easy to believe, given that there were at this time only two inspectors, four assistant inspectors, thirty-eight sub-inspectors and eleven juniors. In 1872 there were 109,324 workshops, and the number of visits reported by forty-eight sub-inspectors over a period of twelve months was 30,664 (this works out at an astonishing average of 638 visits in the course of the year by each sub-inspector).[6] In the report there are lengthy comments on the educational provisions of the acts and on the half-time system introduced by the Factory Act, 1844, but this aspect will be discussed later in this chapter.

All in all, the commission was clearly concerned at the failure to implement the workshop regulations satisfactorily, though they also thought that the factory acts should be extended to hitherto excepted cases. Their list of these included bakehouses and biscuit-making, rope-walks, pot banks, quarries, open-air premises, shipbuilding, cleaning and washing, laundries and boys carrying goods (but not retail shops, even though their hours ranged from 60 to 100 a week; and not public houses or what were termed 'wandering occupations'). Their main recommendation was simply that the factory acts should be consolidated and workshops made 'factories' in law – that is, that the Workshop Regulation Act, 1867 should be repealed. Minor adjustments to the law were also recommended, for example that it should be possible to substitute another day for Saturday as a weekly half-holiday. There were also strong recommendations as to hours of schooling, and also that attendance at school should be enforced by law.[7]

The impression given by this 1876 report is very different from those to be obtained from, say, the reports of the Children's Employment Commission, 1840. Admittedly, the commissioners were concerned with the operation of the existing regulations rather than with the details of the tasks imposed on children. Nevertheless, the opening statement quoted above sets the tone of the whole report – there are certainly few references to children engaged on unsuitable work, or of instances of cruelty to children. The same may be said about the next major investigation of working conditions which resulted from the appointment of a Select Committee of the House of Lords on the Sweating System in 1888. As the name indicates, the committee was appointed to deal with workshop conditions, especially with the sweatshops of the tailoring industry in the East End of London. It also enquired into the nailing and chainmaking workshops of the Black Country. Once more, there are references to over-long hours worked by some adults, but children were not usually employed in the tailoring sweatshops, while few children were brought up to hand nail-making, since it was a languishing trade, as nails were increasingly machine-made.

The last national enquiry into working conditions in the nineteenth century was undertaken by the Royal Commission on Labour, 1892. This commission produced a remarkably detailed and extensive survey of industry divided into three major groups, contained in five massive reports. Yet references to the employment of children are limited, except in the form of discussion from time to time of part-timers. Their employment was conditional on their attaining a certificate of proficiency from school, and they were most numerous in the Lancashire textile mills. The figures given in the Commission's Fifth Report are as follows:

Lancashire	89,234
Yorkshire	47,775
Cheshire	9,639
Rest of England and Wales	24,038
Total	170,686[8]

The report goes on to comment that in Lancashire these figures represent about two out of three children over ten; in Yorkshire, Cheshire and Leicestershire, one in every four; in Staffordshire, one in fourteen; and in the rest of England and Wales, one in thirty-one.

On a first impression, it might seem that substantial numbers of children were still employed on a part-time basis at the end of the nineteenth century, but they were confined to the textile districts. Moreover, the minimum age for part-time work was raised to eleven in 1893 and to twelve in 1899, so that in 1900 no children at all could work part-time below the age of twelve. According to Mann's calculations, the total school population was about 16.8 per cent of the population as a whole, that is, about five million in England and Wales in 1891 (Gillian Sutherland offers the figure of 4.3 million for 1895). Taking five million as a basis, the total of part-timers would constitute only 3.5 per cent of the school population. However, it should be noted that even after 1900 many children could not leave school at twelve unless they acquired partial exemption either under the Factory Acts or by reaching the local authority's standard of proficiency. According to Dr Hurt, just before the First World War about half of the children in elementary schools left school between twelve and fourteen.[9]

There was certainly a considerable amount of discussion concerning the position of part-timers in the hearing of evidence before the Royal Commission of 1892. Clearly, part-timers were favoured in the textile mills where the use of small children on spinning machines and looms had become traditional. It was still argued that it was best for children to start as part-timers as early as possible, because the skills necessary had to be learned at an early age. There were still as many as one child to four adults in the Lancashire mills. Numerous witnesses, including, surprisingly, two factory inspectors, were in favour of part-time work by children, on the grounds not only that the sooner skills were learned the better but also that families needed the children's earnings, and without them the mother would have to go out to work.[10]

Others strongly opposed the whole system. Understandably, teachers' representatives were against it. The spokesman for the National Union of Teachers claimed that the education of the whole school suffered through the presence of the half-timers, for the curriculum had to be arranged to suit their convenience. Timetabling became impossible when a part-timer might attend in any one of five ways – on alternate days, or mornings only, or afternoons only, and so on. Moreover, starting work at too early an age could have a damaging effect on the child – 'part-timers give up the childhood ways of a child too early', it was said. And again, 'When children have been working in the morning, we find very often that they are drowsy, very sleepy, their receptive power is impaired'. Nor was poverty a sufficient excuse for children working part-time – 'Poverty and part-time have very little connection.' One witness, the well-known socialist H. M. Hyndman, claimed that the part-time system had a very bad effect on the physique of the future generation, while another witness, Sidney Webb, thought it 'highly expedient' to raise the age at which children could enter factories, and to extend their school careers.[11]

It seems likely that part-timers suffered a very disruptive conclusion to their school career and that the system was more profitable to the factory owners than to the part-timers themselves; their educational progress on a part-time basis must have been very limited. However, it remains true that the system had only a limited application by 1900. By then, the vast majority of children could not begin work until they were twelve or even older, though this is not to say, of course, that the law was not evaded at times, nor was out-of-school part-time employment unknown. As regards the former, it was still impossible adequately to police the large numbers of small workshops. As the Fifth Report puts it: 'It appears that boys are frequently employed under age, and when the inspector comes round, are hidden, so that the infraction of the law is seldom discovered. The extent of this evil varies, however, very largely in different localities.'[12]

As regards out-of-school part-time employment, this was very common. As we saw earlier in this chapter, children were often employed after school (and, indeed, before school started) in domestic workshops. A variety of jobs was available for them in towns, especially as errand boys, messengers, and delivery boys. Many were employed as van boys, and there was some public concern about the extent of this employment in the early twentieth century, especially in Birmingham, where there was something of a traditional use of part-time child labour.[13] Boys and girls were cheaper to employ than adults, and their employment was widespread. An enquiry in 1908 estimated that nearly 200,000 schoolchildren had jobs outside school hours, excluding half-timers and street traders.[14] Thus in addition to the part-timers who were officially recognised as dividing their time between school and work, there were many more children engaged in part-time work outside school hours for varying lengths of time, from a few hours weekly to a substantial number of hours per week. An extreme instance of this was that of the lather boys in barbers' shops:

> The worst form of shop work is that of the lather boys in barbers' shops. The hours worked by these boys are longer than in any other trade; five hours every evening, with fifteen hours on Saturday, and six or eight on Sunday, are not

uncommon; the sanitary conditions of the shops are sometimes exceedingly bad, and in the lower quarters of the town they are said to be the meeting places of gamblers, and the conversation and surroundings are the worst conceivable for children.[15]

What awaited older children when they entered full-time employment? The major categories of employment in the nineteenth century had changed considerably by the early twentieth century. In particular, boys no longer entered agriculture in such numbers as they had in 1851; the number of boys employed in farming in Britain in 1851 was 120,000, but it had dropped to 39,000 in 1911, greater numbers now being engaged in both textiles and transport. The numbers of boys in textiles had also fallen from 82,000 in 1851 to 46,000 in 1911, though the numbers in mining and in domestic service remained about the same. For girls, textiles was still the major industry in 1911, employing 68,000, together with domestic service (50,000, down from 71,000 in 1851), and dressmaking, which remained about the same at 33,000. In more detail, the figures for the main occupations of boys and girls under fifteen in 1911 are as follows:

Boys			*Girls*		
	(000s)	(%)		(000s)	(%)
Transport	95	27.5	Textiles	68	34.0
Textiles	46	13.3	Domestic Service	50	25.0
Agriculture	39	11.3	Dress	33	16.5
Mines	36	10.4	Food, tobacco, drink, lodging	9	4.5
Metals, machines, implements and conveyances	29	8.4	Paper, printing, books and stationery	8	4.0
Food, tobacco, drink, lodging	16	4.6	Transport	7	3.5
Dress	12	3.5	Metals, machines, implements and conveyances	6	3.0
Domestic Service	9	2.6			
Commercial occupations	8	2.3			
Total employed	346		*Total employed*	200[16]	

A different kind of analysis is provided by R. H. Tawney in his article on Boy Labour published in 1909, where he gives the occupations of 150 boys on leaving school in London and then two years later.[17] It illustrates the concern at the time at the numbers of boys going into dead-end jobs:

Occupation	*On leaving school*	*At sixteen*
Country workers	7	4
Seamen	4	5
Apprentices or learners	8	20
Message boys and milk boys	55	13
Van boys	17	6
Van men	—	9
Boys of labourers in factories or works	40	49
General labourers	9	30

It is clear that in London most boys started work as errand boys or milk boys, or as helpers to industrial labourers, moving on by the age of sixteen to become labourers either in industry or elsewhere. Similar results were obtained by Arnold Freeman in an investigation in Birmingham, and published in his book *Boy Life and Labour: The Manufacture of Inefficiency* (1914). One interesting category to emerge from Tawney's survey is that of the apprentices, who are not shown separately in the preceding table of occupations in 1911.

There have been frequent references in this book to apprenticeship in the nineteenth century, often in the form of the apprenticing of poor law children in husbandry, but also in both workshop and factory. Such apprenticeships were usually a convenient way for poor law authorities to rid themselves of orphan children, and this kind of apprenticeship was too often accompanied by ill-treatment of the children, as we have seen. The traditional form of apprenticeship, however, involving service under indentures for a term of seven years to a skilled trade and the payment of a premium to a master continued thoughout the nineteenth century. Sometimes apprenticeship maintained this formal pattern, but at other times, and more commonly perhaps, it was based on a much looser relationship, the apprentices simply being known as 'learners', and the boy (or girl) being taught not by a master but by one of his workmen. With the great expansion and proliferation of trades in the early nineteenth century, it is understandable that the traditional form of apprenticeship should no longer be thought appropriate for the training of young persons. Fewer apprentices lived in, and many had merely informal verbal agreements with workmen for varying periods of tuition, often much less than the customary seven years. Thus in Birmingham in the 1840s some employers expressed hostility to the whole system; one gave his opinion that 'The system of apprenticeship is quite changed. No respectable manufacturer will trouble himself about them . . . many parents will not bind their children because they hope they will gain a man's wages before the time of their serving expires.'[18] Yet at the same time another manufacturer, a brassfounder, said that although he had only one apprentice, his men had many.[19]

The question therefore arises, how far could working-class children at the end of the nineteenth century expect to be apprenticed? How far was this the way to a skilled and more secure, better-paid job? Earlier writers here took a very pessimistic view of the situation; the author of a standard work, Jocelyn Dunlop, writing in 1912, thought that the 'definite collapse' of apprenticeship began as early as about 1720, when the reorganisation of trades on a capitalist basis was accelerated. The Webbs, in their book *Industrial Democracy* (revised edition, 1902), declared even more strongly that 'over by far the limited field in which apprenticeship once prevailed, the system has gone practically out of use'. These views were supported by Sir John Clapham in 1932 and to a considerable extent by Professor Ashworth as late as 1960.[20]

The older interpretation certainly was that apprenticeship had little national significance by 1900. More recently, however, the subject of de-skilling at the end of the nineteenth century has come under discussion – that is, the extent to which the wider use of more machinery, and of more complicated machinery, led to a loss of the old craft skills. This subject has necessarily involved a study of the teaching of skills, and of how far apprenticeship was still the accepted mode for transmitting industrial skill. The result has been a reassessment of the situation regarding apprenticeship in the early twentieth century. Dr Charles More has provided some valuable information in this respect in his *Skill and the English Working Class 1870–1914*, (1980). According to Dr More, there were, at a rough estimate, over 340,000 apprentices in any one year in the early years of the twentieth century. Apprentices formed the greater part of recruits to engineering fitting, turning, and pattern making, and also to moulding and smithing. In shipbuilding, the platers, riveters and caulkers were largely apprenticed. In building and woodworking, carpenters and joiners, wet coopers and some cabinet-makers, as well as some bricklayers, masons and painters were all apprenticed. In printing (as might be expected) many compositors, lithographers and stereotypers were also apprenticed. The largest number of apprentices in 1906 were in building (100,200) and in engineering(94,100). If a figure of 52,000 in respect of distributive and mercantile marine apprentices were to be added to the figure of 340,000 (refined by More later to 343,200), then a grand total of 395,700 is reached, which is 21 per cent of the total of 1,882,855 of all working males aged between fifteen and nineteen in 1906.[21] On the basis of these figures there seems little doubt that apprenticeship was still of considerable national importance in 1900 and that some working-class children, at the very least, would embark on a form of apprenticeship at the age of fourteen or so.

However, this is not to say that apprenticeship as an institution was actually flourishing about 1900, or had not undergone change in the preceding century. It is simply to assert that in its varying forms it remained a pathway to the acquisition of skills for working-class children, generally from the age of fourteen, and commonly for four, five or six years (though some trades still insisted on seven years, especially printing). Some of the newer trades, however, such as chemicals, had no formal apprenticeship, and it has already been pointed out that the actual form of apprenticeship varied noticeably from trade to trade. Even in engineering there might be little direct teaching of skill. Robert Roberts records that when he became an apprentice in a small engineering works, he was first put on a small machine which polished nuts:

> In three minutes the chargehand had taught me all I needed to know. 'Now gerron with it', he ordered, 'and don't let me catch you scowin'!' Over the next two years, in between brushing the alleys and brewing thirty cans of tea each morning, I performed this simplest of tasks for eight and a half hours every working day. This was called an 'engineering apprenticeship'.[22]

Generally speaking, there was some awareness that the nature of apprenticeship was changing, and that it was, in fact, dying in some sectors of industry. According to the reports of the Royal Commission on Labour, 1892 it played only a very small part in textiles and had fallen more or less into disuse in the boot, shoe and tailoring trades. In the group of industries comprising the chemical, building and miscellaneous trades there were many complaints of the decay of the old system of apprenticeship, which was said to be 'almost obsolete' in London. In the *General Review of the Evidence* of this commission, it is asserted that the system had declined but continued in many small trades in small-scale but not large works or factories. It had a tendency to die out when not made necessary by the skilled nature of the trade or where it was not enforced by strong trade unions. Questions of apprenticeship were most prominent in shipbuilding and in engineering, it was said. However, the commission did not think it necessary to recommend any further efforts to regulate apprenticeship by law – a reference perhaps to the Statute of Apprentices, 1563, which had been removed from the statute book as long ago as 1813.[23]

Another dimension to the problem of apprenticeship about 1900 is the question of de-skilling referred to earlier and the extent to which this was reducing the need for craftsmen and producing a new category of machine-minders who had little need of skills. We have already noted that at the time there was considerable disquiet about blind-alley jobs, and about what was termed the 'Boy Labour problem'. There were fears about national degeneracy as Britain began to lose her industrial supremacy, especially after the revelations of the unfitness for service of many volunteers during the Boer War (1899–1902). There was also concern about the extent of poverty, about unemployment, and about the need for a healthy and thriving working class if the Empire was to be maintained. In his influential article of 1909, Tawney argued that each process had its own machine, and the mechanic was being replaced by a machine-minder, so that the boy labourer was replacing the boy learner or apprentice.[24] Views of this kind led to demands for better industrial training, possibly in day continuation schools. They also helped to bring about the Youth Employment Service, set up under the Labour Exchanges Act, 1909, and the proposal for day continuation colleges in the Fisher Education Act, 1918.

What does all this amount to from the point of view of the average school leaver from a working-class home about 1900? For the great majority of school leavers, full-time work could not begin legally until they reached the age of twelve and according to Tawney most boys in London in 1909 did not start work until they were fourteen. But there were plenty who did start earlier on, and of course there were those employed usually legally enough in a variety of part-time jobs such as errand boys, newspaper sellers, helpers in shops and on market stalls and as the notorious lather boys. The age of starting work therefore seems to have varied greatly, as indeed it had at the beginning of the century, but the introduction and extension of compulsory schooling had in effect raised the age of starting work by five, six or even more years since then. The contrast with the position in 1800 is very marked.

The kind of work which was available for children had also changed. Children still went into the textile industry, but conditions of work were subject to severe regulation, and twice as many boys were in transport as in textiles in 1911. It was otherwise with girls, for whom textiles were still the largest occupation, followed by domestic service. So far as work with machinery is concerned, the effect of de-skilling was probably exaggerated at the time, and certainly there is nothing to show that there was a widespread decline of skilled trades as they were replaced by a machine technology. On the other hand, de-skilling did exist in engineering, and here the use of machinery was advancing with a decreasing demand for the old skills and an increased demand for semi-skilled tradesmen with skills appropriate to operating new machines. This was a sensitive point with the trade unions, who wished to maintain apprenticeship in their own interests. According to the final report of the Royal Commission on Labour, 1892 this was one of the leading points at issue between employers and the employed.[25]

Finally, the concern shown about apprenticeship and dead-end occupations at the end of the century is interesting, though here again it is important to see it in perspective. From today's standpoint, it seems to have been the consequence of a number of developments at the time; above all, perhaps, the realisation that if Britain was to hold her own against her industrial competitors and also to maintain her Empire then it was essential to maintain a healthy, flourishing and fully-employed work-force. Apprenticeship had changed its nature during the course of the nineteenth century in obedience to the economic needs of industry. Thus it disappeared from the textile industry, except for a few of the subsidiary trades such as those of wool sorters, warp dressers and linen lappers. Girl spinners simply learned their skills by being taught for three months for a small fee and without wages, this being done without any reference to the employer, who neither supported nor interfered with the practice.[26] In engineering and shipbuilding, however, a much more traditional form of training was retained, sometimes (as we have seen) without much real substance, but with union support. As for dead-end jobs, that is, unskilled work paid at low rates for juveniles, who after a while would be forced to move on in search of a better-paid job, such employment had always existed in the nineteenth century; but it was the need to examine the role of labour more critically at the end of the century which brought a better understanding of juvenile labour and its problems.

How far did the nature of work really change for children in the last third of the nineteenth century? The common-sense conclusion would appear to be that the revelations of cruelty in previous years coupled with the restrictions on the length and nature of child labour did bring a change in attitude and a greater realisation that children and young persons had to be treated differently. The forming of the National Society for the Prevention of Cruelty to Children in 1889 and the passing of the Prevention of Cruelty Act in the same year are a sufficient indication of changing attitudes. Moreover, there is a significant contrast to be drawn between the controversy over children's working hours in the first decades of the century and the lengthy discussions over Boy Labour when children left school at the end of the century. There was now no dispute over the need for children to attend school until at least the age of twelve, but rather there was argument over the need to give industrial training when they did start work. Nevertheless, the treatment they received at the workplace did not change in nature overnight; the hours might still be very long in the 1890s. According to the fifth report of the Commission on Labour, 1892, even when the law was not broken the work could be too laborious for some boys. For example, in printing some boys under sixteen were found working 36 and 40 hours at a stretch, while in copper works the work was very heavy for ridiculously low pay. In one glass bottle firm the boys had to run twenty-five miles a day.[27] On the other hand, in the Staffordshire mines conditions for boys were subject to numerous regulations and the boys had to pass the Fifth Standard before starting as waggoners and pony drivers. Later on they became loaders and then went on to hew at the pit face.[28] In Birmingham, in the years just before the Great War, boys in unskilled trades often had monotonous and boring jobs to perform, but many seemed able to find time for football in the dinner-hour and for gossip during working hours when work was slack. As a good many changed their jobs frequently, it seems that work at this low level was not difficult to find, though unskilled work had no future and at the age of eighteen the majority would face dismissal when their age qualified them for an adult wage.[29]

To sum up, the contrast between the working conditions of children in 1870 and in 1900 is marked. At the earlier date substantial numbers were still engaged in agriculture, textiles, transport, workshop industry and domestic service. It took time to enforce the factory and workshop legislation of 1867, and schooling was not yet compulsory or free. At the later date factory and workshop legislation had been greatly extended, and in theory at least all children between the ages of five and twelve were to be in school. This then is the classic period in which childhood was transformed, in that by the end of the century schooling replaced work as the recognised occupation of boys and girls from five onwards to at least twelve. Whatever reservations have to be made about this transformation, it remains true that an extraordinary change had taken place in working-class life, a change not always welcome or regarded as necessarily beneficial by all, but one which was inescapable. Full-time child labour under the age of twelve had largely ceased to exist.

Yet substantial qualifications must be made to this picture of working-class children shielded from too early an entry into employment. The first is that illegal employment continued both in the form of under-age working and in the working of excessive hours. It is impossible to quantify this, but undoubtedly it existed, if only to a limited extent. Secondly, part-time work was still possible in 1900 from the age of twelve, provided the necessary standard had been reached; but as we have seen, the numbers involved were not great, except in textiles, and the practice was strongly criticised at the time. It continued until abolished by the Fisher Education Act in 1918.[30] Thirdly, the number of children engaged in part-time work before and after school, at week-ends and in the school holidays was very considerable. It was perhaps this aspect of child labour which caused most concern at the end of the century and before 1914. Estimates of numbers so employed vary. According to Lionel Rose, a questionnaire sent out to schools in 1899 resulted in a figure of 145,000 moonlighters out of a school population of five million. Dr Horn, quoting from the 1901 Interdepartmental Committee report, makes the figure about 150,000, of whom about 40,000 were working for more than forty hours a week. Using the same source, Rose give 200,000, while Dr Sutherland thinks the 1901 figure should be about 300,000. Dr Hurt places the number in 1914 as high as half a million, though this is for those 'dividing their energies between school and work', and may include part-timers.[31] Whatever the true figure, it is evident that the tradition that children should add to the family income died hard. Repeated efforts to stop part-time child labour achieved very little. The Prevention of Cruelty to Children Act, 1894 tried to put an end to street trading by children, but was too limited in its terms; while attempts by the larger cities to control street trading were usually a failure for want of enforcement by the local inspectors. Following the report on street trading by the Interdepartmental Committee, the Employment of Children Act, 1903 permitted local authorities to pass by-laws to restrict street trading, but again the act had only limited success as it was permissive. All in all, the cities provided the scene for most part-time juvenile work before 1914 (though naturally it continued as before on the farms), and it took a variety of forms – street trading, helping in shops, delivering milk and papers and so on. In Birmingham in January, 1914 there were 2,585 elementary school children working 10–20 hours a week, 2,145 working

20–30 hours, and 1,725 working an incredible 30–40 hours a week. In London, an estimated 8 per cent were moonlighters.[32] However, the proportion of spare-time workers among the school population should not be exaggerated. If it was 8 per cent in London, then more than nine out of ten children were *not* so employed.

Lastly, and by way of conclusion to this section, it should perhaps be said yet again that at the beginning of the nineteenth century child labour formed an integral part of the labour force in England and Wales, but that by 1900 it had become merely marginal, as a result of both economic and social forces. As indicated at the end of Chapter Three, with the development of more mechanised production child labour was needed less and the rise in the standard of living made children's earnings less important to working-class family incomes. Yet this did not make their earnings unwelcome to its parents, and there remained a vast number of simple, unskilled and labour-intensive jobs still available to part-time child labour. This is still true at the present day, and many parents, both working-class and middle-class, are happy enough for their children to deliver newspapers and to work in shops. According to a recent joint report by the Low Pay Unit and Birmingham City Council entitled *The Hidden Army* (1991), of nearly 2,000 Birmingham children aged between ten to sixteen, 43 per cent worked, three-quarters illegally. Nationally, the Low Pay Unit estimated that two million children in Britain were at work.[33]

It will be recalled that when working-class schooling in the 1860s was last discussed, it was suggested that it had entered a transitional period in which the outlines of a national system were beginning to emerge, but with numerous gaps and deficiencies. On the other hand, school attendance was becoming increasingly common, usually at the church schools dominated by the Church of England. The annual grant to the church societies, both Anglican and nonconformist, was over half a million pounds a year, and vigorous efforts were made under the Revised Code of 1862 (by Payment by Results) to keep costs down. On the other hand, attendance at school was not yet compulsory, nor was it free – indeed, some parents could see little point in education, and still preferred to send their children out to work as soon as possible, because of the contribution they could make to the family economy. Moreover, even when children did attend school, it was often only for short periods of time, and the instruction they received was of a very limited nature, going no further than the bare essentials of the three Rs. There was very little recognition of the need for any further, secondary education for working-class children to follow what was now being called elementary education. As was noted earlier, Robert Lowe, Vice-President of the Committee of Council for Education, made it clear that there was no intention of giving children an education which would raise them above their station and business in life.

Nevertheless, the tide was beginning to run strongly in favour of further legislation in order to bring within the educational net those children, often from the poorest homes, who still did not attend school.[34] The result was the Education Act, 1870, sometimes known as Forster's Act, after the Vice-President of the Committee of Council for Education, W. E. Forster, who piloted it through the Commons. There was already a good deal of middle-class pressure for reform; the National Education League, which demanded free, compulsory and secular education was established in 1869. Earlier historians have tried to detect other reasons for the passing of this act, for example, the military success of Prussia, which (it was alleged) owed much to the Prussian state system of education. In fact the Newcastle Commission had examined the Prussian system in 1862 and had concluded that its results were not really much superior to the voluntary system in this country; and it does not seem that Prussian efficiency had much influence on the government's policy at the time. Another suggestion has been that Lowe's comment after the passing of the Reform Act, 1867, that 'we must educate our masters', demonstrates the belief that it was necessary to educate the working-class voters enfranchised in the borough constituencies by the act. In actual fact, most of the working-class men entitled to vote under the act were already at least literate (some had had the vote even before 1867), and the amount of working-class pressure for educational reform arising from the new voters was not politically significant. Lowe was a bitter opponent of the 1867 act, but his views did not have much general support in the House of Commons.[35] Clearly this explanation of the origins of the Education Act, 1870 is hardly adequate.

The basic reason for the passing of the Education Act, 1870 is probably mundane enough. Momentum for an extention of working-class schooling had been building up for some time. The Newcastle Commission had favoured it and proposed that it be supported out of local rates – something already advocated by Russell's abortive bill of 1853. By 1870 the financial problems of both church societies were becoming serious; the smaller British and Foreign Schools Society simply lacked the resources to provide sufficient schools, especially in the countryside, where the numbers of nonconformist children were relatively small and it was hardly worth while building small village schools for them. The National Society, of course, was much better-off financially, but even with the support of the Anglican establishment it was hard to keep pace with the ever-increasing number of children of school age. Reluctant as they were to surrender any part of their control over the school system, they were forced to compromise. The result was the Education Act, passed by a Liberal Government under Gladstone, with strong nonconformist support. If the nonconformists could not gain control over the residuum of children not within the educational system, they could at least keep these children out of the clutches of the Church of England. Religion here was not a barrier to advance, as it had been in the past, but it did determine and shape the form that it took.

Forster had to walk very warily in order not to antagonise the church societies. His proposal was not to take away their control of their schools, but instead, as he put it 'to supplement the present voluntary system – that is, . . . fill up its gaps at the least cost of public money, with least loss of voluntary cooperation, and with most aid from parents.'[36] In short, this meant that the existing system should continue, but where there was a need for a new school, it should be provided by a school board elected locally by the ratepayers, and financed both by a local educational rate and by an annual grant. The schools would not be free to parents: fees of up to 9*d* per week could be charged. Nor were they compulsory, though a school board could pass by-laws for attendance between the ages of five and twelve (inclusive), with exemptions (full- or part-time) from the age of ten, dependent on the child's educational attainment. Lastly, any religious teaching in the board schools was, under the Temple–Cowper clause in the act, to be undenominational – there should be 'no religious catechism or religious formulary which is distinctive of any particular denomination'.

Naturally it took some time for the act to be implemented. The church societies were allowed six months to fill up the existing gaps themselves, and there was a flurry of church school building at the end of 1870 – about 3,000 applications were received for building grants in the last five months of 1870; there had been only 226 for the whole of 1869. At the same time, enquiries were carried out by the Education Department in order to establish where there were deficiencies in school provision. Some local communities were confident they had enough school places only to find that the local enquiry conducted by the

Education Department decided otherwise. Problems arose in some rural areas where the population was sparse and the number of adult ratepayers capable of serving on a school board was small. By way of contrast, the larger towns and cities had no difficuties of this kind – the famous London School Board, whose massive buildings with the monogram LSB became a new feature of the inner London townscape, had as its chairman Lord Lawrence, formerly Viceroy of India, while Joseph Chamberlain was a member of the Birmingham School Board.

The appointment of the school boards had important political implications. Working-class ratepayers had a share in their election (twelve votes or even more were usually available for each ratepayer, to be distributed among the candidates or given to any one of them), so that working men or women could be elected. One drawback here, however, was that voting was normally during working hours, when it might be difficult for the working man or woman to get away from work; and even if elected, he or she might have difficulties in attending board meetings held during the day rather than in the evening. Nevertheless, school boards constituted an important democratic advance, even though they met with some opposition from supporters of the voluntary system, especially members of the Church of England, who were not above obstructing the work of school boards or getting them to pay the school fees of poor children at church schools as well as in board schools (in 1876 this power under clause 25 was made over to the poor law guardians).

As for the new schools themselves, they swiftly became prominent in the towns in their new red brick (soon to be darkened by atmospheric pollution). In London the first LSB school opened in 1873; by 1875, there were seventy-nine in all – a remarkably rapid rate of building.[37] They usually took the form of impressive buildings on three floors ('three-deckers'), with large windows and playgrounds. Being newly built, board schools were usually superior in construction to the church schools, which might date back to the early decades of the nineteenth century; but some board schools were simply former church schools, especially schools of the British and Foreign Schools Society, which the societies no longer wished to run. Again, some board schools had to be built in the rougher working-class urban districts where the church societies had not thought it worth while to build. Board schools in these areas had an exceedingly rough clientele; they were really slum schools, and teaching in them was a formidable task. In 1872 *The Schoolmaster* recognised this, referring to 'the younger years of school board life, while the unbroken youth of our country are being raked in from the gutter, the dunghill, and the hedgerow.'[38] Indeed, from early on it was recognised that the particular task of the school boards was to teach the residuum who had not previously attended school, so that while the children of better-off working parents would continue to go to the church schools, the children of the poorest families would attend the board schools. This appears to have been acknowledged by the school boards themselves. By the end of the 1880s the London School Board had 110,000 school places at 1*d* a week, 180,000 at 2*d*, 100,000 at 3*d*, and 60,000 at 4*d* or more. In this way the Board provided for the children of better-paid parents to attend schools which were beyond the reach of the poorest classes.[39] A similar policy of social differentiation seems to have been followed by the Birmingham School Board.[40]

What was the impact of the 1870 act on working-class parents and children? For many parents it brought little that was new. They were already accustomed to sending their children to school, for varying periods of time, of course, and were also used to paying school pence. It was the minority of parents who were affected by the new act, those who for one reason or another had refrained from sending their children and who now found that the local board exercised its option to make attendance compulsory. Few boards did this, as we shall see shortly, but pressure was increasingly exerted on parents to make their children attend. Some working-class parents therefore found themselves confronted by a new figure of authority, the school attendance officer (sometimes known at first with some delicacy as 'the visitor'). A failure to send the child to school or to pay the school fees – children would be sent home on Monday morning if they had not brought their school pence – would result in a court appearance. School fees could be excused on account of poverty, of course, but recourse to the Guardians could be a humiliating experience, and forfeited the right to vote. Meanwhile the hunt was on to identify the poorer parents who had hitherto had nothing to do with schools, and to bring their progeny to the school door. For some of these children, school must have been a frightening experience – their first acquaintanceship with authority other than their parents and also (it could be) with other children better-washed and better-clothed than themselves. In a number of different ways the 1870 act was a monumental piece of legislation, marking a new era in the lives of children, especially those growing up in the most impoverished and restricted of homes. Curiously enough, the one part of the act which had caused some middle-class controversy, that relating to religious instruction, seems to have been implemented without difficulty. What religious teaching was undertaken was not subject to any close definition in the act, and was usually based on simple Bible teaching. Few parents withdrew their children from religious instruction, though seven boards in England and fifty in Wales prohibited all religious teaching. The Birmingham School Board was one of these, the schools being handed over for one hour on two days a week to the Religious Education Society, who sent in their own teachers.[41]

Undoubtedly by the 1870s the image of school as it appeared to children had undergone significant changes since the beginning of the century. In an earlier chapter it was suggested that about 1800 the idea of going to school was something alien to many working-class children; and if they went at all, it would be for only very short periods. Later in the century, however, the idea of school had become increasingly familiar to young children. Put at its simplest, in the course of time the majority of children had begun to attend school (though not all, and still sometimes for short periods only), and as a result school attendance had become an accustomed experience for many. By 1871, as noted in Chapter Five, four out of five bridegrooms and nearly three out of four brides could sign the marriage register – a great improvement in signature-literacy since the beginning of the century, and a good indication of improved school attendance. We can only guess at the attitude of children to school in these changed circumstances, but it seems a fair assumption that there must have been a far wider acceptance of school by then as part of the growing-up process. It was no longer something which might or might not happen. Further, the restrictions placed on child labour meant that school was more and more becoming the necessary experience before starting work, and was no longer a possible alternative to work. In the natural order of things (or so it appeared), boys and girls were to be found at school from the age of five or even earlier. Of course, this did not necessarily make school any more palatable or welcome as an experience, and later in the chapter an attempt will be made to describe some basic aspects of elementary school life towards the end of the century. Some enjoyed their time in school; others emphatically did not. But whatever their reactions, after 1870 schooling increasingly became an established stage in the whole process of growing up, a fate (some might say) from which there was no escape.

In the thirty years following the passing of the 1870 act, further important educational reforms were passed. The first was that of compulsory attendance. In 1876 a first step was taken in this direction when Lord Sandon's Act declared that it was the duty of parents to send their children to school, and also established school attendance committees in areas without school boards, with the authority to compel attendance as could school boards themselves. In this way, pressure was increased on parents to send their children to school. Even then, compulsion existed to only a limited extent. By 1880, only 450, or less than a quarter of the 2,000 school boards, and only 20 of the 190 school attendance committees had made attendance obligatory.[42] Yet there was general agreement that compulsion was necessary. The 1876 Royal Commission on the Factory Acts reported in favour, and the schools were still gravely hampered by irregular attendance. Moreover, they were coming to realise that compulsory attendance would increase their grant. The Inspectorate drew attention to the fact that irregular attendance was fatal to successful work. According to the Revd H. G. Alington, inspector for parts of Kent and Sussex: 'A school of 121 children is open 420 times a year. Three children only have attended 400 times; not more than 34 have been present 300 times . . . What can be more hopeless than such an institution of shreds and patches? How can habits of order be instilled thus by fits and starts?'[43] Another inspector, the Revd C. F. Johnstone, inspector for Huntingdon and Bedfordshire, made the same point: 'Children attend irregularly and they leave school early. This is a prevailing cry, and it is an unanswerable one. During the few years of their school life they are taught by snatches, and they are never able to gain sufficient grasp of any subject to retain it.'[44]

There was the further problem of the numbers of children who still never came to school at all. These would often be the children from the very poorest homes where the parents would genuinely find it very hard to pay the school fees. The inspector for Cumberland and Westmorland commented on this: 'Boards in towns have undoubtedly great difficulties to contend with. At the inspections in Carlisle last year I observed that comparatively few children of the ragged classes seemed to be present, and it is not easy to see how they are to be brought in.'[45]

In fact, there was really only one way in which they could be brought in, and that was by compulsion. This was done when the Liberals returned to office under Gladstone in 1880. By the Education Act of that year attendance became compulsory between the ages of five and twelve, with partial or full exemptions from the age of ten, dependent on the attendance record of the child and his or her educational attainment. These requirements would be determined by the local authority. These reforms excited some controversy, even though they were merely an extension of the powers conferred in the 1870 and 1876 acts. There was a minority who argued that compulsion was an infringement on the personal liberty of the parents. Rather more opponents pointed out the problems faced by the poorest parents in paying fees. For them, this could be a substantial if not an impossible burden. Moreover, some voluntary schools kept their fees relatively high in order to keep out the children of the more feckless and disreputable parents. Yet even respectable parents might fall out of work in periods of depression and be unable to pay, and the 1880s in particular were years of some depression. Of course, fees could be remitted by the poor law guardians, by school managers and by school boards, but the process of applying for relief could be irksome and humiliating. By 1890–91 the proportion of free places in board and church schools was about 5 per cent, while another 4 per cent had fees remitted by the poor law authorities – that is, the total of free places in all elementary schools was still under 10 per cent at this time.[46]

However, in 1891 there came the second major educational reform of the period from 1871 to 1900. This was the passing of Lord Salisbury's Education Act, a Conservative measure which provided an additional grant to schools which abolished fees; parents were also given the right to demand free places for their children. It is curious that the standard histories of education do not say a great deal about this act, and it is true that it took some time to be implemented. Some church schools went on levying school fees in order to exclude children from the roughest homes, and there were parents who accepted this and were willing to pay on a voluntary basis. Nevertheless, Forster's Education Act, together with the acts of 1880 and 1891, provided the foundation for a national system of compulsory and free education for working-class childen, and one which is still the basis a hundred years later. At last, all children between five and ten, and in many cases up to the age of fourteen, had to attend school, and parents could no longer make inability to pay school fees the excuse for not sending them.

Yet having got the children into school, educational reformers found themselves confronted with a new set of problems. There were still the old problems of poor attendance and non-attendance and of what precisely the elementary schools should be aiming to achieve. A new problem was what to do about the children from the poorest homes who had at last been brought within the educational fold. These children might be ragged, without boots or shoes, unkempt, dirty, verminous and undernourished. Headlice and ringworm became familiar enemies in some schools in the poorer quarters. Charles Booth's famous survey of *Life and Labour of the People of London* (in seventeen volumes, 1889–1903) established that 30.7 per cent of the city's population were living in poverty, while 8.4 per cent were living in dire and abject poverty. Rowntree's investigation in York, published in 1901, produced comparable figures of 27.84 per cent and 9.91 per cent.[47] Children from homes suffering from poverty of this order were now to be found in school – often subject to debilitating sickness, with rotten teeth and with defects of hearing and of sight. What was to be done about these casualties of a low standard of living, many of them the product of the worst urban slums? Half-starved children in a wretched physical condition could hardly be expected to learn much.

At the other end of the scale were the children from respectable homes whose parents could afford to keep them on at school beyond the minimum school-leaving age (raised to eleven in 1893 and twelve in 1899), who wanted something more than the basic three Rs for their offspring. Something was done for them by those school boards which set up higher grade schools. More specialised teaching in such schools attracted extra grants from the Department of Science and Art at South Kensington, and students could be entered for public examinations such as those of the City and Guilds Institute in London, or the Royal Society of Arts. By 1894 there were sixty higher grade schools outside London, and by 1900 the London School Board had seventy-nine. How far any of this educational activity could be regarded as providing *elementary* education is a moot point, to which we shall return shortly. Meanwhile, in 1889 the Technical Instruction Act was passed, permitting the new county councils (established in 1888) to raise a penny rate for technical education and to borrow money for new school buildings. Money might also be available from Kensington for evening classes, though it is worth noticing that technical education could be interpreted very liberally to include cookery, laundry work and woodwork.[48]

One last problem to emerge towards the end of the century was the increasing financial difficulties of the church schools. Though under powerful patronage, they still had no direct assistance from the rates, unlike the board schools. The Cross Commission, appointed to survey elementary education, reported in 1888, and once more recommended that church schools should have support from the rates. In 1895 a strong deputation to the Government from the Church of England, led by the two archbishops, sought additional grants for the voluntary schools; but an education bill which was intended to provide this in 1896 came to nothing, such was the opposition of the school boards and of the nonconformists. Meanwhile, another Royal Commission, the Bryce Commission, 1894, reported on the state of secondary education, which included, of course, the new higher grade schools. It recommended that there should be a new government authority to deal with education which would supervise both elementary and secondary education, thus merging the functions of both the Education Department and the Science and Art Department. Further, the county councils (including the county borough councils) should take over all secondary education, including the higher grade schools. All these matters – the state of the poorer children, the issue of the higher grade schools, the financial problems of the church schools and the need for reorganisation of the whole system, both centrally and locally, came to a head at the end of the nineteenth century or shortly thereafter.

To deal with the administrative reforms first: in 1899 the Education Department and the Science and Art Department were merged into a new central body, the Board of Education – in effect, a ministry of Education, though it did not acquire that title until 1944. With a government minister as President, it took over all the powers of the two departments it replaced, plus the educational functions of the Charity Commissioners, who had previously been responsible for the endowed grammar schools. A more difficult problem was presented by the Bryce Commission's recommendations regarding new local authorities with authority over secondary schools. The school boards were very reluctant to surrender control of the higher grade schools, yet their very legality was questionable. Further, the school boards were themselves vulnerable to criticism in some cases as being too small to be efficient – there were 151 boards with fewer than 250 inhabitants in their districts. Moreover, new local authorities had been set up in 1895 for urban and rural districts, in the form of urban and rural district councils and civil parishes. Finally, it was the doubtful legality of using ratepayers' money for higher grade schools and even evening classes which proved the school boards' undoing. In 1899 a carefully arranged complaint to a district auditor, one Cockerton, against the London School Board's use of the rates for education other than in the elementary schools led to such expenditure being declared illegal; and an appeal by the LSB to the High Court against the decision proved unsuccessful. Henceforth all such use of public money had to stop.

This represented a victory for the enemies of the school boards, and two years later their opponents scored another success when the Education Act, 1902 abolished the school boards completely, transferring their powers to the county councils and county borough councils, who were henceforth to be responsible for both secondary and elementary education, with the qualification that in the smaller boroughs and in less populated urban areas the borough councils and urban district councils were to be in charge of elementary or primary education only. The old board schools continued, but under new authorities – they became known as council schools. Supporters of church schools were delighted that their schools were now to gain support from the rates, in return for which the local educational authority could appoint up to one-third of the school managers. One last important provision of the 1902 act was that the new authorities for secondary education were to survey the need for secondary schools in their area, and to take action where they thought it necessary, including the provision of new school buildings.

If Forster's 1870 Education Act was an important step forward in extending elementary education for working-class children, so of at least equal importance is the 1902 Education Act in reorganising the educational administration of the state system and in encouraging secondary education. True, the act had its opponents: those who had supported school boards as a new democratic instrument regretted their replacement by the new local authority bodies; although these, too, were elected, the school committees were nominated. More substantial opposition, perhaps, came from those who objected to the 'church on the rates', that is, to rate support for church schools. Some nonconformists, especially in Wales, took this to the extent of refusing to pay their rates, even going to prison as a result. However, the new educational administration worked well, and was to last for nearly three-quarters of a century. Further, a very important result of the act was the provision of new county secondary schools, run on grammar school lines, with a proportion of free places to be filled by scholarships from the elementary schools, the proportions varying from one authority to another. Critics have lamented the fact that these schools failed to develop the technical and scientific skills of the higher grade schools, but in fact they certainly taught science and were usually better equipped than many old endowed schools. In the terminology of the time, an educational ladder was provided for the academically able working-class boy or girl to climb from the elementary school via the county grammar school to the university. Not many stayed this extremely arduous course, but the opportunity was there and increasing numbers took advantage of it after the Great War. The 1902 Act therefore has great significance for working-class education, even though before 1914 the elementary or council school continued to provide the only schooling for the vast majority of working-class children.

It remains to discuss the problems posed by the state of the children from poorer homes who were brought into the schools after 1880. Their problems were not altogether unknown earlier on, of course, but they certainly attracted more attention later in the nineteenth century as the extent of poverty and unemployment became of increasing concern. Ultimately the educational services which were initiated were to become available to all school children and accepted as an essential part of a state educational system. Perhaps the most urgent need was to do something about the undernourishment of many children from impoverished homes. This was particularly noticeable during periods of trade depression in the 1880s. For example, in 1880 a school board in the Black Country received a letter from the headmaster of one of its schools regarding the mounting arrears of school pence. He claimed that many parents were simply unable to pay, and described 'the tattered clothes and attenuated faces of the children showing that at their homes there had been a protracted struggle for mere existence.'[49] The children, of course, had only what was left of the food after the head of the household had eaten, and that would be little enough when he was unemployed. The provision of meals for needy children had been undertaken as early as the 1860s; some Roman Catholic schools in the poorest parts of London had served meals to their pupils, while Lord Shaftesbury's Destitute Children's Dinner Society gave dinners in a ragged school in Westminster from 1864 onwards.[50] This was opposed in principle by some, who argued that it tended to pauperise the parent. Some even argued further that the children were not actually underfed, but were simply badly fed by their ignorant parents. In 1884 a report to the Education Department by Dr Crichton-Browne emphasised strongly the undernourishment of some schoolchildren, remarking sarcastically: 'These children want blood, and we offer them a little brain-polish; they ask for bread, and receive a problem; and for milk, the tonic sol-fa system is introduced to them.'[51] He went on to claim that 'liberal and regular feeding is necessary in order that a child may be prepared to profit from education'. His forthright views certainly provoked opposition, including a memorandum of dissent from the Board's chief inspector. Nevertheless, towards the end of the century cheap meals (1*d* or ½*d* breakfasts or dinners) were provided by charitable bodies in a number of poor districts, and later on some meals were provided free. Some schools served meals on an impressive scale: the Chaucer Council School, Bermondsey (a very poor part of south London) regularly fed over half its children, 886 out of 1,357.[52] The basic issue, of course, was whether it was right in principle for schools to undertake what was essentially a social service rather than a specifically educational service.

The answer really came when the Interdepartmental Committee on Physical Deterioration, 1904, having received a mass of evidence, including an estimate that 16 per cent of London's school population, about 122,000 children, were underfed, declared that

> With scarcely an exception, there was a general consensus of opinion that the time had come when the State should realise the necessity of ensuring adequate nourishment to children in attendance at school; it was said to be the height of cruelty to subject half-starved children to the process of education, besides being a short-sighted policy, in that the progress of such children is inadequate and disappointing.[53]

So in 1906, among the earliest of the Liberal reforms of the pre-war period to be passed was the Education (Provision of Meals) Act which allowed local authorities to spend a maximum of a ½*d* rate to provide meals for needy children. It recommended that school committees should be set up, known as School Canteen Committees (afterwards called Children's Care Committees). Not all authorities levied the rate immediately, and old prejudices died hard. Where meals had been made available before the act, it had only been after an enquiry into the means of each family, and this kind of officious prying continued after the act. The quality of meals also was often very poor. But all the same, some kind of investigation was necessary and the act was a definite advance. Further, there was to be no loss of the vote as a consequence of accepting free meals.

Closely associated with the subject of undernourishment was the larger question of the general physical condition of schoolchildren. There was increasing alarm, as we have noted, at the continued economic success of Britain's European rivals, especially Germany. During the Boer War (1899–1902), many of those seeking to join up were rejected as unfit – according to Sir Frederick Maurice, as many as 60 per cent. The Interdepartmental Committee put the figure of those who had failed the army's standard tests for weight, height and eyesight at 34 per cent; and in addition to supporting the idea of school meals, the committee recommended a system of medical inspection in schools. Legislation followed in 1907, when Sir Robert Morant, Permanent Secretary to the Board of Education, quietly inserted a clause permitting medical inspection into the Education (Administrative Provisions) Act, 1907. Medical inspection, though having its opponents in the House, was not without precedent and some authorities had already taken action well before this. In 1891 the London School Board appointed its first Medical Officer of Health. In 1904 the London County Council began a campaign against verminous children; the nurses found that more than a third inspected were verminous, but by 1912 the number had dropped to less than a twentieth.[54] Meanwhile, by 1905 there were eighty-five school medical officers, though mostly in urban areas, and the majority part-time.[55] There was also a campaign against ringworm – in London at the end of 1911 there were 2,548 children suffering from this disease. The usual form of treatment for this was by X-rays. As for eyesight and teeth, the new Board of Education issued a circular in 1901 on the need for eyesight tests, though low-level defects were left untreated.[56] Teeth also received attention; the Interdepartmental Committee recommended that the Board of Education take steps to ensure that parents and teachers made children clean their teeth daily and that dental inspections should be held. After 1906 London County Council teachers started toothbrush clubs. At a Totnes church school in the West Country in 1912 the forming of a toothbrush club increased the proportion of children using toothbrushes from 4 per cent to 75 per cent.[57]

Of course, in all the areas of child care so far discussed progress varied greatly from one part of the country to another, especially as between town and country. But progress was certainly not confined to London and the South. In Birmingham in the year ending March, 1914 the total number of meals in the form of breakfasts was 274,069, an average of 751 a day. Dental and medical care was also provided; in the following year (to March, 1915) 11,792 had dental treatment, 468 children had tonsil and adenoid operations and 220 children were X-rayed as treatment for ringworm. In the year ending December, 1914 spectacles at cheap rates were prescribed for 2,533 children, and 4,471 children were treated for minor ailments. Also in 1914 there were 152,769 examinations of verminous children, 38 per cent being found to have nits, 8.2 per cent having other vermin and 53.4 per cent being found to be clean.[58]

Dr John Hurt provides us with a very useful survey of progress made by March 1914.[59] By then, every local education authority had a principal medical officer, though 127 areas had not yet started school clinics, while 139 had one or more clinics. Thirteen clinics provided dental treatment only. Some LEAs (53 in all) made contributions to local hospitals for treatment. There were 84 authorities with dental clinics capable of treating about a quarter of a million children, though there were still about 77 authorities who had done nothing in this respect. About a third of all authorities (125, including 14 county councils) were providing spectacles at low cost or free. The number of children fed peaked in 1912, when 137 authorities fed 358,306 children at some time or other during the year, though this figure is below the 10 per cent or 550,000 in all estimated by the Board of Education as being undernourished. Further, the responsibilities of parents in all these different respects were not forgotten. By the Children's Act, 1908 a local authority could prosecute a parent for failing to give children adequate food, clothing, medical attention or accommodation.

What can we make of all this flurry of activity? The basic causes are not difficult to discern. Partly there was the increasing amount of evidence as to the wretched state of some of the poorer children, while at the same time there was the fear of national degeneracy at a time of increasing world competition, just at a time when society was becoming uncomfortably aware that a third of the working classes were still living in poverty. Add to this the fear that the Empire could not be maintained without a healthy and energetic working class, the scare over the Boer War recruits and the need for national efficiency, and it is not surprising that eugenics and the breeding of a strong and virile race became popular topics among middle-class observers at this time.

When the extent of the new school social services is surveyed, it is clear that as yet they were very patchy. Much was provided in a grudging and parsimonious spirit because of lingering doubts about the propriety of taking over responsibilities thought to belong more properly to parents. Always there was a suspicion that some of the children's problems, at least, were due to parental fecklessness, and this obviously was not to be encouraged. To return to school meals, by way of an example: the act itself laid down the duty of the LEA to recover the cost of the meals from parents whenever possible – a somewhat impractical suggestion, one would have thought. Again, this cost was defrayed at first from purely voluntary funds. Initially no meals were provided at weekends or during the school holidays. As we have just seen, the numbers of children given meals were less than the numbers thought to be undernourished; and the quality of the meals themselves was remarkably poor. As regards other services, similar shortcomings were evident. Once more, the parents were supposed to contribute to their cost. The Local Education Authority (Medical Treatment) Act, 1909 provided that the cost of medical treatment could be charged to parents unless they were too poor to pay. Dental treatment must often have been of a superficial nature. Given the known poor state of children's teeth between the wars, a high proportion of children were likely to have been in need of treatment before 1914. Yet when 200,000 children in London had their teeth examined in 1913, only 40 per cent were said to have decayed teeth and only 16.8 per cent were recommended for treatment.[60] As for eyesight, it has already been noted that only the more serious defects were treated. Arrangements for tonsil and adenoid operations were often very crude. After operations the often blood-stained children were simply laid on the floor until they had recovered sufficiently to go home. Birmingham at least kept the children overnight and then had them return three weeks after the operation for breathing exercises.[61]

Yet again, all these qualifications must be seen in perspective. Given the continued strength of belief in self-help, it is not surprising that the beginnings of social services in the schools were on a small and hesitant scale. Anything more extensive would certainly have been rejected as the unacceptable face of the new liberalism or as smacking of socialism. It was not that the existence of social problems among the poorest children was denied. The dispute was rather about the best way of solving the problems without pampering the parents. The vigorous views of the Charity Organisation Society were still influential. Their essence, it may be said, was that the poor person must be assisted to help him- or her-self. The worst way of doing this was merely to give hand-outs, which would produce an attitude of dependence and subservience. The Liberal Governments were well aware of these beliefs and had to accommodate them in justifying their own reforms as merely helping those who had sunk too far to help themselves or (as in the case of the National Insurance Act) as operating on the insurance principle. When all this is borne in mind, it is remarkable that so much was achieved before 1914. To look at it positively, a start was made on providing a state meals service and also on a medical inspection service, with particular reference to general physical condition, to personal cleanliness, to eyesight and to teeth. Considered in this way, it is an impressive list, whatever its shortcomings might have been in practice at first.

So far this chapter has supplied a more or less conventional picture of the major changes in working-class schooling between 1870 and the outbreak of the Great War. It is fitting that some attempt now be made to end the chapter by providing some idea of how school must have seemed to the working-class boy or girl at the time. In many ways this is an impossible task, given the great variety of elementary schools, yet it is all too easy to omit this entirely when following the customary approach of dealing analytically with the major aspects of the history of working-class education. A composite picture is inevitably hard to achieve, but it is at least worth attempting. To start with buildings; perhaps the easiest approach here is to distinguish between the village school and the town school. At its simplest, the village school consisted of little more than a schoolroom, with perhaps an additional classroom, often dating from early in the century, and built in brick and slate. As was appropriate in the case of church schools, it would be in the conventional Gothic Revival style, and outside would be a playground of sorts, together with earth privies or buckets.[62] It was not always the practice to roof over these offices or necessaries, so that in bad weather children being excused could get very wet. In dry weather there might be time for the more daring to add a comment or two to the graffiti on any wall space available. The Chief Inspector for Surrey and Sussex commented on this in his report for 1875–76: 'Indecent writing on the walls of the offices is happily uncommon. I consider that where it has been found, both managers and teachers have neglected their duty, and I therefore propose in such cases always to recommend a deduction from the grant.'[63]

The smallest village schools would lack cloakrooms even at the end of the century, and the children's hats and coats would be hung up in the schoolroom or piled together in baskets. The schoolroom itself was lit conventionally by casement or later sash windows, the flooring was wooden or tiled and the walls colour-washed or painted. The woodwork would be painted dark brown. Ventilation could be a problem. Schoolrooms were often lofty and under the Revised Code each child was supposed to have a minimum space of eight square feet. There might also be a ventilator in the ceiling. Nevertheless, in the winter, when the windows were kept shut, the atmosphere became stifling; when opened, the windows let in draughts. Heating was usually provided in the form of a stove, duly railed off and sometimes quite inadequate. Mr R. F. Boyle, inspector for West Somerset, remarked on this in the mid-seventies: 'I have more than once had to call a class of children from the desks to stand round me at the stove, and I have found children crying in their places, and on enquiry found that they could not write, as their fingers were too cold to hold the pen.'[64] The children worked at desks, sometimes joined together in units of two, with seats attached by an iron framework, sometimes in units of four, five or six. The modern provision of separate tables and chairs was unknown, even for infants, who had to sit at desks like everyone else, even in the 1880s, when more progressive infant teaching was developing. HMI Burrows reported in 1884 on some infant classes in the South-West Division, where the infant class might be found 'in the hands of a dull monitor, frequently packed away in a dark corner of the main room or in a dingy classroom, where the luckless little creatures have only the opportunity of learning how, without crying, to sit for hours together, with dangling legs and aching backs.'[65] However, Mr C. H. Anderson (Burrows' Chief Inspector), in quoting this passage, remarked that he would be sorry to think that this applied to the majority of infant classes. In larger village schools, infants might be accommodated in a gallery room at the end of the main classroom, with desks arranged in tiers as in a lecture theatre.

The small village school was often housed in ugly buildings, put up to provide the maximum accommodation at the least expense. In the majority of cases it would be a Church of England school, presided over by the local vicar as school manager, though board schools did exist in rural areas, of course, and would at least have the benefit of having been built more recently. Equipment remained rudimentary, with sand trays for the infants, but in the last quarter of the century more reading and writing books became available, and paper and ink replaced slates for the older children. The buildings themselves remained of a primitive kind, based on the shape of a barn for the most part; many continued in use until well after the Second World War. In summer they were hot and airless. In winter, with the windows steamed up and the tiled floors sweating, they were damp and noisome, the smell being compounded of children, wet clothes, stale air, chalk and sometimes a whiff from the offices. This characteristic school smell must have remained in the memory of the many thousands of country children whose sole schooling was in the village elementary schools of the last decades of the nineteenth century; but memories of school of this kind are not necessarily painful or sad. There was more to school than its familiar smells.

Town schools had many of the characteristics of the village schools, but in one particular they could be very different. In the big cities the new board schools could be very large, sometimes accommodating well over a thousand children on three floors. This was certainly so in London, where the largest schools were impressive buildings, often in the new, Queen Anne Revival style with large windows divided by glazing bars into smaller panes. Shortage of building space sometimes meant that after building there was no room left for playgrounds. The Revd T. Sharpe, Senior Chief Inspector of Schools in London, reported in 1895 that 'Within the radius of one mile from Charing Cross there are 25,000 scholars for whom no playground is provided, and in most parts of London there are very few playgrounds worthy of the name.'[66] This was in spite of the requirement of the time that every school attendance had to be broken by an interval given up to recreation. Some London board schools had playgrounds on the roof – one assumes that the roof was specially designed and strengthened. But such was the growth of school population that not all London children could go into new, permanent buildings. In 1889 there were still more than 8,000 children in temporary premises in the form of prefabricated iron huts.[67]

As for the design of the new, larger board schools, it was usual to have separate entrances, sometimes in different streets, for the separate departments of boys, girls and infants. In this way the sexes were segregated, each department usually occupying its own floor. The original design seems to have been for a large central hall which could contain a number of classes, with classrooms off, so that the headmaster in the central hall could supervise the teaching in the classrooms through the glass windows or partitions which divided the classrooms from the hall. The central hall became mandatory in London after 1881.[68] In time this central hall, which could be used for assemblies or physical education, and the adjoining classrooms became the familiar pattern for the large elementary school. By the end of the century there was some dissatisfaction with this design, on the grounds that it lacked adequate ventilation. Just before the war there was support for the building of the more hygienic pavilion school, with ground floor only and more access to the open air, sometimes with wide marching corridors for drill. Only a small minority of children attended schools of this sort before 1914, of course.

Inside, the larger board schools benefited from having been built later in the century than the earlier church schools. They were relatively spacious, had adequate fenestration, gas lighting and tiled walls (white or brown) up to waist height. Cloakrooms were provided, especially after Circular 321 in 1893, which required HMIs to provide details of school buildings; this led to further improvements, especially in voluntary schools. Lavatories, however, often remained outside the main buildings and there was an almost complete lack of specialist rooms such as art rooms or laboratories. Where they did exist, they were to be found in the new central or higher grade schools. In most elementary schools classrooms were regarded as general-purpose rooms, and if in the later board schools there were any specialist rooms, they were also expected to serve as general classrooms as well. In this, unlike the reformed endowed secondary schools, the new, large board schools lacked the kind of specialist accommodation later taken for granted in the secondary school.

What then would a working-class child expect to learn in these surroundings after 1870? The infant stage was very important, if not the most important of all, for here the fundamental three Rs were taught, on which all subsequent learning would be based. The extent to which these skills had been acquired would be tested, usually after two years or so, in Standard I. By the 1870s the techniques of teaching reading were well established, of course, but much would depend on the competence and attitude of the infant teacher; a kindly, motherly teacher could do much to make the early days less frightening, while lengthy periods with a nervous and inexperienced pupil-teacher could make for an uncertain and slow start. By the 1880s the curriculum had widened for infants as knowledge spread of the more enlightened approaches of educationalists such as Froebel, who died in 1852. In addition to the basic three R work, there were ‘occupations’, to which three hours a week were given for the lower classes and two hours for the upper classes. According to HMI Hernaman, responsible for West Lambeth:

> The branches ordinarily taught are –
> *Lower Division* – modelling sand into hills, gardens, etc. Fraying stuff, the threads to be made into brooms, etc. Bead-threading, teaching colour, number, etc. Stick-laying – making letters. Building with cubes.
> *Middle Division* – stick-laying – making letters and forms. Paper-folding – envelopes, boats, trays, etc. Drawing on slates.
> *Upper Division* – plaiting mats – pricking paper for sewing. Making designs for rings. Drawing on slates and paper.[69]

By this time, according to Chief Inspector J. G. Fitch, there was no department of educational work in which improvement was more striking than the infant schools. He commented on the lively spirit in many of these schools: 'It is precisely in those schools which are most distinguished by joyousness and the variety of interesting employments that the children can read, write, and count best, and are best able to face with ease the examination for the First Standard when they reach the proper age.'[70] He went on to explain that all this was not true of smaller country schools, but certainly did apply in London:

> The LSB has taken special pains to secure the services of highly skilled and experienced infant teachers and to equip the schoolrooms with all needful appliances. It has also employed a lady, who has devoted special attention to the study of Froebel's and Pestalozzi's principles, to visit the schools, and to offer help and guidance to the teachers. The district of E. Lambeth is exceptionally fortunate in possessing a considerable number of the brightest, happiest, and most efficient infant schools I have ever seen in either this or in any other country.

This is high praise, indeed, especially when it is remembered that East Lambeth was an inner-city district where there were many impoverished homes, so that the teachers did not have the best of material to work with. There could have been very few children, for example, who started school already able to read.[71]

Here and there in the inspectors' reports of the 1890s there are other references to changing methods in the infant classes. To take one or two instances: the simple teaching of the alphabet by naming of the letters was increasingly replaced by teaching the sound of the letters – 'very different from the old way of learning the ABC', as one inspector's report has it. Another change was the use of word-building in the teaching of reading. According to Chief Inspector the Revd F. F. Cornish, 'In reading, word-building is the latest change, which some people claim to be the only rational way of teaching spelling . . . as yet, few teachers are more than very half-hearted about word-building.'[72] In fact it is probable that most teachers used a combination of methods to achieve the best results, as they do today in combining look-and-say and phonic approaches in reading. Another change could be seen in the teaching of writing. The report just quoted from sums this up well: 'The old flowing commercial hand has been long replaced by the Civil Service style, and in the last year or two, this replaced by a more vertical style, marked by great uniformity, one main object being to take pen off paper as seldom as possible.'[73]

At the end of their stay in the infant classes, children sat the examination under the Revised Code for Standard I. Thereafter they were examined in Standards II, III and IV, at which point some at least would leave school if the local authority gave exemption at this stage. This was so in Portsmouth in 1884, where the bulk of the children still left school at eleven. Thus in this area there was much 'truancy and premature escape', as the local HMI put it.[74] Just what levels of achievement were represented by Standard IV it is difficult to judge. Generally there was rigorous drilling in arithmetic, as can be seen by this example of Standard III arithmetic sums set by the Revd H. G. Alington, inspector for parts of Kent and Sussex, in the mid-1870s:

1. Divide 1,195,250 by 175 (in words)
2. Add together £37 16*s* 9¼*d*, £8 15*s* 6¾*d*, £469 8*s* 10½*d*, £17, £9 13*s* 11½*d*
3. From £100,000 take £1,076 19*s* 9*d* (in words)
4. The sum of £2,698 is left to each of nine persons, what is the total amount left?[75]

According to Alington, the twenty-one girls who sat this exam did very badly. One even supplied as answer to the last question, 'They had nothing left'.

However, it would be wrong to suppose that all the timetable after the infant stage was spent on the three Rs. In the first place, Object Lessons were an important feature of work in Standards I, II and III, and were specifically included in the Code.[76] The class would be supplied with an object, sometimes individually, as a subject for study. According to the Revd Cornish, animals and plants formed the most obvious and most attractive subjects for these lessons.[77] Circular 369 made it clear that Object Teaching should be the basis for instruction in language, drawing, number, modelling and other handwork. Such subjects were known as 'suitable occupations', and the list of such occupations became quite lengthy, and included recitation, weaving, drill and singing.[78] One wonders how teachers could introduce drill or weaving as part of a lesson on a stuffed dog. Presumably teachers had to use their imagination in matching appropriate activities to objects studied. Further, there were 'class' subjects and 'specific' subjects. Class subjects were widened in 1875 by the addition of history (never very popular), geography and grammar. In and after 1893 one class subject was supposed to be taken throughout the school. Specific subjects were higher level subjects, and were confined to Standards IV and V, and comprised such subjects as algebra, animal physiology, physics and domestic economy.[79] Thus although the range of subjects taken by any one child remained very limited, there is no doubt that the timetable was expanding. By the end of the century cookery had become very popular, and both cookery and laundry centres had been set up in London.[80] It should also be mentioned that in addition to industrial schools for wayward and problem children, schools were being erected about this time for deaf, blind and mentally deficient children.[81] The extent of the timetable in the mid-nineties is well set out by HMI Tremenheere, inspector for Berkshire:

> Twenty years ago the great bulk of the schools with which I came into contact taught absolutely nothing beyond reading, writing, and arithmetic, with needlework for girls. Now a representative timetable would show, besides the elements, and needlework for girls and drawing for boys, English or elementary science, geography, recitation, drill, singing, object lessons for the junior classes, and general information lessons (including some on history) for the seniors, manual occupations throughout, and in some cases, one or two specific subjects.[82]

It could be objected that in reality very few children were taught more than the odd class or specific subject in addition to the basics, and there is some truth in this; but by 1914, at least, an increasing number did stay on till fourteen, and so were taught a wider range of subjects. Further, a skilful and energetic teacher could introduce subjects beyond the basics through a wise employment of the object lesson and associated occupations. Certainly he had rather more freedom to plan what he thought appropriate to teach after Payment by Results was finally ended in 1895. Henceforth the annual examinations (apart from the Labour examination giving early release) were replaced by two annual visits by HMIs. Whatever shortcomings were to be found in the elementary schools by the end of the century – and they were still plagued by irregular attendance and early leaving – the curriculum had at least expanded. Another interesting comment on changes in the schools over a period of twenty years was made by HMI Cartwright, inspector for Northants:

> The contrast between the old and new styles would be startling to a teacher of 20 years ago . . . Associated as all our teaching now is with kindergarten principles and varied occupations, and the three Rs being taught on rational and scientific principles, and with regular lessons on common objects from the collections in the school museums which have now so largely taken the place of pictures, our schools have greatly increased the powers of observation of the children.[83]

It remains to consider some general matters arising out of this wide survey. During the last decades of the nineteenth century more and more children attended school, and for longer periods, but what they found there and their reactions would depend on a great variety of factors. Some enjoyed the companionship of the other children, found they could get on with most of the teachers and even found some of the lessons interesting and enjoyable; most children acquired some degree of literacy, even though they might forget much of what they had learned sooner or later. The limited expectations of what constituted a suitable education for a working-class boy or girl were still not very demanding in the 1870s, and were described by HMI H. Smith of Chester:

> That every child should be able on leaving school to read an ordinary English book with ease and therefore with pleasure, to write a legible hand, to make such simple calculations as he will be likely to want in buying his necessaries, or selling his labour, and to have some acquaintance with the world in which he lives, and especially with the geography and history of his own country.[84]

This is not much different from the list drawn up by the Revd James Fraser in 1861 (quoted in Chapter Four), but there is the significant difference that Fraser thought the school should see the last of 'the peasant boy' (as he called him) at ten or eleven, whereas fifteen years later Smith referred to 'what you can expect from children of twelve or thirteen years'; he also went on in his report to discuss the transfer to grammar school of the brightest pupils. The idea of some form of secondary education for these children was beginning to come under consideration.

No doubt a number of children were able to reach Smith's modest standards, and most of these probably thought school tolerable enough. Although the keeping of discipline was severe when compared with present-day practices, and teachers both male and female often used the cane on both boys and girls, the punishment meted out was certainly less harsh than earlier in the century; one has only to think of the kinds of punishments inflicted in the Lancasterian schools. Yet for many different reasons, such as learning difficulties, unfair punishment, bullying, shortage of money at home and so on, some children were only too anxious to leave at the first opportunity. For the individual child, so much depended on the particular circumstances, especially relationships with teachers.[85] Curiously enough, even the worst of slum schools might have their attractions for the more able child. Robert Roberts, after describing the low standards of his slum school in Salford about 1910 goes on to remark, 'But I found it delightful. So did all my siblings, and we blubbered and complained if anything occurred to stop attendance'.[86] Roberts, of course, was an exceptionally gifted pupil from a respectable working-class home. He was also highly critical of authority, but his comments on visits by the 'dreaded HMIs' are worth noting:

> And the great ones duly arrived, putting the fear of God into everyone on the staff. But *we* loved them! Like Dutch uncles they went round the classes, treating us with old-world courtesy, always enquiring, and making us feel that, in school at least, girls and boys were the people who mattered. Among these men were some of the pioneers who dragged the elementary education system kicking and screaming into the twentieth century.[87]

The standards of some schools were still very low, but it seems undeniable that over the thirty years or so after the 1870 act there was a definite improvement in the elementary schools as teachers were better trained, children stayed longer at school, the schools extended their range of activities and school social services were established. Even in the 1880s the Manchester School Board held annual concerts and prize-givings – fifty-five such gatherings were held in 1884, among the prize-winners being 2,698 children who had not missed a single day's attendance in the year.[88] In the 1890s schools were beginning to form school libraries and also to set up school museums (termed by one inspector 'a rather pretentious name for a cabinet with glass doors'). According to the Metropolitan District Senior Chief Inspector, the Revd T. Sharpe, there were few schools in London without a football club and a cricket club.[89] In addition to the elementary schools, the first moves towards secondary education were seen in the form of the higher grade schools and also in the county secondary schools after 1902. It should be mentioned, too, that evening classes were provided in the towns, often including subjects of a vocational nature, such as dressmaking and shorthand, but not excluding arithmetic, reading, writing and composition. In September 1895 in Birmingham twenty-seven evening classes opened with an enrolment of 6,037.[90]

In conclusion, it should perhaps be repeated that all this was not done purely out of consideration for the educational welfare of the individual child; the end of the century saw a great emphasis on Empire, and on the need for youth training with an eye both on defence requirements and the protection of India and the colonies. This was the age when the Boys' Brigade flourished, the Boy Scouts movement was founded and imperial ideas were extolled in the schools.[91] Nevertheless, whatever the motives (and they were a mixture of altruism and self-interest), great changes were taking place, and they were irreversible. At the same time, it goes almost without saying that thc educational standard of some children leaving school about 1900 was still lamentably low. In spite of all the progress which undoubtedly had been made, it is not difficult to find examples of boys and girls who were still barely literate. In fact, it is all too easy to provide instances of the gross ignorance of some school-leavers, of their misunderstanding of what they had supposedly been taught and of their educational regression once they had left school.[92] But it must also be acknowledged that some children did profit from their schooling and in addition to the basic foundation of the three Rs had gained some knowledge of and interest in the wider world, some degree of liberation from their immediate environment. This might well be due to the work of conscientious and persevering teachers, especially dedicated teachers like Jonathan Priestley, of whom his son, J. B. Priestley, said that he was 'not a born scholar but a born teacher with an almost ludicrous passion for acquiring and imparting knowledge'.[93] The increasing professionalism and dedication of the elementary school teachers in the second half of the nineteenth century must not be forgotten. One last contrast: in 1870 there were no central or higher grade schools, and grammar school education was for the middle classes. By 1915 a minimum of 25 per cent of all places in local authority grammar schools (the new county schools) were free, and about 30 per cent of the pupils in these schools were on free scholarships, with children from the unskilled working classes holding about a fifth of these places.[94] Progress may have been limited and slow, but it was unmistakable. Childhood had certainly been transformed from being dominated by full-time work from an early age to being shaped and coloured by school and its widening activities.

References

1 E. H. Hunt, *British Labour History 1815–1914*, 1981, p. 17.

2 B. L. Hutchings and A. Harrison, *A History of Factory Legislation*, 3rd edn, 1926, p. 176; *Report of the Factory and Workshops Commission*, 1876, Vol. I, pp. xiii, xxvi.

3 *Ibid.*, p. xi.

4 *Ibid.*, pp. xii–xiv.

5 *Ibid.*, p. xv.

6 *Ibid.*, p. xcii. One inspector reported his experience of 'catching four or five young children in a brickyard, several of whom were actually rescued from

him by a young woman'; and another said that 'even his stealthy approach by flank marches to certain villages was almost certainly observed and provided against' (p. xciv).

7 *Ibid.*, Recommendations, pp. xcvii, ci, cii.

8 *Royal Commission on Labour*, 1892, Fifth and Final Report, 1894, Pt I, Summary, Group C, Pt I, p. 247. There were further investigations into the number of part-timers and additional figures became available later on. In 1895 the number of part-timers in textile factories in England and Wales was 55,625. By 1897 the total had dropped to 45,993 and by 1907 to little more than 30,000 (*Report of the Inter-Departmental Committee on Partial Exemption from School Attendance* (Committee on Partial Exemption), 1909, p. 12). Another source, numbering part-timers of all kinds, not merely in textiles, gives 110,654 for 1897 and 70,255 for 1911–12 (*Annual Report for 1912 of the Chief Medical Officer of the Board of Education*, 1914, p. 310). See also on this subject F. Keeling, *Child Labour in the United Kingdom*, 1914 and Edmund and Ruth Frow, *A Survey of the Half-Time System in Education*, 1970.

9 J. S. Hurt, *Elementary Schooling and the Working Classes 1860–1918*, 1979, pp. 188, 230.

10 *Royal Commission on Labour*, 1892, First Report, Vol. I, Textiles, pp. 8, 9, and Fifth Report, p. 247. In 1901 mill towns such as Oldham showed 10 to 18 per cent of boys aged ten to thirteen as part-timers, but non-mill towns such as London, Liverpool, Durham and York recorded only 1 per cent of the age range (Lionel Rose, *The Erosion of Childhood*, 1991, p. 5).

11 *Royal Commission on Labour*, 1892, Fifth Report, pp. 247, 353.

12 *Ibid.*, p. 308.

13 For Birmingham see Lawrence A. M. Riley, *Report on Van Boy Labour in Birmingham*, 1913; *Report of the Committee appointed by the Bishop of Birmingham to enqure into Street Trading by Children*, 1910; Arthur Freeman, *Boy Life and Labour: the Manufacture of Inefficiency*, 1914, and Christine Heward and Richard Whipp, 'Juvenile Labour in Birmingham: A Notorious but Neglected Case, 1850–1914', in Anthony Wright and Richard Shackleton (eds), *Worlds of Labour: Essays in Birmingham History*, 1983.

14 John Benson, *The Working Class in Britain 1850–1939*, 1989, p. 31.

15 *Interdepartmental Committee on the Employment of School Children*, 1901, p. 14 (quoted in the 'Report on Boy Labour' by Cyril Jackson in the *Report of the Royal Commission on the Poor Law*, 1909, at p. 22). According to a somewhat sensational account (R. Sherard, *The Child Slaves of Britain*, 1905, p. 333) two barber's boys in Birmingham actually died from overwork, the first a boy of eleven, the other a boy of twelve 'done to death in the same way in Digbeth'.

16 Hunt, *British Labour History*, pp. 14–16.

17 R. H. Tawney, 'The Economics of Child Labour', *Economics Journal*, 1909.

18 *Children's Employment Commission*, 1840, Appendix to Second Report, Report by Theophilus Richards, fols 170, 171.

19 *Ibid.*, fol. 171.

20 For a more extended discussion of the views of these historians, see my 'Were the Webbs wrong about apprenticeship in the Black Country?', *West Midland Studies*, 6, 1973, which surveys the evidence for the survival of apprenticeship in this heavily industrialised area of the West Midlands.

21 Charles More, *Skill and the English Working Class 1870–1914*, 1980, pp. 64, 99–100, 103. See also Harry Hendrick, *Images of Youth: Age, Class, and the Male Youth Problem*, 1990, pp. 41–4, 65–72 and William Knox, 'Apprenticeship and De-Skilling in Britain, 1850–1914', *International Review of Social History*, XXXI, 1986. Further detail is available in Knox's doctoral thesis, 'British Apprenticeship, 1800–1914' (Edinburgh Ph.D. thesis, 1980).

22 Robert Roberts, *A Ragged Schooling*, 1976, p. 159.

23 *Royal Commission on Labour*, 1892, Fifth Report, pp. 250, 313, 16, 105.

24 Tawney, 'Economics of Child Labour'. And see Hendrick, *Images of Youth*, p. 68.

25 *Royal Commission on Labour*, 1892, Fifth Report, General Review of the Evidence, p. 16.

26 *Ibid.*, p. 250 and First Report, p. 22.

27 *Ibid.*, Fifth Report, p. 308.

28 *Ibid.*, First Report, p. 33.

29 Freeman, *Boy Life and Labour*, Chapter V, 'Industrial Conditions', especially pp. 204–5.

30 However, half-time employment was not the only means of escape at the age of twelve. Children living more than two miles from school might be excused attendance, while part-time exemption might be allowed not only on attaining the required standard but also on making a specified number of attendances; see John Hurt, *Elementary Schooling and the Working Classes 1860–1918*, 1979, p. 188.

31 Lionel Rose, *The Erosion of Childhood*, 1991, pp. 22, 27; Pamela Horn, *The Victorian and Edwardian Schoolchild*, 1989, p. 126 and Gillian Sutherland, 'Education', in F. M. L. Thompson (ed.), *The Cambridge Social History of Britain 1750–1950*, 1990, Vol. 3, p. 145; Hurt, *Elementary Schooling*, p. 210. Another recent account gives the 1899 enquiry figures as 144,000 boys and 34,000 girls and the 1901 figure as 200,000: Hugh Cunningham *The Children of the Poor*, 1991, pp. 179–180. A contemporary estimate for 1912 is 280,000 (F. Kealing, *Child Labour in the United Kingdom*, 1914, pp. 59, xxx–xxxi).

32 Eric Hopkins, 'Working Class Education in Birmingham during the First World War', p. 27, in *Labour and Education: Some Early Twentieth Century Studies*, History of Education Society Occasional Publications, No. 6, 1981 and Rose, *The Erosion of Childhood*, p. 27. Rose also has a very informative chapter on juvenile street traders, (pp. 66–79).

33 Reported in *The Times*, 15 May 1991.

34 For good general accounts of working-class education in England between 1870 and 1900 see J. W. Adamson, *English Education 1789–1902*,

1930; Mary Sturt, *The Education of the People*, 1967; S. J. Curtis, *History of Education in Great Britain*, 7th edn, 1967; John Lawson and Harold Silver, *A Social History of Education in England*, 1973; D. Wardle, *English Popular Education 1780–1970*, 1970; Gillian Sutherland, *Elementary Education in the Nineteenth Century*, 1971 and Hurt, *Elementary Schooling*.

35 See Hurt, *Elementary Schooling*, p. 21 for a discussion of the significance of Lowe's words here.

36 Quoted in Lawson and Silver, *Social History*, p. 316.

37 Sturt, *Education of the People*, p. 320.

38 *The Schoolmaster*, 17 December 1872.

39 Hurt, *Elementary Schooling*, p. 71.

40 Carl Chinn, 'Was Separate Schooling a means of Class Segregation in late Victorian and Edwardian Birmingham?', *Midland History*, 1988, Vol. XIII.

41 Hurt, *Elementary Schooling*, pp. 172–8 and Sturt, *Education of the People*, p. 322.

42 Lawson and Silver, *Social History*, p. 321.

43 *Reports of the Committee of Council for Education (England and Wales)* (hereafter *RCCE*), 1876–77, p. 391. The annual reports of the school inspectors are a valuable source of information regarding work and conditions in the elementary schools. Most inspectors had Oxbridge backgrounds, and their reports are sometimes idealistic in tone, but on the whole they provide a realistic and informed appraisal of what they saw; they were no fools. After 1870 they had an increasing influence on educational opinion (see J. E. Dunford, *Her Majesty's Inspectorate of Schools in England and Wales, 1860–1870*, 1980, especially pp. 82–3).

44 *RCCE*, 1876–77, p. 504.

45 *Ibid.*, p. 528.

46 Hurt, *Elementary Schooling*, p. 158.

47 Much has been written about these pioneer surveys. For straightforward accounts see Derek Fraser, *The Evolution of the British Welfare State*, 2nd edn, 1984, pp. 135–37 and Pat Thane, *The Foundations of the Welfare State*, 1982, pp. 4–7. There is also a simple introduction to the subject in Eric Hopkins, *A Social History of the English Working Classes 1815–1945*, 1979, pp. 142–5.

48 *RCCE*, 1895–96, p. 130.

49 *The Advertiser for Brierley Hill, Stourbridge, Dudley, and Kidderminster*, 5 June 1880.

50 Hurt, *Elementary Schooling*, p. 102. Dr Hurt provides a most helpful chapter on the subject of school meals. Ragged schools, founded by Lord Shaftesbury, charged no fees at all. They catered for about 20,000 children in 200 schools in the late 1860s, and still survive here and there in name in the Black Country.

51 Hurt, *Elementary Schooling*, p. 108; a much fuller quotation from the same source is given in Anne Digby and Peter Searby, *Children, School and Society in Nineteenth Century England*, 1981, pp. 123–5.

52 Hurt, *op. cit.*, p. 112.

53 Hurt, *Elementary Schooling*, p. 121; Hopkins, 'Working Class Education', pp. 184–5; Rose, *The Erosion of Childhood*, pp. 154–6.

54 Hurt, *Elementary Schooling*, pp. 132, 133.

55 *Ibid.*, p. 128.

56 *Ibid.*, pp. 129, 136.

57 *Ibid.*, pp. 142–3.

58 Hopkins, 'Working Class Education', pp. 26, 31.

59 Hurt, *Elementary Schooling*, p. 131, pp. 143, 150.

60 *Ibid.*, p. 136.

61 Hopkins, 'Working Class Education', p. 31.

62 A very useful guide to school architecture in this period is Malcolm Seaborne and Roy Lowe, *The English School: its architecture and organisation, Vol. II, 1870–1970*, 1977.

63 *RCCE*, 1875–76, p. 599.

64 *Ibid.*, p. 438.

65 *Ibid.*, 1884, p. 249.

66 *Ibid.*, 1895–96, p. 134.

67 Seaborne and Lowe, *The English School*, p. 27.

68 *Ibid.*, p. 31.

69 *RCCE*, 1884, pp. 300–1.

70 *Ibid.*, pp. 311, 321.

71 But this was not entirely unknown, even in slum areas. Robert Roberts, for example, had been taught to read by his mother before starting school (Roberts, *A Ragged Schooling*, p. 142).

72 *RCCE*, 1895–96, p. 22.

73 *Ibid.*, p. 19.

74 *RCCE*, 1884, p. 243.

75 *Ibid.*, 1875–76, p. 309.

76 *Ibid.*, 1895–96, p. 47.

77 *Ibid.*, p. 27.

78 Hurt, *Elementary Schooling*, p. 182.

79 *RCCE*, 1895–96, p. 47.

80 *Ibid.*, p. 117. In fact, there was an increasing emphasis at the turn of the century on needlework, cookery and domestic science in schools. See Carol Dyhouse, *Girls Growing up in Late Victorian and Edwardian England*, 1981, especially Chapter 3, 'Good Wives and Little Mothers: educational provision for working class girls'.

81 *RCCE*, 1895–96, p. 117. There were also truant schools for persistent truants (in 1911 there were nine such schools in England and Wales). In effect, they were short-term reformatories (Rose, *The Erosion of Childhood*, p. 195).

82 *RCCE*, 1895–96, p. 74.

83 *Ibid.*, p. 76.

84 *Ibid.*, 1875–76, p. 568.

85 The good teacher used his cane only sparingly, of course, and corporal punishment in elementary schools was relatively mild when compared with the ferocious and often sickening beatings still customary in public schools (see Rose, *The Erosion of Childhood*, Chapter 17, 'Pupil Society and School Discipline'). As for school discipline in general, the Revd Sharp, London Schools Senior Chief Inspector, thought that the general atmosphere of the school was all-important – 'Regular attendance depends more on the internal attractiveness of the atmosphere of the school than upon managers, attendance officers, or parents; (*RCCE*, 1895–96, p. 132). This is a sweeping statement, yet in its way a compliment to the teachers who contributed so largely to the tone of their schools.

86 Roberts, *A Ragged Schooling*, p. 141.

87 *Ibid.*, p. 149.

88 *RCCE*, 1884, p. 285.

89 *Ibid.*, 1895–96, p. 135.

90 *Ibid.*, p. 86.

91 Horn, *Victorian and Edwardian Schoolchild*, pp. 147–9, 155–162.

92 Rose, *The Erosion of Childhood*, Chapter 19, 'The Formative Results of Education' provides a good example of this.

93 Horn, *Victorian and Edwardian Schoolchild*, p. 80.

94 Rose, *The Erosion of Childhood*, p. 207.

Chapter Nine

The home environment

In the previous chapter on this subject, which dealt with the period from 1800 to about 1870, emphasis was laid on the nature of the family and familial relationships, on housing, home furnishing, diet, sickness and death. In this chapter the same topics will be discussed, though it should be said at the outset that the period from 1870 onwards saw substantial changes in working-class family life. True, it is a much shorter period, of only thirty years or so (a little longer if the nineteenth century be extended to the climactic year of 1914). Nevertheless, it is a time of considerable change for the family. Earlier in the century countless families had to adjust to living in their new urban surroundings in the great sprawling towns and cities; but after the mid-century, though population continued to expand, the new pattern of existence had become fixed. It was essentially a life lived within towns, and in towns where day-to-day existence was increasingly regulated both at work and at home. In particular, the home environment was affected by the proliferation of by-laws relating to many different aspects of home life, especially housing, sanitation, roads, scavenging, gas and water services and transport. Moreover, as the standard of living rose, diet and home furnishing also improved and mortality fell. Life for working-class children just before the Great War thus acquired a recognisable, early twentieth-century, Edwardian aspect. Street scenes at this time, often in postcard form, are familiar enough to us today – the shops, often with wares stacked on the pavement outside, gas street lamps, much horse traffic but with the occasional motor car, bicyclists here and there and the new electric trams. It is, after all, only the day before yesterday.

Life in the working-class home itself was altered by changes in the nature of the family. In the first place, parents were living longer. Whereas in the mid-nineteenth century the expectation of life was about forty years, by 1911–12 it had risen markedly, to about fifty-two for males and fifty-five for females.[1] As a consequence, more children could expect to grow up with both parents surviving, rather than only one or none at all. The estimated percentage of children losing parents at different ages may be shown as follows:

Percentage losing parent(s)

Cohort born	*By age 10*			*By age 15*			*Median age at losing*	
	Father	*Mother*	*Both*	*Father*	*Mother*	*Both*	*Father*	*Mother*
1861	11	11	1	17	17	3	35	36
1891	9	8	1	14	12	2	37	41
1921	5	4	0	8	6	0	41	47[2]

Thus the phenomenon of the early death of one or more parents during childhood with all its economic and psychological consequences, a familiar enough happening in earlier times, was beginning to disappear by the end of the nineteenth century. One result of this, of course, was that more parents were living long enough to see the birth of their grandchildren and to be available to participate in their upbringing. At the same time infant mortality also dropped from the 1870s onwards, subject only to a still unexplained blip in the 1890s which were characterised by high rates of diarrhoeal fatality; after this, the previous downward trend in the rates was resumed. *Child* mortality (deaths between the ages of one and fifteen) also dropped steadily from the 1870s. The causes of increased longevity at this time are still controversial, but they seem to be a combination of better sanitation, improved diet and the reduced virulence of such diseases as scarlet fever. The improvements in medical science of the time do not appear to have had much effect until the inter-war years. Whatever the root causes, increased longevity was an important and significant aspect of demographic change at the end of the nineteenth century.[3]

Of equal importance to the working-class family was its decline in size from the 1880s onwards. Fertility within the family peaked at 5.7 to 6.2 children born to women who had been born between 1771 and 1831, then fell steadily from the 1870s. Married women born in the 1880s had only half as many children to care for, and their own children in turn had only two-thirds as many to nurture. Thus in two generations the average number of children born to married women fell from around six to only a little over two, though this was offset to some extent by falling mortality, for as we have seen, fewer children were dying young.[4] More specifically, the families of miners, agricultural labourers and unskilled labourers all fell by about a quarter in size between the 1860s and 1891.[5] By 1911 we can be more specific still; textile workers, always known to have relatively small families, then had families with an average of 3.19 children. At the other end of the scale, miners maintained their reputation for having the largest families; they had an average of 4.33 children per family. In between the two extremes and in ascending order were skilled workers, semi-skilled workers, unskilled workers and agricultural labourers.[6] These general statements, of course, do not exclude the fact that at one end of the scale there were married couples with no children at all, and couples at the other end with very large families of eleven or twelve children or more.

Just why these remarkable changes in the size of the working-class family occurred is still not very clear. One possible cause, that of the increasing use of contraceptives such as condoms, can virtually be ruled out; these did not come into widespread use by working-class parents until during and after the Great War, when they were issued to troops as prophylactic devices. Similarly, the notion that parents were no longer interested in having children for economic reasons, since children had lost importance as wage-earners, has very little to recommend it. A more attractive suggestion is that the idea of family limitation had somehow percolated down from the middle classes, who were faced with the increasing costs of education and of domestic service and had begun to restrict the size of their families even earlier. The problem here is to explain exactly how ideas of this kind were actually transmitted from the middle classes to the working classes, with whom they had really very little social contact. As for the actual methods of birth control that were practised, it is likely they were the familiar and obvious methods of sexual abstinence, coitus interruptus, deliberate abortion and possibly the use of the safe period (in reality, often a very *unsafe* period).

The question still remains, why were these forms of family limitation adopted? And why did their use vary from one working-class occupation to another? It has been suggested that the way that ideas percolated from the middle classes to the working classes was principally through the agency of the very large class of domestic servants who passed the newer attitudes on to members of their own class. This explanation is still supported by some historians, though others would lay rather more emphasis on the development of such ideas independently by working-class men and women. In their view, towards the end of the century, women were becoming more self-assertive and less submissive. As religious beliefs began to wane, the idea of regarding children as a gift from God became replaced by a more secular and materialistic outlook. Further, working-class women were becoming better educated and were beginning to take more responsible roles in public life, for example, in trade unionism.[7] They also played a not inconsiderable part in the suffragette movement. When all these different developments are viewed together it becomes possible to argue that the desirability of spacing children out in working-class families owes much to the more independent thinking of wives at the end of the century. However, it would obviously be wrong to exclude entirely the attitude of their husbands in these matters; the more thoughtful and perhaps better-read would also be aware that smaller families might be both feasible and desirable. Pamphlets on birth control methods were supposed to have circulated in textile factories even in the first half of the century, while Mrs Annie Besant's prosecution in 1877 for publishing a pamphlet on the subject (described in the charge as an 'indecent, lewd, filthy, bawdy, and obscene book') helped to give birth control a wide publicity at the time. So by the end of the century increased literacy among both men and women of the working classes would have helped to some degree at least to disseminate knowledge of family planning.

As for variations in the size of families in different occupational groups, this also remains a matter for speculation. It is usual in this connection to focus on the groups at the extremes – the textile families and the families of coalminers. The relative smallness of textile families is usually explained by the fact that textile workers were unique in working in large-scale workplaces employing hundreds of women, some of them married, so that information about family limitation could easily be passed on. Coalminers, on the other hand, lived in small, often isolated communities in which male dominance was a strong characteristic and women's role was traditionally subservient. Another argument has it that the critical division is really between families where the husband is a skilled worker, who did not marry till later in life, when his training was finished, and families where the husband was unskilled or was engaged in heavy manual labour, as in coalmining. Unfortunately, this simple division breaks down when certain skilled tradesmen, such as masons and boilermakers, are found to have had a tradition of large, not small families. Yet another distinction can be drawn between the smaller families in trades subject early on to industrialisation in the form of mechanisation and large-scale organisation, and those in industries still rooted in workshop and handicraft production; but exceptions can be found to this categorisation, too.[8]

Whatever the reason for all these variations, the fact remains that most working-class families began to decline in size towards the end of the nineteenth century, and this had important consequences for the quality of family life. The physical and mental strain engendered by repeated childbearing was lessened, so that mothers had greater reserves of strength to deal with their offspring. Smaller numbers of children meant that more time could be devoted to each child. Fewer children also meant that there were fewer mouths to feed, so that there was more money available to spend on clothing and household goods. If the mother wanted to seek employment, part-time or otherwise, when the children were at school or grown-up, a smaller family made this more possible. All in all, the benefits of smaller numbers to the family as a whole are undoubted, though of course it was not until the closing years of the century that these advantages began to become more generally apparent.

Household size, of course, is different from family size. As family numbers dropped, so did the overall size of the household. In 1851 the estimated mean size of household was 6.2; by 1911 it was down to 5.5. Also in 1851 it has been estimated that 34 per cent of households had 6 or more occupants; by 1911 this percentage had fallen to 27 per cent.[9] The outsiders sharing accommodation with the conjugal family were as before a mixture of distant relatives and lodgers. It should be noted, however, that the housing shortage just before the Great War contributed to the existing degree of overcrowding. In a number of mining communities in Durham and Northumberland, for example, the figure was over 40 per cent.[10] So the decline in the size of the family brought only marginal relief to those families in overcrowded accommodation. It should also be remembered that lodgers came and went as members of the household, dependent on the state of the family economy. When children were small, and the family income under strain, lodgers might well be welcomed. They might have a separate room (if one was available), and often had their meals with the family. In this case, from the children's point of view, the lodger might almost be one of the family, until an increase in the family income might make his presence no longer necessary.

How far did the children see their mother only in the evenings, or at weekends, because she was employed? Not much change can be seen in this aspect of family life between 1870 and the end of the century. Only a minority of married working-class women with children still went out to work in the last decades of the century, though a number continued to have part-time jobs, sometimes in the home, such as taking in washing, or outside the home, such as charring. Employment outside the home varied from district to district; in textile areas, where women traditionally worked in the mills, it was more common than elsewhere (in Lancashire, households containing grandparents were more noticeable than in other areas, possibly because of their usefulness as babysitters). Yet even in textile towns the highest proportions of married women (with or without children) at work in 1911 were not strikingly high – for Blackburn, 23.2 per cent; for Burnley, 22.9 per cent and for Preston, 17.9 per cent. Nationally, the proportion of married women in the age-range 14–24 who were employed in 1911 was only 12.10 per cent; and for older married women, aged 25–34 (many of these presumably with children), the figure was only 9.91 per cent.[11] Hence the number of children who grew up with mother out to work and not at home to greet them on their return from school was relatively small by the end of the century. For most children, home and the presence of their mother were synonymous, unlike the situation at the end of the twentieth century.

When the history of the working-class family after 1870 is reviewed, what stands out as the most significant change is undoubtedly the decrease in its size; and this decline was to continue in the following century. The benefits flowing from this have already been described, though it obviously took time for them to take effect. However, if one of the causes of the family limitation which began to be practised was the increasing independence of working-class wives, this was clearly an important change in familial roles; women must have been becoming less dutiful and submissive than before. This change must not be exaggerated and of course there had always been forceful and indeed dominating working-class wives earlier in the century.[12] But although the change in feminine attitudes may have been limited, it had significance for the future. At the same time, certain other developments were also affecting the role of the father. Earlier in the century he was able to exercise an almost unlimited authority over both wife and children, whom he could beat and batter as he pleased. By 1900 all this had changed. It is true that the law offered protection which was by no means complete, but neighbours usually knew where to find the NSPCC Inspector when cruelty was suspected. More than this, the errant father had to contend with a number of officials who restricted his freedom to tyrannise his family. Among these were local teachers and the attendance inspector, who together exercised authority over the child of school age; and even the liberty to deal with babies and infants as he (or his wife) thought fit was undermined by the setting up of crèches by local authorities and the appearance of missioners or health visitors advising on the care of the very young. In short, parental authority was increasingly eroded by the development of social services (including a national school system) which gradually diminished parental authority in the home. Parents could no longer do what they liked with their own. Or to put it more formally, the multi-functional family in which father's word was law on all matters and could not be challenged was on the way out, as parental authority was increasingly shared with social welfare services and their agents.

To turn to housing, the kind of accommodation in which working-class children grew up in the last decades of the nineteenth century varied from place to place, from region to region, and was always dependent, of course, upon the extent of the family income. Perhaps the most fundamental division was between those children brought up in the countryside and those in the town. For country children, the rural cottage showed little improvement in the period from 1870 to 1900. The two-roomed, damp and insanitary hovel was still everywhere to be seen; some model cottages were built in the 1860s but even then the Agricultural Commission of 1867 criticised the bad housing in a number of counties – Leicestershire, Shropshire, Gloucestershire and Worcestershire – and described the rural cottages in Dorset, Wiltshire and Somerset as being among the very worst.[13] During the long agricultural depression which set in from 1873 onwards cottage-building almost ceased until the end of the century. The one-bedroomed cottage remained very common. Where better housing was available, it would take the form of a living-room, kitchen or scullery and either two or three bedrooms. The Duke of Bedford's model cottages all had two ground-floor rooms, a kitchen with a range, a scullery with a copper, two or three bedrooms, and a WC outside.[14] The vast majority of country children had to grow up in much less favourable housing than this, living under leaky thatched roofs, with draughty windows, damp walls and with an earth privy outside. At the end of the century there was an absolute shortage of rural housing estimated at 120,000, together with a much larger stock of decaying, insanitary and overcrowded cottages. Only under the 1909 Town and Country Planning Act was something done to get rid of the worst rural housing, when some 5,000 cottages were closed under the act.[15] It seems fair to say that at the beginning of the twentieth century the average country child was worse housed than the town child, certainly if the latter had a father in a skilled or semi-skilled occupation.

Urban housing for working-class children was markedly different from rural housing both in its range and in its diversity. Over the period from 1815 to 1911 the urban population had grown by three times, and towns and cities housed 79 per cent of the entire population. Given these facts, it is not surprising that a great variety of accommodation was provided, ranging from common lodging-houses and cellars to terraced housing. As regards the former, though intended only as places to stay overnight, some became long-term hostels for whole families. A contemporary account gives a graphic description of the worst kind: 'Nothing could be worse to the health than these places, without ventilation, cleanliness, or decency, and with forty people's breath perhaps mingling together in one foul choking steam of stench.'[16] In 1854 London officially had 10,824 common lodging-houses, with 82,000 inmates nightly. In Leeds, within a 440 yard semi-circle from Leeds parish church, there were 222 lodging houses with 2,500 inmates, averaging 2.5 persons per bed and 4.5 persons per room.[17] Cellars were also used as living quarters, principally in Liverpool and Manchester, and were perhaps the very worst form of individual housing, being damp, unhealthy and usually lacking windows.[18] (Manchester forbade the use of cellars for living purposes in 1853). Regionally, the principal types of working-class housing varied from through-terraces in the south of England (with divided tenement houses in London) to back-to-back houses in the Midlands, Yorkshire and Lancashire and flatted houses in Tyneside.

However, it would be wrong to think of home for all urban working-class children as an individual dwelling-house, even if only small and slum-like. In fact, many children of poorer parents simply lived in rooms in tenement houses, often grossly overcrowded. The extent of overcrowding was brought out strongly in the report of the Royal Commission on the Housing of the Working Classes, published in 1885. According to Lord Shaftesbury, overcrowding had become more serious than it ever was. The facts produced in evidence, he said, showed plainly how widely the single room system for families was established. Some striking examples were given for London:

In Clerkenwell, at 15 St Helena Place, a house was described containing six rooms, which were occupied at that time by six families, and as many as eight persons inhabited one room. At 1 Wilmington Place, there were 11 families in 11 rooms, seven persons occupying one room. At 30 Noble Street five families of 26 persons in all were found inhabiting six rooms. A small house in Allen Street was occupied by 38 persons, seven of whom lived in one room . . . At 36 Bowling Green Lane there were six persons in an underground kitchen. At 7 New Court there were 11 persons in two rooms, in which fowls were also kept.[19]

In 1891, when overcrowding was defined as having more than two adults to a room, children under ten counting as a half, and infants under one not counting at all, 11.2 per cent of the population of England and Wales lived in overcrowded accommodation. Associated with this overcrowding are the figures for occupancy of rooms. According to the Official Enquiry into Working Class Rents, Housing and Retail Prices, 1908, 18.0 per cent of the population of England and Wales occupied three rooms or less. In London the figure was 38.8 per cent, in Bradford 42.2 per cent and in Newcastle 53.3 per cent. If the figures for occupancy of only two rooms are examined, nearly a quarter of Newcastle's inhabitants (23.9 per cent) had only two rooms, and over a quarter of the inhabitants (26.3 per cent) of Gateshead.[20] Thus substantial numbers of children were growing up in cramped and overcrowded accommodation, and for them real freedom of physical movement was to be found only in the street outside. The reduction in the size of the family discussed earlier in this chapter must ultimately have been an important factor in reducing the strain on children living under such conditions.

Of course, it would be wrong to dwell too exclusively on the very worst housing of the last quarter of the nineteenth century. There are plenty of vivid descriptions available of this kind of housing, especially for the 1880s. Arthur Mearns caused a great stir with his pamphlet *The Bitter Cry of Outcast London*, in which he described some of the worst housing conditions: 'courts reeking with poisonous and malodorous gases arising from accumulations of sewage and refuse scattered in all directions . . . dark and filthy passages swarming with vermin . . . walls and ceilings black with the accretions of filth which have gathered upon them through years of neglect.'[21] Courts of this kind certainly existed, and children grew up in them. Privies were still shared and were grossly over-used, even in the more fashionable parts of London. Thus:

In a street in Westminster, a witness stated that there was only one [closet] for all the houses in the street, 30 or 40 people inhabiting each house; and that it was open and used by all passers-by . . . In some parts of London they are used as sleeping places by the homeless poor of the class who haunt the staircases. In Bristol, privies actually exist in living rooms.[22]

On thc other hand, building regulations were increasingly applied to all new buildings after 1877, and towards the end of the century more and more houses were being supplied with tapped water and with water closets. By 1900 there was a range of accommodation available; at the one end of the scale were the 'reeking courts' – in 1913, Birmingham still had 43,366 back-to-back houses, housing some 200,000 inhabitants – while at the other end of the scale there were new houses, built in monotonous terraces for the most part, and often dark at the rear, but erected in accordance with by-law regulations, and far superior to earlier, jerry-built housing.

This newer building was to set standards for working-class housing in the early decades of the twentieth century. Its major features were those just mentioned – the provision of water-closets and a piped water supply – but in addition in the 1890s there was an increasing provision of gas for both lighting and cooking. To take these advances in order: the most important from the sanitary point of view was undoubtedly the installation of water-closets, usually in the yard at the rear. By 1911 water-closets provided the majority of conveniences in 80 out of the 95 towns in England with over 50,000 inhabitants. In 62 of the towns, they constituted more than 90 per cent of conveniences, though towns in the South and Midlands were ahead of those in the North.[23] These water-closets took a variety of forms, the earlier versions often using waste water – a common type in Lancashire – while later versions with valve systems were often inefficient and noisome; but gradually the modern forms with overhead cisterns operated by chains took over, being dependent, of course, on a piped water-supply to the house. By 1901, in Birmingham, which hitherto had many ashpits and removable pails, over half the houses had water-closets.[24] Of course, this improvement was dependent on the existence of drains to carry away the sewage, so that the increasing use of the water-closet was accompanied by the installation of deep drainage systems in urban areas – a veritable sanitary revolution, of immense consequence for the health and convenience of family life.

The piped water-supply which made water-closets possible also brought tapped water to increasing numbers of houses, sometimes only to the yard at the rear and shared with other families, but often also to the kitchen or scullery sink. In a minority of cases, water might also be taken to a bathroom upstairs, but bathrooms were still very uncommon in working-class houses by 1914. In the new model dwellings built by the Cadburys at Bourneville near Birmingham, the bath was hidden away in the kitchen. Most working-class families still washed at the sink and took a bath on Friday night in a tin tub, using water heated up in the copper, or on the range or stove.[25] As for gas, its use both for public lighting and industrial lighting goes back to the beginning of the nineteenth century, but it was rare in the working-class home until the 1890s, when the invention of the incandescent mantle and also of the slot-meter (first put into use in Liverpool, then in London) led to the rapid replacement by gaslight of the candles and paraffin lamps hitherto used. At the same time, gas cookers provided a much more efficient means of cooking than the often smoky and awkward-to-manage coal-fired range in the kitchen. By 1914 in most towns up to 60 per cent of gas consumers were using gas cookers.[26] These cookers were far from the hygienic and attractive cookers of the present day, often smelling strongly of gas and needing frequent cleaning and black-leading, but they were still a great advance on the old kitchen range.

Water-closets, tapped water, and gas lighting and cooking were thus features of much of the newer working-class housing at the end of the century, and this new by-law building could be seen in particular in the new working-class suburbs which grew up in London as train and tram services improved and permitted working people to live at a distance from their work. West Ham, for example, grew from 19,000 inhabitants to reach a population of 267,000 in the period 1851–1891. By 1905 an estimated 13,000 families were leaving the central parts of London for the suburbs; and according to the London County Council about 820,000 workmen were making extensive journeys to work each day. Nor were these developments confined to the metropolis; they were also to be found in the larger provincial towns and cities.[27] It should be noted in addition that the new amenities were to be found in older houses, too. Because of the cost, many local authorities failed to take the opportunity to build new working-class housing which was conferred by the Housing Act, 1890 (and later extended by the Town and Country Planning Act, 1909), preferring to renovate older property by installing water-closets, a tapped water supply and other improvements such as handrails on stairs. A typical example is provided by Birmingham, where in 1913 a policy was adopted of demolishing one side of courts in order to provide a better circulation of air, at the same time reconditioning about 2,700 houses. Other examples can be found in Black Country towns such as Stourbridge, which also pursued a policy of renovation of older property. According to the Medical Officer of Health's Report for this town for 1911

> There is no considerable amount of overcrowding in houses in this district . . . it is especially favoured regarding open spaces about houses. Nearly all houses have WCs of which about 5 per cent have slop closets, which is undesirable. 66 houses have been given separate water taps, and 84 hand rails put in. Generally speaking, the accommodation for food and coal in many older houses is inadequate. It is usually under the stairs in the living room, and there is no external ventilation. New bye-laws during the year have laid down the distance from the house of pigstys and provide for the weekly removal of manure instead of monthly.[28]

In sum, the new housing offered a far better living environment for those families who could afford the higher rents – often small gardens at the front and back, a parlour, back room or kitchen and scullery, two or three bedrooms above, and all the amenities just described. There are many such houses still in occupation today, usually brought up to date with damp courses, electric lighting, gas or electric cooking, a bathroom, lavatory and central heating. There were also the older houses, modernised by the newer amenities. However, one type of working-class housing which was to become widespread between the wars was conspicuous by its almost complete absence – council house estates. As already noted, local councils were very reluctant to face the expense of building on their own behalf, and there were very few council house tenants before 1914; of all the new houses built between 1890 and 1914, less than 5 per cent were provided by local authorities.[29] The most advanced authority nationally in this respect was the London County Council, building flats centrally and garden villages in the suburbs. It should also be mentioned that some working-class families enjoyed more modern and good-quality accommodation provided by model housing associations such as the Metropolitan Association for improving the Dwellings of the Industrious Classes, the Peabody Trust (1862), Waterlow's Improved Industrial Dwellings Company (1863), and the Artisans, Labourers and General Dwellings Company (1867). By 1885 there were about twenty-eight of these associations in London, housing 29,700 families or 147,000 persons on 254 sites, but this constituted only 4 per cent of London's population and the rents were high in what were well-equipped premises but barrack-like in construction, and usually subject to strict regulations for tenants. Hence they were not regarded with great favour by working people.[30]

What did all these changes signify for the working-class child growing up in an urban environment about 1900? Very few, in all probability, took much notice of the improvements going on in the built environment around them. They simply accepted their homes as they found them, with or without the newer amenities. It has been argued that as life at work became more intensive, and the streets became more orderly and the standard of living rose, a home-based culture of domesticity resulted, manifesting itself in the better-quality housing of the time. Be this as it may, the fact is that children of the skilled working classes became accustomed to a noticeably higher standard of housing than their predecessors earlier in the century. They were the first generation of working-class children to take it for granted that there would be gas lighting in their house and a lavatory which flushed. Children of the less-skilled classes were not so fortunate; their houses lacked gardens, had no separate hallway, and had fewer and smaller rooms – but they might at the same time have a water-closet, and increasingly they were likely to have gas and water supplies. At the bottom of the social pile were the poorly-paid and intermittently unemployed, the very poorest classes, whose homes were in slum buildings as filthy and decrepit as any of fifty years before. Lord Shaftesbury spoke feelingly of children being brought up in such surroundings, especially in London:

> But there is a great deal of suffering among little children in overcrowded districts that does not appear in the death rate at all. In St Luke's, opthalmia, known locally as 'the blight' among the young, is very prevalent, and can be traced to the dark, ill-ventilated, crowded rooms in which they live; there are also found scrofula and congenital diseases, very detrimental to the health of the children as they grow up.[31]

Conditions might be equally bad in small market towns. This description of a working-class house in Stratford-upon-Avon in the 1890s is by its tenant, George Hewins, the father of eight children:

> It was three hundred, four hundred years old, that cottage . . . dark and dirty. Sometimes I thought it must have been there since time began. However much the missus scrubbed the flags, however much I limed the walls, we couldn't keep it clean! Bugs and fleas, it was one long battle, and we was on the losing side. Those we catched was splattered on the wall, blood and all, like pressed flowers. There was one room downstairs with an open fire, where the missus did the cooking and the washing and the ironing, two tiny rooms upstairs – the one we slept in was over the passage. Outside in the yard was the well, and a double-handled pump. When we wanted our side, we pulled the handle; the neighbours pulled it back when they wanted it. A score o' folks or more used that pump –

men, women, and kiddies – and the earth closet. I always went for a crap in the fields on my way to work.[32]

It is pleasing to record that when the Great War came, the Hewins family were allocated one of the first council houses built in Stratford. George recalled that it was 'really modern', with three bedrooms and two rooms downstairs, a 'nice front room' and a kitchen. There were fences between the yards, a good toilet for their own exclusive use, and a long garden.[33]

To turn to house furnishings, here the standard achieved depended for the most part on the family income, and could vary with the number of children, how many mouths there were to feed and so on. A family who had children out to work could clearly afford a better standard than one where all the children were small and a financial liability. In general terms, as was the case earlier in the century, at one end of the scale were the truly impoverished families, where the beds could be mere heaps of rags, and there was very little furniture in the downstairs room or rooms. As was noted in an earlier chapter, investigators into the condition of children on outdoor relief in the early twentieth century often found rooms bare of furniture because there was insufficient money to buy food or boots, and any extra expense had to be met by selling or pawning furniture (it might also be broken up for firewood). On the other hand, the homes of the skilled workers were comfortably furnished and indeed showed an increase in affluence over the period from 1870–1900. Floor-coverings improved with the development of linoleum from 1876 onwards, while wallpaper became more available with machine-printing from the mid-century, and cheaper after the removal of duty in 1861.[34] Furniture itself became cheaper with the development of factory-produced suites towards the end of the century.

The room which best exemplified the increased standard of living of the better-off working classes was, of course, the front-room parlour. The walls were papered, usually having a dado and a frieze, the ceiling whitewashed, and there were curtains at the window, sometimes with wooden venetian blinds. On the floor was a carpet, with stained floor-boards around. The furniture consisted of a heavy table placed centrally, with a fringed woollen cover, a dresser or chiffonier, and several easy chairs, upholstered in horsehair and leather or moquette. On the mantlepiece there would be a clock flanked by innumerable ornaments, vases and so on, with a mirror above and a heavy brass fender on the hearth below. On the walls there were pictures, usually cheap framed reproductions, often of biblical scenes, but in some more artistic households there might be pictures of some discreetly unclothed classical figure or even (a favourite Edwardian scene) an unclothed young woman bathing in what appears to be a lake (the title is 'September Morn'). Everywhere there were framed photographs and knick-knacks of all kinds. The best-furnished rooms would also have an upright piano with candleholders on the front, and a piano stool beneath the keyboard (sheet music was kept in the stool). Everywhere (to modern eyes) there was clutter, the walls covered with pictures and ornaments overflowing on all available surfaces – the mantlepiece, the top of the piano, shelves and what-nots – a cornucopia of cheap, often garish possessions put deliberately on display. For the children this would have been a relatively unfamiliar room, as it was intended only for visitors, and even in summer was rather cool and fusty – it certainly smelt differently from the living-room with its familiar fug. Fires were lit only in winter, and then usually only on Sundays (children practising the piano during the week would have to put up with the cold). The Victorian front parlour has attracted a good deal of criticism in post-Victorian times, at least, but it was a significant indication of the increased affluence of the skilled working classes, with all its clutter and the potted plant in the window (usually an aspidistra, much mocked by Orwell and in a different sense by Gracie Fields). For children it was a sort of holy of holies, visited only infrequently and not part of the business of everyday life.[35]

Upstairs, the most noticeable improvement in furnishing in the better-equipped working-class home was perhaps the popularity of brass bedsteads, complete with wiremesh springing and a horsehair mattress. The floor would be covered with lino, very cold to bare feet in the morning, with one or two mats or rugs. There might be a dressing-table – one was included in a standard list of furniture on offer to newly-weds, requiring an expenditure for all items of only £12 12*s*;[36] but washhand stands, with a large jug, basin and slop-pail, were intended more for the lower middle classes. Chamber-pots were customary, of course, sometimes with tasteful floral designs or even mottoes, and were often put to use in the night.

To sum up, it is impossible, of course, to describe the furnishings of the 'typical' urban working-class home as such, because of the variations in the type of furnishing from the impoverished slum to the respectable by-law terraced dwelling. Nevertheless, it is right to stress the improvement towards the end of the century in both the quality and the quantity of furnishing of the skilled and semi-skilled home. Naturally, younger children took their environment for granted, whatever its nature, but a generation was growing up with a degree of comfort hardly expected earlier in the century. In 1838, the Headmaster of Eton, receiving a deputation who had come to ask for water to be laid on in the College, remarked, 'You will be wanting gas and turkey carpets next!'[37] By 1900 a piped water-supply, water-closets, gas and carpets were increasingly within the reach of the better-off workers, at least and of their children.

There remain to be considered diet and health: as for diet, there can be no doubt that from the 1870s onwards up to the outbreak of the Great War, there was a considerable improvement *overall* in working-class diet. Estimated weekly food consumption figures per head, based on family budget evidence, are as follows:

Date	*No. of Families*	*Bread*	*Potatoes*	*Sugar*	*Fats*	*Meat*	*Milk*
		(lb)	(lb)	(oz)	(oz)	(lb)	(pt)
1863	493	10.9	3.9	7	5.1	0.9	1.4
1890s	153	6.5	2.0	15	5.2	1.8	1.5
1900s	2,332	6.6	3.0	16	7.7	1.2	1.8[38]

These figures must be treated with caution, but it is reasonably clear that bread consumption fell and then levelled off in the later nineteenth century, and so did potatoes, stabilising at around 3 lb per week. Between the 1860s and the 1890s meat consumption probably doubled and began to exceed 1 lb per head per week. Sugar consumption also rose quite remarkably and more than any other foodstuff, also reaching 1 lb a week.[39] Other foodstuffs should also be mentioned: the consumption of butter rose from 11 lb per head per year to 13 lb per head per year in 1900 (margarine, known at the time as 'butterine', was imported from 1876, but had only limited sales). More tea was also purchased, averaging about 2 lb per head in 1851, rising to 6 lb per head per year in 1900. As for beer, its consumption peaked at 34 gallons per head per year in 1875, dropping to under 28 gallons in 1888 and 27 gallons in 1914. The consumption of spirits also declined. Fruit, previously a luxury, was consumed more (14.7 lb a head per year in 1900), while the consumption of bananas shot up sixfold in the period from 1900 to 1914. Condensed milk was widely used from the 1870s, especially for feeding infants and children; although purer than cow's milk, it lacked vitamins

A, D and fats, being made from evaporated skimmed milk. In consequence it often led to rickets in children.[40]

All these improvements in consumption had considerable significance for working-class parents and their children, for food constituted a major part of all working-class budgets; and the lower the income, the higher proportion was devoted to food and drink. Thus, it was estimated in 1885 that 71 per cent of working-class earnings went on food and drink, but only 44 per cent of middle-class earnings. Again, in 1889 Board of Trade returns showed that on a low income of £28 to £40 a year, the proportion spent on food was over 87 per cent, whereas on a higher income of £70 to £80 a year, the proportion dropped to 56 per cent. Further, a skilled engineer earning 30*s* a week would spend 2*s* to 5*s* a week on meat; an unskilled labourer could afford only 1*s* 3*d* to 3*s*.[41] The importance of food expenditure as part of the weekly budget was, therefore, very great.

All this may be illustrated by reference to the weekly household budget (amounting to 12*s* 4½*d*) of a typical workman earning a good wage of 30*s* a week in London, with a careful wife and three children of school age. This budget was printed in the *Cornhill Magazine* in 1901:[42]

¼ lb tea (to last week)	4½*d*	½ lb cheese	3*d*
¼ lb coffee	3*d*	6–7 lb meat (Sunday joint)	2*s* 6*d*
1 lb loaf sugar	2*d*	¼ lb suet	2*d*
3 lb moist sugar	3*d*	fish	10*d*
3 lb jam	7½*d*	potatoes	3*d*
½ lb butter	6*d*	greens	3*d*
8 eggs	6*d*	3 loaves of bread	7½*d*
1 lb bacon	8*d*	½ quarten of flour	3*d*

Later in the week a further 1*s* 3*d* was spend on bread, 2*s* on fish and sausages and 9*d* on extra vegetables to add to the stew. In considering this budget, it should be pointed out that coffee was never as popular as tea, which had gained in favour with the improvement in water supplies and the marketing of cheap tea. Jam was now commonly factory-made, but with a very low fruit content. Bacon was imported from Denmark, Ireland or the USA, while cheese would come from Canada, New Zealand and America. Fish was increasingly popular, its consumption increasing from 25 lb per head per year in the 1890s to 30 lb per head by 1914.

So far attention has been concentrated on urban diet. By the end of the nineteenth century, as already noted, 79 per cent of the population were living in the towns, leaving rural areas as often impoverished backwaters. The poor state of rural housing was matched by a generally poor standard of living and a diet still not far above subsistence level. Some improvement was to be seen by 1900, but rural families continued to eat more starchy food, more potatoes, and more milk than their urban counterparts, who consumed less bread and potatoes and more sugar, fats and meat. The following table showing weekly food consumption in urban and rural working-class budgets brings out the differences very well:

	Date	*No. of familes*	*Bread*	*Potatoes*	*Sugar*	*Fats*	*Meat*	*Milk*
			(lb)	(lb)	(oz)	(oz)	(lb)	(lb)
Urban	1863	125	9.1	2.4	8.0	4.7	0.8	0.8
	1902–13	2,031	6.7	2.9	16.0	8.0	1.3	1.7
Rural	1863	377	11.6	4.4	7.0	5.2	0.9	1.6
	1902–13	301	5.7	4.4	13.0	5.1	0.9	2.0[43]

So although it is true that some improvements in diet took place in rural areas, for example in sugar consumption, on the whole there was not much change for children in the countryside by the end of the period.

Nevertheless, the reasons for the overall changes in food intake are plain enough – lower food prices and the rise in real wages. The retail price of food in the typical workman's budget fell by 30 per cent between 1877 and 1897, and this in turn was due to imports of cheap wheat and meat. Cheap wheat began to come across the Atlantic in the early 1870s, while the first really successful cargo of frozen beef and mutton from Melbourne arrived in London in 1880. Pork from the USA, beef from the Argentine and lamb from New Zealand began to flood the market. At the same time taxes on food gradually fell, especially on tea, on which the tax was lowered from 1*s* 10*d* a pound to 4*d* a pound in 1890.[44]

All these improvements could not fail to take effect on the diet of working-class men, women and children, but at this point important qualifications must be made to the picture presented so far. In the first place, the benefits were felt by only a proportion of the working classes, namely those in steady and relatively well-paid employment. No doubt they constituted a substantial section of the working classes, but the surveys of Booth and Rowntree showed as much as a third of the working population still below the poverty line. It must be remembered, too, that economic conditions varied from one part of the country to another at different times. The so-called Great Depression was a reality in the 1880s in parts of the Black Country, where in some trades real wages actually fell.[45] As a consequence, all turned on family income, and even a relatively well-off family might still not earn enough to provide an adequate nutritional standard. Thus about 1900 a family needed to earn about 30*s* a week before its energy intake began to exceed 2,500 kilocalories a day. This was easily attainable by middle- and lower-middle-class families and by the better-paid working classes, but hardly below that level. Even then, there were likely to be some deficiencies in calcium.[46] The more poorly-paid simply never had enough nutritious food to eat. Many children in towns were ill-fed and undernourished, a fact to which the introduction of school meals in 1906 bears witness.

It should also be remembered that the quality of foodstuffs did not remain unchanged after 1870. In one sense, this was a change for the better, in that food and drink had often previously been adulterated (tea contaminated by floor-sweepings, milk watered, gin and beer sharpened with sulphuric acid, and so on), until the Adulteration of Food, Drink and Drugs Act, 1872 brought the first real improvement. This was an undoubted gain, but against it must be set the fact that by the end of the century the quality of some factory-made products was still relatively low. It has already been mentioned that condensed milk was deficient in both vitamins and in fats, and might even encourage rickets (bow-legged children were not uncommon in late Victorian times). Bread might lose its vitamin content through new methods of milling, butterine did not have added vitamins till the 1930s, and jam might be thin and lacking in fruit. On balance, it certainly seems that more was gained than was lost in preventing food adulteration and introducing higher standards of hygiene, but it must also be taken into account that the poorest always had to buy the cheapest foodstuffs and by 1900 most of the lowest-priced foodstuffs were less nutritious than formerly.[47] Thus it was the poorest families which bought the worst food, and of these families it was those with most children whose standard of living was the lowest, because there was less food to go round.

This leads to another (and concluding) general point about diet: it was pointed out in an earlier chapter that whatever food was available, the breadwinner always had the lion's share. As he was nearly always a manual worker, this made sense because he had to keep up his strength.

This held true at the end of the century as much as at the beginning. Father fed first. Mother took second place and indeed might forgo a proper meal in order to make sure that her husband had his fill. The children came third, especially if infants or still at school. It follows that in spite of the improved diet of the better-off families children as a rule still had to make do with what was left after the adults had eaten. In these circumstances many children grew up without ever having had the satisfaction of eating full and proper meals. The result was that even after the greater consumption levels of the late nineteenth century, children of the poorer working classes were still undernourished. During the Great War some two million men born at the end of the nineteenth century were examined under the Military Service Acts, 1916. Of these men only 36 per cent were placed in Grade I, indicating a 'full normal standard of health and strength'. It is worth quoting the Medical Board's summary of their findings in full:

> Medical examination showed that, of every nine men of military age in Great Britain, on the average, three were perfectly fit and healthy; two were upon a definitely infirm plane of health and strength whether from some disability or some failure in development; three were incapable of undergoing more than a very moderate degree of physical exertion and could almost (in view of their age) be described with justice as physical wrecks; and the remaining man was a chronic invalid with a precarious hold on life.[48]

It may be, of course, that by this time the best of the nation's manhood had already gone to France. Nevertheless, the results provide a striking and significant comment on the nutritional standards of the working classes and of their children.

Lastly, to turn to childhood health and sickness: at the beginning of this chapter it was pointed out that adult longevity increased markedly during the second half of the nineteenth century, with important consequences for relationships within the family. Similarly, infant mortality rates also fell, with the exception of the so-far unexplained rise in the 1890s. This rise in mortality was followed by a remarkable and sustained rise in survival rates in the early 1900s, described by Dr F. B. Smith as an increase in the number of human beings surviving infancy which was probably the largest and swiftest advance in modern British history.[49] Childhood ailments also declined by the end of the century. Vaccination almost eradicated smallpox, and scarlet fever decreased in virulence. Measles could still be a serious illness, but its mortality rate fell from 42.8 per 1000 in 1866–70 to 29.1 in 1906–10. In the years just before the Great War deaths due to whooping cough fell by about a third (1902–07), and there was an important decline of 12 per cent in deaths resulting from diarrhoea and convulsions. This meant an annual saving of some 20,000 lives out of the earlier number of 76,000 deaths from this cause. Dr Smith comments that this must have been due to improved feeding and mothering.[50]

In fact, as indicated earlier in this chapter, there was probably a variety of causes for these changes, such as improved nutrition, better housing and water supply, better sanitation, greater knowledge of hygiene, smaller families and so on. The difficulties lie in establishing precise links between these causes and rising standards of health. For example, it has recently been argued that there was a steady increase in the average height of children between 1860 and 1914 which resulted from better nutrition, but the causal links have still to be fully established.[51] Again, attention has been drawn to the improvements in midwifery training and practice and to the setting-up of crèches from the 1870s onwards, and especially the establishment of health visiting societies. By the late 1890s municipal councils were contributing to the cost of health visitors and in 1907 the City of Westminster Health Society inspected more than 2,000 infants during the course of 10,000 visits by their visitors.[52] However, how far these visits really had an effect is difficult to judge, especially since the poorest mothers viewed the visitors with some suspicion, regarding them as interfering busybodies. In some areas crèches made but a slow advance; weighing of babies and the keeping of records was in some places thought to harm the babies, so that mothers kept away.

All in all it seems undeniable that some changes for the better did take place in children's health from the 1870s onwards, though curiously enough not as a consequence of the major advances in medical practices of the time, which, as we have seen, produced beneficial results between the wars rather than before 1914. These changes for the better received an important and valuable boost with the introduction of school meals on the rates and of the school medical service. By 1914 in Birmingham, for example, an average of 751 meals were served per day, dental and medical treatment was being given, 468 children had operations for tonsils and adenoids, 220 children had X-rays for ringworm, spectacles were prescribed at a cheap rate for 2,533 children and 4,471 children were treated for minor ailments.[53]

Having said all this, we must revert to the need to establish a perspective. Progress is obvious enough, but the question remains, by how much was the children's health improved, and how much poverty remained? Here the spectre at the feast is provided above all by the investigations of Booth and Rowntree, but there is plenty of other evidence as to the wretched conditions of the poorest classes.[54] If indeed a third were living below the poverty line, it is obvious that whatever improvement had taken place overall, much remained to be done to reach acceptable standards of physical well-being. It is salutary to refer in conclusion to the first report of Dr George Newman as Chief Medical Officer of the Schools Medical Service, published in 1910:

> Speaking generally, it may be said that out of the six million children registered on the books of the Public Elementary Schools of England and Wales, about 10 per cent suffer from a serious defect of vision, from 3 to 5 per cent suffer from defective hearing, 1 to 3 per cent have suppurating ears, 6 to 8 per cent have adenoids or enlarged tonsils of sufficient degree to obstruct the nose or throat and thus to require surgical treatment, about 40 per cent suffer from extensive and injurious decay of the teeth, about 30 to 40 per cent have unclean heads or bodies, about 1 per cent suffer from ringworm, 1 per cent from tuberculosis in readily recognisable form, from 1 to 2 per cent are affected with heart disease, and a considerable percentage of children are suffering from a greater or lesser degree of malnutrition.[55]

In Bradford, Dr Ralph Crowley was able to show that children lost weight during the school holidays, when school meals were not available, while in 1913 Mr J. A. Pease, the President of the Board of Education, admitted in the House of Commons that 10 per cent of school children were undernourished.[56] In fact this was probably an underestimate. Clearly, children's health still had far to go before the Great War.

It has been remarked more than once previously in this book that there are substantial problems in describing and commenting on such large subjects as the home life of working-class children. One of the greatest is the difficulty of giving appropriate weight to the component parts of the subject under discussion – was improved diet more important than better housing, or less important than smaller families or better household amenities? Since it is not really possible to quantify these matters, any composite picture is really out of the question. There is another even more unfathomable question: how did it all seem to the children of the time? To see the changes described in this chapter through the eyes of the children is for the most part beyond the art and skill of the historian. As one social historian has put it, there are groups in history like children whose experience can only be seen through the eyes of adults, and who as a consequence will always remain in the shadows.[57] This is well said. All the historian of childhood in the nineteenth century can do is to describe things from the outside, enlightened from time to time by empathy; but even then, he will never know how near he has approached to the truth of the matter.

These caveats having duly been voiced, what can be said by way of final comment on the subject of this chapter? It seems a fair statement that after 1870 home life did begin radically to alter in character. It was not merely the cumulative effect of the detailed changes already discussed, important though they were; it was the result of the transformation of working-class childhood mentioned at the end of the previous chapter on home life – the coming of compulsory education. This was a change of great significance, having profound repercussions for life at home as well as life outside the home, for it introduced new routines and new attitudes into the home, initially for three-quarters of the year at least, but later for the year as a whole. It is true that many children already attended school before 1870, and in their homes, for children to spend their days at school was already familiar enough. It was in the homes of the poorest classes – those of the residuum – that compulsory eduction introduced new daily procedures, and it was in these homes that some kind of rough and ready order had to prevail as school began to dominate the children's lives.

It can be argued then that a force external to the home, that of compulsory education, must be ranked alongside the forces operating within the home. Yet at the same time there was a certain improvement in familial relationships towards the end of the century, as higher standards of conduct were established. It has already been remarked that fathers were becoming less inclined to take their belts off to their children, nor would husbands be so likely to knock their wives about.[58] Of course, it is always possible to provide instances to the contrary. Thus a weekend in the East End of London at the turn of the century has been described as follows: 'From Saturday afternoon, when wages had been paid, till Monday morning, the court was often a field of battle and bloodshed, and Saturday was a pitiable day . . . men kicking their wives around the court like footballs, and women fighting like wild tigers!'[59] However, middle-class social observers did not see it in this way. On the contrary, social workers such as Mrs Bosanquet, Miss Loane, and Lady Bell all commented on the increasing refinement of working-class family life and on the rapid disappearance of physical brawling. They all emphasised the beneficial effects of schooling on demeanour, attitudes, regular habits and on punctuality and self-control. Mrs Bosanquet wrote in 1896 that the

> greatest influence in our parish outside the home is beyond doubt the school . . . For good and evil the rising generation is there receiving instruction and discipline . . . in face of all criticism our children are being firmly and gently brought into line, and helped up the first steep steps of order and knowledge. I do not think we attach nearly sufficient weight to this fact in estimating the advance that has been made towards reclaiming the 'submerged' classes of the community.[60]

Dr McKibbin has observed that all three ladies would have agreed with George Sims, who wrote in 1889 that the crucial division in London was between those who had been to board school and those who had not.[61]

One last point in conclusion: it can be claimed, as it was in the previous chapter on this subject, that in the home all turned on the relationship between father, mother and children, and it was this fundamental relationship which determined all else. This must be true, of course, but this does not advance our argument very far. Some working-class families were loving in their relationships, others less so. Some were torn by internal strife. It has been remarked by one historian that working-class autobiographies do not reveal any very loving relationships between parents and children, and relations, especially with fathers, might often be distant. Another historian, in observing that over the centuries some parents have been passionately affectionate towards each other, while others have been viciously hostile, has reminded us that it is always dangerous to argue from the silence of the record.[62] This is true enough. All that can be done in the present context is to observe and record the various beneficial influences on the home situation before the coming of the Great War. Among these influences must certainly be noted the effect of compulsory education and the increasing transfer of the social conventions governing civilised behaviour from the schoolroom to the home.

References

1 Michael Anderson, 'The social implication of demographic change', in F. M. L. Thompson, (ed.), *The Cambridge Social History of Britain 1750–1950*, Vol. 2, 1990, p. 16. See also the sources given in note 1 to Chapter Four. W. Hamish Fraser, *The Coming of the Mass Market 1850–1914*, 1981, has a succinct description of demographic change in the second half of the nineteenth century in

Chapter I, 'Numbers' (pp. 3–13).

2 Anderson, 'Social implication of demographic change', p. 49.

3 For a recent and useful account of the changes in mortality rates, see Robert Woods, *The Population of Great Britain in the Nineteenth Century*, 1992, Chapter 9, 'Mortality'.

4 Anderson, 'Social implication of demographic change', p. 39.

5 *Ibid.*, p. 43.

6 F. M. L. Thompson, *The Rise of Respectable Society: A Social History of Victorian Britain, 1830–1900*, 1988, pp. 71–2.

7 Woods, *The Population of Great Britain*, p. 53.

8 Thompson, *The Rise of Respectable Society*, pp. 71–4; Woods, *The Population of Great Britain*, p. 52.

9 Anderson, 'Social implication of demographic change', p. 57.

10 *Ibid.*, p. 58. A contributory factor to the heavy overcrowding in some parts of London was that fertility in the poorest districts declined only slowly before 1914; see Ellen Ross, 'Labour and Love: Re-discovering London's Working-Class Mothers, 1870–1918' in Jane Lewis (ed), *Labour and Love: Women's Experience of Home and Family 1850–1900*, 1986.

11 Diana Gittins, *Fair Sex: Family Size and Structure 1900–39*, 1982, pp. 70, 96. See also Elizabeth Roberts, *Women's Work 1840–1940*, 1988, p. 45. Dr Roberts also points out that it can no longer be maintained that children of full-time working mothers suffered higher infant mortality rates than those of mothers staying at home, and that there is little evidence of working mothers neglecting their children, (pp. 46–7).

12 Women's role in the Chartist movement has lately become better defined and there are many examples of strong-minded women in the Black Country in the mid-nineteenth century. In the nailing community at Lye, near Stourbridge, any family dispute in which women played a dominant role was known as a Cole's Wake, after a legendary figure given a severe beating by his wife.

13 John Burnett, *A Social History of Housing 1815–1970*, 1978, p. 129. For general accounts of working-class housing in the nineteenth century, see Chapter Four, note 19.

14 *Ibid.*, p. 133.

15 *Ibid.*, pp. 134, 135.

16 Henry Mayhew, *London Labour and the London Poor*, 1861, vol. I, p. 409.

17 Richard Roger, *Housing in Urban Britain, 1780–1914*, 1989, p. 31.

18 *Ibid.*, pp. 31–2.

19 *Royal Commission on the Housing of the Working Classes*, First Report, 1885, p. 7.

20 Burnett, *Social History*, pp. 142–3, 152, 153.

21 R. Sims (Arthur Mearns), *The Bitter Cry of Outcast London*, 1883.

22 *Royal Commission on Housing*, Second Report, 1885, p. 11.

23 M. J. Daunton, *House and Home in the Victorian City: Working Class*

Housing 1850–1914, 1983, p. 258.

24 *Ibid.*, p. 253.

25 *Ibid.*, p. 247.

26 *Ibid.*, p. 241.

27 Burnett, *Social History*, pp. 161–2.

28 *Annual Report of the Medical Officer for 1911*, Urban District Council of Stourbridge.

29 Burnett, *Social History*, p. 181.

30 *Ibid.*, p. 174.

31 *Royal Commission on Housing*, Second Report, 1885, p. 14.

32 Angela Hewins, (ed.), *The Dillon: Memories of a Man of Stratford upon Avon*, 1982, p. 65.

33 *Ibid.*, p. 138.

34 Daunton, *House and Home*, p. 279; W. Hamish Fraser, *The Coming of the Mass Market*, p. 197.

35 For a good contemporary description of the late Victorian parlour, see Daunton, *House and Home*, p. 283.

36 Robert Roberts, *The Classic Slum*, 1971, p. 35.

37 E. L. Woodward, *The Age of Reform, 1815–1870*, 1938, p. 466.

38 Figures extracted from D. J. Oddy, 'Food, Drink, and Nutrition', in F. M. L. Thompson, *The Cambridge Social History of Britain 1750–1950*, Vol. 2, 1990, p. 269.

39 *Ibid.*, p. 270.

40 Fraser, *The Coming of the Mass Market*, pp. 28–31; John Burnett, *Plenty and Want*, 1966, p. 109.

41 Fraser, *The Coming of the Mass Market*, p. 34.

42 *Ibid.*, pp. 34–5.

43 Oddy, 'Food, Drink, and Nutrition', p. 271.

44 Burnett, *Plenty and Want*, pp. 99, 101.

45 Eric Hopkins, 'Small Town Aristocrats of Labour and their Standard of Living, 1840–1914', *Economic History Review*, XXVIII, 1975.

46 Oddy, 'Food, Drink, and Nutrition', pp. 271, 275.

47 On this interesting point, see W. Ashworth, *An Economic History of England 1870–1939*, 1960, p. 253.

48 Oddy, 'Food, Drink, and Nutrition', p. 279, and 'the Health of the People', in Theo Barker and Michael Drake, *Population and Society in Britain 1850–1980*, 1982, p. 129.

49 F. B. Smith, *The People's Health 1830–1910*, 1979, p. 124.

50 *Ibid.*, pp. 143, 123.

51. R. Floud, K. Wachter and A. Gregory, *Height, Health and History: Nutritional Status in the United Kingdom 1750–1980*, 1990.

52 Smith, *The People's Health*, p. 115.

53 Eric Hopkins, 'Working Class Education in Birmingham during the First World War', *History of Education Society Occasional Publication*, No. 6, 1981.

54 See for example the fictional A. Morrison, *A Child of the Jago*, 1896 and C. F. Masterman, *From the Abyss*, 1902 and *The Condition of England*, 1909.

55 Oddy, 'Health of the People', p. 126.

56 *Ibid.*, p. 127.

57 Leonore Davidoff, 'The Family in Britain', in Thompson, *Cambridge Social History*, Vol. 2, p. 72.

58 It has been argued that neighbourhood public opinion was intensely hostile to those suspected of cruelty to children, and that the NSPCC relied heavily on the testimony of neighbours (Ellen Ross, 'Labour and Love', p. 83).

59 John R. Gillis, *For Better, For Worse: British Marriages, 1600 to the Present*, 1985, p. 251.

60 R. I. McKibbin, 'Social Class and Social Observation in Edwardian England', *Transactions of the Royal Historical Society*, fifth series, Vol. 28, 1978, p. 194.

61 *Ibid.* See also on the improvement in popular behaviour, Thompson, *Rise of Respectable Society*, p. 277.

62 Michael Anderson, 'New Insights in the History of the Family in Britain', *Refresh*, 9, Autumn, 1989.

Chapter 10

Leisure activities

The concept of working-class leisure has received a good deal of attention from historians in recent years, though for the most part it has been adult leisure rather than children's leisure which has come under scrutiny.[1] In the early decades of the nineteenth century most working-class children began work at an early age, so that their time for recreation was often as limited as it was for adults. However, since the time of starting work was often seven or eight, dependent on the physical development of the individual child, there are still the early years before the child began regular work to consider. Further, even when work was begun, there is some evidence to show that children did not immediately abandon play – that is, once they could be spared from household duties.[2] Of course, as attendance at school became more regular, children had to adapt to new educational routines, but school hours were fixed, Saturdays were usually free and there were also the school holidays. As they grew older, children could participate more and more in the leisure pursuits of adults and from even a very early age children went to church, chapel and Sunday school. Towards the end of the century, with the growing sophistication of public entertainment (including the expanding field of urban spectator sports), and taking into account the influence of a national school system which not only produced the first literate generations but also at the same time began to encourage team games, the opportunities for children's leisure activities expanded greatly. Broadly speaking, at the beginning of the nineteenth century most children lived in the country and began work in agriculture, domestic industry or some allied occupation. Agriculture was still the great flywheel of the economy, at least for the early years of the century. By the end of the century most children lived in towns, attended schools till they were twelve or more, and then sought jobs in what had become a heavily industrialised economy.

Against this background, it seems appropriate to make a beginning with the leisure activities of the country children in the first decades of the century. Leisure may be defined in general as time left over after work and other obligations have been completed,[3] but even for very young country children there would be jobs in and around the home which took up a good deal of time, such as gathering and chopping wood for the boys and helping with cleaning and laundry work for the girls. Once household work had been completed, small children were free to explore the local fields and woods. Their activities were very much what one would expect – climbing trees, birdnesting, damming streams and chasing (and persecuting) small animals.[4] In the summer there would be gathering nuts, picking blackberries and searching for mushrooms. Then there was participation in the traditional adult pastimes of the countryside such as Plough Monday, Shrove Tuesday sports, May Day celebrations (including the crowning of the May Queen), Rogation Sunday processions, harvest suppers, following the hunt on foot and so on. Village life might be enlivened from time to time by local visits of fairs or circuses or by occasional entertainments such as penny readings or lantern-shows. Such toys as were available were simple and of a kind popular through the centuries, such as marbles, skipping ropes and hoops. Even at the end of the century, the toys for girls on sale at St Giles's Fair, Oxford, were very crudely fashioned – a roughly-shaped wooden head, body and legs – but they served their simple purpose: 'The kids used to like 'em cos they used to put a cape round 'em, or some kind of apparatus . . . like a frock or shawl . . . an' their little eyes was a bit of black . . . some 'ad black 'air, and that was a doll, you see.'[5] For most children, the woods and fields were their playground, with all the variety of activities possible in a natural habitat, subject only to the demands of their parents for help in the home or in the fields at particular times of the year, as at harvest time.

Leisure time for children in the towns was of a different kind, given the nature of the environment and also the variety of adult entertainments available. Only in one respect were there direct similarities, and that was in the nature of toys and playthings. As with country children, these were of the simplest and crudest kind – the same wooden or rag dolls, marbles, hoops and skipping ropes; and indeed, for the younger children old bits of rag or stick might acquire a special significance and become loved objects, in the same way that modern adults still keep the most battered teddy bears of their childhood. But for the town child, the street was his or her play area, and here a variety of games could be seen and with a good deal of variation from locality to locality. In London, for example, *Punch* complained in 1853 of pavements being made impassable by children playing shuttlecock and tipcat, presumably games especially popular at the time.[6] Many other games were played in the streets and increasingly in playgrounds as school attendance grew during the course of the century; for example, Tom Tiddler's Ground, British Bulldog, Prisoner's Base, Relievo (or Release), Hare and Hounds, Leapfrog and Hi Cockalorum.[7] To these may be added pranks such as tying together adjacent (or even opposite) doorknobs and knocking on one door and then running away. Chalk would always come in handy for marking out wickets or goalposts, or for drawing lines for hopscotch.

To all these urban activities in the first half of the 19th century might be added participation in adult urban pleasures. Some of these took the form of the cruel sports increasingly frowned on by middle-class reformers, such as bull-baiting, cock-fighting, badger-baiting and bear-baiting.[8] Dog fighting was particularly popular in the Black Country. The first bill against ill-treatment of horses and cattle was passed in 1823, due mainly to the efforts of Richard Martin ('Humanity Martin'). In the following year the Royal Society for the Prevention of Cruelty to Animals was established. Bull-baiting was forbidden in London in 1833 and then throughout the country in 1835. This presumably put an end to the bullock-running in Bethnal Green which, we are told, up to 2,000 men and boys left work to attend.[9] Thus the more humane treatment of animals in time removed public spectacles of this kind from the sight of children, though they might still witness public executions up to 1856.

Apart from the barbarous sports more characteristic of the eighteenth century, there were many more forms of entertainment available to working-class children in the towns. Cricket was popular, and a large crowd, estimated at 20,000, watched the Nottinghamshire v. Sussex match at Nottingham in September, 1835. The crowd consisted mostly of working-class men and their families.[10] Other out-of-doors forms of entertainment were pedestrianism (foot-races), horse racing (the Derby drew large crowds of all ages), swimming in local canals (Liverpool opened the first public baths in 1852), and visits to commercially-run pleasure gardens. The Vauxhall Gardens at Ashted, Birmingham, charged an entrance fee of only 1*s* in 1842, which put it within the price range of the better-off working-class parent. In his *Sketches by Boz* (1836) Dickens described pleasure gardens of this sort, referring to the boys and girls he saw there and to 'babies in arms and children in chaises'.[11] Other forms of indoor entertainment included attendance at Saturday evening musical concerts – mechanics, their wives and their children all attended such concerts in Liverpool in the 1840s[12] – and both the theatre and the pantomime, though the latter was patronised more by adults than by children. In the first half of the nineteenth century theatre audiences were not as middle-class as they became by the end of the century. In 1832 the audience at the Coburg Theatre in London, for example, was largely working-class on Mondays, while in the provinces the programme might include three or even more separate plays, seats costing only 6*d* in the gallery. Travelling circuses could be even cheaper, with seats at 6*d* in the pit and 3*d* in the gallery.[13]

However, the most popular form of theatrical entertainment at the mid-century seems to have been the penny gaff, which was cheaper, at a penny, than either the theatre or the new music-halls. These theatrical shows catered for children and young people from about the age of eight to the late teens, almost all from the working classes. They drew audiences of between 150 and 200. In 1838 it was estimated that there were 80 to 100 gaffs in London, many of them in the East End, where their patrons would come mostly from the immediate locality. In 1869 it was claimed that there were at least 20 gaffs within five miles of St Paul's (which seems acceptable enough as an estimate). For a time, they provided a unique form of cheap entertainment (unless the street theatre put on by itinerant jugglers, conjurors, musicians and others be considered even cheaper), and they put on three or four performances per night. Very often they were housed in a former shop and the warehouse at the rear. There is a well-known description of one such penny gaff which Mayhew visited near Smithfield:

> To form the theatre, the first floor had been removed: the white-washed beams, however, still stretched from wall to wall. The lower room had evidently been the warehouse, while the upper apartment had been the sitting room, for the wallpaper was still on the walls. A gallery, with canvas front, had been hurriedly built up, and it was so fragile that the boards bent under the weight of those above. The bricks in the warehouse were smeared over with red paint, and had a few black curtains daubed upon them. The coster-youths required no great scenic embellishment, and indeed the stage – which was about eight feet square – could admit of none. Two jets of gas, like those outside a butcher's shop, were placed on either side of the proscenium, and proved very handy for the gentlemen whose pipes required lighting.[14]

In many gaffs the sexes were segregated, the boys and young men on one side of the gallery and the girls and young women on the other.

There is no doubt that penny gaffs were a very popular form of entertainment, crude though they were. One oddity was that as they were not licensed theatres they could not put on spoken plays with conventional dialogue. The result was that they were forced to confine themselves to dancing and singing acts, ballets (which might require explanatory placards held up by the manager) and lurid melodramas acted in dumb show. There was also conjuring, tight-rope walking and galvanism (the giving of mild electric shocks from a simple generator).[15] Inevitably such a popular form of cheap amusement with such young audiences attracted middle-class criticism, often on the grounds that young patrons would steal to obtain their entrance money; and it was also alleged that the tone of many of the performances was objectionable, and that the gaffs' audiences drew in many undesirables and potential criminals. The journalist James Grant claimed in 1838 that a very large majority of those who afterwards found their way to the Bar of the Old Bailey could trace their career in crime to their attendance in penny theatres.[16] There is little evidence to support these claims for the deleterious effects of visiting penny gaffs, even if, no doubt, many young criminals had been to them in their time, though without being necessarily corrupted.

This brief survey of children's recreations in the first fifty years or so of the nineteenth century merely indicates some of its more outstanding aspects. It cannot possibly list all forms of amusements, of course, and it is possible that the sheer variety of entertainment obtainable in London and the larger towns may be misleading. It is worth repeating that up to the mid-century the majority of working-class children still lived in the country, not in the town. Consequently, most children had to make their own amusements, and they would consist very largely of the traditional pastimes of the countryside. Further, even when the country boy or girl began work, their pay would be only a few pence a week, and it would pass immediately into the family exchequer. Given the low standard of living of the agricultural labourer up to the mid-century and even beyond, and given also the need for children to share household chores, leisure time was limited and forms of amusement and recreation were simple and unsophisticated in the extreme. It was pointed out in Chapter One that earlier in the century children were employed part-time and, later, full-time in agriculture from an early age. Although they would not be given tasks of work until physically strong enough to do them, there was much of a very simple and relatively non-laborious nature that could be done. The lives of most country children would be busy enough from a tender age, what with helping in the fields or domestic duties in the home. There were few idle hours in the summer sun for them.

The town child fared rather better on the whole, but, as always, all depended on the family circumstances, especially the family income. Obviously enough, the child whose father was a skilled man with a steady wage would be better-off than the child of a labourer. The wide variety of town amusements would be available to the former rather than the latter; the artisan's child was in any case much more likely to spend some years in school before starting work. So disparities between the leisure activities of different town children were much more marked than they were in the countryside. Many working-class families were so poor that there was not enough money available to buy sufficient food, let alone to pay for entertainment. In other families, children might attend penny gaffs regularly, together with other forms of urban entertainment, not excluding the public house, from which children were not excluded until the next century. London children, of course, had access to the widest variety of public amusements. In 1851 the Great Exhibition opened in Hyde Park. It was visited not only by Londoners, of course, but also by parties from all over the country, brought to the capital by the new excursion trains – more than six million visitors in all, many of them on the special cheap days, when admission was only 1*s*. Middle-class fears of drunkenness and general disorder proved misplaced; the behaviour of the crowds was very good. The success of the Great Exhibition in the Crystal Palace (later moved to another site at Sydenham in south London) is a good indication not only of the improving standard of living of the better-off working classes but also of the thirst for rational recreation and self-improvement which characterised the mid-Victorian period and influenced very many working-class families.

The second half of the nineteenth century was to witness a marked rise in real wages for the majority of the working classes, though this took effect from the 1870s rather than from the mid-century itself. Once more it must be emphasised that not all the working classes participated in this (it was pointed out in a previous chapter that the surveys of Booth and Rowntree make this clear enough), but there is no doubt that life improved for most people, and this is shown by increased levels of consumption. It is also demonstrated by the further development of leisure activities in the towns, where four out of five of the population now lived. I do not propose to say much about changes in leisure pursuits in the countryside in this period, since there is really little more to be said about changes in children's recreation there, except that after 1880 all children were subject to compulsory education and to the restrictions on leisure time which resulted from this. Children's lives were geared to a new timetable which set a novel pattern of leisure and play. Yet even then there had to be a certain flexibility, especially at harvest time. The demands for labour in summer might even affect city schools; a survey of 60 board schools and 15 voluntary schools in London in 1900 produced a figure of 4,169 schoolchildren absent for an average of four weeks each due to fruit-picking and hop-picking.[17] One other result of compulsory schooling affecting rural children was the introduction of compulsory school games; one historian has referred to schools setting about controlling children's leisure time in the nineteenth century through the invention of compulsory games.[18] This seems rather far-fetched, and in all probability small rural schools were not greatly affected by the introduction of team games. It is likely that the persistence of traditional games in the playground, which were passed on from generation to generation was of greater importance. It has often been stressed that children's lore and culture are conservative in nature, and changed more slowly in the nineteeth century than adult culture.[19] The history of playground games readily confirms this, and little change is to be discerned in them in both rural and urban areas towards the end of the century.

One other general topic requires consideration before we turn to the widening variety of leisure activities in the towns: this is religious observance. In Chapter Five it was argued that attendance at church, chapel and Sunday school by children was an important aspect of the lives of many, and that probably there was a good deal of informal transmission of religious ideas, in however simple, if not garbled, a form, in the majority of working-class families. What happened to church and chapel attendance in the second half of the century? In the absence of any national census similar to that of 1851 it is necessary to rely on local surveys, most of which show a deline in attendance. For example, surveys in the following cities in 1882 show substantial reductions in numbers of attenders as a percentage of population when compared with 1851:

	1851	*1882*		*1851*	*1882*
Sheffield	32.1	23	Southampton	61.1	39
Nottingham	57.7	24	Hull	49.6	31
Liverpool	45.2	20	Bath	79.1	52[20]
Bristol	56.7	40			

London had always been a special case because of its size and social mix, but a census carried out for 1902–03 for the *Daily News* also showed a distinct fall in attendance, and a very marked fall among the upper and middle classes. Overall attendance was 22 per cent of the adult population, with some strikingly small percentages in working-class districts. For example, Church of England attendance in Fulham was 5.7 per cent, in West Ham 5.4 per cent, Poplar 5.4 per cent and Stepney 4.2 per cent. A calculation of percentage attendance per social class, based on Charles Booth's classification in his religious survey of London, 1897–1900, gives the following figures:

The poor	12.2	Middle class	24.6
Working class (unskilled)	13.4	Wealthy suburbs	35.2
Upper working class	16.4	West End	33.1[21]
Lower middle class	19.8		

There seems little doubt that an overall decline took place in urban attendance at least in the last quarter of the nineteenth century, though it should be emphasised that the London figures are not typical of the country as a whole. It may be assumed that children's attendances fell more or less proportionately. The reasons for the decline are not far to seek. One factor was the growing rationalism of the age (Darwin's *Origin of Species* was published in 1859, and his *The Descent of Man* in 1871), but perhaps a more powerful influence was a growing secularism spreading from the top of society, an increasing pursuit of luxury and pleasure by the upper classes (the Prince of Wales held dinner parties on Sundays at Marlborough House and sermons at Sandringham were timed to last not more than ten minutes when he was present). All this naturally took time to affect working-class beliefs and practices, but at the same time Sabbatarianism was being relaxed; in London, the museums and art galleries opened on Sunday afternoons in the 1890s and band concerts were given in the parks. The National Sunday League also held concerts and organised cheap railway excursions on Sundays. Along with these developments went a widening range of leisure activities in the towns which competed powerfully with the churches, so that churches and chapels lost importance as social centres while professional sport, the music-hall and cycling all gained great popularity.[22]

Of course, the churches attempted to resist the spreading secularism in a number of ways. Revivalist campaigns became common, missions were established, and in 1878 the Salvation Army was founded by William Booth. The Pleasant Sunday Afternoon Movement began in 1875 in West Bromwich and by 1913 claimed to have 329 branches nationally and as many as 55,931 members in London. Everywhere churches and chapels widened their activities to include their own social programmes of talks, debates, tea parties, cricket and football teams. There was even a Labour Church movement, founded in Manchester in 1891 to foster the idea of brotherhood inherent in the Labour Movement itself. By 1907 there were about thirty Labour Churches, but they soon became more political than religious; the Labour Church's Statement of Principles in 1912 omitted all references to God. There was also a small number of socialist Sunday Schools.

All in all, the churches and chapels fought a losing battle against the forces of secularism in the last years of the nineteenth century. In theory, there should accordingly have been a sharp decline in the influence of religious thought on both adults and children. Yet this may not necessarily have been the case, and the evidence of oral history seems to show that few working-class families had a consistently secular view of life at this time; and more recent revisionist interpretations tend to play down the purely quantitative approaches to assessing the extent of religious belief in the late nineteenth century. Of course, there were still many children in church schools in 1900 (more than in board schools) and subject to their influence, and most parents were still married in church, had their children baptised there and were buried in the churchyard. Indeed, the Sunday School movement continued to be strong in the second half of the nineteenth century, attendance actually increasing and peaking in 1906. The figures are as follows:

Year	*No. of Students*	*Percentage of Population of England, Scotland and Wales enrolled*	*Percentage in Church of England Schools*
1851	2,614,274	13	36
1881	5,762,038	19	39
1901	5,952,431	16	39
1906	6,178,827	16	39
1911	6,129,496	15	40[23]

These figures are quite remarkable. It seems that even if their parents were not attending services as much as before, they made sure that their children continued to attend Sunday School in considerable numbers, presumably on the grounds that it was good for them and at the same time to get them out of the house and to allow their parents an hour or two of privacy.

However, by the 1870s the teaching of reading and writing in the Sunday Schools had almost completely disappeared, having been replaced by education under the state system. Henceforth religious instruction in the schools became more systematic. According to Professor Lacqueur, secular education was replaced by what he calls 'a plethora of alternative activities', that is, by organisations and activities such as the Christian Endeavour Society, the Band of Hope, branches of the International Bible Reading Association, recreational evening classes and lantern lectures, gymnastic, cricket and cycling clubs, class teas and picnics and so on. In 1883 the Boys' Brigade was founded in Glasgow for Sunday School scholars between the ages of twelve and seventeen, its purpose being 'the advancement of Christ's kingdom among boys'. This was to be achieved on the basis of wearing a simple uniform and of military drill. By 1888 the Brigade had 230 companies, 800 officers and a membership of 11,000 boys. At the same time, the Band of Hope (founded in 1839) expanded considerably, having nearly a million members by 1890.[24]

Nevertheless, although Lacqueur has observed that 'a rosy glow' seems to surround the Sunday School in the second half of the nineteenth century, the fact is that attendance began to decline sometime after 1881 as a proportion of the population. In all likelihood this was the consequence of the growth of rival leisure attractions at the time such as the development of professional football; and at the beginning of the new century there was also the appeal of the cinema and of the new scout and guide movements (though these appealed very largely to middle-class children). The decline was gradual, but proved irreversible. The religious revival which marked the earlier decades of the nineteenth century was over.

So much is readily to be deduced from the attendance figures at both church and Sunday School. Yet as was noted in an earlier chapter, this in itself does not provide any indication of the extent of the loss of religious belief among children. Given the continued emphasis on the Christian religion in the elementary schools, it seems unlikely that there was any substantial loss of faith among children, who in their innocence were still inclined to believe what they were told. By 1900 Sundays may have lost their special quality for some, and the Sabbath was no longer so taken up with church and Sunday School-going, but most children still knew that it was different from other days of the week and was supposed to have a special meaning.

To turn lastly to new forms of public entertainment, especially in the towns, in the last quarter of the nineteenth century: the penny gaff declined in popularity after 1870, its place being taken initially by the music-halls, which were themselves descended from the earlier saloon theatres, which explains the well-known features of a presiding chairman and patrons who were able to combine drinking with watching the turns on stage. According to Mayhew, the majority of the audience at the Victoria Music-Hall were lads aged between twelve and twenty-three, together with young girls, some with babies.[25] By 1868 there were thirty-nine music-halls in London, nine in Birmingham and eight in Manchester and Leeds; over the country as a whole there were about 300, exluding London. By the end of the century the music halls had become very popular, and the most famous performers were known nationwide – Albert Chevalier, Dan Leno, Marie Lloyd, Harry Champion, Gus Elen. The songs they sang were tailored to working-class taste, and gained lasting popularity – 'I'm One of the Ruins that Cromwell knocked abart a bit', 'My Old Man said Follow the Van', 'Any Old Iron', 'My Old Dutch' – and the words became widely known through the sale of cheap sheet music. The music-halls appealed mainly to older children, of course, often those who had started work, and their influence was much deplored by middle-class critics. Thus the Revd Henry Pelham, Domestic Chaplain to the Bishop of Birmingham, speaking even as late as 1914 on the evil influence of the halls on the growing boy: 'The influence of the crowd, the suggestiveness of the performance, and the spectacular appeal to his excitement or emotionalism are rotten to the very core. An occasional visit may do no harm, but the boys usually become habitués, and it is in this that the evil lies.'[26] In fact most of the London music-halls did provide a very robust form of humour and did attract prostitutes in search of clients, though a vigorous cleaning-up campaign by the London County Council did much to improve the moral tone. By the end of the century performances could still be saucy and mildly suggestive, but rarely went beyond what George Robey (himself a famous music-hall star) would call 'good, honest vulgarity'. The corrupting influence of the music-halls on the young was not likely to have been very great.

A different form of entertainment developed out of doors; professional sport, played before large audiences. This was familiar enough in the earlier part of the century, of course, but as Saturday afternoons were increasingly freed from work the way lay open for a great expansion of spectator sport, especially of professional football. The Football Association was established in 1863, in 1871 the first Cup Competition was held, and in the following year the first real international match took place between England and Scotland. By 1885 the Football Association was forced to give official recognition to the employment of paid, professional players. In 1897 there was an attendance of 65,000 at the Cup Final held on the Crystal Palace ground at Selhurst Park. In a remarkably short space of time a middle-class sport, dominated by middle-class officials and middle-class amateur teams such as the Corinthians, had been taken over by the working classes and had become their favourite sport. Football was played not only by adults for a living, of course, but also by boys in back streets and school playgrounds, as well as being watched by many of them on Saturday afternoons, often accompanied by their fathers. More and more London schools had their own football teams by the 1890s; it was noted in Chapter Eight that the London Senior Inspector reported in his 1895–96 report that there were few schools in London without a football club and a cricket club. All this applies, it should be said, to association football. The handling code, or rugby union, remained a middle-class game, played in most public schools and grammar schools. Only in Wales was it a sport played by the working classes before predominantly working-class audiences.

Cricket in the nineteenth century has perhaps a longer history as a spectator sport than football, but it too became organised on a larger scale and on a county basis. Its popularity owed much to an amateur, Dr W. G. Grace, an outstanding figure in the game in the 1870s and 1880s. For long the county game was much under the influence of the amateur gentleman cricketer; in the county games Gentlemen and Players came on to the field through separate gates. Cricket drew rather smaller audiences than football, and games were played in the middle of the week as well as at weekends, thus limiting working-class attendance; nevertheless, between 1891 and 1910 the average crowd size at eighty-one county cricket matches was over 14,000. One significant difference between cricket and association football was the emphasis in the former on good sportsmanship and on keeping strictly to the rules, on self-discipline and on respect for one's opponents. This was very marked in the middle-class approach to the game, where the concept 'Play up, play up, and play the game' (to quote from Newbolt's well-known poem) was part of the public school ethos. No doubt working-class boys took it all rather less seriously, yet it would be wrong to suppose that they were entirely unaffected by the spirit which earnest teachers sought to inculcate in their young charges. It was, incidentally, a spirit which permeated the school fiction of the end of the century, to which subject we shall return later in this chapter.

The earliest cinematograph shows seem to date from 1896, when an exhibition was given at the Regent Street Polytechnic, and another show was presented at a travelling fair at King's Lynn in the same year. By 1914 Charlie Chaplin's two-reel comedies had become very popular, and by this time Birmingham could boast forty-seven picturedromes of various capacities with seats for nearly 33,000 in all. Three afternoon shows were provided and two in the evening. Admission charges were very low; at the Saturday morning matinees for children in Hackney, children could get in for a penny and would be given a comic or a stick of rock as a special treat.[27] The programmes would usually consist of half a dozen or so short films of a varied nature. Arnold Freeman supplies specimen programmes of films available in Birmingham in 1914:[28]

THE STOLEN SYMPHONY	
Bunny all at Sea	Tootles buys a Gun
MUSIC HATH CHARMS	
DUPIN IN SEARCH OF QUIETNESS	
HAWKEYE HAS TO HURRY!	
BLUDSOE'S DILEMMA	

Freeman also quotes from advertisements in the *Kinematograph Monthly Film Record* for April 1913, giving details of individual films. One typical example reads:

> *Leonie* – Landon, an artist, is loved by his model, but he is blind to her affection. He becomes infatuated with Muriel Glean, a rich society girl, who heartlessly leads him on until he declares his passion. Then she scorns him. Dejected and dazed, Landon finds comfort in Leonie, and now he awakens to the fact that he loves her.[29]

According to Freeman the cinema was unquestionably the greatest formative influence at the time in the life of the average working boy. He did not think that there was much that was vicious that was shown, and as entertainment, there was little to be said against the cinema; but he argued that 'the higher powers of the mind are rather lulled to sleep than spurred to activity in a show which leaves nothing to the reason or the imagination'.[30] To judge from the example given, this seems to have been true enough. In common with many of his generation, Freeman still thought that the leisure occupations of the working classes should be eduational and uplifting; 'rational recreation' was still desirable for the lower classes. Whether this view was justified or not, cinema had become an accepted feature of working-class life in Birmingham and elsewhere before 1914 and most boys went to the cinema about twice a week, a trip to the cinema costing not more than a penny or twopence a time and a visit taking up practically the whole evening.[31] By 1914 there were 4,000 cinemas in England, the larger ones having a pianist to provide music appropriate to the action shown on the screen. Some of the older patrons had difficulty in reading the captions, so that the children present would assist by reading them out loud.

Another kind of leisure activity was to develop in the 1880s with the invention of the modern bicycle frame with its two wheels of equal size. This rapidly replaced the earlier penny farthing, and the patenting of the pneumatic tyre by Dunlop in 1888 led to a cycling craze in the 1890s, when it is estimated that there were more than one and a half million cyclists. Many of these cyclists were adults, of course, and many merely used their cycles as a convenient way of getting to work; but there were the younger enthusiasts who joined the more than 2,000 cycling clubs which organised special cycling tours. The Cycling Tourist Club was founded as a national body in 1878, and its badge – a winged wheel – began to be displayed outside village cafés offering suitable refreshment. Smaller-framed bicycles suitable for younger children do not seem to have become popular until later on, but older children soon became familiar with different aspects of cycling lore – the size of frames, types of handlebars and saddles, fixed and free wheels, gears and brakes and lighting equipment (either simple oil lamps or rather smelly acetylene lamps).

The development of seaside holidays was another form of leisure activity which became well known in the second half of the century, though it can be dated to well before the coming of the railways, when trips by sea from London to Gravesend or the Isle of Thanet were common enough. However, it was only in the last quarter of the century that the seaside holiday industry began to develop. Even then, the usual form of seaside visit was a day at the seaside rather than an extended stay. An exception to this was the custom in the 1880s for Lancashire mill-workers to take a week off, and to spend it at Blackpool. The result was an extraordinary increase in the number of visitors to that town. In 1883 during the season they numbered about a million, a figure which had doubled ten years later, rising again to four million in 1914.[32] Meanwhile, other resorts expanded considerably – Morecambe and Llandudno; on the east coast, Bridlington and Scarborough (which developed a low-town area especially for working-class visitors); in Essex, Southend; in Kent, Margate, Broadstairs and Ramsgate; and on the south coast, Brighton, always a favourite for Londoners to visit. Day trips to all these towns were encouraged by the institution of bank holidays in 1871, and these quickly spread to other forms of employment. Thus by 1914 increasing numbers of children were accompanying their parents to the seaside, if only on a day excursion, though naturally enough there were many in homes too poor to permit this and some who grew up never having seen the sea.

As literacy became almost universal in the last decades of the century, it is not surprising that there was an increased output of popular literature aimed at children, and especially at boys. In 1866 *The Boys of England* appeared – the first 'penny dreadful' – which was soon selling 150,000 copies a week, and at least a quarter of a million from 1871 onwards.[33] Alarmed at the success of this periodical, the Religious Tract Society founded *The Boys Own Paper* in 1879, printing more than half a million copies weekly, some of them being distributed free of charge in the London Board Schools. Given its high moral tone, it seems unlikely that many working-class boys bought the *BOP* (it cost 1*d*), preferring to read more thrilling and lurid publications. In 1892 the *BOP* was joined by a similar paper, *Chums*, also at 1*d*, but the Harmsworth Press produced ½*d* papers such as *The Boy's Friend* (1895), *The Union Jack* (1894). and *Pluck* (also 1894). These papers helped to produce a social divide between boys who could afford the *BOP* or *Chums*, and those who could afford only the Harmsworth Press publications. According to A. A. Milne, 'Harmsworth killed the "penny dreadful" by the simple process of producing the ha'penny dreadfuller.' In fact Harmsworth's publications were not especially sensational; *The Marvel* (1893) specialised in stories about buried treasure and about German efforts to invade England. Other publications favoured by Birmingham youths in 1914 were *Illustrated Chips* (1890), *Butterfly* (1904) and *Picture Fun* (1902). Each had four pages of stories and four pages of strip cartoons.

In commenting upon papers of this sort, the 'penny dreadfuls' and 'half-penny comics', Arnold Freeman remarks that although there was a widespread impression that they were of a most pernicious character, in fact their evil influence had been exaggerated; it was not as harmful to a boy as either the picture palace or the music-hall. He then gives five typical titles and synopses, taken from some of the boys' favourite papers. On the evidence they provide, they appear harmless enough to the modern reader. The first example reads as follows:

THE GREAT TURF MYSTERY

Chief Characters in the Story

SEXTON BLAKE	The Great British Detective
TINKER	Blake's Assistant
PEDRO	The Wonderful Bloodhound
GEORGE MARSDEN PLUMMER	The Great Master Criminal
ABE GULWOOD	A Rascally Bookmaker
SPUD LUGGBY	A Through-paced Scoundrel
MR ARTHUR WAYNE-FLEET	A Sporting Millionaire

The First Chapter. Black Maria attacked in the slums. The Escape from the Prison Van. A £250,000 Turf Fraud.[34]

What Freeman deplored about this kind of literature was its utter lack of anything to elevate the mind. As he put it, the boy's senses were 'not open to Nature and Art, but to cheap and tawdry pantomine; his kindling imagination is not nourished with fine, heroic literature, but with the commonest rubbish in print'.[35] His high-mindedness is very evident, though it seems unrealistic to expect much more from material of such ephemeral nature, deliberately designed for popular consumption.

It would have been interesting to have had Freeman's comments on the contents of either *The Gem* (1907) or of *The Magnet* (1908), also published by the Harmsworth Press under its new name of the Amalgamated Press, but, alas, he does not mention them. These two publications were to become great favourites with boys between the wars, when their circulations exceeded 200,000 copies a week. The stories in both were written by Charles Hamilton (better known under his pen-name of Frank Richards), and the adventures of Harry Wharton and the Famous Five of Greyfriars School in *The Magnet* were read avidly week by week. Hamilton's characters included Mr Quelch, the schoolmaster ('A beast, but a just beast'), and Billy Bunter, the fat, bespectacled 'Owl of the

Remove', a comic figure, usually short of money and awaiting a postal order from his parents, and given to great cries of 'Yaroo, you rotters!' when ragged by the other boys. The odd thing about the Greyfriars stories is that according to Robert Roberts many working-class youngsters had become addicted to them even before the First World War. Moreover, Harry Wharton & Co. supplied Roberts and his working-class friends with role models, setting examples of what was supposed to be decent, sporting behaviour. As Roberts puts it, 'Greyfriars gave us one moral code, life another, and a fine muddle we made of it all'. He even goes so far as to claim that in the final estimate, during the first quarter of the twentieth century, Frank Richards might have had more influence on the mind and outlook of young working-class England than any other single person, not excluding Baden-Powell.[36] This may be to exaggerate Richards' influence, especially before the War, but it is an interesting comment on the effect of essentially middle-class popular literature on working-class children.

It remains to provide a round-up of the remaining leisure activities available to children. The Boys' Brigade has already been mentioned. Baden-Powell's *Scouting for Boys* was published in 1906 and scout troops were started about 1907. In 1909 there was a parade of 11,000 boy scouts at the Crystal Palace and in the same year the Girl Guide movement was begun.[37] However, as noted earlier, neither body attracted much working-class support, as the uniforms might cost as much as 15*s*. Joining the Boys' Brigade was much cheaper, as the uniform consisted basically of pill-box hat, bandolier and belt. In the larger towns, boys' clubs were set up in the 1870s and 1880s. A leading example is the Cyprus Boys Club (1872) in Kennington; its membership included about seventy cab-washers, ostlers, coster boys and crossing sweepers.[38] Clubs of this kind were joined in the 1880s by public school and university settlements and missions, especially in the East End of London. In 1886 an offshoot of these settlements took the form of the establishment of the East London Cadet Corps (attached to the Tower Hamlet Rifle Volunteers) at Toynbee Hall. Other cadet corps were later set up in other areas of inner London, usually based on working boys' clubs, themselves often originating in public school missions or university missions; but the numbers recruited were never very large.[39] Reading was encouraged by the increasing number of public libraries. The Libraries Act, 1850 first permitted the use of the rates for this purpose, but progress was slow before philanthropy took a hand. The Scottish-American millionaire Andrew Carnegie helped to establish numerous public libraries towards the end of the century.

Lastly, something more should be said about the public house and about home activities. Normally one might not include going to the public house in any list of children's pastimes, but it must be remembered that for working people the public house was a very common resort after working hours and that it provided free warmth, light, companionship and some degree of comfort, as well as an assortment of games such as draughts, shove ha'penny, cards, dominoes and sometimes skittles. It was the working man's club, and at the end of the century was still open all day. It was not until the inter-war period that any real restrictions were placed on the age of customers, so that before this it was not unusual to see children in the bar, and sometimes the worse for drink.[40] In contrast to this, one may point out that, for most children, home and the street outside the home were where most leisure hours were spent. After carrying out the household tasks time might be spent in a variety of ways ranging from street games to reading, or simply sinking into the reveries and day-dreams characteristic of many thoughtful children. Play, it has been observed, is merely the name we give to children's activities. Perhaps there should be another word to describe periods of non-activity when the child is at leisure but simply day-dreaming. They are an important part of growing up.

When children's leisure activities during the nineteenth century are surveyed as a whole, it will be recalled that it was suggested earlier on that the major changes were the consequence of a transition from life in the countryside to life in the towns. Clearly this is a very broad generalisation, and it is easy to think of qualifications. For some children the toys they played with and the games they played changed little in the course of the century. Nevertheless, the coming of compulsory education produced new patterns of leisure activity and a new uniformity of leisure time which certainly had not existed at the beginning of the century, so that there is both continuity and change in the period. The growth of literacy also produced a significant change in the time given to reading, and this is especially true of literacy among girls, which increased very markedly and rapidly in the second half of the century. It is not known how many female readers of *The Magnet* there were before 1914, but undoubtedly they existed, and Richards also wrote for girls, his stories being based on the girls' school Cliff House School (other writers of stories for girls, like Angela Brazil, attracted a predominantly middle-class clientele). Above all, town life provided an ever-increasing variety of entertainment for those who could afford to pay the usually inexpensive entry changes.

This point requires further emphasis, perhaps. The variety of leisure activities in the towns at the end of the nineteenth century were not enjoyed equally by all, and certainly not by the lowest classes of society. Yet even here the sheer misery and boredom of an impoverished existence might result in the spending of a few pence on entertainment which some might have considered better spent on food; Orwell commented on this phenomenon among the unemployed of the 1930s. Another necessary qualification is that many of the public entertainments listed above were patronised very largely by adults; yet in all the instances given children were undoubtedly present, often in substantial numbers. It seems proper therefore to include them among children's leisure pursuits, though it is not possible to say precisely what proportion of football crowds, for example, were children.

All in all, children's leisure activities show a remarkable resilience throughout the century. There are really no signs of any very marked

public spectacles in the early decades. It used to be argued that adult entertainments such as fairs and wakes were deliberately suppressed by the middle classes as part of the process of social control. It is true that some wakes were brought to an end, usually in the interests of public order, though in Birmingham, for example, their number actually increased in the first half of the century.[41] Fairs, on the other hand, seem to have continued in many places till the end of the century, and they attracted custom from further afield with the development of the railways. Cruder social control theories of the history of leisure during the Industrial Revolution no longer receive much support, though the development of the county police forces after 1839 certainly brought about a reduction in the disorders which accompanied some of the wakes. What is undeniable is the expansion of urban leisure facilities, especially the great and ever-increasing interest in professional sport, particularly football and at the end of the century, in the cinema. All this came about as a result of a combination of factors – an improvement in the standard of living, a vast expansion of the towns, advances in technology and better transport, including the trams which not only made for an easier journey to work, but also allowed families to get out of crowded town centres and out to where the countryside began. In all these ways leisure facilities were transformed in the late Victorian period, and the majority of children shared in the benefits of this transformation.

References

1 See, for example, R. W. Malcomson, *Popular Recreation in English Society 1700–1850*, 1973, Peter Bailey, *Leisure and Class in Victorian England*, 1978, Hugh Cunningham, *Leisure in the Industrial Revolution c.1780–c.1880*, 1980 and John K. Walton and James Walvin (eds), *Leisure in Britain 1780–1939*, 1983. Adolescents at work and play have also become the subject of research. Recent works include John Springhall, *Coming of Age: Adolescence in Britain 1860–1960*, 1986 and Harry Hendrick, *Images of Youth: Age, Class, and the Male Youth Problem 1880–1920*, 1990.

2 See Chapter Two for accounts of children at play after work in ironworks and down the pits.

3 Hugh Cunningham, 'Leisure and Culture', in F. M. L. Thompson, (ed.), *The Cambridge Social History of Britain 1750–1950*, Vol. 2, 1990, p. 279.

4 Keith Thomas, 'Children in Early Modern England', in Gillian Avery and Julia Briggs, (eds), *Children and Their Books*, 1979, p. 61.

5 Pamela Horn, *The Victorian Country Child*, 1974, p. 16.

6 Iona and Peter Opie, *Children's Games in Street and Playground*, 1969, p. 11.

7 For all these games, see the Opies, *Children's Games*, pp. 85, 143, 173, 177, 249, 259. Although the Opies provide historical notes for a number of games, origins are specified only from time to time, so that it is not possible to draw up any definitive list of games played in the nineteenth century. It has also been remarked that most of the earlier precedents for modern children's usage cited by the Opies go back no further than the early nineteenth century (Avery and Briggs, *Children and Their Books*, p. 61). It might also be observed that in a recent interview Iona Opie has pointed out that scatology and sex were omitted from their earlier works, but that sex is more talked about in the playground now, although it was always there (*The Observer*, 14 March, 1993). The 'gross, dirty words' mentioned earlier in this book have a long ancestry, it appears.

8 For these in Birmingham see Eric Hopkins, *Birmingham: The First Manufacturing Town in the World 1760–1840*, 1989, p. 167.

9 Cunningham, *Leisure in the Industrial Revolution*, p. 24.

10 *Ibid.*, p. 27.

11 Hopkins, *Birmingham*, p. 169; Cunningham, 'Leisure and Culture', p. 310.

12 Cunningham, *Leisure in the Industrial Revolution*, p. 104.

13 *Ibid.*, p. 29. There is an excellent collection of Victorian playbills in the Palfrey Collection Scrapbooks in the Hereford & Worcestershire Record Office, on which the last remarks in this paragraph are based.

14 Henry Mayhew, *London Labour and the London Poor*, 1861, Vol. I, p. 41.

15 Springhall, *Coming of Age*, pp. 123–8. See also James Greenwood, *The Seven Curses of London: Scenes from the Victorian Underworld*, 1869.

16 Springhall, *Coming of Age*, p. 126.

17 Pamela Horn, *The Victorian and Edwardian School Child*, 1989, p. 150.

18 Keith Thomas, 'Children in Early Modern England', p. 67.

19 *Ibid.*, p. 70.

20 B. I. Coleman, *The Church of England in the Mid-Nineteenth Century. A Social Geography*, 1980, p. 41; Owen Chadwick, *The Victorian Church*, 1970, p. 226.

21 Hugh McLeod, *Class and Religion in the Late Victorian City*, 1974, pp. 25, 301, 302. The figures for each social class are averages of the percentage attendances for the areas inhabited by that social class. For example, there are twenty separate districts given for the Poor, and twelve for the Working Class.

22 For an interesting discussion of the possible causes of decline in observance see Hugh McLeod, *Religion and the Working Class in Nineteenth Century Britain*, 1984, p. 65.

23 Thomas Lacqueur, *Religion and Respectability: Sunday Schools and Working Class Culture 1780–1850*, 1976, p. 245.

24 *Ibid.*, p. 250.

25 Mayhew, *London Labour*, p. 20.

26 Quoted in Springhall, *Coming of Age*, p. 153.

27 *Ibid.*, pp. 133–135.

28 Arnold Freeman, *Boy Life and Labour*, 1914, p. 136.

29 *Ibid.*, p. 138.

30 *Ibid.*, p. 141.

31 *Ibid.*, p. 133.

32 Cunningham, 'Leisure and Culture', pp. 313–314.

33 Springhall, *Coming of Age*, p. 120. The rest of this paragraph comes from the same source.

34 Freeman, *Boy Life and Labour*, pp. 144, 145.

35 *Ibid.*, p. 151.

36 Robert Roberts, *The Classic Slum: Salford Life in the First Quarter of the Century*, 1973, pp. 160–1.

37 R. C. K. Ensor, *England 1870–1914*, 1936, p. 554.

38 Springhall, *Coming of Age*, p. 148.

39 *Ibid.*, pp. 149–152.

40 The sale of spirits to under-sixteens was forbidden in 1872, but not until 1923 was the sale of liquor banned to under-eighteens, and not until 1933 were under-fourteens forbidden in the bar areas of licenced premises (*The Times*, 20 March 1993).

41 Hopkins, *Birmingham*, pp. 168, 169.

Conclusions and observations

Any historian seeking to investigate the subject of working-class childhood in the nineteenth century is immediately confronted by the problem of sources. Where is he or she to find suitable material? It will not have escaped the attention of the reader of this book that there has been a heavy use of official publications throughout, usually in the form of government reports, and particularly so, perhaps, in the first three chapters, with reference to working conditions. Autobiographical material has also been consulted, especially that relating to the end of the nineteenth and the early twentieth centuries, together with many specialist secondary works on aspects of working-class childhood. Given the fact that at all times it has been necessary to provide generalisations about large numbers of children and their individual life experiences over considerable periods of time, how reliable can all this material be? It is the official reports and perhaps the autobiographical reminiscences which require comment, the specialist works less so, since they form a separate category as secondary sources and have their own standing as works of scholarship.

The government reports of the nineteenth century cover a vast field and of course vary in extent and nature. They present the familiar problem of interpreting a middle-class view of working-class life, based on contemporary assumptions about its nature and about working-class modes of thought and motivation. Very little in the reports themselves comes from below, from the grass roots, though it is otherwise with the evidence provided by working-class witnesses. How far does it matter that what we are given in the reports is often a version of working-class life seen through middle-class eyes? In the 1970s it was fashionable in left-wing historical circles to portray this kind of evidence as tainted by its middle-class origins. Richard Johnson, for example, writing about elementary education, speaks of correcting the bias of the reports, implying that all middle-class opinon is biased, and lamenting the lack of working-class opinion (he does not consider or discuss the possible limitations of working-class evidence.)[1]

Nearly two decades later it seems unwise to adopt such a *parti pris* view of the matter. Of course, many opinions expressed were coloured by middle-class beliefs; of course, some views, such as those of Tremenheere on the 'sensuality and extravagance' of the south Staffordshire miners when in funds seem almost comical today; but this does not necessarily invalidate his many shrewd remarks about the social conditions of the miners, of whom he clearly had considerable knowledge. It certainly does not render irrelevant Michael Sadler's impassioned remarks in the House of Commons about child slavery in British factories, or Southwood Smith's bitter observations on conditions in the towns which were breeding an inferior race, or Henry Mayhew's vivid description of London street children. Nor does it invalidate the enormous mass of factual material, both in the reports and in the evidence presented, to which charges of class bias are quite inappropriate. In all this, the researcher has to pursue his or her customary task of exercising historical common sense in attempting to reach balanced conclusions; and this holds good whether it is a matter of assessing middle-class evidence or evidence provided by working-class witnesses (who may have been got at by their employers, as discussed in Chapter Three, or may simply have been misinformed).

As for working-class biographies, whether in written form or compiled on the basis of oral testimony, they must be assessed in the same way. These sources are not plentiful for the first half of the century, and even later on they have still to be seen as chronicles of individual experience, not necessarily typical of all. There is the further disadvantage of more recent studies based on oral history that understandably they relate to childhoods in Edwardian times and rarely earlier. For reasons of this kind, working-class biographies were not of much assistance in this study. All things considered, the researcher into childhood in the nineteenth century must make the best of whatever materials come to hand. The sad fact remains that only the exercise of historical empathy allows an entry into the inner world of the child, since nearly all the materials available must come from adult observation and experience, as has been remarked more than once. This is likely to be a far greater obstacle than the middle-class nature of the source material or the fact that not a great deal comes from below.

To turn now from sources to an overall view of the subject: there can be little doubt that for the majority of children, the quality of life changed remarkably during the course of the nineteenth century. Those born in its closing years entered a world quite different from that existing at the beginning of the century. It was a world refashioned by the Industrial Revolution, and its great symbol was the industrial city. This enormous economic change is the key to so much which happened, and especially firstly the widespread presence of young children in paid employment, and subsequently their being sent to school, not solely on humanitarian grounds, but also because society could afford to educate them, in the hope of their contributing usefully to the economy in later life. This great change is the central fact in the life of working-class children in the nineteenth century. Along with it there occurred changes in their home environment, in their nutrition, health and mortality, and in their treatment when in need of succour. All this has been demonstrated both quantitatively and qualitatively in the preceeding pages. Nor was it all solely a matter of economic and social change; by the turn of the century, both boys and girls of the English working classes would have the vote when they grew up. When all these aspects of change are taken together, the title of this book has been amply justified. Working-class childhood not only changed, but was indeed transformed in the course of the nineteenth century.

Yet it might still be asked, how far did the changes actually go? How far were some reforms more cosmetic than real? So far as the first half of the century goes, this is not always easy to ascertain; for example, it is hard to establish the real nature of working-class family relationships in this period. All that can be said is that loving relationships certainly did exist, especially between mother and child, but probably, to a lesser degree, between father and son; and at the same time there was a good deal of casual brutality, especially in the workshop, mine and factory. Fathers were accustomed to taking off their belts to their erring sons far into the century (and even to threaten their apprentices with a belting, as in 'Hobson's Choice'). It can be argued, too, that the severe restrictions on female and boy labour imposed by the Mines Act, 1842 were as much the consequence of revelations of sexual improprieties as of concern over long hours and physical cruelty. Factory reformers were often assailed as humanity-mongers – 'bleeding hearts', in modern terminology. As was seen in Chapter Seven, whipping, as a punishment for young delinquents, persisted for most the century. So it is difficult, if not impossible, to judge how far real changes occurred in working-class familial relationships in the first half of the century. In fiction, examples both of compassion (some would say, sentimentality) and of cruelty may be found in the pages of Charles Dickens.

For the second half of the century, and certainly for the last quarter or so, things were different. Here we can speak with greater assurance of an increased awareness of the need for civilised conduct, and the establishment of the NSPCC was a significant advance. New restraints were imposed on heavy-handed parents, parental authority became more limited in a number of ways and children themselves acquired a greater sense of what was and was not permitted by law in day-to-day conduct. As we saw in Chapter Nine, middle-class opinion had it that working-class manners had become more refined in the early twentieth century, and there was much less physical brawling to be seen. The combined effects of compulsory schooling, a rise in the standard of living and an improved enforcement of law and order in urban areas all contributed to this. Of course, individual acts of cruelty were still all too common, but the historian writing in the early 1990s must be wary of how much emphasis to place on this, given the wide publicity afforded in our own time to acts of violence against children, especially of a sexual nature. On the whole, notable strides appear to have been made towards a more civilised treatment of children by the end of the nineteenth century.

What qualifications have still to be made to these generalisations? A recent study of childhood in Britain between 1860 and 1918 concentrates on child oppression, yet concludes that 'the lot of the child at the end of the First World War was a striking improvement on that of the child of the 1860s'. The author goes on to declare that 'the slum child of 1918 was less ill-fed, better clothed, less maltreated and more endowed with time to enjoy the early years of irresponsibility than the child of the 1860s'.[2] It seems then that this author would agree that life did become more tolerable even for slum children by 1918, though his book, strangly enough, is entitled *The Erosion of Childhood*. It would appear to the present writer that it was precisely in the second half of the nineteenth century that childhood acquired new characteristics. Far from being eroded, childhood gained a new status and added respect in this period. In particular, the coming of compulsory education brought into the schools some of the most disadvantaged children from the poorest homes, whose condition led ultimately to the institution of new social services such as school meals and medical inspection in schools. It is true, of course, that advances of this kind were not a simple product of human benevolence; apprehension and a concern both for the economy and for the Empire enters into it, but in fact and for whatever reasons, attention was directed to the state of the poorest children, and advances were undoubtedly made. Once more the importance of the introduction of compulsory education is demonstrated.

A further qualification to the contrast drawn in this book between children at work at the beginning of the century and children in school at the end is suggested in a recent article by Dr Hugh Cunningham, who argues that from the late seventeenth century to the mid-nineteenth century there were large numbers of children for whom no work was available.[3] This is true, he maintains, both in agriculture and in manufacturing and domestic industry. In agriculture, for example, children were a dubious asset, and in most rural areas they were unemployed. Dr Cunningham does well to draw attention to the extent of unemployment in the first half of the nineteenth century, and the intermittent nature of employment has been commented on previously on more than one occasion in these pages. In Chapter One, for instance, reference was made to the report of the Select Committee on Manufacturers' Employment, 1830, with its statement that fluctuations in employment frequently occurred in manufacturing districts and that these produced great distress. Such interruptions in trade were common enough, especially before the coming of the railways. In agriculture it is generally accepted that there was little work for boys in December and January, and not much employment for girls below the age of puberty throughout the year, in the fields, at least.

However, all this is not to accept the proposition that large numbers of children did not work at all in the early nineteenth century. There is a formidable mass of evidence in the 1843 Report on Agriculture to the contrary, detailing the types of jobs performed, the rates of pay and the ages of the children. As was noted in the first chapter of this book, recent commentators on the agricultural scene such as Professor Alan Armstrong have remarked on the importance of children's labour and its contribution to the family income. Barry Reay has referred to the wide range of work for boys in agriculture and to the fact that child labour was an established element of the rural economy.[4] There is also a great deal of evidence in the reports of the Children's Employment Commission, 1840 as to the extent of child labour other than in the textile industry, for example in Birmingham and the Black Country, in the hardware industry in Lancashire, in Yorkshire, in the Nottingham and Leicester areas and in the West Country. It is really very hard to believe that industry offered so few opportunities for employment to young children, given the vast amount of evidence to the contrary which has been examined in the first three chapters of this book. It still seems safe to conclude that many children did in fact work in the early nineteenth century, sometimes from a very early age, in both agriculture and industry. Certainly many parents were anxious for them to do so in order to augment the family income, and for years this remained a stumbling block for educationalists, anxious to improve school attendance. It also explains Tremenheere's Prize Scheme in the Midlands coalfields, since Tremenheere thought that child labour was the main obstacle to better and longer attendance at school.

To turn to another aspect of childhood in the nineteenth century: throughout this book there have been frequent references to the different social roles of girls, and it may be helpful to add to them briefly here. Gender stereotyping was very marked in the nineteenth century, and may even have become more pronounced with the growth of industry. As the factory system developed, more and more female labour was required, especially in spinning, but this did not in itself mean that women and girls acquired any added social importance. On the contrary, if anything the image of womanhood was diminished in a strongly masculine society in which industry and commerce were more and more centred away from the home. The role of women as being essentially domestic was thus reinforced. Their major social function was to marry, keep house and raise children. Those who failed to marry were thought to have been left on the shelf and to have become old maids (an expression which seems to have faded away since the Second World War). Such stereotypes still had great force and influence in the nineteenth century, and only at the end of the period with the increasing demand for women's political rights are there signs of forthcoming change. Even then, the Queen spoke for many in describing women's rights as 'men's lefts', and in wanting to whip the sufragettes.

Inevitably, all this had an effect on the social role of girls in the nineteenth century. In the home they took second place to the boys who had preference in many ways, not excluding the share of food. They were expected to take a full part in the household chores, especially in the cleaning and laundry work, and to help nurse the sick. When employed, they worked the same hours as adults, and though the general assumption was that they were given the lighter tasks, in practice they might undertake very heavy work, as they did in the pits; their pay was usually half that of their male counterparts, thus maintaining the customary differentials between male and female adult workers. The prejudice against married women working continued, and was remarked upon in Chapter Four, 'Children at home'. This prejudice was still to be encountered even between the wars (indeed, it remained strong), when it was still thought that a husband ought to be able to maintain his wife at home. If she was working, it was widely held that both the children and the household would be neglected.

Even after the coming of compulsory education, there are few signs that girls were treated any differently from boys in school. Where instruction was given other than in basic subjects, it would be confined to needlework, cookery or domestic economy – all subjects concerned with household management. Certainly girls were punished in the same way as boys, especially by caning, though on the hand rather than on the bottom (boys might suffer the indignity of having to drop their trousers to be caned). Although working-class girls are often thought to have been more obedient if not actually more servile in school than boys, it has been suggested that this is not necessarily so. Perhaps because they were more afraid of physical chastisement than boys, it has been suggested that girls tended to rely more on evasion and subterfuge, and if driven to it, would use verbal insult and abuse rather than physical assault.[5] This may be so, though kicking and scratching of teachers by girls was not unknown. The fact remains that the caning of girls was still commonplace at the end of the century. All that can be said in concluding this topic is that girls as much as boys must have benefited from the more civilised and less brutal attitudes to children generally which had developed by 1900, but there are not really many signs that the agitation for women's rights had any effect on the gender role of girls by this time.

Another aspect of change in children's lives which deserves comment is that of the changes which took place in the home during the nineteenth century. It is true, of course, that there were noisome slums in 1900 just as there were in 1800, but they were growing proportionately fewer in number. By-law housing was a real step forward and so was the improved standard of furnishing in many homes, the development of the Victorian front room or parlour and the introduction of gas lighting, gas cooking and water-closets. These refinements added greatly to the comfort and hygiene of the home. Moreover, the new housing often had small gardens, both back and front. So the urban environment in particular was slowly getting better and contributing to the reduction of children's diseases, and to the overall improvement in mortality figures, once the hiccup in infant mortality figures of the 1890s had passed. As important an aspect as any of the beneficial changes in the home environment was the reduction in size of the working-class family. As we have seen, its causes are still a matter for conjecture but, obviously enough, it allowed more care for the individual child, made more room available for all and gave a greater share of food for each boy and girl. All this is unquantifiable, of course, but it seems undeniable that smaller families were a great benefit, especially when the gross overcrowding and the bed-sharing of the earlier periods are remembered. It might be added that outside the home the environment also showed substantial improvement in terms of better public lighting, paving and drainage and better local and long-distance transport, not to mention the expansion of amenities such as libraries and museums and of opportunities for entertainment and school sport.

Some additional comment is desirable perhaps on the subject of children and the poor law, although the major changes in this area have been covered in Chapter Six: undoubtedly children suffered under the punitive regime of the New Poor Law after 1834, for the new discipline was deliberately repressive, even though in theory the 'less eligibility' rule was supposed not to apply to them. In the second half of the century children benefited from the more specialised care given to the different classes of the inmates in the workhouse, especially the increasing attempts to get children out of the workhouse and into residential homes and local schools. Even then, the reputation of the workhouse and the stigma of poor relief still marked the workhouse child and also the far more numerous class of children on outdoor relief; but at least the limiting of any healthy child's stay in the workhouse to six weeks in 1913 was a further step forward. As for street children, waifs and strays and criminal children, there was a welcome reduction of the number of children on the streets, and noble efforts were made to care for the orphaned and abandoned. Treatment of criminal children became a little more civilised and better informed; transportation was ended, the need for rehabilitation was more widely accepted and the introduction of juvenile courts and probation were notable advances. Nevertheless, the effective treatment of young offenders had still far to go at the turn of the century, and remains a baffling problem today.

Lastly, a personal observation: when material was first collected for this book, the general intention was to provide an overall picture of changes in attitude to and treatment of children of the working classes in the nineteenth century. However, it was not long before certain impressions were gained of the very considerable extent of the changes which took place and of their far-reaching nature. How far working-class life as a whole was changed during the period as a result of the transition from a largely rural existence to life in the towns would perhaps make a good subject for separate discussion; but there is no doubt in the author's mind that the state of childhood was transformed, not merely changed or modified, and certainly not 'eroded' in the second half of the century; for the majority of children, life provided far greater opportunities for self-fulfilment and for enjoyment in 1900 than in 1800. The basic cause of this transformation, as we have seen, was the transition from life at work at an early age to life in school till the age of twelve or even beyond, to fourteen.

Of course, this statement will immediately invite further qualifications, if not actual objections. What about children still living a wretched existence below the poverty line? What about children in the workhouse, or still roaming the streets, if not actually confined in industrial schools or reformatory schools? What about the poor standards of health and nutrition of so many schoolchildren? But all such objections are really beside the point, which is not that all was for the best in the best of all possible worlds, but that conditions overall had improved in a significant number of ways. This may sound unfashionably Whiggish, but it is surely hard to deny that, for example, it was better for nearly all boys and girls to be able to read and write by 1900 than for substantial numbers to have remained illiterate as they had been earlier in the century.

Indeed, there is an interesting point to be made here. For whatever reasons education for working-class children was advocated in the first half of the century or so, their education was to be of the most utilitarian and limited kind. As was seen in Chapter Five, HMI the Revd James Fraser declared in 1861 that it was not in the best interests of the 'peasant boy' to keep him at school till he was fourteen or fifteen years of age – 'we must make up our minds to get rid of him, so far as the day school is concerned, at 10 or 11'. Half a century later, the 'peasant boy' was in fact often staying on till fourteen, and there was much thoughful debate about the nature of his education and about what kind of work awaited him. In particular, Arnold Freeman was writing in 1914 about the deleterious effects of 'the Picture Palace, and the Music Hall and the Cheap Literature'. According to Freeman, the adolescent was being fed by 'unnatural excitants': 'And all those great cravings that Nature has implanted in him, the intellectual curiosity, the longing for idealism, the splendid ambition, the creative genius, the religious instinct – all of these are dying for lack of nourishment. Or perhaps we should say that the thorns spring up and choke them.'[6] Today we may smile – or perhaps wince – at the outdated sentiment, but this passage illustrates in particular the change in attitudes and expectations over the previous half-century. Cynics may say again, of course, that this enhanced concern for working-class education owed a good deal to an increasing awareness of the need to maintain our economic and imperial supremacy, now clearly threatened by the rise of powerful rivals abroad. Maybe so, but whatever the cause, working-class education and its possibilities were assuming a new importance in the early twentieth century, and the Education Act, 1902 certainly began to open up the prospect of secondary education, however limited in availability at the time, to the working-class boy and girl.

And it was not only the improvement of educational facilities which is significant; the whole approach to childhood had changed over the previous century. Although it is doubtful whether the working-class child had ever been regarded simply as a miniature adult, as it has been argued, and treated accordingly, there is no doubt that by the end of the nineteenth century it was increasingly realised that children pass through well-defined stages of development with different psychological characteristics and needs appropriate to each stage. By this time, school inspectors would refer freely to 'kindergarten principles' and the subject of child psychology was gaining increasing academic acceptance. Add to this the new legislation which provided added safeguards against cruelty and ill-use, and it is clear that childhood in itself had gained a new status by the early twentieth century. Nor should the activities of the Labour Movement before the First World War be forgotten, and its demand for better working-class education. In fact, the wave of national strikes in 1911 actually provoked the first school strikes on anything like a national scale;[7] while after the war the Labour Party produced a trenchant demand for secondary education for the working classes as a whole in its publication in 1922 of *Secondary Education for All*, which scornfully rejected the idea that children of workers had no need for anything beyond elementary education, having less brains than the rich. Altogether the contrast with attitudes towards the children of the lower orders in 1800 is very marked.

Perhaps this is as good a place as any to conclude. Enough and, it may be, too much has been said about the comparisons which can be drawn between the child at work at the beginning of the nineteenth century and the child in school a hundred years later. The change took time, of course; there were both economic and social obstacles to overcome, and what should be taught in the schools still remains a subject of controversy in the 1990s. Yet few would dispute the importance of education for the working classes as an instrument for economic and social advancement and as a powerful agent for social mobility. In this sense, schooling was beginning to appear at the end of the nineteenth century as potentially a great solvent of class differences and certainly a major factor in the transformation of working-class childhood. As we have just noted, the greater availability of secondary education for academically able working-class boys and girls after the turn of the century presented possibilities undreamed of in the early nineteenth century. They were certainly not entertained as possible outcomes by the average peasant boy of that time. How far they have still to become reality by the end of the twentieth century remains an open question and a nice subject for debate.

References

1 Richard Johnson, 'Elementary Education: the Education of the Poorer Classes', in *Government and Society in Nineteenth Century Britain: Commentaries on British Parliamentary Papers*, 1977. It should be remarked that the extent to which the reports on factory conditions can be trusted has already been discussed in Chapter Three.

2 Lionel Rose, *The Erosion of Childhood: Child Oppression in Britain 1860–1918*, 1991, po. 244.

3 Hugh Cunningham, 'The Employment and Unemployment of Children in England *c.*1680–1851', *Past & Present*, 126, February 1990.

4 Barry Reay, 'The Content and Meaning of Popular Literacy: some evidence from nineteenth century rural England', *Past & Present*, 131, May 1991.

5 Stephen Humphries, *Hooligans or Rebels? An Oral History of Working-Class Childhood and Youth 1869–1939*, 1981, pp. 76–7.

6 Arnold Freeman, *Boy Life and Labour: The Manufacture of Inefficiency*, 1914, p. 151.

7 The strikes were against corporal punishment, and are said to have lasted up to three days in places, having spread to hundreds of schools in sixty major towns and cities (see Steve Humphries, Joanna Mack and Robert Perks, *A Century of Childhood*, 1988, pp. 103–5).

Bibliography

Official publications

Census Returns for England and Wales, 1801–1911.
Select Committee on Manufactures, 1816, Report and Evidence.
Select Committee on the Police in the Metropolis, 1828, Report and Evidence.
Select Committee on Manufacturers' Employment, 1830, Report.
Factory Enquiry Commission, 1833, Reports and Examinations.
Select Committee on the Administration of the Poor Law Amendment Act, 1837–38, Reports and Evidence.
Children's Employment Commission, 1840, Reports and Evidence.
Select Committee on the Health of Towns, 1840, Report.
Report on the Sanitary Condition of the Labouring Poor, 1842 (Chadwick's Report).
Commission on the Employment of Women and Children in Agriculture, 1843, Reports and Evidence.
Commission on the State of Large Towns and Populous Places, 1844, 1845, Reports.
Reports of the Committee of Council on Education, 1844–1900.
Poor Law Board, Annual Reports, 1847–71.
Select Committee of the House of Lords on the Execution of the Criminal Law, 1847, Reports and Evidence.
Tremenheere's Report on the Mining Districts of South Staffordshire, 1850.
Home Office Papers, Census Papers, Ecclesiastical Returns, 1851 (HO 129).
Select Committee on Criminal and Destitute Juveniles, 1852, Report and Evidence.
Census of Great Britain, 1851: Education, England and Wales, Report and Tables, 1854.
Reports of the Inspectors of Coal Mines, 1854.
Enquiry into the State of Popular Education in England, 1861, Reports and Evidence.
Children's Employment Commission, 1862, Reports and Evidence.
Reports of the Inspectors of Factories, 1865.

Commission on the Employment of Children, Young Persons, and Women in Agriculture, 1867, Report and Evidence.
Commission on the Working of the Factories and Workshops Acts, 1876, Report and Evidence.
Commission on the Housing of the Working Classes, 1885, Report and Evidence.
Commission on Labour, 1892, Reports and Evidence.
Departmental Committee on Reformatory and Industrial Schools, 1896, Report.
Inter-departmental Committee on the Employment of School Children, 1901, Report.
Reports of the Chief Medical Officer of the Board of Education, 1902–14.
Commission on the Poor Laws, 1905–09, Reports and Evidence.
Inter-departmental Committee on Partial Exemption from School Attendance, 1909, Report.

Books

Place of publication is London unless otherwise stated.

Adamson, J. W., *English Education 1780–1970*, 1970.
Altick, Richard D., *Victorian People and Ideas*, 1974.
Anderson, Michael, *Family Structure in Nineteenth Century Lancashire*, 1971.
Ariès, Phillipe, *L'Infant et la Vie Familiale sous L'Ancien Régime*, 1960, (English translation: *Centuries of Childhood*, 1962).
Ashton, T. S., *Iron and Steel in the Industrial Revolution*, 2nd edn, 1951.
Ashton, T. S. and Sykes, J., *The Coal Industry of the 18th Century*, Manchester, 1929.
Ashworth, W., *An Economic History of England, 1870–1939*, 1960.
Bailey, Peter, *Leisure and Class in Victorian England*, 1978.
Baines, Edward, *History of the Cotton Manufactures in Great Britain*, 1836.
Barker, Theo and Drake, Michael, *Population and Society in Britain 1850–1980*, 1982.
Baxter, G. R. W., *The Book of the Bastilles*, 1841.
Behlmer, George K., *Child Abuse and Moral Reform in England 1870–1908*, Stanford, 1982.
Benson, John, *The Working Class in Britain, 1850–1939*, 1989.
Berg, Maxine, *The Age of Manufactures 1700–1820*, 1985.
Bienefeld, M. A., *Working Hours in British Industry: An Economic History*, 1972.
Birch, A., *The Economic History of the British Iron and Steel Industry 1784–1879*, 1967.
Birchenough, C., *History of Elementary Education in England and Wales*, 1914.
Boyson, Rhodes, *The Ashworth Cotton Enterprise: the Rise and Fall of a Family Firm*, 1970.
Brown, John, *A Memoir of Robert Blincoe*, 1832 (Caliban Books edn, 1977).
Burnett, John, *Plenty and Want*, 1966.
Burnett, John, *A Social History of Housing 1815–1970*, 1978.
Burnett, John, *Destiny Obscure: Autobiographies of Childhood, Education and*

Family from the 1820s to the 1920s, 1982.
Bythell, D., *The Handloom Weavers*, 1968.
Chadwick Owen, *The Victorian Church*, 1970.
Chambers, J. D., *The Workshop of the World*, 1961.
Chambers, J. D., *Population, Economy and Society in Pre-Industrial England*, 1972.
Chapman, S. D., *The Early Factory Masters*, 1967.
Chapman, S. D. (ed.), *The History of Working Class Housing*, 1971.
Checkland, S. G. and E. O. A. (eds), *The Poor Law Report of 1834*, Harmondsworth, 1974.
Church, Roy, *The History of the British Coal Industry, Vol. 3, 1830–1913*, Oxford, 1986.
Cleere, H. and Crossley, D., *The Iron Industry of the Weald*, 1985.
Coleman, B. I., *The Church of England in the Mid-Nineteenth Century: A Social Geography*, 1980.
Crouzet, François, *The Victorian Economy*, 1982.
Crowther, M. A., *The Workhouse system, 1834–1929*, 1981.
Cunningham, Hugh, *Leisure in the Industrial Revolution c.1780–c.1880*, 1980.
Cunningham, Hugh, *The Children of the Poor*, 1991.
Curtis, S. J., *History of Education in England*, 1973.
Daunton, M. J., *House and Home in the Victorian City: Working Class Housing 1850–1914*, 1983.
Davis, George, *Saint Monday, or Scenes from Low Life*, 1790.
Dennis, R., *English Industrial Cities of the Nineteenth Century*, 1984.
Dickinson, H. T., *British Radicalism and the French Revolution 1789–1815*, 1985.
Digby, Anne, *Pauper Palaces*, 1978.
Digby, Anne, *The Poor Law in Nineteenth Century England and Wales*, 1982.
Digby, Anne and Searby, Peter, *Children, School and Society in Nineteenth Century England*, 1981.
Donajgrodski, A. P. (ed.), *Social Control in Nineteenth Century Britain*, 1977.
Dunford, J. E., *Her Majesty's Inspectorate of Schools in England and Wales 1860–1870*, 1980.
Dunlop, Jocelyn, *Apprenticeship and Child Labour*, 1912.
Dyhouse, Carol, *Girls growing up in late Victorian and Edwardian England*, 1981.
Dyos, H. J. and Wolf, Michael (eds), *The Victorian City: Images and Realities*, 1973.
Eden, F. M., *The State of the Poor*, 1797.
Engels, F., *The Condition of the Working Class in England*, 1958 edn.
Ensor, R. C. K., *England 1870–1914*, 1936.
Fitton, R. S. and Wadsworth, A. P., *The Strutts and the Arkwrights 1758–1830*, 1958.
Flinn, Michael W., *The History of the British Coal Industry, Vol. 2, 1700–1830*, Oxford, 1984.
Floud, R., Wachter, K. and Gregory, A., *Height, Health and History: Nutritional Status in the United Kingdom, 1750–1980*, 1990.
Foster, John, *Class Struggle in the Industrial Revolution*, 1974.

Franklin, Bob (ed.), *The Rights of Children*, 1986.
Fraser, Derek, (ed.), *The New Poor Law in the Nineteenth Century*, 1976.
Fraser, Derek, *The Evolution of the British Welfare State*, 2nd edn. 1984.
Fraser, Derek and Sutcliffe, A., (eds), *The Pursuit of Urban History*, 1983.
Fraser, W. Hamish, *The Coming of the Mass Market 1850–1914*, 1981.
Freeman, Arnold, *Boy Life and Labour: the Manufacture of Inefficiency*, 1914.
Frow, Edmund and Ruth, *A Survey of the Half-Time System in Education*, 1970.
Gale, W. K. V., *The British Iron and Steel Industry: A Technical History*, 1967.
Gale, W. K. V., *The Black Country Iron Industry: A Technical History*, 1979.
Galloway, R. L., *Annals of Coal Mining and the Coal Trade*, 2nd series, Vol. 2, 1904.
Gauldie, E., *Cruel Habitations: A History of Working Class Housing 1780–1918*, 1974.
Gilbert, A. D., *Religion and Society in Industrial England: Church, Chapel and Social Change 1740–1914*, 1976.
Gillis, John R., *For Better, For Worse: British Marriages, 1600 to the Present*, 1985.
Gittins, Diana, *Fair Sex; Family Size and Structure 1900–39*, 1982.
Goldstrom, J. M., *The Social Content of Education 1830–50*, 1980.
Greenwood, James, *The Seven Curses of London: Scenes from the Victorian Underworld*, 1869.
Griffin, A. R., *Coalmining*, 1971.
Hampson, E. M., *The Treatment of Poverty in Cambridgeshire*, 1934.
Harris, J. R., *The British Iron Industry 1700–1850*, 1988.
Harrison, J. F. C., *The Early Victorians 1832–51*, 1971.
Hastings, R. P., *Poverty and the Poor Law in the North Riding of Yorkshire, 1780–1837*, York, 1982.
Hayek, F. A. (ed.), *Capitalism and the Historians*, 1954.
Hendrick, Henry, *Images of Youth: Age, Class and the Male Youth Problem 1880–1920*, 1990.
Henriques, U. R. Q., *The Early Factory Acts and their Enforcement*, 1971.
Hewins, Angela (ed.), *The Dillon: Memories of a Man of Stratford upon Avon*, 1982.
Hewitt, Margaret, *Wives and Mothers in Victorian England*, 1958.
Himmelfarb, Gertrude, *Marriage and Morals among the Victorians*, 1986.
Hopkins, Eric (ed.), *The Kinver Parish Chest*, University of Birmingham Extra-Mural Department, 1969.
Hopkins, Eric, *A Social History of the English Working Classes 1815–1945*, 1979.
Hopkins, Eric, *Birmingham: The First Manufacturing Town in the World 1760–1840*, 1989.
Horn, Pamela, *The Victorian Country Child*, 1974
Horn, Pamela, *Labouring Life in the Victoran Countryside*, 1976.
Horn, Pamela, *The Changing Countryside in Victorian and Edwardian England and Wales*, 1984.
Horn, Pamela, *The Victorian and Edwardian School Child*, 1989.
Horner, Leonard, *On the Employment of Children in Factories and other Works in*

the United Kingdom and in some Foreign Countries, 1840.
Houghton, Walter E., *The Victorian Frame of Mind 1830–1870*, 1857.
Hudson, Derek, *Munby: Man of Two Worlds*, 1972.
Humphries, Stephen, *Hooligans or Rebels? An Oral History of Working Class Childhood and Youth 1889–1939*, 1981.
Hunt, E. H., *British Labour History 1815–1914*, 1981.
Hurt, John, *Education in Evolution*, 1971.
Hurt, John, *Elementary Schooling and the Working Classes 1860–1918*, 1979.
Hutchings, B. L. and Harrison, A., *A History of Factory Legislation*, 1911.
Hyde, C. K., *Technological Change and the British Iron Industry*, Princeton, 1977.
John, A. H., *The Industrial Development of South Wales 1750–1850*, 1950.
Jones, M. G., *The Charity School Movement in the Eighteenth Century*, 1938.
Keeling, F., *Child Labour in the United Kingdom*, 1914.
Kendall, Guy, *Robert Raikes, A Critical Study*, 1939.
Lacqueur, Thomas W., *Religion and Respectability: Sunday Schools and Working Class Culture 1780–1850*, 1976.
Laslett, P., *Household and Family in Past Time*, 1972.
Lawson, John and Silver, Harold, *A Social History of Education in England*, 1973.
Lewis, Jane (ed.), *Labour and Love: Women's Experience of Home and Family 1850–1940*, 1986.
Lones, T. E., *History of Coal Mining in the Black Country*, Dudley, 1898.
Longmate, Norman, *The Workhouse*, 1974.
MacDonagh, Oliver, *A Pattern of Government Growth: The Passenger Acts and their Enforcement*, 1961.
MacDonagh, Oliver, *Early Victorian Government*, 1977.
Malcolmson, R. W., *Popular Recreation in English Society 1700–1850*, 1973.
Mann, Horace, *Religious Worship in England and Wales*, 1854.
Marshall, D., *The English Poor in the Eighteenth Century*, 1926.
Marshall, J. D., *The Old Poor Law, 1794–1834*, 2nd edn, 1985.
Masterman, C. F., *From the Abyss*, 1902.
Masterman, C. F., *The Condition of England*, 1909.
Mathias, Peter, *The First Industrial Nation*, 2nd edn, 1983.
Matsumura, A., *The Labour Aristocracy Revisited: the Victorian Flint Glass Makers 1850–1880*, Manchester, 1983.
Mayhew, Henry, *London Labour and the London Poor*, 1861–62.
Mayor, S., *The Churches and the Labour Movement*, 1967.
McCann, P. (ed.), *Popular Education and Socialisation in the Nineteenth Century*, 1977.
McLeod, Hugh, *Class and Religion in the late Victorian City*, 1974.
McLeod, Hugh, *Religion and the Working Class in Nineteenth Century Britain*, 1984.
Memoirs of the Life and Writings of Michael Thomas Sadler, 1842.
Mingay, G. E., *Rural Life in Victorian England*, 1977.
Mingay, G. E., *The Victorian Countryside*, 1981.

Mingay, G. E. (ed.), *The Agrarian History of England and Wales, Vol. VI, 1750–1850*, 1989.

Mitchell, B. R., *British Historical Statistics*, Cambridge, 1988.

More, Charles, *Skill and the English Working Class 1870–1914*, 1980.

Morrison, A., *A Child of the Jago*, 1896.

Musgrave, R. W., *Society and Education since 1800*, 1968.

Musson, A. E. (ed.), *Trade Union and Social History*, 1974.

Musson, A. E., *The Growth of British Industry*, 1977.

Noake, J., *The Rambler*, 1854.

Opie, Iona and Peter, *Children's Games in Street and Playground*, 1969.

Oxley, G. W., *Poor Relief in England and Wales 1601–1834*, 1974.

Parr, Joy, *Labouring Children: British Immigrant Apprentices to Canada 1869–1924*, 1980.

Peacock, Roy (ed.), *Hagley, Worcestershire, from the Eighteenth to the Nineteenth Century*, Hagley, 1985.

Perkin, Harold, *The Origins of Modern English Society 1780–1880*, 1969.

Phillips, G. L., *England's Climbing Boys*, 1949.

Pinchbeck, Ivy and Hewitt, Margaret, *Children in English Society, Vol. II: From the Eighteenth Century to the Children's Act 1948*, 1973.

Plumb, J. H., *England in the Eighteenth Century*, Harmondsworth, 1950.

Pollard, S., *The Genesis of Modern Management*, 1965.

Pollock, Linda, *Forgotten Children: Parent–Child Relations from 1500 to 1900*, 1983.

Pollock, Linda, *A Lasting Relationship: Parents and Children over three centuries*, 1987.

Raistrick, Arthur, *Dynasty of Ironfounders: the Darbys and Coalbrookdale*, 1953.

Razzell, P. E., and Wainwright, W. R., *The Victorian Working Class*, 1973.

Report of the Bishop of Birmingham's Committee on Street Trading in Birmingham, Birmingham, 1910.

Riley, Lawrence A. M., *Report on Van Boy Labour in Birmingham*, Birmingham, 1913.

Roberts, Elizabeth, *Women's Work 1840–1940*, 1988.

Roberts, Robert, *The Classic Slum: Salford Life in the First Quarter of the Century*, 1971.

Roberts, Robert, *A Ragged Schooling*, 1976.

Roger, Richard, *Housing in Urban Britain 1780–1914*, 1989.

Rose, Lionel, *The Erosion of Childhood: Child Oppression in Britain 1860–1918*, 1991.

Rose, M. E., *The English Poor Law 1780–1930*, 1971.

Rose, M. E., *The Relief of Poverty 1834–1914*, 2nd edn, 1986.

Rule, John, *The Labouring Classes in Early Industrial England 1750–1850*, 1986.

Samuel, R. (ed.), *Village Life and Labour*, 1975.

Sanderson, Michael, *Education, Economic Change, and Society in England 1780–1870*, 2nd edn, 1991.

Schubert, H. R., *History of the British Iron and Steel Industry from c.450 BC to AD 1775*, 1957.
Seaborne, Malcolm and Lowe, Roy, *The English School: its Architecture and Organisation*, Vol. II, 1870–1970, 1977.
Senior, Nassau, *Letters on the Factory Act*, 1837.
Sherard, R., *The Child Slaves of Britain*, 1905.
Silver, Harold, *The Concept of Popular Education*, 1965.
Sims, R. (Mearns, Arthur), *The Bitter Cry of Outcast London*, 1883.
Smith, F. B., *The People's Health 1830–1910*, 1979.
Springhall, John, *Coming of Age: Adolescence in Britain 1860–1960*, 1986.
Steedman, Carolyn, *Childhood, Culture and Class in Britain*, 1990.
Stephens, W. B., *Education, Literacy and Society 1830–1870: the Geography of Diversity in Provincial England*, 1987.
Stone, Lawrence, *The Family, Sex, and Marriage: England 1500–1800*, 1977.
Sturt, Mary, *The Education of the People*, 1967.
Sutherland, Gillian, *Elementary Education in the Nineteenth Century*, 1971.
Tarn, J. N., *Five Per Cent Philanthropy: An Account of Housing in Urban Areas between 1840 and 1914*, 1973.
Tate, W. E., *The English Parish Chest*, 1946.
Thane, Pat, *The Foundations of the Welfare State*, 1982.
Thane, Pat and Sutcliffe, Anthony, (eds), *Essays in Social History*, Vol. 2, 1986.
Thomas, M. W., *Young People in Industry 1750–1945*, 1945.
Thomas, M. W., *The Early Factory Legislation*, 1958.
Thompson, F. M. L., *The Rise of Respectable Society: A Social History of Victorian Britain 1830–1900*, 1988.
Thompson, F. M. L. (ed.), *The Cambridge Social History of Britain 1750–1950*, Cambridge, 1990.
Thomson, David, *England in the Nineteenth Century*, Harmondsworth, 1950.
Tobias, J. J., *Crime in Industrial Society in the Nineteenth Century*, Harmondsworth, 1972.
Tranter, N. L., *Population and Society 1750–1940*, 1985.
Ure, Andrew, *The Philosophy of Manufactures*, 1835.
Vincent, David, *Bread, Knowledge and Freedom: A Study of Nineteenth Century Working Class Autobiography*, 1981.
Vincent, David, *Literacy and Popular Culture: England 1750–1914*, 1989.
Walton, John K. and Walvin, James, (eds), *Leisure in Britain 1780–1939*, 1983.
Walvin, James, *A Child's World: A Social History of Childhood 1800–1914*, 1982.
Wardle, D., *English Popular Education 1780–1970*, 1970.
Wearmouth, R. F., *Methodism and the Struggle of the Working Classes 1850–1900*, 1953.
Webb, Sidney and Beatrice, *Industrial Democracy*, 1902 edn.
Webb, Sidney and Beatrice, *English Poor Law Policy*, 1910.
Webb, Sidney and Beatrice, *English Paw Law History*, 1929.
Wickham, E. R., *Church and People in an Industrial City*, 1957.

Williams, Karel, *From Pauperism to Poverty*, 1981.

Wohl, A. S., *The Eternal Slum: Housing and Social Policy in Victorian London*, 1977.

Wohl, A. S. (ed.), *The Victorian Family: Structure and Stresses*, 1978.

Wood, Robert, *The Population of Great Britain in the Nineteenth Century*, 1992.

Woodward, E. L., *The Age of Reform 1815–1870*, 1938.

Wright, Anthony and Shackleton, Richard (eds), *Worlds of Labour: Essays in Birmingham Labour History*, 1983.

Wrigley, E. A., *Continuity, Chance and Change*, Cambridge, 1988.

Articles

Anderson, Michael, 'New Insights into the History of the Family in Britain', *Refresh*, 9, Autumn 1989.

Anderson, Michael, 'The social implications of demographic change', in Thompson, F. M. L. (ed.), *The Cambridge Social History of Britain, 1750–1950*, Cambridge, 1990, Vol. 2.

Chinn, Carl, 'Was separate schooling a means of class segregation in late Victorian and Edwardian Birmingham?' in *Midland History*, Vol. XIII, 1988.

Coats, A. W., 'Changing Attitudes to Labour in the mid-Eighteenth Century', *Economic History Review*, 11, No. 1, 1958–59.

Coats, A. W., 'Economic Thought and Poor Law Policy in the Eighteenth Century', *Economic History Review*, 13, No. 1, 1960–61.

Crafts, N. F. R. and Harley, C. K., 'Output growth and the British Industrial Revolution: A re-statement of the Crafts-Harley view', *Economic History Review*, XLV, 4, November 1992.

Cunningham, Hugh, 'Leisure and Culture', Thompson, F. M. L. (ed.), *The Cambridge Social History of Britain, 1750–1950*, Cambridge 1990, Vol., 2.

Cunningham, Hugh, 'The Employment and Unemployment of Children in England *c.*1680–1851', *Past & Present*, 126, February 1990.

Davidoff, Leonore, 'The Family in Britain', in Thompson, F. M. L. (ed.), *The Cambridge Social History of Britain 1750–1950*, Cambridge 1990, Vol. 2.

Dick, Malcolm, 'The Myth of the Working Class Sunday School', *History of Education*, Vol. 9, 1, 1980.

Dickinson, H. T., 'Thomas Paine's "Rights of Man 1791–2": a bi-centenary assessment', *The Historian*, 32, Autumn, 1991.

Duke, Francis, 'Pauper Education', in Derek Fraser (ed.), *The New Poor Law in the Nineteenth Century*, 1976.

Hair, P. E. H., 'Children in Society 1850–1950', in Barker, Theo and Drake, Michael (eds), *Population and Society in Britain 1850–1980*, 1982.

Henriques, U., 'How Cruel was the Victorian Poor Law?', *Historical Journal*, XI, 1968.

Heward, Christine and Whipp, Christopher, 'Juvenile Labour in Birmingham: a Notorious but neglected Case, 1850–1914', in Wright, Anthony and

Shackleton, Richard (eds), *Worlds of Labour: Essays in Birmingham History*, 1983.

Hopkins, Eric, 'A Charity School in the Nineteenth Century: Old Swinford Hospital School, 1815–1914', *British Journal of Educational Studies*, XVII, 2, June 1969.

Hopkins, Eric, 'Were the Webbs wrong about Apprenticeship in the Black Country?', *West Midland Studies*, 6, 1973.

Hopkins, Eric, 'Tremenheere's Prize Schemes in the Mining Districts, 1851–1859', *History of Education Society Bulletin*, 15, Spring 1975.

Hopkins, Eric, 'Small Town Aristocrats of Labour and their Standard of Living 1840–1914', *Economic History Review*, XXVIII, 1975.

Hopkins, Eric, 'The Decline of the Family Work Unit in Black Country Nailing', *International Review of Social History*, XXII, Pt 2, 1977.

Hopkins, Eric, 'Working Class Housing in the Smaller Industrial Town of the Nineteenth Century: Stourbridge – a Case Study', *Midland History*, IV, Nos 3 & 4, 1978.

Hopkins, Eric, 'Working Class Education in Birmingham during the First World War', in *Labour and Education: Some Early Twentieth Century Studies*, History of Education Society Occasional Publications, 6, 1981.

Hopkins, Eric, 'Working Hours and Conditions during the Industrial Revolution: A Re-appraisal', *Economic History Review*, XXXV, 1, Feb., 1982.

Hopkins, Eric, 'Religious Dissent in Black Country Industrial Villages in the First Half of the Nineteenth Century', *Journal of Ecclesiastical History*, 34, 3, July, 1983.

Hopkins, Eric, 'Working Class Housing in Birmingham during the Industrial Revolution', *International Review of Social History*, XXXI, 1986, Pt. I.

Inglis, K. S., 'Patterns of Worship in 1851', *Journal of Ecclesiastical History*, XI, 1950.

John, Richard, 'Education Policy and Social Control in Early Victorian England', *Past & Present*, 49, Nov., 1970.

Johnson, Richard, 'Elementary Education: The Education of the Poorer Classes', in *Government and Society in Nineteenth Century Britain: Commentaries on British Parliamentary Papers – Education*, 1977.

Knox, William, 'Apprenticeship and De-Skilling in Britain 1850–1914', *International Review of Social History*, XXXI, 1986.

Lacqueur, T. W., 'Working Class Demand and the Growth of English Elementary Education, 1750–1850', in Stone, L., (ed.), *Schooling and Society*, Baltimore, 1976.

Lindert, P. H., and Williamson, J. G., 'English Workers' Living Standards during the Industrial Revolution', *Economic History Review*, 36, 1983.

McKibbin, R. I., 'Social Class and Social Observation in Edwardian England', *Transactions of the Royal Historical Society*, 5th series, 28, 1978.

Mole, David E., 'Challenge to the Church: Birmingham 1815–65', in Dyos, H. J., and Wolf, Michael, *The Victorian City: Images and Realities*, 1973.

Moseley, A. F., 'The Nailmakers', *West Midland Studies*, II, 1968.

Nardinelli, Clark, 'Corporal Punishment and Children's Wages in Nineteenth Century Britain', *Explorations in Economic History*, 19, No. 3, July 1982 (and see the article in response by MacKinnon, Mary, and Johnson, Paul, in *Explorations in Economic History*, 21, no. 2, April, 1984).

Oddy, D. J., 'The Health of the People', in Barker, Theo, and Drake, Michael, (eds), *Population and Society in Britain 1850–1980*, 1982.

Oddy, D. J., 'Food, Drink, and Nutrition', in Thompson, F. M. L., (ed.), *The Cambridge Social History of Britain 1750–1950*, Camb., 1990.

Pickering, W. S., 'The 1851 religious census – a useless experiment?', *British Journal of Sociology*, XVIII, 1967.

Plumb, J. H., 'The new world of children in eighteenth-century England', *Past & Present*, 67, 1975.

Reay, Barry, 'The Content and Meaning of Popular Literacy: some evidence from rural England', *Past & Present*, 131, 1991.

Reid, Douglas, 'The Decline of St Monday, 1776–1867', *Past & Present*, 71, 1976.

Roberts, D., 'How Cruel was the Victorian Poor Law?', Historical Journal, VI, 1963.

Robson, G., 'Between Church and Country: Contrasting Patterns of Churchgoing in the early Victorian Black Country', in Baker, D. (ed.), *The Church in Town and Country, Studies in Church History*, XVI, 1979.

Ross, Ellen, 'Labour and Love: Rediscovering London's Working Class Mothers 1870–1914', in Lewis, Jane (ed.), *Labour and Love: Women's Experience of Home and Family 1850–1914*, 1986.

Sanderson, Michael, 'The Grammar School, and the Education of the Poor', *British Journal of Educational Studies*, XI, 1962.

Simon, Joan, 'Was there a Charity School Movement? The Leicestershire Evidence', in Simon, Brian (ed.), *Education in Leicestershire 1640–1940*, 1968.

Sutherland, Gillian, 'Education', in Thompson, F. M. L. (ed.), *The Cambridge Social History of Britain 1750–1950*, Cambridge, 1990.

Tawney, R. H., 'The Economics of Child Labour', *Economic Journal*, 1909.

Thomas Keith, 'Children in early Modern Endland', in Avery, Gillian and Briggs, Julia, (eds), *Children and Their Books*, 1979.

Thompson, E. P., 'Time, Work-Discipline, and Industrial Capitalism', *Past & Present*, 38, 1967.

Thompson, D. M., 'The 1851 religious census; problems and possibilities', *Victorian Studies*, XI, 1967–68.

Thompson, F. M. L., 'Social Control in Victorian Britain', *Economic History Review*, XXXIV, 1981.

Thompson, F. M. L., 'Social Control in Victorian Britain', in Digby, Anne, and Feinstein, Charles, (eds), *New Directions in Economic and Social History*, 1989.

Vance, J. E., Jr, 'Housing the Worker: Determinative and Contingent Ties in Nineteenth Century Birmingham', *Economic Geography*, XLIII, 1967.

Theses

Davies, E. I., 'The Hand-made Nail Trade of Birmingham and District', Birmingham M.A. thesis, 1933.

Knox, William, 'British Apprenticeship 1800–1914', Edinburgh Ph.D thesis, 1980.

McNaulty, Mary, C., 'Some Aspects of the History of the Administration of the Poor Laws in Birmingham between 1730 and 1834', Birmingham M.A. thesis, 1942.

Pollock, Linda, 'The Forgotten Children', St Andrews Ph.D. thesis, 1981.

Reid, D. A., 'Labour, Leisure and Politics in Birmingham *c.*1800–1875', Birmingham Ph.D. thesis, 1985.

Index